F. Scott Fitzgerald
In His Own Time: A Miscellany

In His Own Time: A Miscellany

EDITED BY

Matthew J. Bruccoli, 1931 - comp.
University of South Carolina

Jackson R. Bryer
University of Maryland

The Kent State University Press

Copyright © 1971 by Matthew J. Bruccoli and Jackson R. Bryer.
All rights reserved.
ISBN 0–87338–108–4.
Library of Congress Card Catalog Number 76–126919.
Manufactured in the United States of America
at Kingsport Press.
Designed by Merald E. Wrolstad.
First edition.

FOR

    MARY,

        KATHRYN,

            JOSEPH,

                JEFFREY,

                    JOSEPHINE,

                        AND ELIZABETH

ABOUT THE EDITORS

Matthew J. Bruccoli is Professor of English at the University of South Carolina and the Director of the Center for Editions of American Authors. His work on Fitzgerald includes the editorship of the *Fitzgerald Newsletter* and its successor, the *Fitzgerald/Hemingway Annual*, as well as the book, *The Composition of Tender Is the Night*. He has edited *As Ever, Scott Fitz—*, the Fitgerald/Ober correspondence.

Jackson R. Bryer, Associate Professor of English at the University of Maryland, is the author of *The Critical Reputation of F. Scott Fitzgerald* and numerous journal articles on Fitzgerald. He is also the editor of *Fifteen Modern American Authors: A Survey of Research and Criticism* and is Head of the American Literature Section of the MLA Bibliography.

Foreword

If, as John Aldridge and other critics would have us believe, the last two decades in American literary history are notable more for the criticism and essays they have produced than for fiction, poetry, or drama, surely one of the not always so desirable by-products of this phenomenon is the astonishing amount of comment on American writers and writing published during this period. One has only to look at the steadily increasing size of the American Literature Section of the annual Modern Language Association of America bibliography to find ample proof: in 1950 there were 512 entries; the 1968 volume lists 1802.

F. Scott Fitzgerald, perhaps as much as any single American writer, can stand as a prime example of how this critical explosion has affected the reputation of an American literary figure. Since 1951, some twenty biographies, critical studies, pamphlets, and collections have appeared which are totally concerned with Fitzgerald and his work. For ten years, 1958–1968, he was the subject of a small journal, the *Fitzgerald Newsletter*, which was superseded by the more ambitious *Fitzgerald/Hemingway Annual*. Bryer's *The Critical Reputation of F. Scott Fitzgerald* is devoted to an annotated listing of the journalism and scholarship on him between 1912 and 1966. And the number of critical articles and book chapters on Fitzgerald which appear in a twelve-month period is now close to fifty.

This situation, obviously, has both its good and bad aspects. It has, undeniably, brought back into critical favor the work of an extremely gifted writer who, while he did not, as the traditional view would have it, die forgotten, was certainly not the subject of much extended or serious comment during the latter part of his life and the decade thereafter. A good deal of valuable literary scholarship, although not nearly enough, has been produced in the last twenty years. However, a curious sort of redundancy has occurred. Commentators, critics, and editors have tended to base their studies on and compile their anthologies and collections from the same well-worn materials. *The Great Gatsby* continues to be the sole or primary subject of well over half of the articles and book sections written about Fitzgerald. Editors select the same short stories as samples of his work—usually "Babylon Revisited," "The Rich Boy," or "Winter Dreams"—in their anthologies of American literature. Critics quote from the same secondary sources—admittedly seminal studies by Malcolm Cowley, Arthur Mizener, and Edmund Wilson—in their new articles and books. And editors, in putting together collections of materials about Fitzgerald, include these same pieces. Again, such oft-reprinted essays as Lionel Trilling's 1945 study in *The Nation* and William Troy's "Scott Fitzgerald—The Authority of Failure" are certainly of lasting importance; but so are John Peale Bishop's long essay-review on *The Beautiful and Damned* and Thomas A. Boyd's three-part interview-essay written in 1922—and neither of them has ever been reprinted. Similarly, while no one would deny that *Gatsby* and "Babylon Revisited" are among Fitzgerald's best and most representative writings, it will be useful to have readily available such lesser-known products of his talent as his book reviews and poetry.

We have assembled this collection to fill some of these gaps. It is divided into two basic parts, which are intended to show the areas of Fitzgerald's career that have been overlooked. He was a professional author writing for money. Everything he published formed his career. He enjoyed fame and was keenly aware of his reputation. That his desire for publicity and his desire for a reputation as a serious writer conflicted is one of the keys to understanding Fitzgerald's image *in his own time*. Therefore, both sections of this miscellany are restricted to material published by or about Fitzgerald while he was living—with the exception of the obituaries. Some of these pieces were hard to locate: this volume will at least save time for other researchers.

The first part of this miscellany consists of forgotten or, at least, unavailable material published by Fitzgerald during his lifetime. Some of it is admittedly ephemeral; but it is worth reprinting here because this volume is designed to facilitate the understanding of Fitzgerald's reputation in his own time. If most of his contemporaries were unwilling to rank him as a major writer—or even as a serious writer—it may have been partly because of the purely popular and commercial material he published, such as "What Became of Our Flappers and Sheiks?" On the other hand, Fitzgerald's book reviews are significant by any standard. Although he reviewed books by Huxley, Tarkington, Dos Passos,

Anderson, Mencken, Hemingway, and Thomas Boyd, only one of these reviews—"How to Waste Material"—has previously been reprinted. The Princeton undergraduate writings are included because they supplement John Kuehl's *The Apprentice Fiction of F. Scott Fitzgerald* (1965) and because they provide inside glimpses of Fitzgerald's talent during its formative stages. The *Tiger,* and the *Lit,* and the Triangle Club were where Fitzgerald developed a style. There was no newspaper or little magazine apprenticeship for Fitzgerald: Princeton was his city room. He worked hard at writing and wasted little time on his studies.

The second part of this volume includes material published between 1915 and 1941; it is about Fitzgerald and again represents to a great extent, previously uncollected selections. This section is presented with two basic intentions: the first is simply to make available in book form to scholars and students the texts of these pieces, many of which can be found only in files of obscure newspapers and magazines. With the ever-increasing amount of research being done on Fitzgerald, the availability of these early interviews, reviews, essays, and editorials should provide an important reference tool. But the second and perhaps more important purpose is to supply a representative sampling of the significant critical attention which F. Scott Fitzgerald received during his lifetime in order to suggest a more realistic and balanced overall view of his total critical reputation than is generally given. The three recent collections of essays on specific Fitzgerald novels, Frederick J. Hoffman's *"The Great Gatsby": A Study,* Ernest Lockridge's *Twentieth Century Interpretations of "The Great Gatsby,"* and Marvin J. La Hood's *"Tender Is the Night": Essays in Criticism* include but one contemporary review among them. The two larger and supposedly more comprehensive collections, edited by Mizener and Alfred Kazin, are heavily weighted to post-1950 essays (Kazin does include a section of earlier comment; Mizener virtually none).

Fitzgerald was interviewed often; his books were reviewed widely; his activities and writings were the subjects of numerous editorials and essays; and his death was commented upon by newspapers and magazines from Los Angeles to New York. And, while a certain percentage of this material is of historical significance only (the review of *The Vegetable* in performance, which we have included, certainly falls into this category), we believe that a substantial number of the selections included in this miscellany can stand independently as important documents. Bishop's review of *The Beautiful and Damned* presents one of the most incisive analyses in print of this relatively neglected work; Malcolm Cowley's review of *Tender Is the Night* deserves a place among the important essays on what is probably Fitzgerald's most critically controversial piece of fiction; and Thomas Caldecot Chubb's review of *The Great Gatsby* is virtually the only contemporary notice which saw this novel in the epic terms as we have come to see it in later decades. Thus, we have assembled this volume to provide researchers with a larger and more informed view of Fitzgerald's literary career as well as with a source-book of material by and about Fitzgerald. Previously reprinted items are included because to have omitted these would have resulted in a distorted and incomplete picture. The section of material by Fitzgerald provides exact reprints of the originals: there are no silent emendations. The selections of material about Fitzgerald have been silently edited to eliminate redundant details about Fitzgerald's life and plot summaries of his works.

The first section of this volume (by Fitzgerald) was edited by Matthew J. Bruccoli; the second section (about Fitzgerald) was edited by Jackson R. Bryer.

In putting together this book, we have incurred many debts, most of which can only be repaid in a token fashion here. First, we thank Frances Fitzgerald Smith for approving this project and for permitting us to see Fitzgerald's scrapbooks, from which we derived material for both sections of this collection. A major debt of gratitude is also owed to Alexander Clark of the Princeton University Library, who has served as god-father to so much Fitzgerald research. He helped us secure texts for both sections of the book, and was always as efficient as he was patient and genial. Ivan von Auw, Jr. of Harold Ober Associates helped with permissions problems. For significant secretarial and editorial assistance in preparing the manuscript, we wish to thank Mrs. Jo Zuppan of the Kent State University Press, Mrs. Carolyn Banks, Mrs. Loretta D'Eustachio, Miss Susan Robinson and Miss Jennifer Atkinson. Thanks are also extended to the General Research Board of the University of Maryland for providing Professor Bryer with a summer grant during a crucial period in the preparation of the volume, and to the University of South Carolina Department of English for providing the same for Professor Bruccoli.

MATTHEW J. BRUCCOLI
JACKSON R. BRYER

Contents

The Princeton Tiger Humor

The Nassau Literary Magazine Humor

Reviews

Introductions and Blurbs

Public Letters and Statements

PART II. MISCELLANY ABOUT FITZGERALD

Interviews

Essays and Editorials

Parodies

Obituary Editorials and Essays

PART I
Miscellany by Fitzgerald

Poems and Lyrics

"FOOTBALL"

By Scott Fitzgerald

Now they're ready, now they're waiting,
Now he's going to place the ball.
There, you hear the referee's whistle,
As of old the baton's fall.
See him crouching. Yes, he's got it;
Now he's off around the end.
Will the interference save him?
Will the charging line now bend?
Good, he's free; no, see that halfback
Gaining up behind him slow.
Crash! they're down; he threw him nicely,—
Classy tackle, hard and low.
Watch that line, now crouching waiting,
In their jerseys white and black;
Now they're off and charging, making
Passage for the plunging back.
Buck your fiercest, run your fastest,
Let the straight arm do the rest.
Oh, they got him; never mind, though,
He could only do his best.
What is this? A new formation.
Look! their end acts like an ass.
See, he's beckoning for assistance,
Maybe it's a forward pass.
Yes, the ball is shot to fullback,
He, as calmly as you please,
Gets it, throws it to the end; he

Pulls the pigskin down with ease.
Now they've got him. No, they haven't.
See him straight-arm all those fools.
Look, he's clear. Oh, gee! don't stumble.
Faster, faster, for the school.
There's the goal, now right before you,
Ten yards, five yards, bless your name!
Oh! you Newman, 1911,
You know how to play the game.

" 'Football,' " *Newman News*, ix (Christmas 1912), 19. Fitzgerald's first published poem.

FIE! FIE! FI-FI!

OPENING CHORUS
ACT I

Chorus of Guests
Cynical, critical, bored and analytical.
Visitors from ev'ry land that sports a millionaire,
Nouveau riche, pedigreed, of a high or petty breed,
Wandering from place to place to get a traveled air.

Guests
Fishing in Sardinia, frightened in Armenia,
Tired to death at Paris, although London makes no glum.
Read a guidebook Litany of Normandy and Brittany;
Since the others bore, to Monte Carlo we have come.

Chorus of Adventuresses
Ou, la, la, love is just a game of chance.
Ou, la, la, love is like Roulette
Ou, la, la,
You may find some romance
Play then tho' it bring regret.

Fie! Fie! Fi-Fi! (Cincinnati, New York & London: John Church, 1914). Princeton University Triangle Club.

Ou, la, la, there's a chance to break the bank,
Ou, la, la, or the hearts of men.
Ou, la, la, if you like excitement
A la mode Parisienne.

Cholmondely
Oh, I'm Tommy Tommy Atkins of the guards
And I'm strolling up and down the Boulevards
When it comes to the art of breaking a heart,
I'm clever as can be,
For I'm Tommy, Tommy Atkins of the guards.

Full Chorus
Oh he's Tommy, Tommy Atkins of the guards,
And he's strolling up and down the Boulevards,
When it comes to the art of breaking a heart,
He's clever as can be,
For he's Tommy, Tommy Atkins of the guards,
He is, yes, he's Tommy, Tommy Atkins of the guards.

Female Chorus
Come on Tommy and flirt with us,
If you've nothing else to do.

Full Chorus
Ou, la, la, love is just a game of chance,
Ou, la, la, love is like Roulette.
Ou, la, la, you may find some romance
Play then tho' it bring regret.
Ou, la, la, there's a chance to break the bank,
Ou, la, la, or the hearts of men.
Ou, la, la, if you like excitement
A la mode Parisienne.

GENTLEMEN BANDITS WE

Del Monti and Bandit Chorus

Del Monti
Striving 'gainst foul conniving
And base contriving
I'm now a bandit.
This once
My council lusty
So true and trusty
Now roams with me.
Tho' we are burned and browned
Instincts will not be downed.

Roaming thro' grove and gloaming
Like pigeons homing
We've reached the city.
Biding
All safe in hiding
Then slyly gliding
We've come to town.
We've taken quite a chance
Risked all to watch a dance.

CHORUS
All
Gentlemen Bandits we
Cultured in Burglary

Del M.
Verily so we are,

All
Merry we, tho' we are lawless!

Del M.
Thieving if done aright
Needn't be impolite

All
So we're gentlemen, gentlemen, gentlemen Bandits,
Yes!

A SLAVE TO MODERN IMPROVEMENTS

[*Clover*]

1. Oh my pa's an old physician with a curious ambition
To be a medical celebritie.
He did see his chance and grab it, so he got into the habit
Of trying all his new ideas on me.
When I foolishly submitted
My ambitious father hit it,
That he might replace my parts with junk and so.
I'm a various collection
Born of modern vivisection.
I must confess I'm false from top to toe.

2. There's the scientific question of our power of digestion,
It worries some, it doesn't worry me.
And of course my father's dictum was that I should be the victim,
Get tested for my true capacity.
So they told me at the table "Eat as much as you are able,
So that we can find out what we want to know."
And they brought me in, a platter,
What it bore, it doesn't matter,
And then producing watches told me "Go."

CHORUS
1. A victim to modern improvements am I,
I've a silver chest and a crystal eye;
A platinum lung and a grafted nose,

Aluminum fingers,
Asbestos toes.
And when I walk I clank and clash,
And rust when damp, you see:
And the wildest lot of anonymous trash
That ever crossed the sea.

2. They fed me a match and a scarlet necktie,
A silver spoon and a croton pie,
Some stuff they called wine but I know they lied,
For I'm pretty sure it was Herpicide
They tried me on ink and Le Page's glue
And some goldfish, two or three,
Then they crowded 'round and they said they had found
My full capacity.

IN HER EYES

Celeste and Archie

1. Arch.   When you're attached in a friendly way.
   Cel.   To a maid?
   Arch.   To a maid,
   Cel.   I see.
   Arch.   It's the duce to pay
         When one's this way,
   Cel.   You're staid:
   Arch.   No afraid;
   Cel.   Dear me.
         Then what makes you dumb?
         Do you fear my scorn?
   Arch.   Not at all.
   Cel.   Not at all?
   Arch.   Oh no.
   Cel.   Well perhaps it's my smile,
         Or my frank open style;
   Arch.   It's your eyes,

Cel.   My eyes?
Arch. That's so:

2. *Arch.* Have you ever met with a villain bold?
   Cel.   I have.
   Arch. Did you find it true
            That the rascal's eyes
            Were full of lies?
   Cel.   I did, didn't you?
   Arch. I do.
            There're some eyes I know,
            That where'er I go seem to haunt me in just that way.
   Cel.   Do you mean to imply
            That the light in my eye
            Is a villain's?
   Arch. Oh, I say:

CHORUS
Both
In her eyes, eyes, eyes,
There's a naughty little devil in her eyes
And he lies, lies, lies slyly waiting there to take you by surprise.
When she sighs, sighs, sighs
He is up in arms prepared to rise,
So be wise, wise, wise
And beware the little devil in her eyes.

WHAT THE MANICURE LADY KNOWS

Sady and Mrs. Bovine

1. *Sady*   Down behind my screen
               While your nails I clean
               Smiling at you, filing at you all the while
               With a gossip ear
               Many things I hear
               Pretty things and witty things that make you smile.

While you wield the soap
You can get the dope
Pattering and chattering the livelong day.
Listen to my plea
Retail some to me;
Gracious me, sagacious be
And tell me what they say.

2. *Mrs. B.* Madame, Major Voe
          Thinks the Count de Trop
  Sady* (dum-de-dum-de-dum-de-dum)
          Is that true?
          Madam Tête-à-tête
          Takes her whiskey straight
  Mrs. B. (dum-de-dum-de-dum-de-dum) so they do.
          Countess Coyne they tell
          Said to go to (dum)
          When she was approached because of daughter's hand.
  Sady Three years on the stage
  Mrs. B. Hates to tell her age;
  Sady Jokes aside, she smokes beside
          And chews to beat the band.

CHORUS
1. *Sady* Count Von Hupp (de-dum) I fear
  Mrs. B. Quite a bit, quite a bit.
  Sady (dum-de-dum-de-dum) I hear
  Mrs. B. Had a fit? Had a fit?
  Sady Because the elder Madam (dum)
          Just starves herself for clothes.
  Both Oh tell me wouldn't you like to hear,
          What the manicure lady knows.

2. *Mrs. B.* (Dum-de-dum-de-dum-de-dum)
  Sady So I've heard, so I've heard;

* The parentheses are whispered to the time of the music

Mrs. B.   (dum-de-dum-de-dum-de-dum)
Mrs. B.   Not a word, not a word.
        My dear, don't speak of it, she paints
        And powders up, her nose.
Both   If you want dope on social taints,
        Why the manicure lady knows.

GOOD NIGHT AND GOOD BYE

Celeste and Archie

Dreams, sweet dreams of you will fill the night and day;
Though the morrow bring us sorrow,
I'll be holding you,
Dream arms enfolding you:
Keep your heart bright for me
And tho' we meet no more
You'll seem real in my dream, dear,
Still mine to adore;

CHORUS
Then we'll say Good Night and Good Bye,
And never a sigh you'll see
Oh the violin's tune
Only sang in June
But a song was enough for me.
Oh, I dreamed my dream, heart alight,
I laughed for a night to the sky,
But my love's gone sped with the dawn;
So I bid you Good Night and Good Bye.

'ROUND AND 'ROUND

Celeste, Archie, Sady and Tracy

1. *Arch.* If Victor's fond of Susie,
       And Susie takes to Sam,
   Cel. And Sam avers that he prefers
       That Mary be his lamb.
   Tracy But Mary quite contrary
       At Sam turns up her nose
   Sady Tho' Victor spurns, for him she yearns.
   All And that is how it goes.

2. *Tracy* If Gwen must marry Peter,
       She straightway takes to Bill,
   Cel. And so one day she runs away,
       To Pete a bitter pill.
   Arch. But Bill now looks at Gladys
       Whose heart old Pete has got
   Sady But Pete don't care, altho' she's fair
       For Gwen is not forgot.

CHORUS
All four
  'Round and 'round and 'round and 'round goes the chain of love.
Brain awhirling, all atwirling,
Chase the dizzy dove:
It's love that makes the world go 'round
So all the sages tell;
But love itself as we have found
Goes 'round and 'round and 'round and 'round
And 'round and 'round and 'round and 'round
And 'round and 'round as well.

CHATTER TRIO

Sady, Mrs. Bovine and Del Monti

Del. I'd like to hear a reason for this terrible commotion,
But if you try to talk so much I can't get any notion;
So re strain yourselves and take your time and let's discuss the
  question.
You act as though you had a touch of chronic indigestion
And as I need a lot of time for ev'ry mental action;
Kindly ease your flow of English, or you'll drive me to
  distraction.

Sady He looks as if he needed time for ev'ry mental action:

Mrs. B. And he must be rather simple if he's driven to distraction.

Sady I was tearing off some ragtime on her fingers just as pretty,
When she makes a flat remark and I says: "gosh! you think
  you're witty"
Then she slung a lot of con about my plebeian position.
So I told her that she had a rather nasty disposition,
And I said that she would make a shapely stove if she was
  thinner;
Then she hit me with a file, and so I stuck the scissors in her.

Mrs. B. It's rather rude to prod a lady just before her dinner.

Del. And it's not a very kindly thing to stick the scissors in her.

Mrs. B. We called you in to settle this by peaceful arbitration,
So I wish you wouldn't listen to this woman's fabrication,
For the matter really started in a row about her money.
I said she overcharged me and she started getting funny
And so it's rather fresh of you to think that I'd begin it,
I'm getting very nervous I shall holler in a minute.

Del.   She didn't hurt your finger much, she only meant to skin it:

Sady.   Well she's going to lose a thumb or two in less than half a
            minute.

FINALE ACT I

Principals and Chorus

Clover
How is it sir, you are with her
When you are pledged to me?

Blossom
Your love inter in sepulchre
We have your promise, see!

Celeste
Do you prefer yon dowager
To one so fair as I?

Archie
Don't make a stir, what they aver
Is some outrageous lie.

Celeste
Oh I dream my dream, heart alight
I laughed for a night to the sky
But my love's gone,
Sped with the dawn,
So I bid you goodnight and goodbye!

Chorus
Ah, they are both on love intent
It's quite the height of sentiment
The question is, will she relent
And ruin this romance

They both adore, yet they must part
And nurse a bleeding broken heart
But still it is the height of art
Which nothing could enhance.

Blossom
Come, cheer up, you still have to-night to be gay,
But farewell to love on the break of day.

All
But tonight, tonight
What may occur tonight?
Wine and life, a lover's kiss,
I'd give all my life for this.
Tonight, Tonight.
Ev'rything may come right
So let's rejoice with merry voice,
And Hail the fair tonight.

ROSE OF THE NIGHT

Del Monti and Chorus

Del Monti
The flower of morning, the violet hue
Is blessed by the month of June.
And showered with kisses the whole Spring through
Are the flowers of afternoon.
Alone in a vale,
Without homage or heart, caressed by the stray beams bright:
And worshipped most madly, but worshipped apart,
Blooms the rose of the fairy night.

Ah, my rose, rose, rose of the night
The Spring moon's bright,
You'll be fair, fair, fair in the spell of midnight air.
So come, come give me just a smile

A kiss under the starry light;
The eve's for play you die with the day,
Little rose of fair tonight.

MEN

Sady

I've lived my life in big hotels
I've seen a lot of men:
From Broadway bums to Newport swells,
From sixty down to ten.
There's the sentimental fellow
Who is rather nice at dusk,
Oh, his voice is sad and mellow
But his manner hints of musk.

To cynics with a manner mild
The ear I turn is deaf;
They think they talk like Oscar Wilde,
But reek of Mutt and Jeff.
There's the ogling man whose attitudes
Don't keep his dullness hid,
He woos you with such platitudes
As "peach" and "oh you kid."

Says the "business" man you read about
"I find I want you." See?
"I'll get you too without a doubt"
It never worked with me.
And the pious youth who dares to say:
I'm anything but slow,
He is toasting me in old Tokay
Before I let him go.

CHORUS
Men, men, I've seen a lot of men,
A peculiar kind of insect you will step on now and then.

A few to love, a few to hate,
You'd better leave them to their fate,
They're harmless
Don't exterminate the men.

IN THE DARK

Dulcette, Giuseppe, Del Monti and Mrs. Bovine

Men   Oh the eve is very dark
So I'm sure we'll not be seen,
If you join us for a lark,
Night will be a perfect screen.
Girls   Who you are we do not know,
But you think convention stuff,
So a little way we'll go
If it's only dark enough.

Girls   When you're sure you're out of sight,
Better throw your cares away,
There are things we do at night
That we wouldn't do by day.
Men   Just a word and we are gone
Far away beyond recall,
We'll be back before the dawn,
Or we won't be back at all.

     CHORUS
All H.
In the dark, dark, dark,
For a lark, lark, lark,
Let's go, let's go.
Oh the moon's never critical,
The stars analytical,
Oh, no, no, no!
We may never know your pedigree or ever see your face

But if we're sure there's no one 'round to hark
We'll go anywhere with anyone at any time or place,
If it's dark, quite dark.

LOVE OR EUGENICS

Celeste and Clover

Clover

1. My figure discloses no finicky poses
    No curve so soft and fair.
    No fashionable bustle but plenty of muscle,
    And Avoirdupois to spare.

Celeste

Now I'm a most popular, tippular, toppular
Maiden born to vex.
And yet he prefers me and always avers me
The queen of the feminine sex.

Clover

2. The rouge and the powder that make you look louder
    I always scorn to use.
    I'd rather be lorn with the face I was born with,
    A face never meant to abuse.

Celeste

You scorn good cosmetics in verses ascetic
But there's a reason alack!
For powder looks smart on, with something to start on,
A something you certainly lack.

CHORUS

Both

Ladies, Here's a problem none of you can flee,
Men, which would you like to come and pour your tea.
Kisses that set your heart aflame,

Or love from a prophylactic dame
Ladies, Take your choice of what your style shall be.

REMINISCENCE

Del Monti and Chorus

Del Monti
The shadows of evening have fallen at last
And memories sweet recall
The dream's gone forever, the joys long past,
The girls and the gaieties all
So fill to the brimming the cup of regret
And drink ere your fancies fly
Better to dream than to try and forgot,
Tho' your dreams bring a tear to your eye:

REFRAIN
Solo
Dreams, dreams, dreams,
They're a part
Of the shimmering heart of the wine,
They whisper of past loves,
Of first loves,
Of last loves,
Of memories half divine.
Drink, drink, drink,
To her smile,
'Mid the fancies the years enhance.
The old loves go by,
But we'll pause for a sigh,
O'er the ashes of dead romance.

Male Quartette
Dreams, dreams, dreams,
They're a part of the shimmering heart of the wine:
They whisper of past loves,

Of first loves,
Of last loves.
Of memories half divine.
Drink, drink, drink,
To her smile,
'Mid the fancies the years enhance.
The old loves go by
But we'll pause for a sigh,
O'er the ashes of dead romance.

FIE! FIE! FIFI!

Sady and Company

Sady   Company
                                    Fie! Fie! Fifi!
                                    We're shocked that you are married.
                                    Sly, sly, Fifi,
                                    Your little plan miscarried.

I only did what I thought best.

                                    The place for you is way out West,
                                    From manicuring take a rest,
                                    For far too long you've tarried.
                                    Fie! Fie! Fifi!

It seems I'm in the way;

                                    Bye-bye, Fifi!

I guess I'll leave today.

                                    Your looks belie,
                                    Without a sigh, we'll say goodbye,
                                    Fie! Fie! Fifi!
                                    Fie! Fie! Fifi!
                                    Fie! Fie!

THE MONTE CARLO MOON

Celeste and Archie

Mem'ries calling sweetly to me
In the summer night:
Cupid with his arrows slew me
When the moon was bright.
We were drifting slowly, sweetly
On a half forgotten day
When he turned and whispered neatly:
"Don't you wish 'twould ne'er be day."
"It won't" said the summer breeze:
"It won't" said the whisp'ring trees.

CHORUS
Underneath the Monte Carlo Moon, dear,
In June dear, we'll stay:
Drifting to a gentle southern tune, dear,
On a sentimental Oriental Bay.
Dreaming in the silver starlight,
'Ere the dawn comes all to soon.
In the summer weather
We'll be there together
Underneath the Monte Carlo moon.

FINALE ACT II

Full Chorus
Underneath the Monte Carlo moonlight
The June night is gay
Laughing, loving, dancing to the music
Of a serenading joy-persuading lay
So the ruby wine is flowing,
Happy we will all be soon
All our woes are over,
Ev'ry one's in Clover,
Underneath the Monte Carlo Moon.

A CHEER FOR PRINCETON

"Glory, Glory to the Black and Orange,
It's the Tiger's turn to-day.
Glory, glory, it's the same old story
Soon as Princeton starts to play.
Eli, Eli, all your hopes are dead
For the Tiger's growling in his lair.
Don't you hear him?
You'll learn to fear him,
Try to face him if you dare.

CHORUS:
Princeton, cheer for Princeton,
Raise your voices, loud and free
Strong and steady
Ever ready
For defeat or victory.
Princeton, cheer for Princeton,
Always sure to win renown,
So we'll raise our praise to Nassau
To the pride of the Tiger town.

"A Cheer for Princeton," *The Daily Princetonian*, October 28, 1915, p. 1. Fitzgerald's lyric won the competition for a new football song.

THE EVIL EYE

ACT I
OPENING CHORUS

Night Watchman
When the weary town is sleeping
Bar the watchman and the owl,
All around the streets we're creeping
Where the thieves and scoundrels prowl;
When the weary town is sleeping
We can hear the night winds howl
Till the tip of dawn come peeping
And the night-clouds cease to scowl.

'Neath the stars serenely beaming
With our eyes alert and wide
And our lanterns softly gleaming
Lest the sneaking rascal hide;
Neath the stars serenely beaming
With our lanterns close beside
While the town is all adreaming
And the trick of thieves defied.

Oh, the sleepy-head,
Best get out of bed,
Dream your dreams no more;
See the morn is here,
Night has gone, dear,
Sandman's fled from your door.
He's forsaken you,
We will waken you,
Send us not away;
Shut your eyes and count to ten,
Better get up, 'tis day!

The Evil Eye (Cincinnati, New York & London: John Church, 1915).
Princeton Triangle Club.

(*Entrance of Fishermen*)
Fishermen of character are we,
Picturesque and sturdy don't you see,
Up in the early morning
Bound for the stormy shore.
First we'll sing and then we'll disappear,
We'll be back directly don't you fear
'Though we be lonely
For the only girls we adore right here.

Ensemble
Come we'll sing a song of Brittany,
Ah! We'll tell our little history
All of a lonely maiden
Sighing in vain for love
Please applaud us till our course be run,
Jacques and Margot,
Claude and ev'ryone;
Dawn-bells are ringing,
Time for singing,
On with the play,
'Tis morn!

I'VE GOT MY EYES ON YOU

Margot

Rumor says I'm very catty,
Rumor lies.
I admit I'm rather chatty,
Somewhat wise;
Air all guilt in the beginning,
As the sinners keep on sinning;
What there be to it
I'll see to it
It flies.

I but said that Missus Burt had turned Brunette;
She passed by with head averted
When we met.
Surely taking down a beauty
Should be ev'ry woman's duty;
Soon you'll yearn for it,
You'll burn for it,
I'll bet.

CHORUS
So to my cause I'm true
I've got an eye on you
I can tell you I'm a real reformer,
Born to censor the haughty, punish the naughty.
Watch your step
Or you will lose your rep.
Conversation fattens on reputation,
Tho' it's just duty that's all.

 ON DREAMS ALONE

Claude and Dulcinea

Dear heart, tho' night be dreary,
The stars of hope may gleam;
Faint stars make me but weary,
I'm tired of dreaming dreams.
Ah, then ever I'm lonely for some once longed for June, dear,
Dream on, I love you only,
And I'll come soon, dear.

Love's own paradise near us,
And yet we answer not;
Love's own ears wait to hear us,
And still our love's forgot.
Doubts, cares, sorrows we'll banish, if only you will wake me;
Else my dreams will all vanish,
And love forsake us.

CHORUS
I'm dreaming all the while
My dreams grow bright at your smile.
Oh, I'll dream forever and aye
If dreams bring you some day,
Come live as love has shown.
Enough I call you my own;
For love, it seems
Can live on dreams,
On dreams alone.

THE EVIL EYE

Jacques

When I go harmlessly down the street,
They spread to left and to right.
If ever I'm near
They tremble with fear
And frequently die of fright.
I view a building; it's soon condemned;
I see some ships and they sink.
I look at a wife,
Her husband for life
Immediately takes to drink.
Ha, ha, ha, ha, ha, ha, ha, ha, ha.
A panic begins when I wink.

The Church collection on Sunday morn
Is not passed overly near.
They fear for its fate,
I'll shatter the plate,
And dollars will change to beer;
And all Theatres are closed to me,
The sleight-of-hand shark can't shine;
The lady that stars
On parallel bars

Collapses and breaks her spine.
Ha, ha, ha, ha, ha, ha, ha, ha, ha.
The bald-headed row change to swine.

CHORUS
Beware lest I look behind
If anyone's sick
By chance or trick
I'm fined.
The devil also others of my adopted brothers
By comparison are most kind.
Beware of my passing glance
"It's worse than any curse," they cry
It's all a story but just the same
I wish I had it, I'd play the game.
Beware, Beware, Beware, The Evil Eye.

WHAT I'LL FORGET

[*The Girl*]

I'm a girl who hasn't any memory,
It doesn't worry me at all;
Chorus girl or cast girl, prim girl, fast girl,
Dance, or just dance hall.
I've forgotten all the ills the doctor wants,
Appendicitis haunts me not;
May be I am ailing, slowly, surely, failing,
But I've quite forgot.

I'll forget the furry shoes they wear about,
Or rather tear about in, now,
Winter garden dollies,
Cafés, "Follies,"
Dance—I don't know how.
I've forgotten all the stone age sentiment
That used to find a vent in me;

When they say I'm pretty, then I think they're witty,
Such simplicity!

CHORUS
I've forgotten all the fashions and the passions
That are current in the present century,
All my past, perhaps a hot one, husband if I've got one,
And may be I'm a refugee;
I've forgotten all the Balkan situation,
I've forgotten whether hoops are stylish yet;
But the wonderful sensation of
This mental dislocation,
That's the only thing I can't forget.

I've forgotten all the hints to beauty seekers
Which the Sunday supplement will give you free,
All my past, perhaps a hot one, husband if I've got one,
And may be I'm a refugee;
I've forgotten if my age is worth concealing,
I've forgotten ev'ry bill and ev'ry debt;
But the wonderful sensation of
This mental dislocation,
That's the only thing I can't forget.

OVER THE WAVES TO ME

Jacques and The Girl

I've dreamt alone on the ocean track
When the stars were pale and cold
And the night clouds gathered scowling black
Of a face I should once behold,
A whisper sweet in a midnight blow,
A smile on a twilight wave;
But who was a fisher to dream on so
I, a dreamer to dreams a slave.

The sea that sang to a heart of stone on the cliffside years ago
Sang its hope to one who was lost alone
With the surge of its breakers low;
"Oh, bring my love and my life," I cried,
"And bring back my heart to me;"
And here as its answer you're by my side;
You're a wonderful friend,
Oh sea.

CHORUS
Over the waves,
O sea,
Bring my true love to me;
Promise to seek her far away,
Seek her where'er your billows play.
Then while I dream a lone
She whom I call my own
Over the seas, born by the breeze,
Comes to my heart, to me.

ON HER EUKALALI

The Mayor, Margot, Boileau, Dulcinea

William Jones to Honolulu went and on the beach
Feeling tender
Spied a slender
Hula Honolula peach.
Tho' he knew no
Honolulu talk, her heart knew best;
She kept strumming, softly humming things he guessed.

Bye and bye they married by the sea and care defied;
Surf board riding,
Seaward gliding,
She was always by his side.

His fiancée back in Bangor, Maine could vainly call.
Tho' he missed her like a sister, that was all.

CHORUS
Oh upon her Eukalali
She'd chatter to him gaily;
He could almost guess the things she meant,
She was from the orient.
She knew that he was saying,
"My boat has gone, I'm staying."
She smiled and just kept playing;
And they managed to find a way.

JUMP OFF THE WALL

Boileau

I'm very fond of fisher maids,
They're innocent and demure;
But still they say the city gay has such a mighty lure.
You'd like to try the Moulin Rouge and rule the feast alone;
But safe and high against the sky,
You'd better keep your throne.
With compliments inane
The city calls in vain.

The Paris lights, on August nights,
Keep humming your heart atune;
But simple maids, in caps and braids, prefer the harvest moon.
Au "Dansant Boire" the café noir is stronger far than wine;
So bob your hair, I'll pay your fare,
Romance is next in line.
The belles of Brittany
Have rung their last for me.

CHORUS
Fisher maids as brown as copper,
You'll get lonesome bye and bye,

Paris tho' is quite improper
Country walls are safe and high.
Come, we'll take a look at Maxim's
Some night we'll do them all.
On the boulevards, dears,
You'll be drawing-cards, dears,
Little girls jump off the wall.

FINALE ACT I

CHORUS
Jacques we're very sorry for the company you're keeping,
And you'd better go to prison or you'll stab us while we're sleeping,
For we're much afraid your sinking to a lower, lower level
When you spend you time in country roads and gossip with the devil.
We knew "La Rire" was written for the devil's humor, drat him!
You were reading all the risqué jokes and may be laughing at 'em;
The scales will soon be growing on your chest and on your tummy;
But the scales will give you character,
You're such an awful rummy.
Soon Satan will commence to golf and bridge with all the fellows,
And next install a telephone and flirt with all the "Hellos;"
The high brow social register will want at once to list him,
And the débutantes of Naiserie will brag because they've kiss'd him;
And such an awful state of things will drive us to distraction
You'd better try the jail a while and muse upon your action.
So stick to your level
And herd with the devil, go 'way.

Jacques
True to me now, oh sea,
Take not my love from me,
Mine when I kept her safe from harms,
Mine when I held her in my arms.
And tho' I stand alone,
She is my love, my own;
Tho' we may part,
Here in my heart
She will be mine, mine, mine.

ENSEMBLE
Oh, Jacques, you're really to blame,
These things are truly a shame,
Our town will loose its good name,
For you have reached your level
When you gossip with the devil,
We feel for Miss I-don't-know;
She's no experience, so
She had better take the fellow while she can,
True love is so beautiful,
Happy and dutiful;
He looks good to me
She'd better let it be.

ACT II

OPENING CHORUS

Dulcinea
Out of the sea returning,
Worn with their weary stay,
Now to their homes they are turning
Just at the close of day,
Draw in your nets full laden,
Hoist when the sun meets sea,
Here is a lonely maid en,
Waiting for Thee, for thee,
Here is a lonely maiden,
Waiting for thee, waiting for thee, waiting for thee.

(*Entrance of Fishermen*)
Sail on,
Sail on,
While the lapping wavelets kiss the side
Sail on,
Sail on,
Mermaids will ride beside
Sail on,

Sail on,
Lucky blows the homing wind, good men
Sail on,
Sail on,
Westward ho!
We're drifting home again.

HARRIS FROM PARIS

Mr. Harris

You're looking at a man
Who's modelled on a plan,
The up-to-date detective.
In Sunday magazines,
You've read of my machines
For making jails selective.
The intimate affairs
Of multi millionaires
Are vested safe within me;
For money in advance,
I'll find the King of France
And prove his ancestry.

The crooks of other times
Were judged upon their crimes;
It's now their circulation;
Deduction will not serve,
You test their pressure curve
And try their chest inflation.
Craig Kennedy's the King;
The lab'ratory thing
Is getting quite au fait,
The burglar is so wise
He laughs at your disguise;
This progress makes me gray.

CHORUS
Harris from Paris,
The dread of the crook,
Sleuth-hound from Broadway,
You're down in his book.
Knifers and lifers
Turn pale at his call;
Gangmen thereabout learn to care about Harris,
That's all.

TWILIGHT

A *Gypsy*

Come, wander where the firefly gleams;
Night's mingling with day.
Come soon for all the summer beams
Fade slowly away.
Night will burn you with its kisses;
Day will charm you with its eyes,
I'm waiting for the twilight time
Where mystery lies.

Love's sweeter in the afterglow
Born over the years;
Red roses when their beauties go
Hold laughter and tears.
Gold is fading in the yellow,
Yellow melting into gray;
Eve's perfumed with the Jessamine,
Farewell to the day.

CHORUS
Twilight, shylight,
Thro' the shadow land we'll stroll
Dreaming,
Dreaming,
While the mellow night-bells toll

Softly,
Softly
Fade the summer daylight while
I'm peace at last obtaining
In the waning twilight time.

"THE NEVER, NEVER LAND"

Jacques, The Girl, Claude, Dulcinea

MEN
    Just listen, I'll tell you of a plan, dear,
    A hunch for a gay honeymoon;
(*Girls*) I'll listen and listen all I can, dear,
    Keep talking from now till June;
(*Men*) Discovered an undiscovered country,
    On shores of the sea I-don't-know.
(*Girls*) You haven't told us yet;
(*Men*) The truth is, we forget;
(*All*) But we know how to get there when we go.

MEN
    Its' lure is forever calling you, dear;
    Enchanted the fair skies above;
(*Girls*) The laws are but one, that you'll be true, dear,
    The password is only Love.
(*Men*) The song of the nation is an old one,
    It's only, I love you alone.
(*Girls*) This land preserves, you see,
    It's own neutrality
(*All*) And even guards of lovers are unknown.

REFRAIN
To the land of the never, never
Where we can love forever,
We will sail away;
So put the ring where it ought to linger,
On your engagement finger,

Pack your little grip, we'll leave today;
And there's no room for care and sorrow,
We'll not be back tomorrow,
Carefully we've planned;
There'll be no one around when we're departing, starting
For the never, never land.

MY IDEA OF LOVE

Mme. Mirliflore and Mr. Harris

A drug clerk, "Mike," from Yonkers
Loved Esmerelda Sage;
One evening he proposed that she
Should share his humble wage;
And when he'd gotten calmer,
She cooly answered, "Mike,
I'll meet some day my fiancée,
I'll tell you what he's like."

Young Stuyvesant, worth millions,
Came touring through the town;
He met Miss Sage, and asked her age,
And wished to settle down.
The day that they were married,
He said with fond appeal,
"My eyes so blue have won me you;"
She told him her ideal.

CHORUS
Give him a swell name like Astor,
Give him a great big limousine,
Show me the mansion where he's master,
Add just the touch that keeps the
Brain from tinkling, clothes from wrinkling,
Give him a face that won't scare you
Fringed with a little hair above;
Hand me the silken halter

That will lead him to the altar,
That's my idea of love.

OTHER EYES

Jacques and Quartette

When one at last
Denies his past
To honor and obey
With fervor and sighs
You swear that her eyes
Are brighter than you can say
She says, "How nice!"
She blushes twice;
On compliments she's fed;
But you know well
You'll never tell
Of ghosts that aren't quite dead
A lot of things you've left unsaid.

The loves of old
That once unfold,
The heart with tender bliss
Are folded away
With dreams of the day
That smiled on another kiss
The songs and sighs
To the other eyes
Have sung and sighed their last;
But in your breast,
Tho' unconfessed,
Your heart could still beat fast
For all the youthful romance past.

CHORUS
Solo
  Tell her of the other eyes
  That call you in the night,
Tenor I
  Tell her of the other eyes
   That call you in the night, dark night.
Tenor II
Base I
Tell her of the other eyes
   That call you in the night, dark night.
Base II

  Eyes of sadness,
  Eyes of gladness, past delight,
  Eyes of sadness,
  Eyes of gladness, past delight, her tears still shining,
  Eyes of sadness,
  Eyes of gladness, past delight, her tears still shining,

  Ne'er forgetting, half regretting other sunny skies
  Ne'er forgetting, half regretting other sunny skies ne'er fading
  Ne'er forgetting, half regretting other sunny skies ne'er fading

  How they haunt you,
  Seem to want you, other eyes.
  How they haunt you,
  Seem to want you, other eyes.
  How they haunt you,
  Seem to want you, other eyes.

THE GIRL OF THE GOLDEN WEST

Jacques

Cowboys are what I can dote upon,
Like those Puccini wrote upon
Roaming the plains of the golden west;
Girls who are quick with the gun or knife,

Tho' they're still quicker to be your wife.
I'm going to start upon a merry quest.
I know that soon I'll flit,
Out where Puccini got it.

Fair ladies staged so dramatic'ly,
Brave deeds done operatic'ly
Give me a wonderful thrill for fair;
Bad men who rampage and run about,
Carelessly swinging a gun about,
Add such a bristle to my curly hair.
High are the horse-thieves hung;
I want to hear the deed sung.

CHORUS
Ride your horse right to my heart,
(*All a-whirl, all a-whirl, for my little girl.*)
Tied am I by cowgirl art
(*To a tree, to a tree, hanging over me,*)
We await the hour
When we can round 'em up again
In that operatic style.
I'm happy while Caruso twirls his rope
While the hills while the hills, ring with tenor trills,
You could swear he had the dope
(*On the names, on the names, such as Jesse James,*)
Don't know whether to bide or go
To the borders of Idaho
Oh—Puccini, do it some more.

WITH ME

The Girl, Mme. Mirliflore, Mr. Harris and Boileau

There's a proverb I have heard:
"Two heads are better than one;"
Two together in any old weather
Have ever so much more fun;
So don't be stingy with yourself,

Show generosity;
No solo you get can beat a duet,
Come form a trust with me.

Solo dancing's all the rage;
Nevertheless it is true,
Give me a lady who's never old-maidy
But saves up a lot for you.
I'd rather dance with Mary Brown
Than look at Miss Deslys;
So give me your hand and signal the band,
You're going to dance with me.

CHORUS
Play, play, play with me,
Promise you'll come and stay with me.
I could love you, dear, quite a bit,
Even tho' we should fight a bit.
Hide, ride, bide with me,
Merry we two shall be
And ev'ry single thing you do,
Promise you'll do with me.

SAFETY FIRST!

(A) PROLOGUE

Spirit of the Future

Hail to the spirit of the muse of Youth,
Dear to the hardest heart!
Hail to the sunny seekers after Truth,
That herald modern art!
Hail to the century of foolish fads,
Best century and worst!
Be this the gist of our satire,

Safety First! (Cincinnati, New York & London: John Church, 1916).
Princeton University Triangle Club.

To make your rule Safety First!
Eyes up!
We're off!

(B) GARDEN OF ARDEN

Spirit of the Future, Ralph, Bill, Betty and Cynthia

Garden of Arden in fairyland,
When love and art linger hand in hand;
Far from the passions, the hobbies and fashions,
Glad beyond measure, rich in our search for pleasure,
You are invited to wander there.
We'll be delighted you know;
Always it's June, 'neath the Calcium Moon,
To the Garden of Arden we'll go.

Act I

OPENING CHORUS

Howard, Percy and Chorus

Art Studends
  Prettily painting,
  Frequently painting,
  Weak with art,
  Braving the yawning
  Depths of the dawning,
  Set apart,
  Trying to roll in some of our soul in pictures that don't come true;
  Work! work! the gallery waits for all we do.
  Hail, Cubo!
  Jitney muse of post-impression!
  We make confession
  You're all for show,
  You're a very gentle grafter;
  Bouillon cubes they named you after;

Excuse our laughter,
Ha ha ha, Cubo!

SEND HIM TO TOM

The Convicts

Dear old Ding Ding, home of the blest, Invalid's rest,
after leaving the court, you're my summer resort:
Since my father Shermy, the worm, finished his term,
Osborne Merry has made it very seductive to one sport:

We're so bored with people who dare not to prepare,
Men who worship their purse, women probably worse;
Some day soon we'll send them a way, send them to stay,
Up the river to help their liver They seem to need a nurse:

When the Allies finally win, capture Berlin,
Here's the problem they'll get, one they'll never forget;
What to do with William the King, nasty old thing,
This solution will suit the "Roosian" as well as any yet:

CHORUS
Send him to Tom,
Send him to Tom,
There he'll better his ways
Kings of the trust,
Bankers that bust,
Pass the rest of their days,
Knitting neckties for Belgiums
Cutting down their aplomb,
There they will cure weep for the poor
Just send them to Tom.

Send them to Tom,
Send them to Tom,
Far from whispers of war

Needles and Thread,
Early to bed,
Paper dollies galore,
Parsons pink and pacific
Bryan bearing his palm,
Ivory domes nobody homes
Just send them to Tom.

Send him to Tom,
Send him to Tom,
Sword and speeches and "Hochs",
Give him a year,
Serve him no beer,
Start him darning his socks,
Read him stories by Henry
Keep him quiet and calm,
Put him to work chained to a Turk
Just send him to Tom.

ONE-LUMP PERCY

Percy

1 Snakes were once despised of beasts
And unappreciated,
They were not invited to the feasts,
To eat alone were fated;
But now a diff'rent brand of snake
Does Cleopatra handle,
For it feeds on tea and angel cake
And knows the latest scandal.

2 Some girls like them "big and strong"
And some prefer them mental,
But I'd rather listen all day long,
When you grow sentimental;
Your line is stocked with artifice

And other people's humor,
For you draw conclusions from a kiss
And scandal from a rumor.

CHORUS
One lump Percy, Percy, the parlor snake,
Please have mercy, Percy for mercy's sake,
Tender hearts you're breaking,
Some one forsaking;
When upon your knee your tea you balance,
We lose sight of other gallants,
King of parlor talents,
Percy the parlor snake.

WHERE DID BRIDGET KELLY
GET HER PERSIAN TEMPERAMENT?

Ralph and Chorus

I'm oh so very blue today;
I haven't got a thing to say!
My Bridget has torn my loving heart in two,
I don't know what I shall do!

I could'nt sleep a wink last night;
I'm looking for a man to fight!
Tony with his curly muspistachios,
I'll get him and spoil his clothes!

CHORUS
Where did Bridget Kelly get her Persian temp'rament?
I'm a very angry man at her,
For she left her cop,
Goes with that Tony wop,
Eats his peanuts in his dirty shop,
Soon she'll dress up in jewels and veils;
All her beautifull vermillion hair
Is dyed away,

Now she's got an oriental air;
She's smoking Meccas
Murads and Fatimas,
Since my Bridget got her temp'rament.

IT IS ART

Percy

We're kneeling at the shrine of post-impression,
The art whose patron saint is Doctor Cook;
Our chief and only patrons,
Are feebleminded Matrons,
And dilettantes who have to have a cook.
There are no strict requirements for a cubist,
You only need a dipper full of paint,
A little distance bring it
And at your canvas fling it,
Then shut your eyes and name it what it ain't.

For anything's a subject if it's ugly,
And anything's a picture if it hangs;
I'm using as a sitter,
A young banana fritter,
And painting her in pantalettes and bangs.
We try to sketch the passion in the onion,
We never do the hair, we paint the part;
We've passed through ev'ry stage
And reached the golden age
When anything and ev'rything is art.

REFRAIN
Art, Art, the period is o'er
When your standards stand apart;
Mister Comstock's indignation
Gives a picture reputation
And doubles its sale as Art.

Art, Art, you're getting rather deep,
Common Sense and you must part;
For a complex cubist dimple
Makes the "Mona Lisa" simple,
There's no "Safety First" in Art.

SAFETY FIRST

Ralph, Bill, Betty, and Cynthia

Sages for ages have said to hasten slowly,
To stay away from phoney tricks
And never hit a cop,
When one rocks the boat a bit
The undertakers gloat a bit
They'll place you in a two-by-six
And they'll hammer down the top.

Fair ones are rare ones for never picking winners,
They like the man with wavy hair
Who looks like Bruce McRae,
Who's able to walk about
And competent to talk about
Their color and their baby stare
And why New York is gay.

CHORUS
Oh, you might be careful
If you won't be good,
The aeroplane is beautifull and new,
But Mother Earth is good enough for you,
'Though you like her dancing
And you know her name,
This love is just a game of chance,
She'll try to do her worst;
So hide your watch before you dance,
For Safety First!

For the men who thrill you
May be clerks by day,
So wed a man who's prosperous tho' meek
Or else you'll take in washing by the week;
Though he's most entrancing
And he knows new steps,
And calls himself a Duke or Count
Or Baron at the worst,
Just ask to see his bank account,
For Safety First!

CHARLOTTE CORDAY

Ralph, Cynthia and Chorus

Back where Robespiere ruled
In frivolous fickle France,
That's when someone was fooled
And fooled in a bold way, fooled in the old way.
Young Miss Charlotte Corday
Of the "Follies of Ninety three,"
Asked old Marat to buy her a hat,
Oh, mercy on me!
So Marat he had it sent,
And to her little flat it went,
Oh!

Poor old Mister Marat,
He never was more surprised,
For he ordered the hat
To get him in strong there,
He was in wrong there.
When she looked in the glass,
For, oh, she was very trim,
Found it too big, it mussed up her wig;
So she showed him;
She had him at her nod and beck

And so he got it in the neck,
Oh!

CHORUS
Charlotte Corday, Charlotte Corday,
You had them all on the string;
Gee, they were mean to guillotine
A sweet, little innocent thing!
Got the hat when you wanted it,
Tried it on, but it didn't fit,
Then you joined the wrath club,
Stabbed him in his bathtub,
Served him just right, he was a fright,
You were impulsive through life.
Many a dame, does just the same,
But stabs with her eyes, not a knife;
Still we've thought upon it,
And we wear your bonnet;
Charlotte Corday, Charlotte Corday,
You were some girl in your day!

UNDERNEATH THE APRIL RAIN

Bill, Cynthia and Chorus

One day ere May had brought one wonderful flower,
'Twas in a stummering shower, I saw her pass by,
I stared, I dared to be an impudent fellow,
To spread my big umbrella, tell her that she was welcome.

We walked, we talked and thought no more of the weather;
We stayed so closely together we didn't get wet,
The rain in vain dripped on attempting to drown us;
But drops that fell around us found us quite unobserving.

CHORUS
April rain,
Dripping happily,

Once again catch my love and me;
Beneath our own umbrella cosy,
The world will still seem gay and rosy.
Drip, drip, drop, while we're strolling down
Through the stunning town;
And since it's turning colder,
I'll hold her, enfold her
Under the Thunder with love and the rain.

FINALE ACT I

"DANCE, LADY, DANCE"

Ralph and Chorus

Ralph
Afar in the distance again
A violin takes up the strain,
So you to the waltz as the leaf to the rose,
Come dance with me in dreams that dances will disclose!
So

CHORUS
1st time: Ralph
2nd time: Ensemble
dance, dance, Lady, dance, weaving in the same design with eyes
    and lips that cling to mine;
And love, love, love while you may,
For the rose in the day will wither.
Dear, dear, hold me near,
Mine the hour ere the dawn,
For youth and love will soon be gone;
    [1] we'll glide, glide in to the night While the waning moon is bright.
    [2] And as soft violins sigh, as the violins sigh.
One long goodbye,
Dance, Lady, dance ere the night goes by!

ACT II

(A) SAFETY FIRST

Chorus

CHORUS
When the 'cello's sighing
And the lights are low,
The new loves seem much nearer than the old
Remember all that glitters is'nt gold;
Tho' the wine forgetfull
Turns your soul aglow,
The chilly dawn will quench the fire,
And thunder storms may burst;
So keep enough for Taxi hire
For safety First.

(B) HELLO TEMPTATION *

Ralph and Chorus

Ralph
    I've a friend who does'nt know tomorrow.
Girls
    (He's very nice very nice.)
Ralph
    Lives his life today for fun and fame.
Girls
    (what a thrill what a thrill what a thrill!)
Ralph
    Makes a hit with all of us

---

* A leaf of the songbook has been reversed, so that pages 51 and 52 are mis-numbered and mis-ordered. The ordering of the lyric is here corrected.

And plays a bit with all of us
And Lord Temptation's his name.
Ralph
    Miss temptation's just as nice as Mister.
Girls
    (She's quite a kid, quite a kid.)
Ralph
    Takes her suitors old and rather bald.
Girls
    (pretty bald pretty bald pretty bald,)
Ralph
    Dances like Pavlowa does
    And charms you like a boa does
    And Miss Temptation she's called.

    CHORUS
    Hello Temptation I'll play with you,
    Tempt me with something I should'nt do, stolen sweets are best,
    We've stolen much, we'll steal the rest
    Before we leave you;
    Take me and make me your fav'rite child,
    Lead me
    Let's go!
    Oh, resist you I can't, Sir,
    Just page me, I'll answer,
    Temptation, hello!

WHEN THAT BEAUTIFUL CHORD CAME TRUE

The Pianist and Chorus

    One day I sat, took a pat
    At my baby grand, my Chickering
    Glued to the stool, like a fool,
    I was musically bickering;
    Played something pash with a dash,
    That was Spanish in its temp'rament

Then all those keys came true,
Each one a maid, a laughing maid,

Often I've dreamed that it seemed
Ev'ry melody must have a heart,
Were all the notes from the throats
of a chorus in a world apart?
Sprites from above or perhaps
little Demons from a place below
Even a blonde or so?
And soon I knew it could be true,

CHORUS
When that joyfull chord came true,
And the notes hurried out ran about,
Then that room turned sickly blue,
And I reeled almost keeled from the stool.
A was a Persian petter,
B natural knew no better,
Little C was sentimental
She was horribly oriental,
Each in harmony a grees,
(Little G pours my tea ev'ry day,)
As they dance upon the keys
gleaming bright, black and white, in the night;
I've acted like the dickens
With those harmonic chickens,
Beautiful chord, now that you've come true.

RAG-TIME MELODRAMA

Convicts, Detectives and Chorus

Convicts
Surprise will fell you
When we will tell you
In strictest confidence
We are not really masquerading,
But rather Uncle Sam evading.
The clothes we've got on
Are really not on
To help the merriment
But for protection
From life election
Back to the cell we'll be sent!

Detectives
Oh, here we come, we're going some!
The cops are strolling up the avenue
In little Fords
With running boards to hold our captives
to hold our captives who will have a new number of their own,
Not a telephone;
For they have no bells in their private cells.
Whom have we here Horatio?

Convicts
Ah!

Detectives
Oh! Clue!

Convicts
No!

Detectives
We can't be wrong,

The clues are strong,
we'd better take them into custody!

Convicts
Oh, we've got a date,
We're sorry to run away,
Yes we're late.
Tut, Tut! put your gun away!
See you soon, Goodbye!

Detectives
Whats the rush!

Convicts
Goodday!

Ensemble
Got a date, got a date, got a date, got a date,
Got to see a fellow who is terribly sick!
Better wait, better wait, better wait better wait!
Stick around a minute and we'll show you a trick!

Convicts
Handcuffs weren't made for me,
Just give me liberty,

Ensemble
Got a date, got a date, got a date, got a date,
Must hurry along!

SCENE II

Spirit of the Future

Stop! what's the row? what's all
This commotion
In our colony formed for quietude?
Cease now, let's have peace now!
You have shocked my sober sobrietude!
Why this scurry and hateful hurry?
The tree trunks themselves are all nervous and quivery.
Hush your clatter, your childish chatter!
You act like a boy with a Special Delivery!
What's all this commotion
In our colony formed for quietude?
Cease now, let's have peace now!
You have shocked my sober sobrietude!

TAKE THOSE HAWAIIAN SONGS AWAY

Bill, Cynthia and Chorus

Now'days from giddy Piccadilly
Back to the snores of sleepy Philly,
You can hear the strum of the euralali,
Mingled with the sliding guitar;
I'm not too strong for Claude Debussy
Or for this Russian Charlotte "Russey,"
But now they push Hawaii too far;
I'm tired of hearing:

Once all the world was growing dippy
For Alabam' and Mississippi,
Franz Lehar once kept us in time with him
With his waltzes dreamy and loud;
Next ev'ry debutante was whirlin'

Round at the will of Irving Berlin,
Lately he's joined the popular crowd
And now he writes like:

CHORUS
Oo-ley Bool-ey wool-ey-ing
By the Cool-ey ool-ey-ing
On her Eu-ki-wak-i-wee,
She would ick-y ick to me
This is all they sing about,
Stuff like this they fling about,
When will they shift to a new locality?
Iona Bologna is her name,
Each Hula dame
Is named the same
As the others.
Honolulu go away,
You have more than had your day!
Take those Hawaiian songs away,
Eu-ka-la-li-oo-li-ay!

THE VAMPIRES WON'T VAMPIRE FOR ME

Percy and Sal

Oft en I have seen on the screen,
Pictures living and snappy,
Girls quite a fistfull ingenues wistful,
Loving I look at that makes me unhappy;
Tell me why are girls that I meet,
Always simple and slow?
I want a brunette like those I met,
Back in the seven reel show.

Lik ing striking blondes as I do,
Hair that's golden and rippling,
Why don't I meet a few that are'nt sweet but

Act very much like the ladies in Kipling?
Dolls are very numerous now,
Many wonders Ive seen;
But I'd like a wife early in life,
Someone who learned on the screen.

CHORUS
Theda Bara they say,
Drives depression away,
What Olga Petrova knows won't go in the censored shows!
Why are ladies I meet
Never more than just sweet?
Girls seem to be Vampires,
But they won't vampire for me.

THE HUMMIN' BLUES

Ralph, Bill, Percy and Guild Master

My love has gone away,
She would'nt stay,
She left today,
I'm feeling' mighty lonely,
For I want her, want her only!
The little bird she knew
Has gone along away and left me too;
He's not returnin',
I miss the yearnin'
Hummin' songs he used to sing.
Oh

The shadows gather near,
The stars appear,
Why don't I hear,
The song we heard together,
In some other summer weather?
Oh, little bird I know

You wouldn't go away, we loved you so.
I know you want me,
Your hummin's haunt me,
Hum a sadder melody.
Oh

CHORUS
Hummin' bird, Hummin' bird,
Hummin' thro' the lingerin' twilight,
Sing in' sad for your lad
'Cause he's got the blues melodious blues;
Seems as tho'
You must know
My longin' heart is ayearnin',
Lovin' bird, I need you with your hummin' blues!
My little ever lovin' blues!

DOWN IN FRONT

Ralph, Bill, Percy, Howard, the Guild Master and the Convicts

I've been around triangling,
I'm used to angling you know;
I've travelled o'er this ground before,
As you'll have found out before I go.
Once while singing something clinging I beheld the girl
I'd been seeking,
Primly peeking at me.

So, like a fool I married her,
Ha! ha! And carried her away,
Drew out a check on father dear,
Then settled down prepared to stay.
Since she'd known me as a pony in triangle plays,
Hooking dresses, I confess, is my job.

REFRAIN

Down in front, there the lady sat
gazing on me, eyes upon me, just like that!
Watched me act,
That's a fact,
Heard her laughter, met her after,
Tipped my hat;
Liked her fine,
Liked her lilac eyes entrancing,
Liked her line,
Liked her face and liked her dancing,
She's my wife, mine for life,
I loved her when she was down in front.

Down in front, 'round and up in back,
Thus I hooked her till she looked her very best;
Night and day, that's the way;
Such a deadlock in the wedlock, never rest!
I was rash,
Her dressmakers must be gluttons,
Belt and sash,
Hooks and eyes and holes and buttons!
"Oswald" dear, hurry here!
You've got to hook my dress down in front.

FINALE

Entire Cast and Chorus

Oh, the play is over
And the song is sung,
The paint comes off,
The wig is put away,
The violin's dumb until another day;
For the pony ballet
With their figures Trim
Can stand no more this awful pest, their corsets most accursed
And now they'll give themselves a rest for Safety First!

Goodbye, Temptation,
We're tired of you;
Tempt us
No more for we're really through.
You have said your say,
Just go away
We've won the day
And you're resisted;
Time was we courted and welcome you
Nor were you shy;
But since we out did you,
We cheerfully bid you,
Temptation, goodbye.

TO MY UNUSED GREEK BOOK

(Acknowledgments to Keats)

Thou still unravished bride of quietness,
    Thou joyless harbinger of future fear,
Garrulous alien, what thou mightst express
    Will never fall, please God, upon my ear.
What rhyme or reason can invest thy shape
    That is not found in countless syllibi?
What trots and cribs there are, what ponies rich,
    With all thou sing'st and in a clearer key.
Expose thee to a classroom's savage rape?
    Nay! better far remain within thy niche.

Tasks all complete are sweet, but those untried
    Are sweeter, therefore little book, with page
Uncut, stay pure, and live thy life inside,
    And wait for some appreciative age.
Oh, Author, most admired and left alone,
    Thou cans't not ever see the garish day.
Editor, never, never wilt thou speak,
    But yellow grow and petrify to stone
Where I shall throw thee after tests next week;
    Yet grieve not—ever thou'lt have much to say.

Oh happy, happy, leaves that cannot shed
   Their ink, or ever bid the print adieu;
Oh happy, happy, bard who never bled
   At verse of his droned out with meaning new.
No words are penciled in a barbarous tongue
   Above thy dactyls oft misunderstood;
Caesuras are not marked to shame thy taste;
   Thy song is as you sing it, though unsung.
If not of use at least thou'rt noble waste;
   Let stand thy native accent as it should.

—F. Scott Fitzgerald

"To My Unused Greek Book (Acknowledgments to Keats)," *The Nassau Literary Magazine*, LXXII (June 1916), 137.

RAIN BEFORE DAWN

The dull, faint patter in the drooping hours
   Drifts in upon my sleep and fills my hair
   With damp; the burden of the heavy air
Is strewn upon me where my tired soul cowers,
Shrinking like some lone queen in empty towers
   Dying. Blind with unrest I grow aware:
   The pounding of broad wings drifts down the stair
And sates me like the heavy scent of flowers.

I lie upon my heart. My eyes like hands
Grip at the soggy pillow. *Now the dawn*
Tears from her wetted breast the splattered blouse
Of night; lead-eyed and moist she straggles o'er the lawn,
Between the curtains brooding stares and stands.
Like some drenched swimmer—Death's within the house!

—F. Scott Fitzgerald

"Rain Before Dawn," *The Nassau Literary Magazine*, LXXII (February 1917), 321.

PRINCETON—THE LAST DAY

The last light wanes and drifts across the land,
The low, long land, the sunny land of spires.
The ghosts of evening tune again their lyres
And wander singing, in a plaintive band
Down the long corridors of trees. Pale fires
Echo the night from tower top to tower.
Oh sleep that dreams and dream that never tires,
Press from the petals of the lotus-flower
Something of this to keep, the essence of an hour!

No more to wait the twilight of the moon
In this sequestrated vale of star and spire;
For one, eternal morning of desire
Passes to time and earthy afternoon.
Here, Heracletus, did you build of fire
And changing stuffs your prophecy far hurled
Down the dead years; this midnight I aspire
To see, mirrored among the embers, curled
In flame, the splendor and the sadness of the world.

—*F. Scott Fitzgerald*

"Princeton—The Last Day," *The Nassau Literary Magazine*, LXXIII (May 1917), 95.

ON A PLAY TWICE SEEN

Here in the figured dark I watch once more;
　There with the curtain rolls a year away,
　A year of years—There was an idle day
Of ours, when happy endings didn't bore
Our unfermented souls, and rocks held ore:
　Your little face beside me, wide-eyed, gay,

Smiled its own repertoire, while the poor play
Reached me as a faint ripple reaches shore.

Yawning and wondering an evening through
   I watch alone—and chatterings of course
      Spoil the one scene which somehow *did* have charms;
You wept a bit, and I grew sad for you
   Right there, where Mr. X defends divorce
      And What's-Her-Name falls fainting in his arms.

                —F. Scott Fitzgerald

"On a Play Twice Seen," *The Nassau Literary Magazine*, LXXIII (June 1917), 149.

THE CAMEO FRAME

I

Golden, golden is the air,
   Golden is the air,
Golden frets of golden mandolins,
Golden notes of golden violins,
     Fair . . . Oh wearily fair;
Skeins from woven basket
   Mortal may not hold,
Oh what young extravagant god,

   Who would know or ask it . . .
    Who could give such gold . . .

     Oh the proud page
     In the gold gloaming,
     When the light whispers
     And the souls roaming,
     Ports the grey train,
     Sees the gold hair

In the gay
The golden air

She posed that day by the marble pool
    At half after five, so her fancy led;
Her slim grey pages, her lord, her fool
    Clacked various clacks as they watched the head
Acomba was doing . . . his own request . .
    Her head—just from swirling hair to throat,
With clinging silk for a shoulder sheath
And half the curve of a breast beneath.

"Head to the left . . so . . Can you stand
    A little more sun on hair and face?"
Then as he lightly touched her hand
    She whispered to him a time, a place
Then he aloud "Here's the very light,
    My Lord, for the gold and rose effect . .
Such a light over pool and sky
As cameo never was graven by."

Over her grey and velvet dress
    Under her molten, beaten hair
Color of rose in mock distress
    Flushes and fades and makes her fair
Fills the air from her to him
    With light and languor and little sighs
Just so subtly he scarcely knows
Laughing lightening, color of rose.

And grey to rose, and rose to gold
    The color of day is twain, is one;
And he blinds his eyes that his heart may hold
    This cameo on the setting sun,
And lip and fingers as lip and lip
    Burn together and chill apart
And he turns his head as he sees her go,
Beautiful, pitiful, cameo.

Oh the proud page
In the green gloaming,
When the grass whispers
And the souls roaming,
Ports the grey train,
Sees the gold hair
In the gay
The golden air.

II

The night was another fragile frame
    Tall and quiet and fair to fill;
It made for Acomba when he came
    A silver setting . . . He watched until
She fluttered down from the guarded hall
    A weary leaf from a dreary tree,
Fluttered to him where the breezes cool
Made pale love to the marble pool.

Then the moon and his heart sank low . . .
    All that he knew of a sudden there
Was just that the light on the cameo
    Was not the light that had made it fair . .
Not the grey and not the rose,
    Not the gold of the afternoon,
So he kissed it sadly and spoke a name
And he pressed it back in its silver frame.

And youth in anger, and time in tears
    Sat at his feet and bade him take . .
"Once a day for a thousand years
    Think of the gold her hair will make . .
Shaper of lips you may not kiss
    Scorn you the soul where colors touch
Kept for you in a golden sleep! . . . ."
But he could never say why . . . or weep.

So ice by day and ghost by night
    The cameo lay till its moment came
And blushed for the sunset bold and bright
    Gold and rose in its velvet frame,
And he who made it would stand and smile,
    Pause and pity and count the years,
Watch and watch till the frame turned blue
Knower of things was he . . . . he knew . .

Golden, golden is the air,
    Golden is the air,
Golden frets of golden mandolins,
Golden notes from golden violins,
    Fair, oh wearily fair;
Skiens from woven basket
    Mortal may not hold
Oh what young extravagant god
    Who would know or ask it
    Who could give such gold!

—F. Scott Fitzgerald

"The Cameo Frame," *The Nassau Literary Magazine,* LXXIII (October 1917), 169–172.

CITY DUSK

Come out . . . . out
To this inevitable night of mine
Oh you drinker of new wine,
Here's pageantry. . . . . Here's carnival,
Rich dusk, dim streets and all
The whisperings of city night. . . . .

I have closed my book of fading harmonies,
(The shadows fell across me in the park)
And my soul was sad with violins and trees,

And I was sick for dark,
When suddenly it hastened by me, bringing
Thousands of lights, a haunting breeze,
And a night of streets and singing. . . . .

I shall know you by your eager feet
And by your pale, pale hair;
I'll whisper happy incoherent things
While I'm waiting for you there. . . . .

All the faces unforgettable in dusk
Will blend to yours,
And the footsteps like a thousand overtures
Will blend to yours,
And there will be more drunkenness than wine
In the softness of your eyes on mine. . . . .

Faint violins where lovely ladies dine,
The brushing of skirts, the voices of the night
And all the lure of friendly eyes. . . . . Ah there
We'll drift like summer sounds upon the summer air. . . . .

—*F. Scott Fitzgerald,*
Lieutenant 45th Infantry

"City Dusk," *The Nassau Literary Magazine,* LXXIII (April 1918), 315.

MY FIRST LOVE

All my ways she wove of light
  Wove them half alive,
Made them warm and beauty-bright . . .
  So the shining, ambient air
  Clothes the golden waters where
    The pearl fishers dive.

When she wept and begged a kiss
   Very close I'd hold her,
Oh I know so well in this
   Fine, fierce joy of memory
   She was very young like me
     Tho half an aeon older.

Once she kissed me very long,
   Tip-toed out the door,
Left me, took her light along,
   Faded as a music fades. . . . .
   Then I saw the changing shades,
   Color-blind no more.

          —*F. Scott Fitzgerald,* '18

"My First Love," *The Nassau Literary Magazine,* LXXIV (February 1919), 102.

MARCHING STREETS

Death slays the moon and the long dark deepens,
   Hastens to the city, to the drear stone-heaps,
Films all eyes and whispers on the corners,
   Whispers to the corners that the last soul sleeps.

Gay grow the streets now torched by yellow lamplight,
   March all directions with a long sure tread.
East, west they wander through the blinded city,
   Rattle on the windows like the wan-faced dead.

Ears full of throbbing, a babe awakens startled,
   Sends a tiny whimper to the still gaunt room.
Arms of the mother tighten round it gently,
   Deaf to the patter in the far-flung gloom.

Old streets hoary with dear, dead foot-steps
   Loud with the tumbrils of a gold old age

Young streets sand-white still unheeled and soulless,
   Virgin with the pallor of the fresh-cut page.

Black streets and alleys, evil girl and tearless,
   Creeping leaden footed each in thin, torn coat,
Wine-stained and miry, mire choked and winding,
   Wind like choking fingers on a white, full throat.

White lanes and pink lanes, strung with purpled roses,
   Dance along the distance weaving o'er the hills,
Beckoning the dull streets with stray smiles wanton,
   Strung with purpled roses that the stray dawn chills.

Here now they meet tiptoe on the corner,
   Kiss behind the silence of the curtained dark;
Then half unwilling run between the houses,
   Tracing through the pattern that the dim lamps mark.

Steps break steps and murmur into running,
   Death upon the corner spills the edge of dawn
Dull the torches waver and the streets stand breathless;
   Silent fades the marching and the night-noon's gone.

—F. Scott Fitzgerald, '18

"Marching Streets," *The Nassau Literary Magazine*, LXXIV (February 1919),
103–104.

THE POPE AT CONFESSION

The gorgeous vatican was steeped in night,
   The organs trembled to my heart no more,
But with the blend of colors on my sight
   I loitered through a sombre corridor
And suddenly I heard behind a screen
   The faintest whisper, as from one in prayer,
I glanced around, then passed, for I had seen
   A hushed and lonely room . . . . and two were there—

A ragged friar, half in a dream's embrace
Leaned sideways, soul intent, as if to seize
The last grey ice of sin that ached to melt
And faltered from the lips of him who knelt—
A little bent old man upon his knees
With pain and sorrow in his holy face.

—*F. Scott Fitzgerald*, '18

"The Pope at Confession," *The Nassau Literary Magazine*, lxxiv (February 1919), 105.

A DIRGE

(*Apologies to Wordsworth*)

By F. Scott Fitzgerald

It lay among the untrodden ways,
'Twas very small in size;
A bar whom there were none to praise,
And few to patronize.

But when the drought had well begun
One winked a wicked eye!
—'Twas like a star when only one
Is shining in the sky!

It served unknown and few could know
The wink that fixed the tea;
But now it too is closed, and, oh,
The difference to me!

"A Dirge (Apologies to Wordsworth)," *Judge*, lxxvii (December 20, 1919), 30.

SLEEP OF A UNIVERSITY

Watching through the long, dim hours
Like statued Mithras, stand ironic towers;
Their haughty lines severe by light
Are softened and gain tragedy at night.
Self-conscious, cynics of their charge,
Proudly they challenge the dreamless world at large.

From pseudo-ancient Nassau Hall, the bell
Crashes the hour, as if to pretend "All's well!"
Over the campus then the listless breeze
Floats along drowsily, filtering through the trees,
Whose twisted branches seem to lie
Like *point d'Alencon* lace against a sky
Of soft gray-black—a gorgeous robe
Buttoned with stars, hung over a tiny globe.

With life far off, peace sits supreme:
The college slumbers in a fatuous dream,
While, watching through the moonless hours
Like statued Mithras, stand the ironic towers.

"Sleep of a University," *The Nassau Literary Magazine*, LXXVI (November 1920), 161. Fitzgerald's revision of a poem by Aiken Reichner—see *Fitzgerald/Hemingway Annual 1971*.

TO ANNE

1

"Like the mellow wisp of an ancient moon,
  "On a night of long ago.
"Like the fragrant breeze of a by-gone June
  When the wee winds whisper low,
Or wild in a night of pleasure gay

Or sweet in the calm of an April day—
Dear Anne!

2

Girl of my dreams, 'neath the midnight gleams,
   A whisper echoes "Anne," An answer echoes "Anne."
Enveloped by all romance, fair in my fancies flight,
   Star shot by legend and [s]lowed by tale,
   Queen of some fair tonight, dear Anne!
Queen of some fair tonight!

3

Some time when the stars kiss the roses,
   We'll meet in the never land,
When the violet night discloses
   I'll take you by the hand.
Dear Anne! Some day and some day!"

[UNTITLED]

"For the lands [sic] of the village triumph,
   "Honest, not brilliant like me,"
"So I turn again to St. Paul
   "For my old popularity.

"For handsome is as handsome does,
   And the hands of time won't turn back.
Girls, be they friend, crush or sister,
   Dont love me, in Hackensack!

"To Anne" and Untitled Poem, Peggy Mitchell, "Novelist Loved Atlanta Girl's Picture," Atlanta *Journal*, September 30, 1923, p. 5. Interview with Martin Amorous, Fitzgerald's Newman School roommate—by the future author of *Gone With the Wind*.

LAMP IN A WINDOW

Do you remember, before keys turned in the locks,
  When life was a closeup, and not an occasional letter,
That I hated to swim naked from the rocks
  While you liked absolutely nothing better?

Do you remember many hotel bureaus that had
  Only three drawers? But the only bother
Was that each of us argued stubbornly, got mad
  Trying to give the third one to the other.

East, west, the little car turned, often wrong
  Up an erroneous Alp, an unmapped Savoy river.
We blamed each other, wild were our words and strong,
  And, in an hour, laughed and called it liver.

And, though the end was desolate and unkind:
  To turn the calendar at June and find December
On the next leaf; still, stupid-got with grief, I find
  These are the only quarrels that I can remember.

—*F. Scott Fitzgerald*

"Lamp in a Window," *New Yorker*, xi (March 23, 1935), 18.

OBIT ON PARNASSUS

Death before forty's no bar. Lo!
  These had accomplished their feats:
Chatterton, Burns, and Kit Marlowe,
  Byron and Shelley and Keats.

Death, the eventual censor,
  Lays for the forties, and so
Took off Jane Austen and Spenser,
  Stevenson, Hood, and poor Poe.

You'll leave a better-lined wallet
    By reaching the end of your rope
After fifty, like Shakespeare and Smollett,
    Thackeray, Dickens, and Pope.

Try for the sixties—but say, boy,
    That's when the tombstones were built on
Butler and Sheridan, the play boy,
    Arnold and Coleridge and Milton.

Three score and ten—the tides rippling
    Over the bar; slip the hawser.
Godspeed to Clemens and Kipling,
    Swinburne and Browning and Chaucer.

Some staved the debt off but paid it
    At eighty—that's after the law.
Wordsworth and Tennyson made it,
    And Meredith, Hardy, and Shaw.

But, Death, while you make up your quota,
    Please note this confession of candor—
That I wouldn't give an iota
    To linger till ninety, like Landor.

—*F. Scott Fitzgerald*

"Obit on Parnassus," *New Yorker*, xiii (June 5, 1937), 27.

The Princeton Tiger Humor

There was once a second group student who lived in Holder. He thought that solitude would give him a first group. So he moved to Patton, where he lent an unwilling ear to the following:

1:30–2:30 P.M.—Shrill soprano shrieks of soccer team.
2:30–3:30 " "   Session of the gun club.
3:30–4:30 " "   Interclass baseball game on Brokaw.
              (Continous cheering.)
4:30–5:30 " "   Engines puffing up and down for their afternoon exercise.
7:00–8:00 " "   Mandolin or banjo in Brokaw,
8:00–9:00 " "   Triangle pactice in Casino.

* * *

The next day the student moved back to Holder.

"There was once a second group student . . ." *The Princeton Tiger*, xxv (December 1914), 5. Attributed to Fitzgerald on the basis of clipping in the Fitzgerald Papers, Princeton University. Fitzgerald's earliest identifiable *Tiger* contribution.

MAY SMALL TALK

To get a reputation for ability to chatter
You must learn this little system for your common campus patter.
First you ask about exams and how your victim thinks he's doing,
Speak of war and shake your head and say you think there's trouble
    brewing.
A word about your bills, and on the chapel question, too,

Then "Gee, but it was mighty tough—you know about the crew."
"Yes, Charlie Chaplin's at the show—a mighty funny thing;"
"Going over Campus now, to hear the Seniors sing?"
"I s'pose since you're a parlor snake you'll bring a girl in June?"
"Oh! eat your soup, for movie show is starting pretty soon."
"Well, these are busy days for me"—"You've always been a bummer,"
"Yes, meet me here at Morey's School," and "What's the dope this
　　summer?"
You must always ask the heeler, 'How he's coming with the Prince,"
And "Coming back here early?" makes the guards and centers wince:
For this is always easier and better far for mine,
Than a continental, trancendental consequental line!

"May Small Talk," *The Princeton Tiger*, xxvi (June 1915), 10. Attributed
to Fitzgerald on the basis of clipping in the Fitzgerald Papers, Princeton
University.

HOW THEY HEAD THE CHAPTERS

A. Detective Story.

Chapter I.—The Affair at Brownwill.
Chap. II.—In The Dark.
Chap. III.—The Hound Hits The Trail.
Chap. IV.—A Ray Of Light.
Chap. V.—Fresh Developments.
Chap. VI.—Gone!
Chap. VII.—Caught!
Chap. VIII.—Old Jacques Speaks.
Chap. IX.—Solved!

B. Chobert Rambers Story.

Chap. I.—Auction Bridge.
Chap. II.—At Seabreeze.
Chap. III.—The Shooting Party.
Chap. IV.—A Kiss In The Dark.
Chap. V.—A Gentleman's Gentleman.
Chap. VI.—Rector's.

Chap. VII.—Champagne.
Chap. VIII.—Arms And The Man.

C. Any Best Seller.

Chap. I.—Third Avenue.
Chap. II.—Fifth Avenue.
Chap. III.—The Big Man With The Lame Head
And The Little Girl With The Lame Back.
Chap. IV.—A New Start.
Chap. V.—Contentment.
Chap. VI.—The Operation.
Chap. VII.—"Guardian, I Can Walk."
Chap. VIII.—The Little Girl And The Big House.
Chap. IX.—"The Greatest Of These Is Charity."

"How They Head the Chapters," *The Princeton Tiger*, xxvi (September 1915), 10. Attributed to Fitzgerald on the basis of clipping in the Fitzgerald Papers, Princeton University.

NOTE:—Many articles have appeared lately in our current magazines stating how simple it is for Germany to conquer this country. Is it? the TIGER asks. Read on, oh, gentlissimo!

THE CONQUEST OF AMERICA

(*as some writers would have it*)

(Mr. Fitzcheesecake, who has written this article, needs no introduction. He has held numerous official positions: he was on three different beats in Trenton, and was for one year Deputy Garbage Man of Bordentown; and we feel that what he writes will be authoritative.)—THE EDITORS.

The American Atlantic fleet has been sunk. The Germans were coming in three thousand transports and were about to land in New York. Admiral Von Noseitch was swimming across with the fleet. Pandemonium reigned in the great city, women and tenors were running frantically up and down their rooms, the men having all left; the police force also, fearing to be called to the colors, had been in Canada for two months. Who was to raise and equip a vast army? The New York

Baseball Team had finished in the second division, so Mgr. McGraw gave up all hope and volunteered; the new army, for secrecy, used a subway car to drill in. No help could be had from Boston, for they had won the pennant, and there was nothing on the front pages of the papers to warn the people of the imminent danger. General McGraw intrenched himself in the middle of Brooklyn for, so he thought, not even a German would go there. He was right, but three stray cannon balls came his way, and he struck out. The Statute of Liberty had been invested, New York's six million people were all captured; the Germans were upon them before preparation could be accomplished. Generals Von Limburger, Munchener, and Frankfurter held a consultation in Busty's the first night: General Von Limburger was going to attack General Bryan and his army of the Raritan in New Jersey; General Frankfurter was going to take a Day-Line boat to Albany and thence to Canada, where three-fourths of the citizens of the U. S. capable of bearing arms had fled for a much-needed rest; while General Munchener with thirty picked men would hold New York. Gen. Von Limburger took the 7 P.M. train to Princeton, near which place Bryan was reported to have fled. Meanwhile all the United States had been captured, save this section of New Jersey. The Pacific Squadron, however, was intact; they had been taken for fishing boats and had escaped without any injury. The besieging army was fast approaching the city; preceptors could be seen running madly to and fro, mostly fro. Bryan drew up his army in the "Tiger" Office; they voted five votes to one not to let a German live.

It was February. Glory Be! And meant all fortune to the United States! The Germans advanced. They were held up at Rocky Hill. They readvance; they column right around the old mill; they pass the Prep; they leave the outskirts far behind. They cluster round the Chem. Lab. and then—Bei Reichstag, was ist? The Polar's Recess and the poisonous gases of the Lab hit that vast army at one fell swoop! Long had it been since they had heard the sound of guns and the shock of Polar's Recess made them sore afraid. Some fled to the Nass. It was closed. Some rushed to Joe's. The promise of a small check cashed was too much for them. Some dove toward the Jigger Shop where a raspberry marshmallow nut marangue laid a hundred more beside their graves. Some sank upon the benches on Nassau Street. Both collapsed, each under the strain of seeing the other. Some tried to p-rade around the Cannon, but the prestige of Whig and Clio drove them off to Penn's Neck. And the one man left cried out, "I'm Gish—I touched the Cannon." Bryan's army rushed out of the TIGER Office and stuck him with the point of a joke—a joke preserved for these many years. America was saved, saved, SAVED, yes—saved by the point of a joke. YE GODS!

"The Conquest of America," *The Princeton Tiger*, xxvi (Thanksgiving 1915), 6. Attributed to Fitzgerald on the evidence of the reference to "Mr. Fitzcheesecake." But Fitzgerald did not preserve a clipping in his scrapbook.

Yais

Wouldn't it be nais
to sit on a dais
with Thais.

"Yais," *The Princeton Tiger*, xxvii (June 1916), 13. Attributed to Fitzgerald by John McMaster, '19, an editor of the *Tiger*, who supplied the title. Fitzgerald did not preserve a clipping in his scrapbook.

LITTLE MINNIE McCLOSKEY.

A Story for Girls.

EDITOR'S NOTE—*Not since Little Women have we had so moving a picture of girlhood hopes and dreams.*

It was midnight in Miss Pickswinger's Select Seminary for Young Ladies (country location, hot and cold water, wrestling, bull-baiting and other out-door sports; washing, ironing, and Bulgarian extra). A group of girls had gathered in a cozy room. There was going to be a midnight feast. Oh, goody! There was but little light, for, fearing to turn on the acetylene, they had built a bonfire on the table, and one girl was appointed to feed the faint flames with false hair and legs which she wrenched quietly from the chairs and tables. A saddle of venison for their little supper was turning over and over on a spit in the cooking stove in the corner, and the potatoes were boiling noiselessly in the steam radiator. Perched like a little queen on the armchair sat Louise Sangfroid the hostess, on the mantle-piece lay Mary Murgatroid in red and white striped pajamas while balancing on the molding sat Minnie McCloskey in a nightshirt of yaeger flannel. Other girls sat around the room, two on a trunk which they had ingeniously improvised as a chair, one on an empty case of beer and three on a heap of broken glass and tin cans in the corner.

Girls will be girls! Ah, me! They would have their little frolic; a cask of Haig and Haig, stolen from Miss Pickswinger's private stock, was behind the door and the mischievous girls had almost finished it.

Minnie McCloskey was the school drudge; she was working for her education. At three every morning she rose, made the beds, washed the dishes, branded the cattle, cut the grass, and did many other tasks. She was known affectionately to her companions as "Piggy" McCloskey (all the girls had nicknames. How they got them no one knew. Amy Gulps was called "Fatty," perhaps because she was fat; Mary Munks was called "Red" conceivably because she had red hair. Phoebe Cohop was called "Boils" possibly because—(but enough, let us continue).

"Girls," said Bridget Mulcahey, a petite little French girl, whose father had been shot at Soissons (for deserting), "let's play a prank."

A chorus of ohs! and ahs! and girlish giggles greeted this suggestion.

"What shall we do?" asked Gumpsa LePage.

"Something exciting," said Bridget, "let's hang Miss Pickswinger." All assented enthusiastically except Minnie McCloskey.

"'Fraid cat," sneered the others, "'fraid you'll get punished."

"No," said Minnie, "but think of all she's done for me."

They struck her savagely with chairs, locked her in and rushed off. There was but one chance. Minnie quickly braided a rope out of rugs, lowered herself from the window, quickly weaved another rope out of grass, raised herself to Miss Pickswinger's window. They were not there. There was yet time to outwit them. Suddenly she gasped in horror.

* * *

A moment later the rollicking crowd of girls was confronted in front of Miss Pickswinger's door by a slender figure. It was Minnie.

"You cannot pass," she said sternly.

"Do you mean to say we cannot hang Miss Pickswinger if we wish?" cried Louise, indignantly.

Minnie shivered with emotion and sneezed with emotion. Then she spoke.

"There is no need. She has gotten one of her bedroom slippers in her mouth and choked to death."

The girls rushed off shouting "Holiday" and striking each other playfully on the head with stones, but Minnie, in the room above, threw herself down upon the heap of glass in the corner and sobbed as if her heart would break.

"Little Minnie McCloskey," *The Princeton Tiger*, xxvii (December 1, 1916), 6–7. Attributed to Fitzgerald on the basis of clipping in the Fitzgerald Papers, Princeton University.

One from Penn's Neck.

Baby Ben, Baby Ben, you annoy a lot of men
With your aggravating tinkle at about eight-ten.
I'm dreaming pretty dreams about the girls who love me—when
I hear your voice a calling, Baby Ben.

"One from Penn's Neck," *The Princeton Tiger*, xxvii (December 18, 1916), 7. Attributed to Fitzgerald by Henry Dan Piper on the basis of a clipping in the Fitzgerald Papers, Princeton University.

A Litany of Slang.

From "Knockouts"—   Great Von Hindenburg deliver us.
From "dopeless" people—   Great Von, etc.
From "sardines"—   Great Von, etc.
From "trick" things—   Great Von, etc.
From "trick" people—   Great Von, etc.
From "I'll say"—   Great Von, etc.
From lads who "have it"—   Great Von, etc.
From lads who "lack it"—   Great Von, etc.
From "nice fellow you are"—   Great Von, etc.
From "Hotstuff"—   Great Von, etc.
From "Persian Petters"—   Great Von, etc.
From all last years' slang—   Great Von Hindenburg do deliver
                                us if you get time.   Amen.

"A Litany of Slang," *The Princeton Tiger*, xxvii (December 18, 1916), 7. Attributed to Fitzgerald by Henry Dan Piper on the basis of a clipping in the Fitzgerald Papers, Princeton University.

"Triangle Scenery by Bakst."

Princetonian,

We are glad to see that this scene designer has broken his fifty-thousand-dollar contract with the Russian Ballet. The Triangle Club must be prospering. Next year's score by Claude DeBussy?

" 'Triangle Scenery by Bakst,' " *The Princeton Tiger,* xxvii (December 18, 1916), 7. Attributed to Fitzgerald by Henry Dan Piper on the basis of a clipping in the Fitzgerald Papers, Princeton University.

Futuristic Impressions of the Editorial Boards.

The Prince—A merry-go-round game of "who read the proof?" with solid gold-filled radicalism every morning before breakfast.

The Lit—Half a dozen men who agree, at the price of appearing in print, to listen to each other's manuscript.

The Pic—The tall man with the black box who gets in front of the umpire all through May.

THE TIGER—A lot of lo—yes, sir; all right, sir, a collection of artists and side-splitting humorists.

"Futuristic Impressions of the Editorial Boards," *The Princeton Tiger,* xxvii (December 18, 1916), 7. Attributed to Fitzgerald by Henry Dan Piper on the basis of a clipping in the Fitzgerald Papers, Princeton University.

"A glass of beer kills him."

New York Sun.

brought forth "Ex Princetoniensi non erat"

from the *Yale Record.*

Right again. Probably some one threw it at an Eli.

" 'A glass of beer kills him,' " *The Princeton Tiger,* xxvii (December 18, 1916), 7. Attributed to Fitzgerald by Henry Dan Piper on the basis of a clipping in the Fitzgerald Papers, Princeton University.

Oui, le backfield est from Paris
Quel les Eli studes adore,
C'est Messieurs Laroche and Neville
Messieurs Jaques et LeGore.
—*Maxim of General Joffre.*

"Oui, le backfield est from Paris," *The Princeton Tiger*, xxvii (December 18, 1916), 7. Attributed to Fitzgerald by Henry Dan Piper on the basis of a clipping in the Fitzgerald Papers, Princeton University.

"When you find a man doing a little more than his duty, you find that kind of patriotism not found in Blair or Campbell."—Oliver Wendell Holmes.

We were under the impression that Mr. Holmes went to Harvard, but he evidently roomed in North Edwards.

" 'When you find a man doing a little more,' " *The Princeton Tiger*, xxvii (December 18, 1916), 7. Attributed to Fitzgerald by Henry Dan Piper on the basis of a clipping in the Fitzgerald Papers, Princeton University.

Things That Never Change! Number 3333.

"Oh, you fr-shm-n, where shall we go. Let's go to J—'s. I want to get a sm-ll check c-shed. We g-t g—d M-j-st-c s-ndw-tches there."

THE TIGER's reward for the most complete solution will be a m-j-st-c s-ndw-tch at J—'s.

"Things That Never Change! Number 3333," *The Princeton Tiger*, xxvii (December 18, 1916), 7. Attributed to Fitzgerald by Henry Dan Piper on the basis of a clipping in the Fitzgerald Papers, Princeton University.

THE OLD FRONTIERSMAN

A *Story of the Frontier*

It was the middle of the forest. A figure might have been noticed crawling along, sniffing at the ground. It was Old Davy Underbush, the frontiersman and b'ar hunter. He was completely invisible and inaudible. The only way you could perceive him was by the sense of smell.

He was dressed as a frontiersman (*cf*. "what the men will wear," theatre programs of 1776.) On his feet he wore moccasins made from the skin of the wood weasel. Around his legs were coonskin spats which ran into his trousers made of sheepskin; these extended to the waist. He wore a belt made of an old rattlesnake and a long bearskin coat. Around his head was wrapped a fishskin hat. At his hip hung horrible trophies of Indian warfare. One scalp of Object the Ojibway still wet with Oleaqua hung there beside the pompadour of Eardrum the Iroquois and the cowlick of Bootblack the Blackfoot. By his side walked "Tres Bien," his trusty Eskimo cheese-hound.

He carried a muzzle loading shotgun, an old horse-pistol, and a set of razors. He was on the trail of Sen-Sen the Seneca and Omlette the Omega. They had come into the clearing and drunk all the fire-water from the fire-water factory. As they left they had, in the usual Indian manner, carved their initials on each tree they passed and it was by this that the astute old frontiersman had been sent out to track them.

It was now too dark to read the initials plainly and Davy often got them mixed up with those of other savages who had passed that way before. For three weeks the old b'ar hunter had followed them, living on the berries from the bushes and sometimes when no berries were to be found, snatching great handfuls of grass and dry leaves and devouring them.

As he crawled along he was thinking. If he did not find the redskins soon he would have to eat his moccasins. His scarred brow was knit with worry.

All around him were the noises of the forest; the long sad "Hoo" of the Huron, the plaintive sigh of the Sioux, and the light cackle of the Apache. Suddenly a new sound broke the stillness. It was the dry harsh cawing of the Seneca. Davy ran forward noiselessly. He was careful to make no sound. He ran with his feet completely off the ground to leave no clue for the watchful redmen. Sure enough the savages were in a little clearing in the forest playing on their primitive musical instruments. Sen-Sen the Seneca sat playing "The Last Rose of Summer" on an old comb wrapped in tissue paper and Omlette the Omega accompanied him on the snare Tom-Tom. The old frontiersman burst in on them waving his gun at them and threatening their scalps with one of his tempered razors.

The fight which ensued was furious.

The savages pulled his coat over his ears and hit him on the head with their bows and arrows. One would kneel behind Davy and the other would push the old frontiersman over him. Sen-Sen combed all the hair of his sheepskin trousers the wrong way and frantic with pain the old b'ar hunter fought on.

Finally Omlette the Omega withdrew to a distance and taking a station behind the old frontiersman let fly an arrow at him which passed through his sheepskin trousers and pierced his catskin underwear. The old b'ar hunter expired.

The savages fried him for dinner but found, to their disappointment that he was all dark meat owing to his lifelong exposure to the sun.

"The Old Frontiersman," *The Princeton Tiger,* xxvii (December 18, 1916), 11. Attributed to Fitzgerald on the basis of a clipping in the Fitzgerald Papers, Princeton University.

Boy Kills Self Rather Than Pet.

—New York Journal.

Nice fellow ! !

"Boy Kills Self Rather Than Pet," *The Princeton Tiger,* xxvii (February 3, 1917), 12. Attributed to Fitzgerald on the basis of a clipping in the Fitzgerald Papers, Princeton University.

PRECAUTION PRIMARILY

The scene is a paint box. Large green and whites form the back, a blue leans against the side and many small greens edged with orange are scattered around artistically. As the curtain rises music is falling gently from the strange melancholy individuals who sit in front dressed in their blacks and whites. They all look sadly at the stage which is now filled with people dressed in purple splotched with mauve sitting on pale violets.

The chorus can be heard to remark vaguely in the old English in which all opening choruses are written

> Oh gleeumph wax wash ich
> Vil na wan in bun oh
> Bun-gi-wow
> Il bur lee burly. Oh Gish Bush!

They accompany this by the appropriate dance. The audience lean back wearily and wait for the play to begin.

(Enter the football team disguised as chorus men and the Prom committee in pink tights.)

Cue: "Look back in your score books; look at Hank O'Day."

> *Song.*
> Henry O'Day, Henry O'Day,
> 　King of the neutrals were you;
> Kaisers or Kings, Hughie Jenni*ngs*

> All were impartially blue.
> 　Called a ball
> 　　When you meant a strike;
> Heard them call
> 　"For the love of Mike," etc.
> 　　*(Pause.)*

(*Enter two mere striplings, stripped, boiled in grease paint and decorated in Hawaiian straw.*)

Song.

Junior, shave your mustache, you're souring all the milk.

(*At the back of the Casino the long-haired authors walk up and down feeling about as comfortable as the Kaiser's own before another offensive.*)

FIRST AUTHOR—How do you think the thing's going?

SECOND DITTO—Fine! not two minutes ago I heard a laugh in the eighteenth row. It was my joke about the—

FIRST AUTHOR—Your joke, Ha-Ha! you make me laugh—Did my line about—, etc.

FIRST MUSIC WRITER (aside)—As if anyone listened to the dialogue.

SECOND MUSIC WRITER—How my songs do stand out.

LYRICIST—Remarkable how a good lyric redeems a bad tune. (*Listens to the silent audience and wishes the senior in the front row would control his whooping-cough until the dialogue begins again.*)

(*Behind the scenes.*)

CORINNE—Knockout girl in the front row.

CHLORINE—No dope.

CORINNE—She likes my eyes.

CHLORINE—Wait till she sees your legs in the next chorus.

FLUORINE (the leading lady)—Don't spoil my entrance.

BROMINE—Grab on, freshman—one—two—pull! (Blankety-blank! dash! dash!)

IODINE—All right, everybody—Hurry up! Get your pink silk over-coats.

THE WHOLE HALOGEN FAMILY (*simultaneously*)—

A bas with the pony ballet,
Ha-Ha to the pony ballet,
　　Their faces are phoney,
　　On places they're bony,
Scorn chases the pony ballet.

ENTHUSIASTIC YOUNG PRECEPTOR—Progressive! Ah! After the true Washington Square manner.

AVERAGE STUDENT (*who doesn't know what he wants and kicks when he gets it*)—Where's the plot?

Moral of the show: You can't please all of the people all of the time. Curtain. *F. S. F.*

"Precaution Primarily," *The Princeton Tiger*, xxviii (February 3, 1917), 13–14. Attributed to Fitzgerald on the basis of initials.

Things That Never Change. No. 3982.

Is it $\left\{ \begin{array}{c} \text{hot} \\ \text{cold} \end{array} \right\}$ enough for you?

"Things That Never Change. No. 3982," *The Princeton Tiger*, xxvii (February 3, 1917), 12. Attributed to Fitzgerald on the basis of a clipping in the Fitzgerald Papers, Princeton University.

McCaulay Mission—Water Street.
Service at five. Drunkards especially invited.

—*N. Y. Sun.*

If we send a delegation to Northfield, we should certainly be represented here.

"McCaulay Mission—Water Street," *The Princeton Tiger*, xxvii (March 17, 1917), 10. Attributed to Fitzgerald on the basis of a clipping in the Fitzgerald Papers, Princeton University.

Popular Parodies—No. 1.

I'm off to the Math. School
To pass it or bust.
If Conics don't get me
Then Politics must.

Chorus.
Professor how long
Do I have to wait?
Do you debar me now
Or will you hesitate?

"Popular Parodies—No. 1," *The Princeton Tiger*, xxvii (March 17, 1917), 10. Attributed to Fitzgerald on the basis of a clipping in the Fitzgerald Papers, Princeton University.

THE DIARY OF A SOPHOMORE.

Sunday—March 18th.

Felt nervous all day—temperature 99 8/10. Jim and Heck and Joe came in after dinner. We are going to stick together. Everybody says "stick to your friends"—I'm sticking like a leech—they can't shake me off. Hope I get a *Seaweed* bid.

Monday—

No mail—Jim, Heck and Joe not in rooms, college in anarchy—shall not leave room until I get a bid. Temperature 89.7.

Tuesday—

No mail—except a bill from Sinclair's. Sophomores wanted me to join commons club—Told them I'd like to but I'd promised to stick with my friends. Got Jim, Heck and Joe bids to commons club. Why don't they come to see me.

Wednesday—

Joe came over and said he and Heck were in the *Pillbox* section— Jim is going *Star and Garter*. I have a good chance for *Pillbox*—Turned down commons again.

Thursday—

We are all going *Star and Garter*. I'm glad I waited. We shook hands on it and Jim and Heck wept. Emotion is in the air. Temperature, 100.

Friday—

Peter Hype told me to hold off for *Lung and Coatcheck*. I told him I was going to stick with my friends. Hope he didn't think I meant it.

Saturday—

Bid for *Lung and Coatcheck*. I hate to leave Joe and Heck. Shook hands with all the "Lungs." Was introduced to several fellows in my class.

Sunday—

Awful excitement. Temperature 102.

Monday—

Signed up *Seaweed*. Jim was foolish to throw away his chances. It's everyman's business to look out for himself. Heck and Joe were a drag on me. They'll be very happy in *Star and Garter*. Wrote Doris about it. Temperature, normal.

F. S. F.

"The Diary of a Sophomore," *The Princeton Tiger*, xxvii (March 17, 1917), 11.

UNDULATIONS OF AN UNDERGRADUATE.

I've been for North Edwards selected,
 I've roomed in a cupboard in Blair
In Witherspoon dark and dejected,
 I've slept without sunshine or air.
My janitress kept me from study,
 And awfully long-winded she were,
Her mouth didn't shut so I overcut,
 And I learned about college from her.

A senior who came from our city
 And practically lived for the glass,
Would tell me in epigrams witty
 The way to be big in my class.
He took me to hatters and tailors
 And coached me on how to look slim;
He taught me to drink but forbade me to think,
 And I learned about college from him.

A girl that I met at the seashore
  And took for a summer-day sail
Told stories of brothers at Princeton
  Of friends and fiancees at Yale.
She knew all the men who played hockey,
  She knew when the promenades were,
She thought me a bore till I asked her to four,
  And I learned about college from her.

The dean, since my marks were pathetic,
  Had sent me a summons to call,
He greeted me, apologetic,
  And smiled, "This is social, that's all."
He said if I chanced to the city
  I might be remembering him
To Babbie Larove at the Cocoanut Grove,
  And I learned about college from him.

"Undulations of an Undergraduate," *The Princeton Tiger*, xxvii (March 17, 1917), 20. Attributed to Fitzgerald on the basis of a clipping in the Fitzgerald Papers, Princeton University.

Yale's swimming team will take its maiden plunge to-night.

—*New York Sun.*

How perfectly darling!

"Yale's swimming team will take its maiden plunge to-night," *The Princeton Tiger*, xxvii (April 28, 1917), 8. Attributed to Fitzgerald on the basis of a clipping in the Fitzgerald Papers, Princeton University.

"Kenilworth Socialism," *The Princeton Tiger*, xxvii (March 17, 1917), 22.

"True Democracy," *The Princeton Tiger*, xxvii (March 17, 1917), 18. Attributed to Fitzgerald [by Henry Dan Piper] on the basis of a clipping in the Fitzgerald Papers, Princeton University. Presumably Fitzgerald supplied the idea for the cartoon.

A FEW WELL-KNOWN CLUB TYPES AND THEIR FUTURES.

"A Few Well-Known Club Types and Their Futures," *The Princeton Tiger*, xxvii (March 17, 1917), 7. Attributed to Fitzgerald on the basis of a clipping in the Fitzgerald Papers, Princeton University. Presumably Fitzgerald supplied the idea for the cartoon.

THE PRINCE OF PESTS

A Story of the War.

It was night in July, 1914. A man and his board of directors sat around a table in a palace at Berlin. The man was tall, with a moustache and a short arm. Who was he?—oh, reader, can you guess? He wore a military uniform, green with grey facings; his pants were blue with red facings.

"Your Highness," Von Boodlewaden was saying, "everything is ready."

The Kaiser shook his head sadly and folded his arms, at least he tucked the short one in with the other. Then he took his short leg and crossed it over his long one, and having scratched his long ear come to business.

"Nietzsche," he said, and waited for his words to have effect. Von Nicklebottom immediately sprang upon the table and led the customary cheer for Nietzsche—three locomotives with three sidels of beer on the end.

"Nietzsche," continued the Kaiser, "has said it. We will conquer by the sword." As he said this he ran his hand lovingly along his sword, then trying its edge on a bit of celery which he munched tentatively.

"Your Highness," cried Von Munchennoodle, "Belgium must be sacrificed."

The Kaiser bit his lip until the blood ran slowly down to the table where it spread into little livid pools of red and yellow liquid. His councillors dipped their fingers in it and reverently crossed themselves. Deeply affected the Kaiser pledged them.

"And what of America?" asked Pistachio, Chancellor of the Domino Club.

"America?" said the Kaiser, rising to his full height. "Charles II had his Cromwell, Caesar had his Brutus, and Wilson—"

There were cries of "plagiarism" and the Kaiser paused.

"'Daniel Webster was a German," he continued, rather abashed. Turning to the man on his center, Baron Badenuf, Chancellor of the Shakespearegoetheteutonic League, he commanded him.

"Look him up, Baddy."

There was an hour while Badenuf looked up Webster, during which an absolute silence was maintained, broken only by the Kaiser as he ran his sword rapidly up and down his neck, where he had caught prickly heat the summer before playing leap-frog on the beach at Ostend with Czar Nicholas. Badenuf finally returned.

"I find in the life of Webster," he announced, "the relevant news that he once stopped at the Sauerkraut Inn while passing through Pennsylvania. This proves the case, for no one but a German would stop at a German Inn unless he has to, and Daniel didn't."

There were three wild cheers at this and according to the ancient German custom they prepared to pledge each other in the royal blood. The Kaiser tried his lip again but all the blood had gone out of it long ago. So he opened an artery in his leg with an olive fork.

They all gulped it down heartily while a German band played "Ach du lieber Augustine" and the Kaiser's valet strapped his paralyzed arm to his sword so he could have his picture taken.   *F. S. F.*

"The Prince of Pests," *The Princeton Tiger*, xxvii (April 28, 1917), 7.

"These rifles * * * will probably not be used for shooting, although they are of a powerful type capable of before commencing actual firing reaching a distance of two miles"
> —*The Daily Princetonian.*

Some rifles! Lord help Germany!

" 'These rifles * * * will probably not be used,' " *The Princeton Tiger*, xxvii (April 28, 1917), 8. Attributed to Fitzgerald on the basis of a clipping in the Fitzgerald Papers, Princeton University.

"It is assumed that the absence of submarines from the Pacific will not necessitate American naval activities in that ocean."
> —*New York Evening Post.*

Will it not not?

" 'It is assumed that the absence of submarines,' " *The Princeton Tiger*, xxvii (April 28, 1917), 8. Attributed to Fitzgerald on the basis of a clipping in the Fitzgerald Papers, Princeton University.

Ethel had her shot of brandy while she powdered for the ball,
If a quart of wine was handy she was sure to drink it all;
People thought she was a dandy—called her Ethyl Alcohol.

"Ethel had her shot of brandy," *The Princeton Tiger,* xxvii (April 28, 1917), p. 8. Attributed to Fitzgerald on the basis of a clipping in the Fitzgerald Papers, Princeton University.

THE STAYING UP ALL NIGHT.

The warm fire.
The comfortable chairs.
The merry companions.
The stroke of twelve.
The wild suggestion.
The good sports.
The man who hasn't slept for weeks.
The people who have done it before.
The long anecdotes.
The best looking girl yawns.
The forced raillery.
The stroke of one.
The best looking girl goes to bed.
The stroke of two.
The empty pantry.
The lack of firewood.
The second best looking girl goes to bed.
The weather-beaten ones who don't.
The stroke of four.
The dozing off.
The amateur "life of the party."
The burglar scare.
The scornful cat.
The trying to impress the milkman.
The scorn of the milkman.
The lunatic feeling.

The chilly sun.
The stroke of six.
The walk in the garden.
The sneezing.
The early risers.
The volley of wit at you.
The feeble come back.
The tasteless breakfast.
The miserable day.
8 P. M.—Between the sheets.

F. S. F.

"The Staying Up All Night," *The Princeton Tiger*, xxviii (November 10, 1917), 6.

Intercollegiate Petting-Cues.
2. "You really don't look comfortable there."

"Intercollegiate Petting-Cues," *The Princeton Tiger*, xxviii (November 10, 1917), 8. Attributed to Fitzgerald on the basis of a clipping in the Fitzgerald Papers, Princeton University.

OUR AMERICAN POETS.

I

Robert Service.

The red blood throbs
 And forms in gobs
 On the nose of Hank McPhee.
With a wild "Ha-Ha!" he shoots his pa
 Through the frozen artic lea.

II

Robert Frost.

A rugged young rhymer named Frost,
Once tried to be strong at all cost
    The mote in his eye
    May be barley or rye,
But his right in that beauty is lost.

Though the meek shall inherit the land,
He prefers a tough bird in the hand,
    He puts him in inns,
    And feeds him on gins,
And the high brows say, "Isn't he grand?"
                    F. S. F.

"Our American Poets," *The Princeton Tiger*, xxviii (November 10, 1917), 11.

CEDRIC THE STOKER.

(*The true story of the Battle of the Baltic.*)

The grimy coal-hole of the battleship of the line was hot, and Cedric felt the loss of his parasol keenly. It was his duty to feed the huge furnace that sent the ship rolling over and over in the sea, heated the sailors' bedrooms, and ran the washing machine. Cedric was hard at work. He would fill his hat with a heap of the black coals, carry them to the huge furnace, and throw them in. His hat was now soiled beyond recognition, and try as he might he could not keep his hands clean.

He was interrupted in his work by the jingle of the telephone bell. "Captain wishes to speak to you, Mr. Cedric," said the girl at the exchange. Cedric rushed to the phone.

"How's your mother," asked the Captain.

"Very well, thank you, sir," answered Cedric.

"Is it hot enough for you, down there?" said the Captain.

"Quite," replied Cedric, courteously.

The Captain's voice changed. He would change it every now and then. "Come to my office at once," he said, "we are about to go into action and I wish your advice."

Cedric rushed to the elevator, and getting off at the fourth floor, ran to the office. He found the Captain rubbing his face with cold cream to remove sunburn.

"Cedric," said the Captain, sticking a lump of the greasy stuff into his mouth, and chewing it while he talked, "You are a bright child, rattle off the binomial theorem."

Cedric repeated it forwards, backwards, and from the middle to both ends.

"Now name all the salts of phosphoric acid!"

Cedric named them all, and four or five extra.

"Now the Iliad!"

Here Cedric did his most difficult task. He repeated the Iliad backwards leaving out alternately every seventh and fourth word.

"You *are* efficient," said the Captain smilingly. He took from his mouth the cold cream, which he had chewed into a hard porous lump, and dropped it back into the jar. "I shall trust you with all our lives." He drew Cedric closer to him.

"Listen," he whispered; "the enemy are attacking in force. They are far stronger than we. We outnumber them only five to one: nevertheless we shall fight with the utmost bravery. As commander of the fleet, I have ordered the crews of all my ships to struggle to the last shell and powder roll, and then to flee for their lives. This ship is not so fast as the others so I guess it had better begin fleeing now!"

"Sir—" began Cedric, but he was interrupted by the stacatto noise of the huge forward turret pop-guns as the two fleets joined in battle. They could hear the sharp raps of the paddles as the bosuns spanked their crews to make them work faster. Their ears were deafened by the cursing of the pilots as the ships fouled one another. All the hideous sounds of battle rose and assailed them. Cedric rushed to the window and threw it open. He shrank back, aghast. Bearing down upon them, and only ten miles away, was the huge *Hoboken*, the biggest of all ferry-boats, captured by the enemy from the Erie Railroad in the fall of '92. So close she was that Cedric could read her route sign "Bronx West to Toid Avenoo." The very words struck him numb. On she came, and on, throwing mountains of spray a mile in front of her and several miles to her rear.

"Is she coming fast, boy?" asked the Captain.

"Sir, she's making every bit of a knot an hour," answered Cedric, trembling.

The Captain seized him roughly by the shoulders. "We'll fight to the end," he said; "even though she is faster than we are. Quick! To the cellars, and stoke, stoke, STOKE!!"

Cedric unable to take his eyes from the terrible sight, ran backwards down the passageway, fell down the elevator shaft, and rushed to the furnace. Madly he carried coal back and forth, from the bin to the furnace door, and then back to the bin. Already the speed of the ship had increased. It tore through the water in twenty-foot jumps. But it was not enough. Cedric worked more madly, and still more madly. At last he had thrown the last lump of coal into the furnace. There was nothing more to be done. He rested his tired body against the glowing side of the furnace.

Again the telephone bell rang. Cedric answered it himself, not wishing to take the exchange girl away from her knitting. It was the Captain.

"We must have more speed," he shouted: "We must have more speed. Throw on more coal—more coal!"

For a moment Cedric was wrapped in thought, his face twitching with horror. Then he realized his duty, and rushed forward * * * * *

Late that evening, when they were safe in port, the Captain smoking his after-dinner cigar, came down to the stoke-hole. He called for Cedric. There was not a sound. Again he called. Still there was silence. Suddenly the horror of the truth rushed upon him. He tore open the furnace door, and convulsed with sobs, drew forth a Brooks-Livingstone Collar, a half-melted piece of Spearmint gum, and a suit of Yerger asbestos underwear. For a moment he held them in his arms, and then fell howling upon the floor. The truth had turned out to be the truth.

Cedric had turned himself into calories.

F. S. F.

J. B.

"Cedric the Stoker," *The Princeton Tiger*, xxviii (November 10, 1917), 12. With John Biggs, Jr.

The Nassau Literary Magazine Humor

"Our Next Issue," *The Nassau Literary Magazine*, LXXII (December 1916). Unsigned. Attributed to Fitzgerald on the basis of a clipping in the Fitzgerald Papers, Princeton University.

THE USUAL THING

By Robert W. Shameless

Synopsis of Preceding Chapters.

John Brabant, adopted son of Jules Brabant, the South American Peccadillo Merchant, reaches New York penniless. He has, however, six letters of introduction, one of them unsigned, unsealed, and in fact unwritten. He presents all five of them, including the sixth, to John Brabant. John Brabant, a young South American, is in love with pretty Babette Lefleur, the daughter of Jules Lefleur, a merchant from South America. Upon Jules presenting four of the six letters of introduction which Babette Brabant has written to Jules Lefleur, John begins to realize that Jules, John, and Babette are in league against Brabant and Lefleur for some sinister purpose. Upon presenting the unwritten letter, he realizes that of the five letters Jules or possibly Babette has given Brabant, the only clue to the case of Lefleur and his connection with Babette. At this point Jules and Fefleur meet in Central Park, and Jules presenting the sixth or fifth letter, finds that Babette has given Brabant the letter than Jules presents to John. Confused by this, and in fact, not realizing the importance of the third or fourth letter, he takes tea in his boudoir one day with Brabant. Brabant believes that some sinister connection with Lefleur has driven Babette from South America, where John had been employed in Lefleur's peccadillo factory. He takes boat to South America and on board, sees Brabant also bound South on some secret mission. They decide to combine forces and destroy the second letter. Meanwhile, on the same ship, unknown to the other two, Brabant is disguised as a steward with the first, third and part of the fifth letters of introduction in his possession. As they pass through the Suez Canal a boat rows out from Cairo, and Brabant boards the ship. The other four notice his arrival, but fearful for the safety of the fourth and part of the sixth letter, decide among themselves not to mention peccadillo's or South America in general. Meanwhile, Babette and Lefleur, still in Newport, are falling more and more deeply in love. Lefleur hears of this, and unwilling that Babette should become involved in an affair with this man, leaves his peccadillo factory in the charge of an employee named Brabant and comes North. George meets him in Troy at the business firm of Dulong and Petit, and boarding the train, they rush to Tuxedo Park to join the others, and incidently to seize the sixth letter, if the Countess has not already written it. Arriving in New York, they take rooms at the Ritz, and begin the seach for Brabant. Babette, in her boudoir, is sorting towels when the door suddenly bursts open and Genevieve comes in.

CHAPTER XXXI

Tea was being served at the VanTynes. On the long lawn, the pear trees cast their shadows over the parties of three and four scattered about. Babette and Lefleur had secured a table in a secluded nook, and as the sun glimmered and danced on the burnished silver tea set, she told him the whole story. When she had finished neither spoke for a minute, while he reached into the little mother-of-pearl satchel that hung at his side for cigarettes.

He selected one; he lit a match.

She held it for him.

The cigarette instantly lighted.

"Well?" She smiled up at him, her eyes ringed with those long eyelashes that had evoked Rembrant's enthusiastic praise in Holland the previous summer.

"Well?" He equivocated, shifting his foot from one knee to the other; the foot that had so often booted Harvard to victory on the gridiron.

"You see I am nothing but a toy after all," she sighed, "and I've wanted to be so much more—for you." Her voice sank to a whisper.

"That night," he exclaimed impetuously. "You did, didn't you?"

She blushed.

"Perhaps."

"And that other time in the Chauncy Widdecombs limousine when you————."

"Hush, she breathed, "the servants, one is never alone. Oh! I'm tired of it all, the life I lead. I go to breakfast, what do I eat—grapefruit. I ride—where—the same old places. Do I see life? No!"

"Poor girl," he sympathized.

"It's horrible," she went on, "nothing to eat but food, nothing to wear but clothes, nowhere to live but here and in the city. She flung her hand in a graceful gesture towards the city.

There was a silence. An orange rolled from the table down to the grass, then up again on to a chair where it lay orange and yellow in the sun. They watched it without speaking.

"Why can't you marry me," he began.

She interrupted.

"Don't, don't let's go over that again. Do you think I could ever live on your income? I—live over a stable, with the smelly horses smelling of horses. No—I'm selfish!"

"Not selfish, dear," he interrupted.

"Yes, selfish," she went on. "Do you think I could go around and bear the covert sneers of those who call themselves my friends. Yes, they would sneer at me riding around in your Saxon. No, Gordon— this morning I went down town in sections in two Pierce Arrows. I've got to have it."

"But dear," he broke in again, "I————."

"No, don't apologize. You say we do not need a box at the opera. We can sit in the stalls. But I can't sleep except in a box. I should be kept awake the whole time to bear the covert sneers of those who call themselves my friends. Yes, they would sneer at me."

He mused a moment, making the old clanging noise by snapping his lips together, that he used to make, when, as two little friends, they played together in Central Park, then his family home.

He took her hand in his, his hand that had won so many baseball games for Yale, when known as Beau Brabant, he had been the pitcher. He thought of the hot langurous days of the previous summer, when they had read Gibbon's history of Rome to each other, and had thrilled over the tender love passages.

Mrs. VanTyne came tripping down the lawn, tripped over the grass, and tripped over the tea table.

"What are you two dears doing here?" she asked kindly, but suspiciously. "The others are waiting." She turned to Jules, "They think you have hidden the polo balls for a joke, and they are furious at you."

He smiled wearily. What had he to do with polo balls and other gilded ornaments of the world he had renounced forever.

"They are in the kitchen," he said slowly, "in the drawer with the soap." He ran slowly toward the walk with the famous dogtrot that had made him Captain of the running team at Princeton.

Babette turned angrily to her mother.

'You have hurt him," she cried. "You are cold and cruel, mercenary and heartless, big and fat." She pushed her mother into the tea table.

The sun slowly sank out of sight, and long after the others were dressing and undressing for dinner Babette sat and watched the orange roll up and down from the lawn to the table, and wondered if, in its own dumb way, it had solved the secret of things.

CHAPTER XXXII

As Babette left the house, followed by a deferential butler carrying her suit cases, she glanced back and saw the Countess Jenavra silhoutted in the doorway.

"Good trip," shouted the Countess.

Lefleur, his Saxon purring with energy, was waiting at the gates. She stepped in the front seat. Muffled in fur robes, blankets, overcoats, old sacking, and cotton batton, she gazed once more back at the house. The brilliant Cedric I exterior was punctuated by flashes denoting early English windows. In the Elizabethian doorway stood the Colonial figure of Babette's mother.

The butler gave the car a deferential push, and they started bowling down the long highway alone. The trees bent as if to intercept them, swooping back, however, as they burst by. Lefleur, his foot upon the cylinder, felt a wild exhilaration sweeping over him as they bobbed madly up and down, to and fro, towards the city.

"John," she began, "I know—" she paused and seemed to breath— "that you think," her voice sank to a whisper, then lower still. Nothing could be heard but the rasping of her teeth against her jaws.

"Unghlt," she said, as they passed Bridgeport. It was not until Greenwich, that she got his answering "Gthliuup."

The town was a mere speck as they sped by. He increased the speed. Leaning back against his shoulder, she felt a deep, perfect content surge through her. Surely this was living or more than living. The cold air surging by turned her senses cold and tense. Sharp as a whip, everything, all her life, stood out against the background of this ride. She wondered if all things could not be solved in this way, with the sting of the fresh night and the rat-tat of the motor.

Up to this time he had been running on two cylinders. He now threw on two more, and the car, careening up for a second on its front wheels, righted itself and continued with its speed redoubled. However, in the confusion of the change, his right arm had become disengaged and thrown around her. She did not move it.

Faster they went. He pressed harder on the steering gear, and in response to his pressure, the car sprang forward like a well-trained steed. They were late, and realizing it, he threw on the last two cylinders.

The car seemed to realize what was demanded of it. It stopped, turned around three times, and then bounded off at twice its former speed.

Along they went. Suddenly the car stopped, and with the instinct of a trained mechanic, he realized that something was the matter. After an inspection, he saw that one of the tires was punctured. He looked to see what damage had been done. They had run over a hairpin, and the rubber was torn and splintered to shreds. They looked around for another tire. They looked in the back seat, they looked under the car, they looked behind the bushes on the edge of the road. There was no tire. They must fix the old one. John put his mouth to the puncture and blew it up, sticking his handkerchief into the hole.

They started off, but after several miles, the grueling strain of the road wore through the handkerchief, little by little, and the car stopped again. They tried everything, leaves and gravel, and pieces of the road. Finally Babette sacrificed her gum to stop up the gaping aperture, but after several miles this too wore out.

There was but one thing to do, to take off the tire, run into town on three wheels, and hire a man to run along beside the car and hold up the fourth side. No sooner had they had this thought than they put it into action. Three whistles, and a cry of "buckwheats," brought a crowd of Yokels in a jiffy, and the most intelligent looking one of the lot was engaged for the arduous task.

He took his place by the fender, and they again started off. They increased the speed soon, driving along at the rate of forty miles an hour. The Yokel, running beside with a long easy stride, was panting and seemed to have difficulty in keeping up the pace.

It was growing darker. Sitting up close to John's huge ratskin coat, Babette felt the old longing to see his eyes close to hers, and feel his lips brush her cheek.

"John," she murmured. He turned. Above the clatter of the motor and the harsh plebian breathing of the peasant, she heard his heart heave with emotion.

"Babette," he said.

She started, sobbing softly, her voice mingling with the roar of the fan belt.

He folded her slowly, dignifiedly, and wilfully, in his arms and ki————.

The next installment of Mr. Shameless' fascinating story will appear in the July number.

"The Usual Thing," *The Nassau Literary Magazine,* LXXII (December 1916), 223–228. Unsigned. Attributed to Fitzgerald on the basis of a clipping in the Fitzgerald Papers, Princeton University.

JEMINA

A Story of the Blue Ridge Mountains

By John Phlox, Jr.

It was night in the mountains of Kentucky.

Wild hills rose on all sides. Swift mountain streams flowed rapidly up and down the mountains.

Jemina Tantrum was down at the stream brewing whiskey at the family still.

She was a typical mountain girl.

Her feet were bare. Her hands, large and powerful, hung down below her knees. Her face showed the ravages of work. Although but sixteen, she had for over a dozen years been supporting her aged pappy and mappy by brewing mountain whiskey.

From time to time she would pause in her task, and filling a dipper full of the pure invigorating liquid, would drain it off—then pursue her work with renewed vigor.

She would place the rye in the vat, thresh it out with her feet, and in twenty minutes the completed product would be turned out.

A sudden cry made her pause in the act of draining a dipper and look up.

"Hello," said a voice. It came from a man in hunting costume who had emerged from the wood.

"Hi, thar," she answered sullenly.

"Can you tell me the way to the Tantrums' cabin?"

"Are you uns from the settlements down thar?"

She pointed her hand down to the bottom of the hill where Louisville lay. She had never been there, but once, before she was born, her great-grandfather, old Gore Tantrum, had gone into the settlements in the company of two marshalls, and had never come back. So the Tantrums from generation to generation had learned to dread civilization.

The man was amused. He laughed a light tinkling laugh, the laugh of a Philadelphian. Something in the ring of it thrilled her. She drank off a dipper of whiskey.

"Where is Mr. Tantrum, little girl?" he asked kindly.

She raised her foot and pointed her big toe toward the woods.

"Thar in the cabing behind those thar pines. Old Tantrum air my ole man."

The man from the settlements thanked her and strode off. He was fairly vibrant with youth and personality. As he walked along he whistled and sang and turned handsprings and flapjacks, breathing in the fresh, cool air of the mountains.

The air around the still was like wine.

Jemina Tantrum watched him fascinated. No one like him had ever come into her life before.

She sat down on the grass and counted her toes. She counted eleven. She had learned arithmetic in the mountain school.

Ten years before, a lady from the settlements had opened a school on the mountain. Jemina had no money, but she had paid her way in whiskey, bringing a pail full to school every morning and leaving it on Miss Lafarge's desk. Miss Lafarge had died of delerium tremens after a year's teaching, and so Jemina's education had stopped.

Across the still stream still another still was standing. It was that of the Doldrums. The Doldrums and the Tantrums never spoke.

They hated each other.

Fifty years before old Jem Doldrum and old Jem Tantrum had quarrelled in the Tantrum cabin over a game of slapjack. Jem Doldrum had thrown the king of hearts in Jem Tantrum's face, and the old Doldrum, enraged, had felled the old Tantrum with the nine of diamonds. Other Doldrums and Tantrums had joined in and the little cabin was soon filled with flying cards. Hartsrum Doldrum lay stretched on the floor writhing in agony, the ace of hearts crammed down his throat. Jem Tantrum, standing in the doorway, ran through suit after suit, his face lit with fiendish hatred. Old Mappy Tantrum stood on the table wetting down the Doldrums with hot whiskey. Old Heck Doldrum, having finally run out of trumps, was backed out of the cabin, striking left and right with his tobacco pouch, and, gathering around him the rest of his clan, they mounted their cows and galloped furiously home.

That night old man Doldrum and his sons, vowing vengeance, had returned, put a tick-tock on the Tantrum window, stuck a pin in the doorbell and beaten a retreat.

A week later the Tantrums had put Cod Liver Oil in the Doldrum's still, and so, from year to year, the feud had continued, first one family being entirely wiped out and then the other.

Every day Jemina worked the still on her side of the stream, and Boscoe Doldrum worked the still on his side.

Sometimes, with unborn hatred, the feudists would throw whiskey at each other, and Jemina would come home smelling like a Bowery saloon on election night.

But now Jemina was too thoughtful to look across. How wonderful this stranger had been and how oddly he was dressed! In her innocent way she had never believed that there were any settlements at all, and she had put it down to the credulity of the mountain people.

She turned to go up to the cabin, and as she turned something struck her in the neck. It was a sponge soaked in whiskey, and thrown by Boscoe Doldrum—a sponge soaked in whiskey from his still on the other side.

"Hi thar, Boscoe Doldrum," she shouted in her deep base voice.

"Yo', Jemina Tantrum. Gosh ding yo'!" he returned.

She continued up to the cabin.

The stranger was talking to her father. Gold had been discovered on the Tantrum land, and the stranger, Edgar Edison, was trying to buy the land for a song.

She sat upon her hands and watched him.

He was wonderful. When he talked his lips moved.

She sat upon the stove and watched him.

Suddenly there came a blood-curdling scream. The Tantrums rushed to the windows.

It was the Doldrums.

They had hitched their cows to trees and concealed themselves behind the bushes and flowers and soon a perfect rattle of stones and bricks beat against the windows, bending them inward.

"Father, father," shrieked Jemina.

Her father took down his slingshot from his slingshot rack on the wall and ran his hand lovingly over the elastic band. He stepped to a loophole. Old Mappy Tantrum stepped to the coal-hole.

The stranger was aroused at last. Furious to get at the Doldrums, he tried to get out of the house by crawling up the chimney. Then he thought there might be a door under the bed, but Jemina told him there was not one. He hunted for doors under the beds and sofas, but each time Jemina pulled him out and told him there were no doors there. Furious with anger, he beat upon the door and hollered at the Doldrums, but cowed, they could not answer him, but kept up their fusillade of bricks and stones against the window. Old Pappy Tantrum knew that as soon as they were able to effect an aperture they would pour in and the fight would be over.

Old Heck Doldrum, foaming at the mouth and spitting on the ground left and right, led the attack.

The terrific slingshots of old Pappy Tantrum had not been without their effect. A master shot had disabled one Doldrum, and another, shot three times through the abdomen and once through the stomach, fought feebly on.

Nearer and nearer they approached the house.

"We must fly," shouted the stranger to Jemina. "I will sacrifice myself and bear us both away."

"No," shouted Pappy Tantrum, his face begrimmed with cold cream and grease paint. "You stay here and fit on. I will bar Jemina away. I will bar Mappy away. I will bar myself away."

The man from the settlements, pale and trembling with anger, turned to Ham Tantrum, who stood at the door throwing loophole after loophole at the advancing Doldrums.

"Will you cover the retreat?"

But Ham said that he too had Tantrums to bear away, but that he would leave himself here to help the stranger cover the retreat if he could think of a way of doing it.

Soon smoke began to filter through the floor and ceiling. Shem Doldrum had come up and touched a match to old Japhet Tantrum's breath as he leaned from a loophole and the alcoholic flames shot up on all sides.

The whiskey in the bathtub caught fire. The walls began to fall in.

Jemina and the man from the settlements looked at each other.

"Jemina," he whispered.

"Stranger," she answered in an answering answer.

"We will die together," he said. "If we had lived I would have taken you to the settlements and married you. With your ability to hold liquor, your social success was assured."

She caressed him idly for a moment, counting her toes softly to herself. The smoke grew thicker. Her left leg was on fire. She was a human alcohol lamp.

Their lips met in one long kiss, and then a wall fell on them and blotted them out.

When the Doldrums burst through the ring of flame ten minutes later, they found them dead where they had fallen, their arms around each other.

Old Jem Doldrum was moved.

He took off his hat.

He filled it with whiskey and drank it off.

"They air daid," he said slowly. "They hankered after each other. The fit is over now. We must not separate them."

So they threw them together into the stream and the two splashes they made were as one.

"Jemina," *The Nassau Literary Magazine*, lxxii (December 1916), 210–215; reprinted in *Vanity Fair*, xv (January 1921) and *Tales of the Jazz Age*.

"The Vampiest of the Vampires" (*The Nassau Literary Magazine*, lxxii [December 1916], 216) is attributed to Fitzgerald in Henry Dan Piper's checklist (*The Princeton University Library Chronicle*, xii [Summer 1951]) on the basis of a clipping in the Fitzgerald papers. But "The Vampiest of the Vampires" is on the verso of the last page of "Jemina," which makes this attribution shaky. Fitzgerald did not save a clipping of "The Apotheosis of the Amateur," which is a companion piece to "The Vampiest of the Vampires."

Reviews

PENROD AND SAM

Penrod and Sam, by Booth Tarkington, '93, another collection of "Penrod" stories, is the typical second book of a series. At times it maintains the rather high level of humor set by its predecessor *Penrod*, but certain of the stories seem to have been turned out solely to fill a contract with the Cosmopolitan magazine.

The same set of characters figure once more. Mr. Tarkington has done what so many authors of juvenile books fail to do: he has admitted the unequaled snobbishness of boyhood and has traced the neighborhood social system which, with Penrod and Sam at the top, makes possible more than half the stories. Herman and Verman, the colored brethren, may be socially eligible, but Maurice Levy, barely a "regular fellow," is never quite admitted as an equal. Georgie Basset, "the best boy in town," and Roddie Bitts, the hot-house plant, are clearly outside the pale; although we claim that there is still hope for Roddy, there is a certain disagreeableness about him which is too sure to be despised. It is to be regretted that Carlie Chitten, a future Machiavelli, figures in only one story. He and Penrod are truer types of success than are to be found in the intricacies of a dozen psychological novels.

The first two stories, "The Bonded Prisoner" and "Bingism," belong distinctly in the filler class, although both have Tarkington touches. The third story, "The In-or-in," the history of an ill-fated secret society, is really funny, and so is the next one, "The Story of Whitney", the horse that was rescued in spite of himself. "Conscience" and "Gypsey" are not so good, but the following tale, "Wednesday Madness", is uproariously funny. It is as good as the best parts of *Seventeen*. Penrod tries to pass off a rather sentimental letter of his sisters as his own composition, in answer to a demand made at school for a model letter to a friend. This leads to a wild Wednesday of fights, flights, and fatalities, the last of which is the spanking which awaits him as he trudges home at seven-thirty.

"Penrod's Busy Day" and "On Account of the Weather" are both amusing; the "Horn of Fame" is rather poor. The book ends with "The Party", easily the best story. From the sleek advent of Carlie Chitten to Marjorie's confession, that she loves Penrod because of his capabilities for wit, it is extremely well done, and brings back a dozen like experiences to the reader's memory. Where Mr. Tarkington gets his knowledge of child psychology, I am unable to understand. It has become a tradition to mention Tom Brown as an ideal boy's story, but as a matter of fact, the heroes of Owen Johnston, Compton McKenzie, and Booth Tarkington are far more interesting and far truer to facts.

(Penrod and Sam, *by Booth Tarkington. Doubleday Page & Co., New York. $1.35 net.*)

—*F. S. F.*

Review of Booth Tarkington's *Penrod and Sam, The Nassau Literary Magazine,* LXXII (January 1917), 291–292.

DAVID BLAIZE

Of late years there have been really good boys' stories, with the boy treated from a subjective point of view neither cynically nor sentimentally. In the class belong *The Varmint, Youth's Encounter, Seventeen,* and perhaps a new book, *David Blaize,* by E. F. Benson, author of *Dodo.* Benson, by the way, is one of the famous Benson triology with Arthur C. Benson and the late Monsiegnuer Robert Hugh Benson. The book carries the English hero through his last year at a "private" school and through three forms at an English public school, presumably Eton under the name of Marchester.

Frank Maddox, David's first and last hero, is the strongest personality in the book, David being rather a peg on which the author hangs virtues and adventures. The book starts well and until three-quarters the way through is very interesting. Then follows a long and, to an American, dry and unintelligible account of a cricket match in which, by careful sounding, we fathom that the hero and his idol Frank Maddox, in the orthodox Ralph Henry Barbour manner, win the day for the school.

Mr. Benson's indebtedness to Compton MacKenzie and Kipling is very great. Swinburne introduces David to literature as he did Michael in *Youth's Encounter* and the disagreement of David with the prefects is very like certain chapters in Stalkey's career. The one incident which forms the background of the book is foreign to anything in our preparatory schools and although handled with an overemphasized delicacy, seems rather unnecessary and unhealthy from our point of view.

One of the great charms of the book lies in the chapters where Frank first lights upon David near the old cathedral and where David is visiting Frank at the seashore. The chapter on David's love affair is poorly written and seems a half-hearted attempt to make him seem well-rounded. The last melodramatic incident, the injury and recovery of the hero is well done, but does not go for unity. The first two-thirds of the book is immensely entertaining, the last third disappointing.

(David Blaize, *by E. F. Benson, The George Doran Company, New York. $1.35 net*).

—F. S. F.

Review of E. F. Benson's *David Blaize, The Nassau Literary Magazine,* LXXII (February 1917), 343–344.

THE CELT AND THE WORLD

After his most entertaining *End of a Chapter,* Mr. Leslie has written what I think will be a more lasting book. *The Celt and the World* is a sort of bible of Irish patriotism. Mr. Leslie has endeavored to trace a race, the Bretton, Scotch, Welsh, and Irish Celt, through its spiritual crises and he emphasizes most strongly the trait that Synge, Yeats and Lady Gregory have made so much of in their plays, the Celt's inveterate mysticism. The theme is worked out in an era-long contrast between Celt and Teuton, and the book becomes ever ironical when it deals of the ethical values of the latter race. "Great is the Teuton indeed," it says, "Luther in religion, Bessemer in steel, Neitzche in philosophy, Rockefeller in oil—Cromwell and Bismarck in war." What a wonderful list of names! Could anyone but an Irishman have linked them in such damning significance?

In the chapter on the conversion of the Celt to christianity, is traced the great missionary achievements of the Celtic priests and philosophers, Dungal, Fergal, Abelard, Duns Scotus and Ereugena. At the end of the book that no less passionate and mystical,, although unfortunate, incident of Pearse, Plunkett and the Irish Republic, is given sympathetic but just treatment.

To an Irishman the whole book is fascinating. It gives one an intense desire to see Ireland free at last to work out her own destiny under Home Rule. It gives one the idea that she would do it directly under the eyes of God and with so much purity and so many mistakes. It arouses a fascination with the mystical lore and legend of the island which "can save others, but herself she cannot save." The whole book is colored with an unworldliness, and an atmosphere of the futility of man's ambitions. As Mr. Leslie says in the foreword to *The End of a Chapter* (I quote inexactly) we have seen the suicide of the Aryan race, "the end of one era and the beginning of another to which no Gods have as yet been rash enough to give their names."

The Celt and the World is a rather pessimistic book: not with the dreary pessimism of Strinberg and Sudermann, but with the pessimism which might have inspired "What doth it profit a man if he gaineth the whole world and loseth his own soul." It is worth remarking that it ends with a foreboding prophecy of a Japanese-American war in the future. The book should be especially interesting to anyone who has enjoyed *Riders to the Sea,* or *The Hour-Glass.* He will read an engrossing view of a much discussed race and decide that the Irishman has used heaven as a continued referendum for his ideals, as he has used earth as a perennial recall for his ambitions.

(The Celt and the World, *by Shane Leslie,* New York; *Charles Scribner's Sons.*)

—*F. S. F.*

Review of Shane Leslie's *The Celt and the World, The Nassau Literary Magazine,* LXXIII (May 1917), 104–105.

VERSES IN PEACE AND WAR

Mr. Leslie, after starting out as a sort of Irish Chesterton, now produces a diminitive volume of poetry under the title of *Verses in Peace and War*. In this poetical era of titles like "Men Women and Ghosts," and "Sword Blades and Poppy Seeds," Mr. Leslie is liable to be out-advertised by that dashing soubrette of American rhyming, Miss Amy Lowell, but if one desires poetry instead of the more popular antics of the School of Boston Bards and Hearst Reviewers, let him sit down for an hour with Mr. Leslie's little book. At first, one gets the impression of rather light verse, but soon finds that it is the touch rather than the verse which is light. The same undercurrent of sadness which runs through Mr. Leslie's prose is evident in his poetry, and gives it a most rare and haunting depth. In the series, "Epitaphs for Aviators," two are particularly apt. The one on Lieutenant Hamel:

> Nor rugged earth, nor untamed sky,
> Gave him his death to die,
> But gentlest of the Holy Three;
> The long grey liquid sea.

And the one on Lieutenant Chavez:

> One flying past the Alps to see
> What lay behind their crest—
> Behind the snows found Italy;
> Beyond the mountains—rest.

There is a savor of the Greek in his poem "The Hurdlers," dedicated to two of England's representatives in the last Olympian games, since killed in Flanders. The lines:

> Oh, how are the beautiful broken
> And how are the swiftest made slow—

sound as if they'd scan as well in Greek as in English. The lighter poems such as "Nightmare" and "Rubies," are immensely well done as are the Irish poems "The Two Mothers" and "A Ballad of China Tea," but the brightest gem of the coffer is the poem "The Dead Friend," beginning:

> I drew him then unto my knees
> My friend who was dead,
> And I set my live lips over his,
> And my heart to his head.

Mr. Leslie has a most distinct gift, and the only pity is that his book is so small. Poets are really so very rare that it seems almost unfair for them to become essayists. Despite Mr. Taine, in the whole range from Homer's Oddysey to Master's idiocy, there has been but one Shakespeare, and every lost name leaves a gap that it, and it only, could have filled.

(Verses in Peace and War *by Shane Leslie; Scribner's.*)

—*F. S. F.*

Review of Shane Leslie's *Verses in Peace and War, The Nassau Literary Magazine,* LXXIII (June 1917), 152–153.

GOD, THE INVISIBLE KING

The fad of rediscovering God has reached Mr. Wells. Started by Tolstoi (who has since backed his case by fathering a brand new revolution) it has reached most of the Clever People, including Bernard Shaw, who tried to startle us last year with his preface to *Androcles and the Lion.* But Mr. Wells has added very little. Like Victor Hugo, he has nothing but genius and is not of the slightest practical help. Neither a pacifist nor a crusader, he has been wise enough to keep God out of the war, which is only what the sanest people have been doing all along; if any war was ever made on earth it is this one.

If there is anything older than the old story it is the new twist. Mr. Wells supplies this by neatly dividing God into a creator and a Redeemer. On the whole we should welcome *God, the Invisible King,* as an entertaining addition to our supply of fiction for light summer reading.

(God, the Invisible King *by H. G. Wells; MacMillan Co.*)

—*F. S. F.*

Review of H. G. Wells' *God, The Invisible King, The Nassau Literary Magazine,* LXXIII (June 1917), 153.

THE BALTIMORE ANTI-CHRIST

By F. Scott Fitzgerald

The incomparable Mencken will, I fear, meet the fate of Aristides. He will be exiled because one is tired of hearing his praises sung. In at least three contemporary novels he is mentioned as though he were dead as Voltaire and as secure as Shaw with what he would term "a polite bow". His style is imitated by four-fifths of the younger critics—moreover he has demolished his enemies and set up his own gods in the literary supplements.

Of the essays in the new book the best is the autopsy on the still damp bones of Roosevelt. In the hands of Mencken Roosevelt becomes almost a figure of Greek tragedy; more, he becomes alive and loses some of that stuffiness that of late has become attached to all 100% Americans. Not only is the essay most illuminating but its style is a return to Mencken's best manner, the style of "Prefaces", with the soft pedal on his amazing chord of adjectives and a tendency to invent new similes instead of refurbishing his amusing but somewhat overworked old ones.

Except for the section on American aristocracy there is little new in the first essay "The National Letters": an abundance of wit and a dozen ideas that within the past year and under his own deft hand have become bromides. The Knights of Pythias, Right Thinkers, On Building Universities, Methodists, as well as the corps of journeyman critics and popular novelists come in for their usual bumping, this varied with unexpected tolerance toward "The Saturday Evening Post" and even a half grudging mention of Booth Tarkington. Better than any of this comment, valid and vastly entertaining as it is, would be a second Book of Prefaces say on Edith Wharton, Cabell, Woodrow Wilson—and Mencken himself. But the section of the essay devoted to the Cultural Background rises to brilliant analysis. Here again he is thinking slowly, he is on comparatively fresh ground, he brings the force of his clarity and invention to bear on the subject—passes beyond his function as a critic of the arts and becomes a reversed Cato of a civilization.

In "The Sahara of Bozart" the dam breaks, devastating Georgia, Carolina, Mississippi, and Company. The first trickle of this overflow appeared in the preface to "The American Credo"; here it reaches such a state of invective that one pictures all the region south of Mason-Dixon to be peopled by moron Catilines. The ending is gentle —too gentle, the gentleness of ennui.

To continue in the grand manner of a catalogue: "The Divine Afflatus" deals with the question of inspiration and the lack of it, an old and sad problem to the man who has done creative work. "Examination of a Popular Virtue" runs to eight pages of whimsical excellence—a consideration of ingratitude decided at length with absurd but mellow justice. "Exeunt Omnes", which concerns the menace of death, I choose to compare with a previous "Discussion" of the same subject in "A Book of Burlesques". The comparison is only in that the former piece, which I am told Mencken fatuously considers one of his best, is a hacked out, glued together bit of foolery, as good, say, as an early essay of Mark Twain's, while this "Exeunt Omnes", which follows it by several years, is smooth, brilliant, apparently jointless. To my best recollection it is the most microscopical examination of this particular mote on the sun that I have ever come across.

Follows a four paragraph exposition of the platitude that much music loving is an affectation and further paragraphs depreciating opera as a form. As to the "Music of Tomorrow" the present reviewer's ignorance must keep him silent, but in "Tempo di Valse" Mencken, the modern, becomes Victorian by insisting that what people are tired of is more exciting than what they have just learned to do. If his idea of modern dancing is derived from watching men who learned it circa thirty-five, toiling interminably around the jostled four square feet of a cabaret, he is justified; but I see no reason why the "Bouncing Shimmee" efficiently performed is not as amusing and as graceful and certainly as difficult as any waltz ever attempted. The section continues with the condemnation of a musician named Hadley, an ingenious attempt to preserve a portrait of Dreiser, and a satisfactory devastation of the acting profession.

In "The Cult of Hope" he defends his and "Dr. Nathan's" attitude toward constructive criticism—most entertainingly—but the next section "The Dry Millennium", patchworked from the Ripetizione Generale, consists of general repetitions of theses in his previous books. "An Appendix on a Tender Theme" contains his more recent speculations on women, eked out with passages from "The Smart Set".

An excellent book! Like Max Beerbohm, Mencken's work is inevitably distinguished. But now and then one wonders—granted that, solidly, book by book, he has built up a literary reputation most to be envied of any American, granted also that he has done more for the national letters than any man alive, one is yet inclined to regret a success so complete. What will he do now? The very writers to the press about the blue Sabbath hurl the bricks of the buildings he has demolished into the still smoking ruins. He is, say, forty; how of the next twenty years? Will he find new gods to dethrone, some eternal "yokelry" still callous enough to pose as intelligenzia before the Menckenian pen fingers? Or will he strut among the ruins, a man beaten by his own success, as futile, in the end, as one of those Conrad characters that so tremendously enthrall him?

Prejudices. Second Series. By H. L. Mencken. Alfred A. Knopf.

"The Baltimore Anti-Christ": Review of H. L. Mencken's *Prejudices, Second Series, The Bookman*, LIII (March 1921), 79–81.

THREE SOLDIERS

A Review by F. Scott Fitzgerald

With the exception of a couple of tracts by Upton Sinclair, carefully disguised as novels but none the less ignored by the righteous booksellers of America, "Three Soldiers" by a young Harvard man named John Dos Passos is the first war book by an American which is worthy of serious notice. Even "The Red Badge of Courage" is pale beside it. Laying "Three Soldiers" down I am filled with that nameless emotion that only a piece of work created in supreme detachment can arouse. This book will not be read in the West. "Main Street" was too much of a strain—I doubt if the "cultured" public of the Middle Border will ever again risk a serious American novel, unless it is heavily baited with romantic love.

No—"Three Soldiers" will never compete with "The Sheik" or with those salacious sermons whereby Dr. Crafts gives bilogical thrills to the wives of prominent butchers and undertakers,—nor will it ever do aught but frighten the caravanserie of one hundred and twenty-proof Americans, dollar a year men and slaughter crazy old maids who waited in line at the book stores to buy and read the war masterpiece of the

Spanish Zane Grey, the one that is now being played in the movies by a pretty young man with machine oil on his hair.

To a dozen or so hereabouts who require more seemly recreation I heartily recommend "Three Soldiers." The whole gorgeous farce of 1917–1918 will be laid before him. He will hear the Y.M.C.A. men with their high-pitched voices and their set condescending smiles, saying "That's great, boys. I would like to be with you only my eyes are weak. * * * Remember that your women folk are praying for you this minute. * * * I've heard the great heart of America beat. * * * O boys! Never forget that you are in a great Christian cause."

He will hear such stuff as that and he will see these same obnoxious prigs charging twenty cents for a cup of chocolate and making shrill, preposterous speeches full of pompous ministers' slang. He will see the Military Police (the M.P.'s) ferociously "beating up" privates for failure to salute an officer.

He will see filth and pain, cruelty and hysteria and panic, in one long three-year nightmare and he will know that the war brought the use of these things not to some other man or to some other man's son, but to himself and to his OWN son, that same healthy young animal who came home two years ago bragging robustly of the things he did in France.

Dan Fuselli, from California, petty, stupid and ambitious, is the first soldier. His miserable disappointments, his intrigues, his amiable and esurent humanities are traced from the camp where he gets his "training" to postwar Paris where, considerably weakened in his original cheap but sufficing fibre, he has become a mess-cook.

The second soldier, Chrisfield, a half-savage, southern-moralled boy from Indiana, murders his fancied oppressor—not because of any considerable wrong, but simply as the reaction of his temperament to military discipline—and is A. W. O. L. in Paris at the end.

These two inarticulate persons are woven in the pattern with a third, a musician, who is in love with the mellifluous rythms of Flaubert.

It is with this John Andrews, the principal protagonist of the story, that John Dos Passos allows himself to break his almost Flaubertian detachment and begin to Britling-ize the war. This is immediately perceptible in his style, which becomes falsely significant and strewn with tell-tale dots. But the author recovers his balance in a page or two and flies on to the end in full control of the machine.

This is all very careful work. There is none of that uncorrelated detail, that clumsy juggling with huge masses of material which shows in all but one or two pieces of American realism. The author is not oppressed by the panic-stricken necessity of using all his data at once lest some other prophet of the new revelation uses it before him. He is an artist—John Dos Passos. His book could wait five years or ten or twenty. I am inclined to think that he is the best of all the younger men on this side.

The deficiency in his conception of John Andrews is this: John Andrews is a little too much the ultimate ineffectual, the Henry-Adams-in-his-youth sort of character. This sort of young man has been previously sketched many times—usually when an author finds need of a mouthpiece and yet does not wish to write about an author.

With almost painstaking precaution the character is inevitably made a painter or a musician, as though intelligence did not exist outside the arts. Not that Andrews' puppet-ness is frequent. Nor is it ever clothed in aught but sophistication and vitality and grace—nevertheless the gray ghosts of Wells' heroes and those of Wells' imitators seem to file by along the margin, reminding one that such a profound and gifted man as John Dos Passos should never enlist in Wells' faithful but aenemic platoon along with Walpole, Floyd Dell and Mencken's late victim, Ernest Poole. The only successful Wellsian is Wells. Let us slay Wells, James Joyce and Anatole France that the creation of literature may continue.

In closing I will make an invidious comparison: Several weeks ago a publisher sent me a book by a well-known popular writer, who has evidently decided that there is better pay of late in becoming a deep thinker, or to quote the incomparable Mencken "a spouter of great causes." The publishers informed me that the book was to be issued in October, that in their opinion it was the best manuscript novel that had ever come to them, and ended by asking me to let them know what I thought of it. I read it. It was a desperate attempt to do what John Dos Passos has done. It abounded with Fergus Falls mysticism and undigested Haeckel and its typical scene was the heroic dying Poilu crying "Jesu!" to the self-sacrificing Red Cross worker! It reached some sort of decision—that Life was an Earnest Matter or something! when it was not absurd it was so obvious as to be painful. On every page the sawdust leaked out of the characters. If anyone wishes to cultivate the rudiments of literary taste let him read "The Wasted Generation" by Owen Johnston and "Three Soldiers" by John Dos Passos side by side. If he can realize the difference he is among the saved. He will walk with the angels in Paradise.

F. SCOTT FITZGERALD.

Review of John Dos Passos' *Three Soldiers, St. Paul Daily News,* September 25, 1921, feature section, p. 6.

THREE CITIES

By F. Scott Fitzgerald
Author of "This Side of Paradise", "Flappers and Philosophers"

It began in Paris, that impression—fleeting, chiefly literary, unprofound —that the world was growing darker. We carefully reconstructed an old theory and, blonde both of us, cast supercilious Nordic glances at the play of the dark children around us. We had left America less than one half of one per cent. American but the pernicious and sentimental sap was destined to rise again within us. We boiled with ancient indignations toward the French. We sat in front of Anatole France's house for an hour in hope of seeing the old gentleman come out—but we thought simultaneously that when he dies, the France of flame and glory dies with him. We drove in the Bois de Boulogne—thinking of France as a spoiled and revengeful child which, having kept Europe in a turmoil for two hundred years has spent the last forty demanding assistance in its battles, that the continent may be kept as much like a bloody sewer as possible.

In Brentano's near the Café de la Paix, I picked up Dreiser's suppressed "Genius" for three dollars. With the exception of "The Titan" I liked it best among his five novels, in spite of the preposterous Christian Science episode near the end. We stayed in Paris long enough to finish it.

Italy, which is to the English what France is to the Americans, was in a pleasant humor. As a French comedy writer remarked we inevitably detest our benefactors, so I was glad to see that Italy was casting off four years of unhealthy suppressed desires. In Florence you could hardly blame a squad of Italian soldiers for knocking down an Omaha lady who was unwilling to give up her compartment to a Colonel. Why, the impudent woman could not speak Italian! So the *Carabinieri* can hardly be blamed for being incensed. And as for knocking her around a little—well, boys will be boys. The American ambassadorial tradition in Rome having for some time been in the direct line of sentimental American literature, I do not doubt that even they found some compensating sweetness in the natures of the naughty *Bersaglieri*.

We were in Rome two weeks. You can see the fascination of the place. We stayed two weeks even though we could have left in two days —that is we *could* have left if we had not run out of money. I met John Carter, the author of "These Wild Young People," in the street one day and he cashed me a check for a thousand lira. We spent this on ointment.

The ointment trust thrives in Rome. All the guests at the two best hotels are afflicted with what the proprietors call "mosquitos too small for screens." We do not call them that in America.

John Carter lent us "Alice Adams" and we read it aloud to each other under the shadow of Caesar's house. If it had not been for Alice we should have collapsed and died in Rome as so many less fortunate literary people have done. "Alice Adams" more than atones for the childish heroics of "Ramsey Milholland" and for the farcical spiritualism in "The Magnificent Ambersons." After having made three brave attempts to struggle through "Moon Calf" it was paradise to read someone who knows how to write.

By bribing the ticket agent with one thousand lira to cheat some old general out of his compartment—the offer was the agent's, not ours— we managed to leave Italy.

"*Vous avez quelque chose pour déclarer?*" asked the border customs officials early next morning (only they asked it in better French).

I awoke with a horrible effort from a dream of Italian beggars.

"*Oui!*" I shrieked, "*Je veux déclare que je suis trés, trés heureux a partir d'Italie!*" I could understand at last why the French loved France. They have seen Italy.

We had been to Oxford before—after Italy we went back there arriving gorgeously at twilight when the place was fully peopled for us by the ghosts of ghosts—the characters, romantic, absurd or melancholy, of "Sinister Street," "Zuleicka Dobson" and "Jude the Obscure." But something was wrong now—something that would never be right again. Here was Rome—here on the High were the shadows of the Via Appia.

In how many years would our descendents approach this ruin with supercilious eyes to buy postcards from men of a short, inferior race—a race that once were Englishmen. How soon—for money follows the rich lands and the healthy stock, and art follows begging after money. Your time will come, New York, fifty years, sixty. Apollo's head is peering crazily, in new colors that our generation will never live to know, over the tip of the next century.

"Three Cities," *Brentano's Book Chat*, ı (September–October 1921), 15, 28.

POOR OLD MARRIAGE

By F. Scott Fitzgerald

Although not one of the first I was certainly one of the most enthusiastic readers of Charles Norris's "Salt"—I sat up until five in the morning to finish it, stung into alertness by the booming repetition of his title phrase at the beginning of each section. In the dawn I wrote him an excited letter of praise. To me it was utterly new. I had never read Zola or Frank Norris or Dreiser—in fact the realism which now walks Fifth Avenue was then hiding dismally in Tenth Street basements. No one of my English professors in college ever suggested to his class that books were being written in America. Poor souls, they were as ignorant as I—possibly more so. But since then Brigadier General Mencken has marshaled the critics in aquiescent column of squads for the campaign against Philistia.

In the glow of this crusade I read "Brass" and suffered a distinct disappointment. Although it is a more difficult form than "Salt" and is just as well, perhaps more gracefully, constructed, the parallel marriages are by no means so deftly handled as the ones in Arnold Bennett's "Whom God Hath Joined". It is a cold book throughout and it left me unmoved. Mr. Norris has an inexhaustible theme and he elaborates on it intelligently and painstakingly—but, it seems to me, without passion and without pain. There is not a line in it that compares with Griffith Adams's broken cry of emotion, "Why, I love you my girl, better than any other God damned person in the world!"

There was a fine delicacy in Frank Norris's work which does not exist in his brother's. Frank Norris had his realistic tricks—in "McTeague" for instance where the pictures are almost invariably given authenticity by an appeal to the sense of smell or of hearing rather than by the commoner form of word painting—but he seldom strengthens his dose from smelling salts to emetics. "Brass" on the contrary becomes at times merely the shocker—the harrowing description of Leila's feet could only be redeemed by a little humor, of which none is forthcoming. Early in the book one finds the following sentence:

He inflated his chest . . . pounding with shut fists the hard surface of his breast, alternately digging his finger-tips into the firm flesh about the nipples.

Here he has missed his mark entirely. I gather from the context that he has intended to express the tremendous virility of his hero in the early morning. Not questioning the accuracy of the details in themselves it is none the less obvious that he has chosen entirely the *wrong* details. He has given a glimpse not into Philip's virility but into the Bronx zoo.

Save for the pseudo-Shavian discussion on marriage near the end Mr. Norris manages to avoid propaganda and panacea. Some of the scenes are excellent—Philip's first courtship, his reunion with Marjorie after their first separation, his final meeting with her. Marjorie and Philip's mother are the best characters in the book, despite the care wasted on Mrs. Grotenberg. Leila is too much a series of tricks—she is not in a class with Rissie in "Salt."

Had this novel appeared three years ago it would have seemed more important than it does at present. It is a decent, competent, serious piece of work—but excite me it simply doesn't. A novel interests me on one of two counts: either it is something entirely new and fresh and profoundly felt, as, for instance, "The Red Badge of Courage" or "Salt", or else it is a tour de force by a man of exceptional talent, a Mark Twain or a Tarkington. A great book is both these things— "Brass", I regret to say, is neither.

Brass, A Novel of Marriage. By Charles G. Norris. E. P. Dutton and Co.

"Poor Old Marriage": Review of Charles G. Norris' *Brass, The Bookman*, LIV (November 1921), 253–254.

ALDOUS HUXLEY'S "CROME YELLOW"

Reviewed by F. Scott Fitzgerald

Now this man is a wit. He is the grandson of the famous Huxley who, besides being one of the two great scientists of his time, wrote clear and beautiful prose—better prose than Stevenson could ever master.

This is young Huxley's third book—his first one, "Limbo," was a collection of sketches—his second, "Leda," which I have never read, contained one long poem and, I believe, a few lyrics.

To begin with, Huxley, though he is more like Max Beerbohm than any other living writer (an ambiguity which I shall let stand, as it works either way), belongs as distinctly to the present day as does Beerbohm to the '90's. He has an utterly ruthless habit of building up an elaborate and sometimes almost romantic structure and then blowing it down with something too ironic to be called satire and too scornful to be called irony. And yet he is quite willing to withhold this withering breath from certain fabulous enormities of his own fancy—and thus we have in "Crome Yellow" the really exquisite fable of the two little dwarfs which is almost, if not quite, as well done as the milkmaid incident in Beerbohm's "Zuleika Dobson."

In fact I have wanted a book such as "Crome Yellow" for some time. It is what I thought I was getting when I began Norman Douglas' "South Wind." It is something less serious, less humorous and yet infinitely wittier than either "Jurgen" or "The Revolt of the Angels." It is —but by telling you all the books it resembles I will get you no nearer to knowing whether or not you will want to buy it.

"Crome Yellow" is a loosely knit (but not loosely written) satirical novel concerning the gay doings of an house party at an English country place known as Crome. The book is yellow within and without—and I do not mean yellow in the slangy sense. A sort of yellow haze of mellow laughter plays over it. The people are now like great awkward canaries trying to swim in saffron pools, now like bright yellow leaves blown along a rusty path under a yellow sky. Pacid, impoignant, Nordic, the satire scorns to burn deeper than a pale yellow sun, but only glints with a desperate golden mockery upon the fair hair of the strollers on the law; upon those caught by dawn in the towers; upon those climbing into the hearse at the last—beaten by the spirit of yellow mockery.

This is the sort of book that will infuriate those who take anything seriously, even themselves. This is a book that mocks at mockery. This is the highest point so far attained by Anglo-Saxon sophistication. It is written by a man who has responded, I imagine, much more to the lyric loves of lovers long dust than to the contemporary seductions of contemporary British flappers. His protagonist—what a word for Denis, the mocked-at mocker—is lifted from his own book, "Limbo." So is Mr. Scoogan, but I don't care. Neither do I care that it "fails to mirror life;" that it is "not a novel"—these things will be said of it, never fear. I find Huxley, after Beerbohm, the wittiest man now writing in English.

The scene where Denis was unable to carry Anne amused me beyond measure.

And listen to this, when Huxley confesses to a but second-hand knowledge of the human heart:

"In living people one is dealing with unknown and unknowable qualities. One can only hope to find out anything about them by a long series of the most disagreeable and boring human contacts, involving a terrible expense of time. It is the same with current events; how can I find out anything about them except by devoting years of the most exhausting first-hand studies, involving once more an endless number of the most unpleasant contacts? No, give me the past. It does not change; it is all there in black and white, and you can get to know about it comfortably and decorously, and, above all, privately—by reading."

Huxley is just 30, I believe. He is said to know more about French, German, Latin and medieval Italian literature than any man alive. I refuse to make the fatuous remark that he should know less about books and more about people. I wish to heaven that Christopher Morley would read him and find that the kittenish need not transgress upon the whimsical.

I expect the following addenda to appear on the green jacket of "Crome Yellow" at any moment:

"Drop everything and read "Crome Yellow." —H-yw-d Br-n.

———

"Places Huxley definitely in the first rank of American (sic!) novelists."

—General Chorus.

(The "sic" is mine. It is not harsh as in "sic 'im!" but silent as in "sick room.")

————

"It may be I'm old—it may be I'm mellow,
 But I cannot fall for Huxley's "Crome Yellow."

—F. P. A.

————

 "Exquisite. Places Huxley among the few snobs of English literature."

—G-tr-de Ath-r-t-n.

("Crome Yellow," by Aldhous Huxley, George H. Doran Co. $2.)

Review of Aldous Huxley's *Crome Yellow, St. Paul Daily News,* February 26, 1922, Feature section, p. 6.

TARKINGTON'S "GENTLE JULIA"

A Review by F. Scott Fitzgerald

Tarkington's latest consists of half a dozen excellent short stories sandwiched in between half a dozen mediocre short stories and made into an almost structureless novel on the order of "Seventeen." But it has not "Seventeen's" unity of theme nor has it a dominant character to hold it together like the Penrod books. In fact, the book could be called after little Florence as well as after her popular older cousin, Julia. Nevertheless, in parts it is enormously amusing.

The stories which make up the narrative were written over a period of ten years. They concern Herbert, age 14; his cousin Florence, age 13, and their cousin Julia, age 19—and Julia's beaux, in particular one unbelievably calfish one named Noble Dill. From much interior evidence I doubt whether they were originally intended to form a continuous story at all. For instance, the Julia who is cross and peremptory with Florence in the early chapters, is scarcely the gentle Julia who can not bear to hurt a simple suitor's feelings in the last—and in addition the book jumps around from character to character in a way that is occasionally annoying, as it proceeds from the lack of any unity of design. Add to this that Tarkington seems a bit tired. He has used material throughout the book practically identical with material he has used before. The dance is the dance of "Seventeen," though not so fresh and amusing. The little girl, Jane, grown up, is legitimately new but the little boy repeats the experiences of Hedrick in "The Flirt"— it is held over his head by a shrewd female that he has made love to a little girl, he lives in torture for awhile and finally when the secret is exposed he becomes the victim of his public school.

All the above sounds somewhat discouraging, as if Tarkington, our best humorist since Mark Twain, had turned stale in mid-carer. This is not the case. Parts of the book—the whole scene of the walk, for example, and the astounding abuse of Florence's poem by the amateur printers—are as funny as anything he has ever done. Even the inferior parts of the book are swiftly moving and easily readable. When Noble Dill flicked his cigaret into the cellar I howled with glee. When Florence waved her hand at her mother and assured her that it was "all right," I found that I was walking with the party in a state of almost delirious merriment. In fact, the only part of the book which actively bored me was the incident of the bugs—which had the flavor of Katzenjammer humor. I expected this incident to be bad because Edward J. O'Brien, the world's greatest admirer of mediocre short stories, once gave it a star when it appeared in story form under the title of "The Three Foological Wishes."

The book is prefaced by a short paragraph in which Mr. Tarkington defends, for some curious Freudian reasons, his right to make cheerful books in the face of the recent realism. But no one questions it and the greatest whoopers for "Three Soldiers" and "Main Street" and "My Antonia" has admitted and admired the sheer magic of "Seventeen." We simply reserve the right to believe that when Mr. Tarkington becomes mock-sociological and symbolical about smoke as in "The Turmoil," he is navigating out of his depth and invading the field of such old-maids' favorites as Winston Churchill. His ideas, such as they are, are always expressed best in terms of his characters as in the case of "Alice Adams" and parts of "The Flirt." Mr. Tarkington is not a thoughtful man nor one profoundly interested in life as a whole and when his ideas can not be so expressed they are seldom worth expressing. "Ramsey Milholland," one of the most wretched and absurd novels ever written, showed this. So did the spiritualistic climax of "The Magnificent Ambersons."

It is a pity that the man who writes better prose than any other living

American was brought up in a generation that considered it a crime to tell the truth.

But read "Gentle Julia,"—it will give you a merry evening. With all its fault it is the best piece of light amusement from an American this past year.

Review of Booth Tarkington's *Gentle Julia, St. Paul Daily News*, May 7, 1922, Feature section, p. 6.

"MARGEY WINS THE GAME"

By F. Scott Fitzgerald

MARGEY WINS THE GAME. By John V. A. Weaver. Knopf.

This here story's about a Jane named Margey that used to rub the 3-in-1 off the tall part of straight chairs whenever she tried to step out on the polished pine, until none of her dresses never had no backs to them. She shook a mean Conrad, but she thought Chicago was a city instead of a patent shimmee.

All she wanted was to light the candles and vamp teachers with them jazz proverbs they call epa grams. She was no Gloria Swanson, but she wouldn't gag you in a close-up. The trouble was her duds looked like she was trying to say it with towels, and she had no more line than a cow has cuticle.

Well, her brother was a mean guy, and he told her that as a flapper she was the bunk. That made this Souse Baker sore, and as he was sort of a simple duke that had been a school inspector all his life he said lay off. And that starts the signal for the jazz to begin.

Well, this guy Souse Baker he dressed this Margey up like she was a super in a Cecil B. de Mille Civil War feature and then he blind-folded her and shoved her in front of a lot of pink-blooded he-men at a cake-eaters' ball. From her shoes up to the roll of her stockings she was Ziegfeld stuff, so they fell for Souse's bunk and began chasing her around like she would give them a job or something.

By the time they got the blinders off her she had a lot of them bound and gagged, and they stuck around just from habit because everybody was there and they didn't want that they should be lonesome. But this Souse guy was getting stuck on her hisself, so he had a tough time whenever she went to some swell dive with one of the other cake-eaters. But the Jane thought it was all the bunk anyways.

She wanted to light up the tallows and swap highbrow jokes with a book-weasel from the big school. She didn't let on though for a while because she was sorry for the guy Souse, so she kept shaking the weight off her shoulders until she got a bid to the gas-fitters' ball, which was considered swell—and which was what she wanted so everybody would think she was a big cheese and then she could sneak back to the bulge-brain that she was really nuts about. . . .

. . .

I give up. I can't do it. It requires a Rabelasian imagination and a patent Roth memory. Let me introduce you to John V. A. Weaver, who can.

After the immediate and deserved success of "In American" he has bubbled over into semi-dialect prose. The new book—it runs, I imagine, into less than 20,000 wards—is called "Margey Wins the Game," a bright, ebullient story, shot through with sentiment and dedicated to the proposition that personal magnetism can be captured in the set snare of self-confidence.

Marge (she becomes Marge once she's past the title) is a wealthy wall flower—something rare in New York, but easily to be found in a thousand mid-Western country clubs. She lives in Chicago, thinly veiled under the name of Dearborn, amid those mysterious complexities of North Side and South Side and in that smoky, damp and essentially romantic atmosphere which overhangs our second metropolis and makes it so incomprehensible to all but the initiated inhabitant.

We meet the "Nebraska Glee Club," a touch of exceptional humor, and attend a raid on an Italian café. The cross-section of gay Chicago is well done. The people, hastily sketched, are types, but convincing as such. The story is admirably constructed, and it seems to me that the author should do others of the same type and go a little more thoroughly into the matter, for the field is large and unexplored and he is well equipped to deal with it.

At present he has merely touched the surface with a highly amusing, swiftly moving tale of the jazz-nourished generation. But why only one story? My appetite is whetted for more.

Review of John V. A. Weaver's *Margey Wins the Game, New York Tribune*, May 7, 1922, section IV, 7.

HOMAGE TO THE VICTORIANS

By F. Scott Fitzgerald

THE OPPIDAN. By Shane Leslie. Charles Scribner's Sons.

Now, Shane Leslie is the son of an Anglo-Irish baronet. He is an old Etonian and he is chamberlain to the Pope. He is half a mystic, and he is entirely a cousin of the utilitarian Winston Churchill. In him there is a stronger sense of old England, I mean a sense not of its worth or blame, but of its *being*, than is possessed by any one living, possibly excepting Lytton Strachey.

It is almost impossible to review a book of his and resist the temptation to tell anecdotes of him—how a hair-pin fell from heaven, for instance, and plumped into the King of Spain's tea, of a certain sentimental haircut, of the fact that he has been the hero of two successful modern novels—but with such precious material I can be no more than tantalizing, for it belongs to his biographer, not to me.

He first came into my life as the most romantic figure I had ever known. He had sat at the feet of Tolstoy, he had gone swimming with Rupert Brooke, he had been a young Englishman of the governing classes when the sense of being one must have been, as Compton Mc-Kenzie says, like the sense of being a Roman citizen.

Also, he was a convert to the church of my youth, and he and another, since dead, made of that church a dazzling, golden thing, dispelling its oppressive mugginess and giving the succession of days upon gray days, passing under its plaintive ritual, the romantic glamour of an adolescent dream.

He had written a book then. It had a sale—not the sale it deserved. "The End of the Chapter," it was; and bought by the snap-eyed ladies who follow with Freudian tenseness the missteps of the great. They missed its quality of low, haunting melancholy, of great age, of a faith and of a social tradition that with the years could not but have taken on a certain mellow despair—apparent perhaps only to the most sensitive but by them realized with a sensuous poignancy.

Well, he has written another book—with a wretched, puzzling title, "The Oppidan," which to an American means nothing, but to Leslie an intriguing distinction, that has endured since Henry VIII. An Oppidan is an Etonian who either lives in college or doesn't—I am not quite sure which—and what does it matter, for the book is all of Eton. Once, years ago I picked up a novel called "Grey Youth," and I stared fascinated at that perfect title. I have never read it nor heard tell of it—I'm sure it was worthless—but what two words!

And that is what Leslie's new book should be named—a tale of that gray, gray cocoon, where the English-butterfly sheds its cocoon. It should have been called "Grey Youth." Once in it and you are carried back to the time of Shelley, or day-long fights with occasionally tragic, nay, fatal culminations, of Wellington's playing fields, of intolerable bullyings and abominable raggings. And even more intimately we are shown Eton of the late 90s, and the last magnificence of the Victorian age is spread in front of us, a play done before shadowed tapestries of the past.

The book interested me enormously. Mr. Leslie has a sharp eye for the manners of his age. If he does not plumb the motives of his people or his creations with the keen analysis of Strachey it is because he refers to finer judgments to the court of the Celtic deity which he has accepted for his own—and where the inscrutability of men is relinquished beyond analysis, to fade into that more immense inscrutability in which all final answers and judgments lie.

Those who are interested in the great patchwork quilt picture of Victorian England, which is being gradually pieced together from the memories of survivors and the satire of their commentators, will enjoy "The Oppidan."

"Homage to the Victorians": Review of Shane Leslie's *The Oppidan*, *New York Tribune*, May 14, 1922, section IV, 6.

A RUGGED NOVEL

THE LOVE LEGEND. By Woodward Boyd.
New York: Charles Scribner's Sons. 1922.

Reviewed by F. Scott Fitzgerald

This is a rugged, uneven, and sometimes beautiful novel which concerns four girls, sisters, of Chicago's middle class. These girls believed in —— Listen:

> Ward Harris, at twenty, wore a virginal look like golden rain infiltrated through the stuff of a morning meadow; a look that came from her trust in the love legend, in which she had put all the capital of her youthful hopes, since her mother's whispered story of the prince who was to come and change the world with a magic kiss.

That sentence, a lovely, ill-constructed sentence, opens the book. Ward was the Mary of the family—her three sisters were Marthas. Ward believed in the love legend which "like hope, is deathless." One sister, Sari, who wanted a career on the stage, became absorbed in the business of life, the business of poverty, the business of children. Another sister wanted to be a writer. She had a story accepted by a "Mr. Hopkins," whom I suspect of being a composite Mencken and Nathan. In one of the few artificial scenes in the novel she discovers she cannot marry a fool. She goes on writing. Nita, less intelligent than the others but more shrewd, marries well in the Far West, and, because of this, incurs the faint hostility of the author.

And Ward goes on believing in the love legend, which, like hope, is deathless.

This novel is enormously amusing. The incidental portraits, the Jewish family into which Sari marries, for example, and the environment of the man "Oz," whom Ward loves, are excellent. They're convincing and they're intensely of Chicago—couldn't have existed anywhere else. Easily the best picture of Chicago since "Sister Carrie." All done in little circles and eddies and glimpses with no mooning about the heart or voice or "clangor" or smell of the city. Suddenly you're there. Suddenly you realize that all these people you are reading about —possibly excepting Ward—talk with slightly raised voices and are enormously self-confident.

.   .

The book is obviously by a woman, but her methods of achieving an effect are entirely masculine—even the defects in the book are masculine defects—intellectual curiosity in what amounts to a riot, solid blocks of strong words fitted into consecutive pages like bricks, a lack of selective delicacy, and, sometimes, a deliberately blunted perception. Read the scene where Cecil goes to work in the machine shop and try to think what other women writers could have written it.

This is not a perfect first novel—but it is honest, well written, if raggedy, and thoroughly alive. Compare it, for instance, with "Dancers in the Dark" as a portrait of young people and the modern young mind. Of course, this is hardly fair because "Dancers in the Dark" is merely a jazzed-up version of the juvenile sweetbooks—and the characters are merely puppets who have read flapper editorials. The characters in the "Love Legend" are real in conception, and where the author fails to get her effects it is because of inexpertness and uncertainty rather than because of dishonesty or "faking."

The book is formless. In first novels this is permissible, perhaps even to be encouraged, as the lack of a pattern gives the young novelist more of a chance to assert his or her individuality, which is the principal thing. The title is excellent and covers the novel adequately as it jumps from character to character. The only one of the girls I liked was Ward —the other three I detested. A good book—put it upon the shelf with "Babbitt" and "The Bright Shawl" and watch and pray for more such entertainment this autumn.

"A Rugged Novel": Review of Woodward Boyd's *The Love Legend, The Literary Review, New York Evening Post* October 28, 1922, p. 143.

SHERWOOD ANDERSON
ON THE MARRIAGE QUESTION

A Review by F. Scott Fitzgerald

MANY MARRIAGES. By Sherwood Anderson. B. W. Huebach, Inc.

In the last century literary reputations took some time to solidify. Not Tennyson's or Dickens's—despite their superficial radicalism such men flowed with the current of popular thought. Not Wilde's or De Musset's, whose personal scandals made them almost legendary figures in their own lifetimes. But the reputations of Hardy, Butler, Flaubert and Conrad were slow growths. These men swam up stream and were destined to have an almost intolerable influence upon succeeding generations.

First they were esoteric with a group of personal claqueurs. Later they came into a dim rippling vogue. Their contemporaries "tried to read *one* of their books" and were puzzled and suspicious. Finally some academic critic would learn from his betters that they were "the thing," and shout the news aloud with a profound air of discovery, arguing from interior evidence that the author in question was really in full accord with Florence Nightingale and Gen. Booth. And the author, old and battered and with a dozen imitators among the younger men was finally granted a period of wide recognition.

The cultural world is closer knit now. In the last five years we have seen solidify the reputations of two first class men—James Joyce and Sherwood Anderson.

"Many Marriages" seems to me the fullblown flower of Anderson's personality. It is good enough for Lee Wilson Dodd to write a kittenish parody for the Conning Tower. On the strength of "Many Marriages" you can decide whether Anderson is a neurotic or whether you are one and Anderson a man singularly free of all inhibitions. The noble fool who has dominated tragedy from Don Quixote to Lord Tim is not a character in "Many Marriages." If there is nobility in the book it is a nobility Anderson has created as surely as Rousseau created his own natural man. The genius conceives a cosmos with such transcendental force that it supersedes, in certain sensitive minds, the cosmos of which they have been previously aware. The new cosmos instantly approximates ultimate reality as closely as did the last. It is a bromide to say that the critic can only describe the force of his reaction to any specific work of art.

I read in the paper every day that, without the slightest warning, some apparently solid and settled business man has eloped with his stenographer. This is the central event of "Many Marriages." But in the glow of an unexhaustible ecstasy and wonder what is known as a "vulgar intrigue" becomes a transaction of profound and mystical importance.

The book is the story of two moments—two marriages. Between midnight and dawn a naked man walks up and down before a statue of the Virgin and speaks of his first marriage to his daughter. It was a marriage made in a moment of half mystical, half physical union and later destroyed in the moment of its consummation.

When the man has finished talking he goes away to his second marriage and the woman of his first marriage kills herself out of a little brown bottle.

The method is Anderson's accustomed transcendental naturalism. The writing is often tortuous. But then just as you begin to rail at the short steps of the truncated sentences (his prose walks with a rope around the ankle and a mischievous boy at the end of the rope) you reach an amazingly beautiful vista seen through a crack in the wall that long steps would have carried you hurriedly by. Again—Anderson feels too profoundly to have read widely or even well. What he takes to be only an empty tomato can whose beauty he has himself discovered may turn out to be a Greek vase wrought on the Ægean twenty centuries before. Again the significance of the little stone eludes me. I believe it to have no significance at all. In the book he has perhaps endowed lesser things with significance. In the case of the stone his power is not in evidence and the episode is marred.

There is a recent piece of trash entitled "Simon Called Peter," which seems to me utterly immoral, because the characters move in a continual labyrinth of mild sexual stimulation. Over this stimulation play the colored lights of romantic Christianity.

Now anything is immoral that consoles, stimulates or confirms a distortion. Anything that acts in place of the natural will to live is immoral. All cheap amusement becomes, at maturity, immoral—the heroin of the soul.

"Many Marriages" is not immoral—it is violently anti-social. But if its protagonist rested at a defiance of the fallible human institution of monogamy the book would be no more than propaganda. On the contrary, "Many Marriages" begins where "The New Machiavelli" left off. It does not so much justify the position of its protagonist as it casts a curious and startling light on the entire relation between man and woman. It is the reaction of a sensitive, highly civilized man to the phenomenon of lust—but it is distinguished from the work of Dreiser, Joyce and Wells (for example) by utter lack both of a concept of society as a whole and of the necessity of defying or denying such a concert. For the purpose of the book no such background as Dublin Catholicism, middle Western morality or London Fabianism could ever have existed. For all his washing machine factory the hero of "Many Marriages" comes closer than any character, not excepting Odysseus, Lucifer, Attila, Tarzan and, least of all, Conrad's Michaelis, to existing in an absolute vacuum. It seems to me a rather stupendous achievement.

I do not like the man in the book. The world in which I trust, on which I seem to set my feet, appears to me to exist through a series of illusions. These illusions need and occasionally get a thorough going over ten times or so during a century.

The man whose power of compression is great enough to review this book in a thousand words does not exist If he does he is probably writing subtitles for the movies or working for a car card company.

"Sherwood Anderson on the Marriage Question": Review of Sherwood Anderson's *Many Marriages, New York Herald*, March 4, 1923, section 9, p. 5.

MINNESOTA'S CAPITAL
IN THE RÔLE OF MAIN STREET

By F. Scott Fitzgerald

Along comes another of those annoying novels of American manners, one of those ponderous steel scaffoldings upon which the palaces of literature may presently arise. It is something native and universal, clumsy in its handling of an enormous quantity of material; something which can be called a document, but can in no sense be dismissed as such.

Grace Flandrau's "Being Respectable" * the book of the winter and in all probability of the spring, too—is superior to Sinclair Lewis's "Babbitt" in many ways, but inferior in that it deals with too many characters. The characters are complete and excellently motivated in themselves, but there is no one Babbitt or Nostromo to draw together the entire novel. It is a satirical arraignment of the upper class of a Middle Western city—in this case St. Paul, Minnesota, as "Babbitt," speaking generally, was concerned with the upper middle-class of Minneapolis. Poor Minnesota! Sauk Center, Minneapolis and St. Paul have been flayed in turn by the State's own sons and daughters. I feel that I ought to take up the matter of Duluth and make the thing complete.

Now St. Paul, altho a bloodbrother of Indianapolis, Minneapolis, Kansas City, Milwaukee and Co., feels itself a little superior to the others. It is a "three generation" town, while the others boast but two. In the fifties the climate of St. Paul was reputed exceptionally healthy. Consequently there arrived an element from the East who had both money and fashionable education. These Easterners mingled with the rising German and Irish stock, whose second generation left the cobbler's last, forgot the steerage, and became passionately "swell" on its own account. But the pace was set by the tubercular Easterners. Hence the particular social complacency of St. Paul.

"Being Respectable" starts with a typical family of to-day—the sort of family that Tarkington sketched brilliantly but superficially in the first part of "The Magnificent Ambersons." There is the retired father, a product of the gilded eighties, with his business morality and his utter lack of any ideas except the shop-worn and conventional illusions current in his youth. His son, Charles, is the typical healthy vegetable which Yale University turns out by the hundred every year. The younger daughter, Deborah, is a character frequently met with in recent fiction—and also in life—ever since Shaw shocked the English-speaking world with his emancipated woman of 1900. In her very Carol-Kennicotting against the surrounding conventions Deborah is the most conventional character of all. Her conversations (which, of course, consist of the author's own favorite ideas) are the least important part of the book. The unforgetable part is the great gallery of dumb-bells of which the elder sister, Louisa, is Number One.

* BEING RESPECTABLE. By Grace Flandrau. New York: Harcourt, Brace & Co. $2.00.

Louisa is a woman completely engrossed in St. Paul's passionate imitation of Chicago imitating New York imitating London. Every once in a while some woman's imitation becomes ineffective. The woman "gets in wrong and drops out." The society itself, however, goes on in its distorted and not a little ridiculous fashion. It is a society from which there is no escape. On one side there is nothing but the "common fast set" and just below are the thousand Babbitts, who from time to time furnish recruits to society itself.

Louisa is the real protagonist of the book—Louisa and her young married crowd. They are portraits to the life, differing by less than a hair from each other and from the women on whom they are modeled. They are set down here in all their energy, their dulness, their fear, their boredom—forty well-drest automatons moving with deft, unpleasant gestures through their own private anemic and exclusive Vanity Fair. It is a fine accomplishment to have captured them so—with sophistication, satire, occasional bitterness, and a pervading irony.

A thoroughly interesting and capable novel. The writing is solid throughout, and sometimes beautiful. Like Sinclair Lewis and Woodward Boyd, the author has little sense of selection—seems to have poured the whole story out in a flood. The book lacks the careful balance of "Three Soldiers," and it is not nearly so successful in handling its three or four protagonists. It skips from character to character in a way that is often annoying. But there it is, the newest and in some ways the best of those amazing documents which are (as Mencken might say) by H. G. Wells out of Theodore Dreiser, and which yet are utterly national and of to-day. And, when our Conrad or Joyce or Anatole France comes, such books as this will have cleared his way. Out of these enormous and often muddy lakes of sincere and sophisticated observation will flow the clear stream—if there is to be a clear stream at all.

Incidentally, the remarkable portrait of Valeria is the best single instance of artistic power in the book. The entire personality and charm of the woman is conveyed at second-hand. We have scarcely a glimpse of her, and she says only one line throughout. Yet the portrait is vivid and complete.

"Minnesota's Capital in the Rôle of Main Street": Review of Grace Flandrau's *Being Respectable, The Literary Digest International Book Review*, 1 (March 1923), 35–36.

UNDER FIRE

THROUGH THE WHEAT. By Thomas Boyd.
New York: Charles Scribner's Sons. 1923. $1.75.

Reviewed by F. Scott Fitzgerald

I did not know how good a man I was till then. . . . I remember my youth and the feeling that will never come back any more—the feeling that I could last forever, outlast the sea, the earth, and all men . . . the triumphant conviction of strength, the heat of life in the handful of dust, the glow in the heart that with every year grows dim, grows cold, grows small, and expires, and expires too soon—before life itself.

So, in part, runs one of the most remarkable passages of English prose written these thirty years—a passage from Conrad's "Youth"—and since that story I have found in nothing else even the echo of that lift and ring until I read Thomas Boyd's "Through the Wheat." It is the story of certain privates in a marine regiment which, the jacket says, was rushed into action under a bright June sunlight five years ago to stop the last thrust of the German Army towards Paris. These men were sustained by no democratic idealism, no patriotic desperation, and by no romance, except the romance of unknown adventure. But they were sustained by something else at once more material and more magical, for in the only possible sense of the word they were picked men— they were exceptionally solid specimens of a healthy stock. No one has a greater contempt than I have for the recent hysteria about the Nordic theory, but I suppose that the United States marines were the best body of troops that fought in the war.

Now, young Hicks, Mr. Boyd's protagonist, is taken as an average individual in a marine regiment, put through a short period of training in France, a trench raid, a long wait under shell fire (a wait during which, if C. E. Montague is to be believed, the average English regiment of the last year would have been utterly demoralized), and finally ordered forward in the face of machine gun fire through an endless field of yellow wheat. The action is utterly real. At first the very exactitude of the detail makes one expect no more than another piece of expert reporting, but gradually the thing begins to take on significance and assume a definite and arresting artistic contour. The advance goes on—one by one the soldiers have come to know, know fragmentarily and by sudden flashes and illuminations, go down and die, but young Hicks and the rest go on, heavy footed and blind with sweat, through the yellow wheat. Finally, without one single recourse to sentiment, to hysteria, or to trickery, the author strikes one clear and unmistakable note of heroism, of tenuous and tough-minded exaltation, and with this note vibrating sharply in the reader's consciousness the book ends.

There is a fine unity about it all which only becomes fully apparent when this note is struck. The effect is cumulative in the sheerest sense; there are no skies and stars and dawns pointed out to give significance to the insignificant or to imply a connection where there is no connection. There are no treasured-up reactions to æsthetic phenomena poured along the pages, either for sweetening purposes or to endow the innately terrible with a higher relief. The whole book is written in the light of one sharp emotion and hence it is as a work of art rather than as a textbook for patrioteer or pacifist that the book is arresting.

Already I have seen reviews which take it as propaganda for one side or the other—in both cases this is unfair. The fact that both sides claim it tends to prove the author's political disinterestedness. As Thomas Boyd has been one of the loudest in praise of "Three Soldiers" and "The Enormous Room," it is to his credit that he has not allowed any intellectualism, however justified, to corrupt the at once less thoughtful and more profound emotion of his attitude. Still less has he been influenced by the Continental reaction to the last year of war. This, too, is as it should be, for that poignant despair, neatly as our novelists have adapted it to their ends, could not have been part of the mental make-up of the Fifth and Sixth Marines. Dos Passos and Elliot Paul filtered the war through an artistic intellectualism and in so doing attributed the emotions of exhausted nations to men who for the most part were neither exhausted nor emotional.

To my mind, this is not only the best combatant story of the great war, but also the best war book since "The Red Badge of Courage."

"Under Fire": Review of Thomas Boyd's *Through the Wheat, The Literary Review, New York Evening Post*, May 26, 1923, p. 715.

HOW TO WASTE MATERIAL

A *Note on My Generation*

By F. Scott Fitzgerald

Ever since Irving's preoccupation with the necessity for an American background, for some square miles of cleared territory on which colorful variants might presently arise, the question of material has hampered the American writer. For one Dreiser who made a single minded and irreproachable choice there have been a dozen like Henry James who have stupid-got with worry over the matter, and yet another dozen who, blinded by the fading tail of Walt Whitman's comet, have botched their books by the insincere compulsion to write "significantly" about America.

Insincere because it is not a compulsion found in themselves—it is "literary" in the most belittling sense. During the past seven years we have had at least half a dozen treatments of the American farmer, ranging from New England to Nebraska; at least a dozen canny books about youth, some of them with surveys of the American universities for background; more than a dozen novels reflecting various aspects of New York, Chicago, Washington, Detroit, Indianapolis, Wilmington, and Richmond; innumerable novels dealing with American politics, business, society, science, racial problems, art, literature, and moving pictures, and with Americans abroad at peace or in war; finally several novels of change and growth, tracing the swift decades for their own sweet lavender or protesting vaguely and ineffectually against the industrialization of our beautiful old American life. We have had an Arnold Bennett for every five towns—surely by this time the foundations have been laid! Are we competent only to toil forever upon a never completed first floor whose specifications change from year to year?

In any case we are running through our material like spendthrifts— just as we have done before. In the Nineties there began a feverish search for any period of American history that hadn't been "used", and once found it was immediately debauched into a pretty and romantic story. These past seven years have seen the same sort of literary gold rush; and for all our boasted sincerity and sophistication, the material is being turned out raw and undigested in much the same way. One author goes to a midland farm for three months to obtain the material for an epic of the American husbandmen! Another sets off on a like errand to the Blue Ridge Mountains, a third departs with a Corona for the West Indies—one is justified in the belief that what they get hold of will weigh no more than the journalistic loot brought back by Richard Harding Davis and John Fox, Jr., twenty years ago.

Worse, the result will be doctored up to give it a literary flavor. The farm story will be sprayed with a faint dilution of ideas and sensory impressions from Thomas Hardy; the novel of the Jewish tenement block will be festooned with wreaths from "Ulysses" and the later Gertrude Stein; the document of dreamy youth will be prevented from fluttering entirely away by means of great and half great names—Marx, Spencer, Wells, Edward Fitzgerald—dropped like paper weights here and there upon the pages. Finally the novel of business will be cudgeled into being satire by the questionable but constantly reiterated implication that the author and his readers don't partake of the American commercial instinct.

And most of it—the literary beginnings of what was to have been a golden age—is as dead as if it had never been written. Scarcely one of those who put so much effort and enthusiasm, even intelligence, into it, got hold of any material at all.

To a limited extent this was the fault of two men—one of whom, H. L. Mencken, has yet done more for American letters than any man alive. What Mencken felt the absence of, what he wanted, and justly, back in 1920, got away from him, got twisted in his hand. Not because the "literary revolution" went beyond him but because his idea had always been ethical rather than æsthetic. In the history of culture no pure æsthetic idea has ever served as an offensive weapon. Mencken's invective, sharp as Swift's, made its point by the use of the most forceful prose style now written in English. Immediately, instead of committing himself to an infinite series of pronouncements upon the American novel, he should have modulated his tone to the more urbane, more critical one of his early essay on Dreiser.

But perhaps it was already too late. Already he had begotten a family of hammer and tongs men—insensitive, suspicious of glamour, preoccupied exclusively with the external, the contemptible, the "national" and the drab, whose style was a debasement of his least effective manner and who, like glib children, played continually with his themes in his maternal shadow. These were the men who manufactured enthusi-

asm when each new mass of raw data was dumped on the literary platform—mistaking incoherence for vitality, chaos for vitality. It was the
"new poetry movement" over again, only that this time its victims were
worth the saving. Every week some new novel gave its author membership in "that little band who are producing a worthy American literature". As one of the charter members of that little band I am proud to
state that it has now swollen to seventy or eighty members.

And through a curious misconception of his work, Sherwood Anderson must take part of the blame for this enthusiastic march up a blind
alley in the dark. To this day reviewers solemnly speak of him as an
inarticulate, fumbling man, bursting with ideas—when, on the contrary,
he is the possessor of a brilliant and almost inimitable prose style, and of
scarcely any ideas at all. Just as the prose of Joyce in the hands of, say,
Waldo Frank becomes insignificant and idiotic, so the Anderson admirers set up Hergesheimer as an anti-Christ and then proceed to imitate
Anderson's lapses from that difficult simplicity they are unable to understand. And here again critics support them by discovering merits in the
very disorganization that is to bring their books to a timely and unre-
gretted doom.

Now the business is over. "Wolf" has been cried too often. The public, weary of being fooled, has gone back to its Englishmen, its memoirs
and its prophets. Some of the late brilliant boys are on lecture tours (a
circular informs me that most of them are to speak upon "the literary
revolution"!), some are writing pot boilers, a few have definitely abandoned the literary life—they were never sufficiently aware that material,
however closely observed, is as elusive at the moment in which it has its
existence unless it is purified by an incorruptible style and by the catharsis of a passionate emotion.

Of all the work by the young men who have sprung up since 1920
one book survives—"The Enormous Room" by E. E. Cummings. It is
scarcely a novel; it doesn't deal with the American scene; it was
swamped in the mediocre downpour, isolated—forgotten. But it lives
on, because those few who cause books to live have not been able to
endure the thought of its mortality. Two other books, both about the
war, complete the possible salvage from the work of the younger generation—"Through the Wheat" and "Three Soldiers", but the former despite its fine last chapters doesn't stand up as well as "Les Croix de
Bois" and "The Red Badge of Courage", while the latter is marred by
its pervasive flavor of contemporary indignation. But as an augury that

someone has profited by this dismal record of high hope and stale failure comes the first work of Ernest Hemingway.

II

"In Our Time" consists of fourteen stories, short and long, with fifteen vivid miniatures interpolated between them. When I try to think of any contemporary American short stories as good as "Big Two-Hearted River", the last one in the book, only Gertrude Stein's "Melanctha", Anderson's "The Egg", and Lardner's "Golden Honeymoon" come to mind. It is the account of a boy on a fishing trip—he hikes, pitches his tent, cooks dinner, sleeps, and next morning casts for trout. Nothing more—but I read it with the most breathless unwilling interest I have experienced since Conrad first bent my reluctant eyes upon the sea.

The hero, Nick, runs through nearly all the stories, until the book takes on almost an autobiographical tint—in fact "My Old Man", one of the two in which this element seems entirely absent, is the least successful of all. Some of the stories show influences but they are invariably absorbed and transmuted, while in "My Old Man" there is an echo of Anderson's way of thinking in those sentimental "horse stories", which inaugurated his respectability and also his decline four years ago.

But with "The Doctor and the Doctor's Wife", "The End of Something", "The Three Day Blow", "Mr. and Mrs. Elliot", and "Soldier's Home" you are immediately aware of something temperamentally new. In the first of these a man is backed down by a half breed Indian after committing himself to a fight. The quality of humiliation in the story is so intense that it immediately calls up every such incident in the reader's past. Without the aid of a comment or a pointing finger one knows exactly the sharp emotion of young Nick who watches the scene.

The next two stories describe an experience at the last edge of adolescence. You are constantly aware of the continual snapping of ties that is going on around Nick. In the half stewed, immature conversation before the fire you watch the awakening of that vast unrest that descends upon the emotional type at about eighteen. Again there is not a single recourse to exposition. As in "Big Two-Hearted River", a picture—sharp, nostalgic, tense—develops before your eyes. When the picture is complete a light seems to snap out, the story is over. There is no tail, no sudden change of pace at the end to throw into relief what has gone before.

Nick leaves home penniless; you have a glimpse of him lying

wounded in the street of a battered Italian town, and later of a love affair with a nurse on a hospital roof in Milan. Then in one of the best of the stories he is home again. The last glimpse of him is when his mother asks him, with all the bitter world in his heart, to kneel down beside her in the dining room in Puritan prayer.

Anyone who first looks through the short interpolated sketches will hardly fail to read the stories themselves. "The Garden at Mons" and "The Barricade" are profound essays upon the English officer, written on a postage stamp. 'The King of Greece's Tea Party", "The Shooting of the Cabinet Ministers", and "The Cigar-store Robbery" particularly fascinated me, as they did when Edmund Wilson first showed them to me in an earlier pamphlet, over two years ago.

Disregard the rather ill considered blurbs upon the cover. It is sufficient that here is no raw food served up by the railroad restaurants of California and Wisconsin. In the best of these dishes there is not a bit to spare. And many of us who have grown weary of admonitions to "watch this man or that" have felt a sort of renewal of excitement at these stories wherein Ernest Hemingway turns a corner into the street.

"How to Waste Material—A Note on My Generation": Essay and Review of Ernest Hemingway's *In Our Time, The Bookman,* LXIII (May 1926), 262–265.

F. SCOTT FITZGERALD IS BORED
BY EFFORTS AT REALISM IN 'LIT'

Not Flesh and Blood Characters but Petulant Phantoms
Appear in Stories in March Issue.

POETRY EARNS MORE PRAISE

Griswold's Sonnets Outstanding Feature of Issue—
Careful Work by Barnouw and Day is Noted.

By F. Scott Fitzgerald '17.

In my days stories in the *Lit* were bout starving artists, dying poilus, the plague in Florence and the soul of the Great Khan. They took place, chiefly, behind the moon and a thousand years ago. Now they all take place on Nassau Street, no longer back than yesterday. Playing safe they are more "real", but by reason of their narrow boundaries they are desperately similar to each other.

There is the sensitive under-graduate who, perhaps because he is the author, is never given a recognizable skin; there is mention of Nassau Street and Gothic towers; without once seeing or feeling the visual world, without being fresh or tired, without being desperate or ecestatic, neither eating nor loving, and drinking only as a mannerism of the day, this petulant ghost moves through a vague semi-adventure with a girl, a parent, the faculty or another shadow labelled his room-mate. Acted upon but never acting, limp and suspicious, he lacks even the normal phosphoresence of decay.

He drifts through the two best stories in this month's *Lit*—in one he barely attains a stale-mate with his father, due to the latter's advantage of being flesh and blood, since he is observed, however superficially from the outside. *Stranger* by Charles Yost is really a pretty good story, though like all tales of futility and boredom it unavoidably shares the quality of its subject—but it is intelligent, restrained and with some but not enough excellent writing.

A. Z. F. Wood's *St. George and the Dragon* is even a little better. Offended by the manners of his home town the ghost grows angry and knocks down not a yokel but another ghost by mistake. We are left to imagine his humiliation. If the author had been a little less facile about Jim's real motives the story would have carried a great deal of conviction, for it is credible, well written and interesting throughout.

H. M. Alexander's *Peckham's Saturday Night* is a good story. *Waking Up* by A. S. Alexander is below the author's standard. *The Old Meeting House* by H. A. Rue is Gray's Elegy copiously watered—it might have come out of the *Lit* of forty years ago.

The poetry is better. Griswold's two sonnets show imagination and power and, I dare say, a great deal of honest toil. They are incomparably the best thing in the issue, cheering even exciting. Erik Barnouw's lighter piece is excellent. So is Price Day's poem—it has feeling, not a few real felicities and, again, welcome signs of patience and care. Wilfred Owen's *Brass Moon* has quality—his shorter pieces are trite; we have such feeble lines as "walk solemnly single file", "piquant turned-up nose", "creep in upon the window sill' etc. *Harlem and the Ritz* by H. T. B. is trivial but I like the form of his long poem. *Defiance* by Grier Hart is fair. The remaining verse is of no interest.

To conclude: This is a dignified but on the whole unadventurous number of the oldest college magazine in America. The present reviewers strongest reaction is his curiosity as to the fate of Mr. Yost's and Mr. Wood's phantoms. One is sure, of course, that they will in a few years refuse to go into their fathers' businesses, one hardly blames them—but what then? The American father, under the influence of his wife, will immediately yield and the ghost will carry his pale negatives out into the world. Those to whom life has been a more passionate and stirring affair than one must suppose it now is at Princeton, will not envy him his hollow victory.

"F. Scott Fitzgerald Is Bored By Efforts At Realism In 'Lit' ": Review of March 1928 issue of *The Nassau Literary Magazine*, *The Daily Princetonian*, March 16, 1928, pp. 1, 3.

Introductions and Blurbs

SCOTT FITZGERALD says: "BABEL is a beautifully written story pervaded with a lovely, haunting melancholy. The author's graphic atmospheres in London and Paris and New York are flawless. It is sprinkled with concise and thoughtful aphorisms which cover without dogmatism almost the whole range of current ideas. Its love affair is the love affair of hundreds of thousands of people, one of the most real and human love episodes in recent fiction."

This clipping in Fitzgerald's scrapbook is an unlocated advertisement for John Cournos' *Babel* (New York: Boni & Liveright, 1922). The text of the Fitzgerald blurb which appeared on the dust jacket is a condensed version of this advertisement.

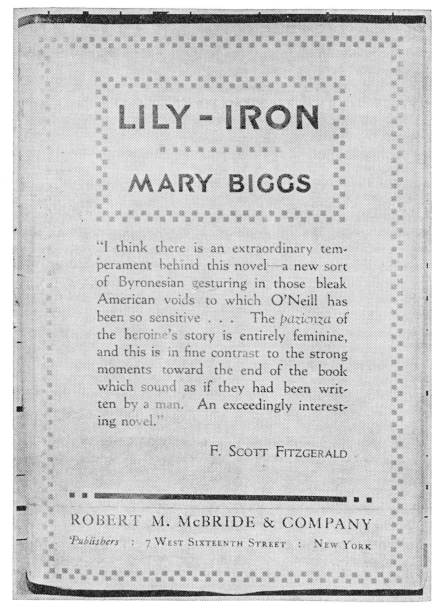

LILY - IRON

MARY BIGGS

"I think there is an extraordinary temperament behind this novel—a new sort of Byronesian gesturing in those bleak American voids to which O'Neill has been so sensitive . . . The *pazienza* of the heroine's story is entirely feminine, and this is in fine contrast to the strong moments toward the end of the book which sound as if they had been written by a man. An exceedingly interesting novel."

F. SCOTT FITZGERALD

ROBERT M. McBRIDE & COMPANY
Publishers : 7 WEST SIXTEENTH STREET : NEW YORK

Blurb for Mary Biggs' *Lily-Iron* (New York: McBride, 1927, dust jacket). The author was the sister of Fitzgerald's Princeton friend, John Biggs.

INTRODUCTION TO *THE GREAT GATSBY*

To one who has spent his professional life in the world of fiction the request to "write an introduction" offers many facets of temptation. The present writer succumbs to one of them; with as much equanimity as he can muster, he will discuss the critics among us, trying to revolve as centripetally as possible about the novel which comes hereafter in this volume.

To begin with, I must say that I have no cause to grumble about the "press" of any book of mine. If Jack (who liked my last book) didn't like this one—well then John (who despised my last book) *did* like it; so it all mounts up to the same total. But I think the writers of my time were spoiled in that regard, living in generous days when there was plenty of space on the page for endless ratiocination about fiction—a space largely created by Mencken because of his disgust for what passed as criticism before he arrived and made his public. They were encouraged by his bravery and his tremendous and profound love of letters. In his case, the jackals are already tearing at what they imprudently regard as a moribund lion, but I don't think many men of my age can regard him without reverence, nor fail to regret that he got off the train. To any new effort by a new man he brought an attitude; he made many mistakes—such as his early undervaluation of Hemingway—but he came equipped; he never had to go back for his tools.

And now that he has abandoned American fiction to its own devices, there is no one to take his place. If the present writer had seriously to attend some of the efforts of political diehards to tell him the values of a métier he has practised since boyhood—well, then, babies, you can take this number out and shoot him at dawn.

But all that is less discouraging, in the past few years, than the growing cowardice of the reviewers. Underpaid and overworked, they seem not to care for books, and it has been saddening recently to see young talents in fiction expire from sheer lack of a stage to act on: West, McHugh and many others.

I'm circling closer to my theme song, which is: that I'd like to communicate to such of them who read this novel a healthy cynicism toward contemporary reviews. Without undue vanity one can permit oneself a suit of chain mail in any profession. Your pride is all you have, and if you let it be tampered with by a man who has a dozen prides to tamper with before lunch, you are promising yourself a lot of disappointments that a hard-boiled professional has learned to spare himself.

This novel is a case in point. Because the pages weren't loaded with big names of big things and the subject not concerned with farmers (who were the heroes of the moment), there was easy judgment exercised that had nothing to do with criticism but was simply an attempt on the part of men who had few chances of self-expression to express themselves. How anyone could take up the responsibility of being a novelist without a sharp and concise attitude about life is a puzzle to me. How a critic could assume a point of view which included twelve variant aspects of the social scene in a few hours seems something too dinosaurean to loom over the awful loneliness of a young author.

To circle nearer to this book, one woman, who could hardly have written a coherent letter in English, described it as a book that one read only as one goes to the movies around the corner. That type of criticism is what a lot of young writers are being greeted with, instead of any appreciation of the world of imagination in which they (the writers) have been trying, with greater or lesser success, to live—the world that Mencken made stable in the days when he was watching over us.

Now that this book is being reissued, the author would like to say that never before did one try to keep his artistic conscience as pure as during the ten months put into doing it. Reading it over one can see how it could have been improved—yet without feeling guilty of any discrepancy from the truth, as far as I saw it; truth or rather the *equivalent* of the truth, the attempt at honesty of imagination. I had just re-read Conrad's preface to *The Nigger*, and I had recently been kidded half haywire by critics who felt that my material was such as to preclude all dealing with mature persons in a mature world. But, my God! it was my material, and it was all I had to deal with.

What I cut out of it both physically and emotionally would make another novel!

I think it is an honest book, that is to say, that one used none of one's virtuosity to get an effect, and, to boast again, one soft-pedalled the emotional side to avoid the tears leaking from the socket of the left eye, or the large false face peering around the corner of a character's head.

If there is a clear conscience, a book can survive—at least in one's feelings about it. On the contrary, if one has a guilty conscience, one reads what one wants to hear out of reviews. In addition, if one is young and willing to learn, almost all reviews have a value, even the ones that seem unfair.

The present writer has always been a "natural" for his profession, in so much that he can think of nothing he could have done as efficiently as to have lived deeply in the world of imagination. There are plenty other people constituted as he is, for giving expression to intimate explorations, the:

—Look—this is here!

—I saw this under my eyes.

—*This* is the way it was!

—No, it was like this.

"Look! Here is that drop of blood I told you about."

—"Stop everything! Here is the flash of that girl's eyes, here is the reflection that will always come back to me from the memory of her eyes.

—"If one chooses to find that face again in the non-refracting surface of a washbowl, if one chooses to make the image more obscure with a little sweat, it should be the business of the critic to recognize the intention.

—"No one felt like this before—says the young writer—but *I* felt like this; I have a pride akin to a soldier going into battle; without knowing whether there will be anybody there, to distribute medals or even to record it."

But remember, also, young man: you are not the first person who has ever been alone and alone.

F. Scott Fitzgerald

Baltimore, Md.
August, 1934.

Introduction to *The Great Gatsby* (New York: Modern Library, 1934, pp. vii–xi).

CAST DOWN THE LAUREL

F. Scott Fitzgerald: "Beautifully written, startling in form, and promising other equally good things to come. It pleases me beyond measure that Arnold Gingrich has brought off this book, which has the same scope and appeal of his editorial ventures."

Blurb for Arnold Gingrich's *Cast Down the Laurel* (New York: Knopf, 1935, dust jacket).

COLONIAL AND HISTORIC HOMES OF MARYLAND

The undersigned can only consider himself a native of the Maryland Free State through ancestry and adoption. But the impression of the fames and the domains, the vistas and the glories of Maryland followed many a young man West after the Civil War and my father was of that number. Much of my early childhood in Minnesota was spent in asking him such questions as:

"—and how long did it take Early's column to pass Glenmary that day?" (That was a farm in Montgomery County.)

and:

"—what would have happened if Jeb Stewart's cavalry had joined Lee instead of raiding all the way to Rockville?"

and:

"—tell me again about how you used to ride through the woods with a spy up behind you on the horse."

or:

"Why wouldn't they let Francis Scott Key off the British frigate?"

And since so many legends of my family went west with father, memories of names that go back before Braddock's disaster such as Caleb Godwin of Hockley-in-ye-Hole, or Philip Key of Tudor Hall, or Pleasance Ridgeley—so there must be hundreds and hundreds of families in such an old state whose ancestral memories are richer and fuller than mine.

But time obliterates people and memories and only the more fortunate landmarks survive. In the case of this fine book, it is upon the home above all that Don Swann has concentrated his talents and his painstaking research—the four walls (or sixteen as it may be) of Baronial Maryland, or the artistic result of the toil and sweat that some forever anonymous craftsman put into a balcony or a parquet. And outside this general range, the etcher has also paused here and there to jot down some detail of plainer houses that helps to make this a permanent record of the history of the Free State.

His work, naturally, will speak for itself, and, to allow it to do so, I cut short this prelude with the expression of high hopes for this venture by one of the State's adopted sons.

F. Scott Fitzgerald

Foreword to Don Swann's *Colonial and Historic Homes of Maryland* (Baltimore: Etchcrafters Art Guild, 1939, 1).

WHAT MAKES SAMMY RUN?

December 13, 1940

DEAR BENNETT CERF:

I told Budd I was going to write you a word about his novel with permission to quote if you wanted. I read it through in one night. It is a grand book, utterly fearless and with a great deal of beauty side by side with the most bitter satire. Such things *are* in Hollywood—and Budd reports them with fine detachment. Except for its freshness and the inevitable challenge of a new and strong personality it doesn't read like a first novel at all.

It is full of excellent little vignettes—the "extra girl" or whatever she is and her attitude on love, and the diverse yet identical attitude of the two principal women on Sammy. Especially toward the end it gets the feeling of Hollywood with extraordinary vividness. Altogether I congratulate you on publishing this fine book and I hope it has all the success it deserves.

Sincerely,
(Signed) *F. Scott Fitzgerald*

Letter for Budd Schulberg's *What Makes Sammy Run?* (New York: Random House, 1941, dust jacket).

THE DAY OF THE LOCUST

F. Scott Fitzgerald: "The book, though it puts Gorki's 'The Lower Depths' in the class with 'The Tale of Benjamin Bunny,' certainly has scenes of extraordinary power—if that phrase is still in use. Especially I was impressed by the pathological crowd at the premiere, the character and handling of the aspirant actress and the uncanny almost medieval feeling of some of his Hollywood background set off by those vividly drawn grotesques."

Blurb for Nathanael West's *The Day of the Locust* (New York: New Directions, 1950, dust jacket).

Public Letters and Statements

SELF-INTERVIEW

AN INTERVIEW
WITH F. SCOTT FITZGERALD

By F. Scott Fitzgerald

In 1920, a few weeks after the publication of "This Side of Paradise,"
F. Scott Fitzgerald suggested to John William Rogers, then book adver-
tising manager of Scribner's, that he might write an interview with
himself for use in publicizing his book. A few days later Fitzgerald
handed him a rough pencil draft. The interview was not used, however,
because, as Mr. Rogers recalls, "Fitzgerald was just one more young
man with a promising first novel. An interview giving impressions of
him and his literary opinions was of very little interest to anybody."
Recently Mr. Rogers came across Fitzgerald's manuscript, which had
been filed away for nearly forty years, and made it available to SR. The
manuscript, printed here exactly as the twenty-four-year-old Fitzgerald
wrote it, has been given by Mr. Rogers to the Dallas Public Library.

With the distinct intention of taking Mr. Fitzgerald by surprise I ascended to the twenty-first floor of the Biltmore and knocked in the best
waiter-manner at the door. On entering my first impression was one of
confusion—a sort of rummage sale confusion. A young man was standing in the center of the room turning an absent glance first at one side
of the room and then at the other.

"I'm looking for my hat," he said dazedly, "How do you do. Come
on in and sit down on the bed."

The author of "This Side of Paradise" is sturdy, broad shouldered and just above medium height. He has blond hair with the suggestion of a wave and alert green eyes—the mélange somewhat Nordic—and good looking too, which was disconcerting as I had somehow expected a thin nose and spectacles.

We had preliminaries—but I will omit the preliminaries. They consisted in searching for things [,] cigarettes, a blue tie with white dots, an ash tray. But as he was obviously quite willing to talk, and seemed quite receptive to my questions we launched off directly on his ideas of literature.

"How long did it take to write your book?" I began.

"To write it—three months, to concieve [sic] it—three minutes. To collect the data in it—all my life. The idea of writing it occurred to me on the First of last July. It was sort of a substitute form of dissipation."

"What are your plans now?" I asked him.

He gave a long sigh and shrugged his shoulders.

"I'll be darned if I know. The scope and depth and breadth of my writings lie in the laps of the Gods. If knowledge comes naturally, through interest, as Shaw learned his political econemy [sic] or as Wells devoured modern science—why, that'll be slick. On study itself—that is in 'reading up' a subject—I haven't ant-hill moving faith. Knowledge must cry out to be known—cry out that only I can know it and then I'll swim in it to satiety as I've swum in—in many things."

"Please be frank."

"Well, you know if you've read my book. I've swum in various seas of adolescent egotism. But what I meant was that if big things never grip me—well, it simply means I'm not cut out to be big. This conscious struggle to find bigness outside, to substitute bigness of theme for bigness of perception, to create an objective *Magnum Opus* such as the "Ring in the Book" [sic]—well, all that's the antithesis of my literary aims.

"Another thing," he continued, "My idea is always to reach my generation. The wise writer, I think, writes for the youth of his own generation, the critic of the next and the schoolmasters of ever afterward. Granted the ability to improve what he imitates in the way of style, to choose from his own interpretation of the experiences around him what constitutes material, and we get the first-water genius."

"Do you expect to be—to be—well, part of the great literary tradition?" I asked, timidly.

He became excited. He smiled radiantly. I saw he had an answer for this. "There's no great literary tradition," he burst out. "There's only the tradition of the eventual death of every literary tradition. The wise literary son kills his own father."

After this he began entheusiasticly [sic] on style.

"By style, I mean color," he said. "I want to be able to do anything with words: handle slashing, flaming descriptions like Wells, and use the paradox with the clarity of Samuel Butler, the breadth of Bernard Shaw and the wit of Oscar Wilde, I want to do the wide sultry heavens of Conrad, the rolled-gold sundowns and crazy-quilt skies of Hichens and Kipling as well as the pastelle [sic] dawns and twilights of Chesterton. All that is by way of example. As a matter of fact I am a professed literary thief, hot after the best methods of every writer in my generation."

The interview terminated about then. Four young men with philistine faces and conservative ties appeared, and looking at each other exchanged broad winks. Mr. Fitzgerald faltered and seemed to lose his stride.

"Most of my friends are—are like those," he whispered as he showed me to the door. "I don't care for literary people much—they make me nervous."

It was really rather a good interview, wasn't it!

Self-Interview, 1920, *Saturday Review*, XLIII (November 5, 1960), 26, 56. Although the *Saturday Review* stated in 1960 that this self-interview was never used, it was in fact printed as Carleton R. Davis' interview with Fitzgerald, *New York Tribune*, May 7, 1920.

Copyright by White

The Author's Apology

I don't want to talk about myself because I'll admit I did that somewhat in this book. In fact, to write it took three months; to conceive it—three minutes; to collect the data in it—all my life. The idea of writing it came on the first of last July: it was a substitute form of dissipation.

My whole theory of writing I can sum up in one sentence: An author ought to write for the youth of his own generation, the critics of the next, and the schoolmasters of ever afterward.

So, gentlemen, consider all the cocktails mentioned in this book drunk by me as a toast to the American Booksellers Association.

MAY, 1920

Sincerely

Scott Fitzgerald

"The Author's Apology," tipped into copies of the third printing of *This Side of Paradise* (April 1920), distributed at the American Booksellers Association convention, May 1920.

THE CREDO OF F. SCOTT FITZGERALD

Dear Boyd: It seems to me that the overworked art-form at present in America is the "history of a young man." Frank Norris began it with "Vandover and the Brute," then came Stephen French Whitman with "Predestined" and of late my own book and Floyd Dell's "Moon Calf." In addition I understand that Stephen Benet has also delved into his past. This writing of a young man's novel consists chiefly in dumping all your youthful adventures into the readers' lap with a profound air of importance, keeping carefully within the formulas of Wells and James Joyce. It seems to me that when accomplished by a man without distinction of style it reaches the depth of banality as in the case of "Moon Calf." * * * Up to this year the literary people of any pretensions—Mencken, Cabell, Wharton, Dreiser, Hergesheimer, Cather and Charles Norris—have been more or less banded together in the fight against intolerance and stupidity, but I think that a split is due. On the romantic side Cabell, I suppose, would maintain that life has a certain glamour that reporting—especially this reporting of a small Midwestern town—cannot convey to paper. On the realistic side Dreiser would probably maintain that romanticism tends immediately to deteriorate to the Zane Grey-Rupert Hughes level, as it has in the case of Tarkington, fundamentally a brilliant writer. * * *

It is encouraging to notice that the number of pleasant sheep, i.e., people who think they're absorbing culture if they read Blasco Ibanez, H. G. Wells and Henry Van Dyke—are being rounded into shape. This class, which makes up the so-called upper class in every American city, will read what they're told and now that at last we have a few brilliant men like Mencken at the head of American letters, these amiable sheep will pretend to appreciate the appreciable of their own country instead of rushing to cold churches to hear noble but intelligible lords, and meeting once a week to read papers on the aforementioned Blasco Ibanez. Even the stupidest people are reading "Main Street," and pretending they thought so all the time. I wonder how many people in St. Paul ever read "The Titan" or "Salt" or even "McTeague." All this would seem to encourage insincerity of taste. But if it does it would at least have paid Dreiser for his early struggles at the time when such cheapjacks as Robert Chambers were being hailed as the "Balzacs of America."

—*F. Scott Fitzgerald*

Public letter to Thomas Boyd, *St. Paul Daily News*, February 20, 1921, Feature section, p. 8.

WHAT I WAS ADVISED TO DO— AND DIDN'T

By F. Scott Fitzgerald

Author of "The Beautiful and Damned," etc.

"Good morning, Mr. Fitzgerald," said the man with horn-rimmed spectacles, "I was asked to come down to the copy department and speak to you about writing. I understand that you received $30 for a story. Now I have had five stories in the Saturday Evening Post during the last ten years and I know the game from A to Z. There's nothing in it. It's all right for picking up a little spare cash, but as for making a living at it, it won't do. You're dreaming. It would take ten years before you'd even begin to get a start. In the meanwhile, you'd starve. Take my advice, give up writing and stay at your job."

I didn't!

"What I was Advised to Do—and Didn't," *Philadelphia Public Ledger*, April 22, 1922, p. 11.

HOW I WOULD SELL MY BOOK
IF I WERE A BOOKSELLER

By F. Scott Fitzgerald

Author of "This Side of Paradise" "Flappers and Philosophers" and "The Beautiful and the Damned."

Mr. Fitzgerald (unusually fortunate in instantaneous popularity) was born in St. Paul, Minn., in the fall of 1896. After his graduation from Princeton University, he served in the war as first lieutenant of the 45th Infantry as aide-de-camp to General T. A. Ryan. He worked at advertising for five months and so cordially hated it that he gave it up, went back to St. Paul and wrote "This Side of Paradise," which was accepted before his 23rd birthday. His writing career began at eleven years of age. Nothing else really interested him. He wrote two Triangle Club plays at Princeton, but the impetus which produced "This Side of Paradise" and the eight short stories in "Flappers and Philosophers," written in the short space of five months, was the desire to get married, which he did in 1921.

I believe that a book by a well-known author should be given a full window display—I don't believe a mixed window display of four books for four days is nearly as effective as that of one book for one day. To attract attention it might be a coy idea to set all the books upside down and to have a man with large spectacles sitting in the midst of them, frantically engrossed in the perusal of a copy. He should have his eyes wide with rapt attention and his left hand on his heart.

Seriously, the above title puzzles me. If I were a bookseller I should probably push the most popular book of the season, whether it was trash or not.

The vogue of books like mine depends almost entirely on the stupendous critical power at present wielded by H. L. Mencken. And it is his influence at second hand that is particularly important. Such men as Weaver, in *The Brooklyn Eagle*; Bishop, in *Vanity Fair*; Boyd, in the *St. Paul News*, and dozens of others, show the liberal tendencies which Mencken has popularized.

The growing demand for likely American books is almost directly created by these men, who give no room to trash in their columns and, city by city, are making the work of living writers acceptable to the wavering and uncertain "better public."

I did not know "This Side of Paradise" was a flapper book until George Jean Nathan, who had read parts of it before publication, told me it was. However, I do not consider any of my heroines typical of the average bob-skirted "Dulcy" who trips through the Biltmore lobby at tea time. My heroine is what the flapper would like to *think* she is—the actual flapper is a much duller and grayer proposition. I tried to set down different aspects of an individual—I was accused of creating a type.

I think that if I were a bookseller with a real interest in better books I would announce the new good books as the publisher announced them to me and take orders from customers in advance.

"See here," I would say; "this is a novel by Fitzgerald; you know, the fella who started all that business about flappers. I understand that his new one is terribly sensational (the word 'damn' is in the title). Let me put you down for one."

And this would be approximately true. I am not in love with sensationalism, but I must plead guilty to it in this instance. And I feel quite sure that, though my books may annoy many, they will bore no one.

"How I Would Sell My Book If I Were a Bookseller," *Bookseller and Stationer*, xviii (January 15, 1923), 8.

CONFESSIONS

F. Scott Fitzgerald, the first chronicler of the flapper, in "This Side of Paradise" makes this explanatory reply when I asked him what book he would rather have written than any other:

Dear Miss Butcher:

I'd rather have written Conrad's "Nostromo" than any other novel. First, because I think it is the greatest novel since "Vanity Fair" (possibly excluding "Madame Bovary"), but chiefly because "Nostromo," the man, intrigues me so much. Now the Nostromo who exists in life and always has existed, whether as a Roman centurion or a modern top sergeant, has often crept into fiction, but until Conrad there was no one to ponder over him. He was dismissed superficially and abruptly even by those who most admired his efficient handling of the proletariat either in crowds or as individuals. Kipling realized that this figure, with his almost autocratic disdain of weakness, is one of the most powerful props of the capitalistic system, and under various names he occurs in many of Kipling's stories of Indian life—but always as a sort of glorified servant. The literary attitude toward him has been that of an officer sitting in his club with a highball during drill.

"Well, I've got nothing to worry about. Sergt. O'Hare has the troop and——" this with a patronizing condescension—"I believe he knows just about as much about handling them as I do."

Now Conrad didn't stop there. He took this man of the people and imagined him with such a completeness that there is no use of any one else pondering over him for some time. He is one of the most important types in our civilization. In particular he's one that always made a haunting and irresistible appeal to me. So I would rather have dragged his soul from behind his astounding and inarticulate presence than written any other novel in the world.

Sincerely,

F. Scott Fitzgerald

Public letter to Fannie Butcher, *Chicago Daily Tribune*, May 19, 1923, p. 9.

IN LITERARY NEW YORK

F. Scott Fitzgerald Says Appearance in January of Mencken and Nathan's American Mercury Will Be Event of the Year—Tom Boyd Writing for Scribner's Magazine.

GREAT NECK L. I.

Dear Bernard: You ask me for the news from literary New York. Outside of the fact that Rebecca West and Frank Swinnerton are in town, there isn't any. Tom Boyd, after being feted on all sides by admirers of his books, got off for France and is sending back short stories for Scribner's Magazine by every boat.

The books of the fall seem to have determined themselves as "A Lost Lady," Thomas Beer's life of Stephen Crane and Eleanor Wylle's "Jennifer Lorn," a remarkable period romance which just misses—but misses —being a classic. Floyd Dell's new book ("Janet March") is a drab, dull statistic throughout. How such an intelligent, sophisticated man can go on year after year turning out such appalling novels is a question for the psychoanalysts, to whom, I understand, he resorts.

Aldous Huxley's "Antic Hay," while a delightful book, is inferior on all counts to Van Vechten's "The Blind Bow-Boy."

But the real event of the year will, of course, be the appearance in

January of the American Mercury. The Smart Set without Mencken and Nathan is already on the stands, and a dreary sight is is. In their nine years' association with it those two men had a most stupendous and far reaching influence on the whole course of American writing. Their influence was not so much on the very first-rate writers, though even there it was considerable in many cases as on the cultural background. Their new venture is even more interesting. We shall see what we shall see.

You ask for news of me. There is little and that bad. My play ("The Vegetable") opened in Atlantic City and foundered on the opening night. It did better in subsequent performances, but at present is laid up for repairs.

—*Scott Fitzgerald*

"In Literary New York," unlocated (fall-winter 1923). Clipping in Fitzgerald's scrapbooks.

CENSORSHIP OR NOT

Then Mr. Fitzgerald:
"The clean-book bill will be one of the most immoral measures ever adopted. It will throw American art back into the junk-heap where it rested comfortably between the Civil War and the World War. The really immoral books like 'Simon Called Peter' and 'Mumbo Jumbo' won't be touched, they'll attack Hergesheimer, Drieser, Anderson and Cabell, whom they detest because they can't understand. George Moore, Hardy and Anatole France who are unintelligible to children and idiots will be supprest at once for debauching the morals of village clergymen."

"Censorship Or Not," *The Literary Digest*, LXXVII (June 23, 1923), 31, 61. Statements by various people about campaign against unclean books by Justice Ford of Supreme Court of New York State.

FITZGERALD SETS THINGS RIGHT
ABOUT HIS COLLEGE

"Dear Mr. Olmsted:
"Your article in The Washington Herald of May 9th is inaccurate in that it places the Princeton freshmen enrollment at 2200. That is the

total enrollment. The freshmen are limited to about 600 less than at Yale and Harvard: and Princeton is still the hardest institution to get in to and stay in (and leave!) in America.

"Sincerely,

"F. Scott Fitzgerald."

"Fitzgerald Sets Things Right About His College," *Washington Herald,* June 28, 1929, II, p. 1. Public letter to Stanley Olmsted.

UNFORTUNATE "TRADITION"

Editor, the *Weekly*
Sir:

It seems to me a pity that the *Alumni Weekly* and the Press Club keep harping on the "tradition" that a lineman shall captain Princeton football teams. It is not a very hoary or venerable tradition—as late as 1922 Halfback Gilroy was Captain-elect, and at any moment it might be necessary to honor it in the breach. There are fine linesmen whose nerves go to pieces under strain, and there are backs with temperaments as steady and imperturbable as sergeants of Marines—I need only mention Buell of Harvard and Mallory of Yale.

My point is that a star prep school back with quite justifiable ambitions for glory—say a born quarterback with a gift for leading and driving—might read of this "tradition" and say to himself "What's the use of bucking up against that kind of discrimination?" Imagine the effect of an annual boast that only outfielders could captain the nine, or that sprinters were too unreliable to lead a track team!

Why not put a quietus on this "tradition" until it has the endorsement of at least a decade?

NINETEEN-SEVENTEEN

February 4, 1929.

"Unfortunate 'Tradition,' " *Princeton Alumni Weekly,* xxix (February 15, 1929), 562. Attributed to Fitzgerald on the basis of a clipping in his scrapbooks.

FALSE AND EXTREMELY
UNWISE TRADITION

Graduate Finds Cause for Fear in Advertisement of
Erroneous "Sacred Old Football Tradition."

To the Editor of the Princetonian:

Sir:—I see that the fact of a lineman being elected Football Captain is still being sent out to the papers as a "sacred old tradition." As the present writer pointed out in the *Alumni Weekly* last winter, there is no such tradition—Ralph Gilroy was Captain-elect in 1922—and the report serves merely to fill two lines of space for unimaginative Press Club members each year. The point is that I believe it directly responsible for the fact that no first class backs have entered Princeton for four years; where Roper used to make tackles out of extra halfbacks he is now compelled to make fullbacks out of guards and quarterbacks out of air. If anyone believes that rival colleges don't make full use of this alleged discrimination in winning over prospective triple threats, he is simply an innocent; for American boys have a pretty highly developed desire for glory.

It will take five years to kill this rumor, but the Athletic Association has obviously done nothing—and no matter what steps are taken now we can scarcely expect any more Slagles, Miles, Wittmers and Caulkins until 1940.

"Seventeen."

Paris, January 24, 1930.

"False and Extremely Unwise Tradition," *The Daily Princetonian*, February 27, 1930, p. 2. Attributed to Fitzgerald on the basis of a clipping in his scrapbooks.

CONFUSED ROMANTICISM

Editor, the *Weekly*
Sir:

I have just been reading the debate between Mr. Casement and Mr. Van Arkel in the *Alumni Weekly*. I am enlightened rather than astonished by Mr. Casement's indifference to any conception of education more modern than the British public school spirit of the middle 'nineties. The two men are talking across a chasm, as the resignation in both their rebuttals clearly shows. It has become a truism that the salient points of character are fixed before the age of twelve. At eighteen you can change a young man's superficial habits, teach him the ethics of a profession, expose him to broadening or narrowing influences—but the deeper matters of whether he's weak or strong, strict or easy with himself, brave or timid—these things are arranged in the home, almost in the nursery. It is preposterous to ask a university to take over such a task.

Is it required of Oxford, Cambridge, Göttingen, Heidelberg, Paris? The Honor System, to take an example, was and is successful as a *contract* ("You don't watch us and we won't cheat you"). When it was extended into a headmaster's harangue ("Now, boys, you won't copy your themes, will you—you give me your word of honor, don't you, boys"), it showed signs of going to pieces. The Honor System is a fine thing precisely because it is not the sort of paternalism Mr. Casement seems to advocate. And I may add that the students lost their cars chiefly because the cars had become a nuisance to the university at large.

Mr. Casement's attitude reminds me of that of the father who sends his timid son to a military school "to make a man out of him." To a boy who grew up as I did—playing at football and baseball and going through the average rough and tumble—the rushes and their like were only a good roughhouse. To other boys they were a nuisance, and one would be blind not to admit after fifteen years that these boys included some of the best.

Modern Princeton cannot devote itself primarily to moulding the regimented Samurai that Mr. Casement admires, without sacrificing the intellectual freedom and choice which distinguishes a university from a prep school. It does not interfere with such men; but it merely insists that they shall be, intellectually, officers and not privates. It gives a special break to those who will presumably be scholars, scientists, and artists, and this Mr. Casement simply can't understand. Nevertheless, his argument would not seem so intemperate if he would admit that there are many human instruments of good and his ideal is just possibly not the only one. Kingdoms have been built by consumptives and hunchbacks, and the "well rounded man" of the 'nineties—the Roosevelt-Churchill-Soldier-of-Fortune type—takes on with time an increasing aspect of papier maché. It survives as an ideal for the eternally juvenile and the latest immigrants in such legends as "Knute Rockne, Builder of Men." It is a type valuable in time of war, especially when stiffened with a rigorous technical training. That it should have the preempted place in a great university, dedicated to preserving "what the world will not willingly let die"—well, Mr. Casement believes that it should have such a place. To younger men he seems to be merely voicing the confused romanticism of that generation into which he was born.

F. Scott Fitzgerald '17

Baltimore.

"Confused Romanticism," *Princeton Alumni Weekly*, xxxii (April 22, 1932), 647.

AN OPEN LETTER TO FRITZ CRISLER

By F. Scott Fitzgerald '17

Dear Fritz: You write me again demanding advice concerning the coming season. I hasten to answer—*again* I insist that using a member of the Board of Trustees at left tackle to replace Charlie ("Asa") Ceppi and Christian ("Dean") Eisenhart, would be a mistake. My idea is a backfield composed of Kipke, Eddie Mahan, President Lowell and anybody we can get for the left side—Pepper Einstein in the center—and then either bring back Light Horse Harry Lee, or else you fill in yourself for the last place. Or else shift Kadlic to center and fill in with some member of the 75-lb. team.

Failing that, it *is* as you suggest in your round-robin, a question of using a member of the Board of Trustees. Then who? and where? There is "Hack" Kalbaugh. There is the late President Witherspoon—but where is he? There is Harkness Hall, but we can't get it unless we pay for the whole expressage *at this end!*

The best suggestion is probably to put Rollo Rulon Roll-on at full, and return to the Haughton system.

Now Fritz, I realize that you and I and Tad know more about this thing than I do—nevertheless I want to make my suggestion: all the end men and backfield men and members of the Board of Trustees start off together—then they all reverse their fields led by some of the most prominent professors and alumni—Albie Booth, Bob Lassiter, etc., and almost before we know it we are up against the Yale goal—let me see, where was I? I meant the Lehigh goal—anyhow some goal, perhaps our own. Anyhow the main thing is that the C.W.A. is either dead, or else just beginning, and to use again that variation of the "Mexican" shift that I suggested last year will be just *disastrous*. Why? Even I can follow it! Martineau comes out of the huddle—or topples back into it—he passes to some member of past years' teams—(who won't be named here because of the eligibility rules) and then—well, from then on we go on to practically anything.

But not *this* year, Fritz Crisler, if you take my advice!

THE TEAM.

"An Open Letter to Fritz Crisler," *Princeton Athletic News*, II (June 16, 1934), 3. Crisler was the Princeton football coach.

COMMENTS ON STORIES

F. Scott Fitzgerald has supplied these comments in regard to the origin of four of his best-known short stories: "Baby Party: Went to one—saw just a moment of bitterness between two women. Was drawn in spiritually on wife's side. Imagined the same scene among stupid people with less self-control—and its consequences. Also Maupassant's 'Piece of String.' Imagination.

"Rags Martin Jones: Struck by personality of girl just home from Europe and hating America. Also gossip about Prince of Wales. Invention.

Huckleberry Finn took the first journey back. He
was the first to look back at the republic from the perspective of
the west. His eyes were the first eyes that ever looked at us
objectively that were not eyes from overseas. There were mountains
at the frontier but he wanted more than ~~that~~ mountains to look at with his res
less eyes--he wanted to find out about men and how they lived toget
And because he turned back we have him forever.

[signature: F. Scott Fitzgerald]

F. Scott Fitzgerald.

Statement on Huck Finn, Collection of Matthew J. Bruccoli. This statement
was read at the banquet of the International Mark Twain Sociey marking
the hundredth anniversary of Mark Twain's birth, November 30, 1935.

"Absolution: Memory of time when as a boy told a lie in confession. Also glimpse of a very bored passionate celibate priest one day. Imagination.

"Winter Dreams: Memory of a fascination in a visit paid to very rich aunt in Lake Forest. Also my first girl 18–20 whom I've used over and over and never forgotten. Imagination."

Comments on stories, *These Stories Went to Market*, ed. Vernon McKenzie (New York: McBride, 1935, p. xviii).

ANONYMOUS '17

*The second of the alumni contributions is written by a man who prefers that his name not be mentioned * inasmuch as he is revealing the secrets of the 1917 team. It is in the author's words "an account of activities of 1916–17" and may be taken as the general prologue to this history.*

The 1916–17 team was perhaps the strongest in Princeton history with an undefeated record of six issues and no suppressions. At quarterback Edmund B. Wilson using an open style of play used notable headwork in his mingling of straight stuff and trick plays. At fullback John Peale Bishop starred. Already represented in the *Century* he could always be counted on to pick up a few meters. F. Scott Fitzgerald was perhaps the fastest of the halfbacks though there have been faster ones since. His mate John Biggs Jr. plunged brilliantly close to center in a way that prophesied his legal success. Charlie Bailey alternated with him at the position.

At one end we had Hamilton Fish Armstrong, later an All-American Book-of-the-Month man. At the other was Townsend Martin whose later life as a playrite was featured by his connection with "A Most Immoral Lady." Herbert Agar, the critics' choice as American Pulitzer Prize winner, Alexander McKaig, later producer of "The Racket", and

* The editors are privileged to say that this sporting information is given by a member of the team named above. There is no prize for solution, but the editors, who have read "This Side of Paradise", can make a guess.

Elliot Springs, the War Bird, turned out for the tackle posts, while at guard the poets Hardwick Nevin, Henry Chapin, and Harry Keller could be depended upon to plug up any holes in the line. Stephen Benet's team at Yale was easily snowed under, though the charges of professionalism against the Tigers were easily proved a few years later.

Needless to say the above account is not typical of the style employed, which is why the sports writer remains anonymous.

"Anonymous '17," statement about the *Lit, The Nassau Literary Magazine*, xcv (June 1937), 9.

TO HARVEY H. SMITH

January 9, 1939

Dear Harvey:—

. . . only a note from Sap Donohoe at Coronado and a short visit with Bert Hormone whom I hadn't seen since Triangle Days. He came out here first with the Federal Theatre project, was spotted by Selznick I believe and took a test for the part of Rhett Butler. The rumor is that they wanted somebody with a more roguish face and Bert still has the same bland innocence of twenty years ago. New Year's I saw him again in the front row at the Trojan-Duke game. He was cheering on his sophomore son who is Tipton's substitute and expected to be a big shot next year. When I asked Bert about the disloyalty he gave the usual alibi "Princeton was too hard to get in to." I understand how he feels because my off-spring couldn't get into Princeton either—so this fall she went to Vassar instead.

Best wishes always.
Scott Fitzg

Public Letter to Harvey H. Smith, Secretary, class of '17, *Princeton Alumni Weekly*, xxxix (February 3, 1939), 369.

Love, Marriage, and Sex

"Why Blame It on the Poor Kiss if the Girl Veteran of Many Petting Parties Is Prone to Affairs After Marriage?"

Once past the age of thirty all civilized persons realize that many of our institutions are no more than conspiracies of silence.

When the clergyman assumes for the sake of his sermon that there is a great body of men and women who "live a moral life" he does not mean, if he is a man of any intelligence, that every week and every year this body is composed of the same people. He means rather that on any given date more people are engaged in keeping the rules than are engaged in breaking them. And he also means that these people who are at the moment engaged in being virtuous will combine against the people who are outraging the morals of the time.

The libertine sits in the jury box and votes against the divorce case defendant as heartily as does the pillar of the church. Three days later the pillar of the church may elope with the sexton's wife and five hundred unfaithful husbands read the news aloud at breakfast in shocked and horrified tones.

So in discussing the question as to whether we human beings are really capable of a happy monogamy, I don't want to start from the angle that four-fifths of us are approximately lily white and the other fifth a rather dingy shade of gray. I assume that at present there are a large majority of couples on this continent who are true to each other and a minority who are at present tangled up in some fascinating but entirely illegal affair.

Monogamy a Theory

We believe, from our racial experience, that monogamy is the simplest solution of the mating instinct. It tends to keep people out of messes and less time is required to keep up a legal home than to support a chorus girl. There are disadvantages—marriage is often dull for at least one of the parties concerned and the very security of the bond tends, not infrequently, to make an unconscious bully of the man or a shrew of the woman. But on the whole the advantages outweigh the disadvantages, and the only trouble is—that it isn't really monogamy because one party is so frequently not true to the other.

This, despite the angry denials of thousands of pew-holders, is the unfortunate truth. The more the opportunity the greater is the tendency for young men and women to experiment in new fields. Some professions are proverbially dangerous in this respect—stage people "on the road," travelling salesmen, men of great means and great leisure, poor people who are thrown, by crowding conditions, into close proximity—all these men and women drift frequently into liaisons in what seems to them the most natural way in the world.

The truth is that monogamy is not (not yet at least) the simple natural way of human life. But we are officially pledged to it as the only possible system in the western world and at present it is kept working by a series of half artificial props—otherwise it may collapse and we may drift, quite naturally, into an age of turmoil and confusion.

A Faithful Couple

I know a man named Harry, a girl named Georgianna (these, strange to say, are their real names) who married in those happy radical days before the war, when experiment was in the air. The understanding was that, when the first flush was over, Harry and Georgianna were to be free to ramble. They were exceptionally well-mated, exceptionally congenial, and the fascination endured well into the fourth year of their marriage.

Then they made two discoveries—that they were still in love with each other, and that they were no longer completely unaware of the other men and women in the world. Just as they made these discoveries, circumstances threw them suddenly into gayest New York. Harry, through the nature of his occupation, came into almost daily contact with dozens of charming and foot-loose young women, and Georgianna began to receive the attentions of half a dozen charming and foot-loose young men.

If ever a marriage seemed bound for the rocks this one did. We gave them six months—a year at the outside. It was too bad, we felt, because fundamentally they loved each other, but circumstances had undoubtedly doomed them—as a matter of fact, they are now in process of living happily together forever after.

Jealousy Aids Love

Did they decide that the best way to hold each other was to let faithfulness be entirely voluntary? They did not. Did they come to an arrangement by which neither was to pry into the other's life? They did not. On the contrary they tortured each other into a state of wild, unreasoning jealousy—and this solved the problem neatly in less than a week.

Despite the sentimentalists, jealousy is the greatest proof of and prop to love. Harry and Georgianna, with the relentless logic of jealousy—poor, abused, old jealousy—forced concessions out of each other. They decided that the only sensible course was to remain always together. Harry never goes to see a woman alone nor does Georgianna ever receive a man when Harry is not there. Women over sixty and men over eighty are excepted.

Harry does not say:

"You mind my taking Clara to the theatre? What nonsense! Why, her husband is one of my best friends."

Nor does Georgianna protest:

"Are you mad because I sat out with Augustus? What nonsense! Why, Augustus hasn't got three hairs on top of his head."

Dangerous Intruders

They know that the wives of best friends and the men with less than three hairs on their heads are the most dangerous of all. Any one can protect his or her household against Apollo and Venus—it is the club-footed man and the woman with honest freckles who will bear watching.

If Harry goes away on a trip Georgianna goes with him. They go to no mixed parties unless both of them are able to go—and if there is any jealousy in the air neither of them strays out of the other's sight.

As I write this it sounds like a self-enforced slavery—a double pair of apron strings—but in the case of Harry and Georgianna, two highly strung and extremely attractive young people, it had the inestimable advantage of working admirably. I think they are the happiest couple I know.

As to "Compatability"

The Experience of the Race (that stupid old man who every once in a while gets a few truths through his head) has found certain things violently unfavorable to a contended monogamy. Two of the most obvious things are a great disparity in age and a surrounding atmosphere of excessive alcoholic stimulation—two factors which occur chiefly among the well-to-do classes.

A heart-balm expert, in discussing the matter of successful marriages, the other day alluded to a "spirit of kindliness" between husband and wife—as if kindliness were a thing that can be acquired by wanting to acquire it or can be turned off and out in our hearts like a water faucet.

"She spoke of "intellectual compatibility." It is one of her favorite phrases. The trouble is that when people are in love it is horribly hard to find out just how intellectually compatible they are—for they will bluff and lie and conceal and pretend interests that will never materialize after the celebrated words are murmured at the altar.

"Petting Parties"

But there are several essentials to successful monogamy that are not talked about in the women's magazines. A genius may some day arise who will find a way of presenting physiological facts to youth without shocking youth's sensibilities into an infuriated disgust. The long list of current "sex books," while they may have a certain value to married people, have absolutely no effect on the young except to arouse pruriency and sometimes to kill the essence of romance. It is the toss of a coin which is the worst—knowledge so acquired, or ignoranc itself. And yet should such knowledge be acquired before marriage rather than after? If so, how?

It is only recently that the "petting party" has become almost as conventional a term as "afternoon reception" among the upper and middle classes, but in some more primitive communities a sustained physical courtship has preceded marriage. Such a courtship is the natural, not the vicious; the romantic, not the sordid; the ultra-ancient, not the ultra-modern preparation, for married life.

I have heard otherwise intelligent people speak of "petting parties" as if they were accidental and immoral phenomena in an entirely non-physical world—instead of an introduction to life, intended by nature to ameliorate the change between the married and unmarried state. We have given them a new tag, married and the unmarried state.* tied them up in some curious way with cocktails, opium, "The Sheik" and sheer perversity, but they have always existed and, it is to be hoped, always will.

One of the favorite questions of the recent controversy was:

"What kind of wife will the girl make who has had numerous petting parties before marriage?"

The answer is that nobody knows what kind of wife any girl will make.

"But," they continue, "won't she be inclined to have petting parties after she's married?"

"Why Blame the Kiss?"

In one sense she will. The girl who is a veteran of many petting parties was probably amorously inclined from birth. She'll be more prone to affairs after marriage than the girl who didn't want any parties. But why blame it on the poor kiss? It is a question of temperament. The alarmist believes not in cause and effect, but that one effect produces the other.

It may even be true that petting parties tend to lessen a roving tendency after marriage. A girl who knows before she marries that there is more than one man in the world but that all men know very much the same names for love is perhaps less liable after marriage to cruise here and there seeking a lover more romantic than her husband. She has discovered already that variety is not half as various as it sounds. But if petting parties had been so named in 1913 we would have been assured that they caused the war.

Here is a more worthy scapegoat—the one-child family. Because of

* Thus in the original published text.

our breathless economic struggle, it has become almost an American institution. Women with one child are somehow more restless, more miserable, more "nervous" and more determined to pay any price for the attention of men than women with several children or no children at all. The child often becomes a pest and a bore and a continual subject for heated discussion at the dinner table. For some reason parents do not mind losing both temper and dignity before one child. They will hesitate in the presence of two.

For "Easy Divorce"

Now I have discussed a number of things that war against a true and enduring marriage, rather than offering remedies for making every home a paradise in twelve lessons. Believing as I do that all questions worth solving are entirely insoluble, it is the only angle from which I can sincerely approach the subject. On the constructive side I can only say that I believe in early marriage, easy divorce and several children.

All in all nothing can tarnish the cheerful fact that a sincerely happy marriage under exclusive monogamy—one marriage in five, in ten—sometimes I think one in a hundred—is the most completely satisfactory state of being in this somewhat depressing world.

Copyright 1924, Metropolitan Newspaper Service.

" 'Why Blame It on the Poor Kiss if the Girl Veteran of Many Petting Parties Is Prone to Affairs After Marriage?' " *New York American*, February 24, 1924, LII, p. 3. Syndicated by the Metropolitan Newspaper Service and published with variant titles.

Does a Moment of Revolt
Come Some Time to Every Married Man?

By F. Scott Fitzgerald
Author of "This Side of Paradise," etc.

Any decent, self-respecting marriage should have a percentage of from three to seven revolts every day. Otherwise, it's not a marriage—it's a defeat. Or rather it's a sitting on the lukewarm sidelines watching somebody else play.

In the first place no sooner does a man marry his reproachless ideal than he becomes intensely self-conscious about her. In a sort of panic he tries to make her into a thorough conservative as quickly as possible. It doesn't matter how beautiful her complexion looked to him before they were married—the first time he sees her at her easel applying complicated pigments to her eyelids and the lobes of her ears, the horrible suspicion seizes him that she has an immoral streak, and what's worse that she is conspicuously overdoing it and will probably be hailed in the streets.

In consequence—a double revolt is immediately enacted before her mirror, a revolt ending with that celebrated masculine statement:

"Well, you're *not!* And that's all there is to it!"

Is he sensitive? Mr. Egg, the young husband? Horribly! Did you ever go to a young married party and see the husbands, one by one whisper to their wives not to do what the other wives are doing?

If it's anybody else except Mrs. Egg she can do all these things and you'll be one of the husbands who gather admiringly around her. But Mrs. *Egg*—well, you'd rather she'd sit in the corner with Mrs. Yoke and discuss whether you drop four stitches when you purl.

So after awhile young Mrs. Egg begins to feel that if Mr. Egg has demands on her, she has demands on him too, and then the revolt of Mr. Egg begins.

There is, for instance, that ghastly moment once a week when you realize that it all depends on you—wife, babies, house, servants, yard and dog. That if it wasn't for you, it'd all fall to pieces like an old broken dish. That because of those things you must labor all the days of your life, when otherwise you could go to the poorhouse or murder your office boy or spend the summer in Monte Carlo and the winter in Sing Sing prison. But you can't! How did it happen? Where is the gay young man, the length of whose rambles was measured only by the size of his pocketbook?

After awhile you forget the gay young man and enter the third stage of revolt which endures through Mrs. Egg's palmy days—that is, as long as she is still attractive to other men. These are the days of:

"Here I've been working all day and you want to go out and dance all night. Well, you can't. I'm through. I'm an old man. I want to sit by the fire and bore the very pattern off the wallpaper!"

"I wish I was dead—God forbid!" says Montague Glass. In the same spirit I have often wished that I had never laid eyes on my wife—but I can never stand for her to be out of my sight for more than five hours at a time.

"Does a Moment of Revolt Come Some Time to Every Married Man?" *McCall's*, LI (March 1924), 21, 36. One of several comments on this question.

What Kind of Husbands Do "Jimmies" Make?

How about the sons and daughters of the rich? Those whose engagements and marriages are this day announced on society pages the country over. What kind of a success will they make of marriage and what sort of ideals are they capable of passing on to their children? Consider:

The door captain at the Mont Mihiel Restaurant approaches Eddie, the head waiter, with a distraught expression in his eyes.

"Young Mr. Jimmy Worthington is outside," he says.

"Drunk?" asks Eddie.

"He can hardly stand up."

"Is he dressed?" Eddie does not mean: Is he in his underwear?— though this would not surprise him a great deal. He means: Does he have on a dinner coat?

"Yes."

"All right," says Eddie. "Show him in."

Jimmy's Ideas About Life

And into the Mont Mihiel cafe reels that peerless aristocrat, that fine flower of American civilization, young Mr. Jimmy Worthington. His father made a fortune hoarding food during the war but the son scorns commerce and has gone in for aristocracy on a large scale.

I have often talked to Jimmy and tried to find out his ideas about life. It is an enlightening if somewhat alarming experience, for Jimmy's conversation is chiefly a history of his more recent dissipations. He has heard his father make remarks about "these dangerous radicals," so Jimmy thinks of all the policemen and soldiers in America as a sort of bodyguard to protect his person from the "lower classes."

He thinks that when he is arrested for running his car 60 miles an hour he can always get out of trouble by handing his captor a large enough bill—and he knows that even if he has the bad luck to run over someone when he's drunk, his father will buy off the family and keep him out of jail. This is a complete summary of Jimmy's attitude toward the government under which he lives.

Fashions In Behavior

It has been the fashion for the last five years to blame rich girls for the "wildness" of the younger generation. Women, however, are always just what men make them. In 1840, women were required to faint to show their delicacy—in 1924, women are required to dissipate to show their sportsmanship. Occasionally the revulsion from some orgy throws Jimmy in a panic into the arms of a girl of character. But, as a rule, he marries someone like himself.

Jimmy and Mrs. Jimmy have a year of dissipation together. Mrs. Jimmy is "a good sport"—she has to be; if she ceased being one Jimmy would find another lady to be a good sport in her stead. Perhaps at the end of a year or two, there is a single child—not particularly wanted nor particularly unwanted; not the center of the household, apparently, nor the result of any scheme of life—simply a child which exists through its infancy in a sort of vacuum; not unloved but, somehow, an incongruity inasmuch as its parents, though they may have three houses, have not yet succeeded in establishing anything in the nature of a home.

On the contrary, they are already drifting apart. Their bonds were never very close, for in the world of continual stimulation in which they moved they never really regarded marriage as a permanent thing.

Jimmy's Children

The psychological effect of the child on Mrs. Jimmy begins a new era in their marriage. Something is wrong and she knows it. She is torn between her natural love for the child and the idea that she's got to keep up with Jimmy. But the problem is solved for her by Jimmy, who has learned to amuse himself without her. To all intents and purposes their marriage is over.

Let us suppose though that Jimmy and Mrs. Jimmy remain together after a fashion and have a series of three children over an interval of 10 years. Is Jimmy in any position to supervise their education? Not he. He hasn't even the wisdom to leave them intelligently alone.

He knows by this time that there is something wrong with his life and his one idea is that his children shall be unlike himself. And of all the intolerant, mean and unjust parents in the world, an ex-libertine is the worst. He looks with horror on the mildest escapade.

While at no period in the world's history, perhaps, has a larger proportion of the family income been spent upon display, an even worse phenomenon is observable in those who come into direct contact with the irresponsible rich. Every wealthy set in the big cities has many couples who, from their inability to pay the heavy financial cost of post-prohibition entertaining, have become nothing more than sponges and parasites.

I know dozens of boys who have never been able to live down expensive educations—who have come into contact with the rich, wasting class at the big prep-schools and universities and never realized that what young Midas wastes today was once paid for by old Midas, his grandfather, and that what he himself wastes is going to be sweated out of his parents' inadequate bank book. He sees young Midas reel through life like Jimmy, or if he wants to work, become a director in six companies on his twenty-fifth birthday. So the poor but lazy young man gets a confused, jealous and distorted picture of the world.

Is Jimmy, lasting a month in Wall Street, to blame for his failure to hold a job? What possible attraction can Wall Street hold for him? Joy in the work? He hates the work—he is too dull and slow for it. Money? He knows there's plenty of money at home and his for the asking. Pride? But he need feel no shame in being a parasite since half the rich young men he knows are just as lazy and useless as himself. Responsibility?

Here we come to something that sets the American "leisure class" off from the leisure class of all other nations—and makes it probably the most shallow, most hollow, most pernicious leisure class in the world. It has frequently no consciousness that leisure is a privilege, not a right, and that a privilege always implies a responsibility.

Look for a minute at the so-called English aristocracy, a favorite butt of American comics. Mention it, and you bring up before the small town eye a picture of an anaemic, weak-chinned individual with a small coronet on the side of his head. This picture is, of course, about as lifelike as the antiquated British idea that Americans were engaged in a permanent buffalo hunt.

Sons of the Newly Rich

In the first place, the young Englishman of wealth heretofore has made an honest attempt to go into politics and run his government. He may not have been brilliant at it, but he was rich and he didn't need bribes and stock presents and tips on the market—and that's why the British Government has been incomparably the cleanest government in the world. Compared to it, recent developments would make the American Government appear to be a barnyard of scandal and corruption. Can you imagine the Teapot Dome oil disclosures or wounded-veteran graft having happened in the British Isles?

There is, of course, the Jimmy in England too, but he is in a minority there. Here, since the war, at least, Jimmy has become a majority of the rich boys of the land. He occurs most frequently among the newly rich. The older families often have some tradition of responsibility. Their boys go into politics if they can afford it or into law or one of the arts. They are sent to carefully chosen schools—schools which realize that the rich boy must be broken into habits of work and discipline when he is young. And they are given no such allowances as the Jimmies are given.

There was a boy in my class at Princeton who was the son of one of the oldest and wealthiest families in the Middle West. During his freshman year he kept an account book with a record of every dollar he spent. I make no comment on the value of this particular practice, but it shows how necessary it seemed to this boy's father that he should have a sense of responsibility—if not to the country, at least to the fortune he was some day to control.

One Encouraging Fact

Probably the most encouraging thing about the Jimmies is that they don't survive—survive, I mean, as rich men. The largest purse has a bottom, and though Jimmy never works while he can bluff and sponge and borrow his way along, his children will have to take what scraps remain and start again in the middle class.

Since I was seven years old, just 20 years ago, I have seen in my own experience the break up of five sizable fortunes. Out in St. Paul, where I was born, a dozen houses still stand that were once inhabited by one-generation "aristocrats." The "aristocrats" are dead now and their fortunes have melted away; their children, who had no sense of responsibility, even toward their father's money, are bad examples around the streets or, at best, starting life over again with nothing but their own talents and a pioneer name.

This phenomenon, remember, is peculiarly American. English families seldom, if ever, decay with such rapidity, because they are founded not on sand but on aristocracy. And real aristocracy, whatever its faults, is willing to undergo a discipline of its own.

A Pretentious Mockery

The leisure class of England are not soft. They have their scandals, their wastrels, their roues—but in London one never gets the impression that one does sometimes in New York, that all society is a silly, pretentious, vicious mockery of a defunct feudal regime.

Let the American rich have their summer and winter places which tower over our suburban bungalows; let them keep 12 suits and servants to our one. The founder of a great family has been shrewd and successful and bought his descendants soft, fine things that no relative has seen fit to provide for us.

Theoretically, at least, we have the same chance for a marble mausoleum as all the Astors in England and America. It is not so much what the rich do as what they don't do that becomes more and more deplorable each year. They grow softer and softer—and Jimmy's father is now just as soft as Jimmy. Let two dozen workmen meet behind a barn and he bursts out in a cold sweat, casts aside eight centuries of justice and tries to get half a dozen bewildered foreigners sent to Leavenworth for 10 years. He stocks his cellar with liquor and then votes righteously for prohibition "for the good of the masses."

And Jimmy's father after a hard office day looks for his ideals—to his wife.

The effect of this on the children of the rich has been enormous. Women are not public-spirited and they are not natural idealists—they are too "practical" to be concerned with anything that is not their own. When they make standards they are inclined to make violently selfish and unchivalric standards.

Can you imagine the usual very rich woman urging her son to go into politics for the good of the country—if, say, he were making a big success in business? The thing is inconceivable. Women do have vast dreams for their children, but when it comes down to cases their desire is that their children shall take no chances and, at all costs, keep out of trouble.

Many American rich boys of this generation get what ideals they have from their mothers. The boy watches his mother's almost insane strivings toward a social position commensurate with her money. He sees her change her accent, her clothes, her friends, her very soul, as she pushes her way up in life, pulling her busy husband with her. Jimmy's idea of politics becomes the remembrance of some preposterous women's club that met at his mother's house one day. Politics, he thinks, is a thing where ugly women read long dull papers made up out of the month's newspaper editorials.

By the time he is twenty-one Jimmy is about as public-spirited as a rattle-snake. He is not told that his father grew rich because America is the richest country in the world and his father was somewhat shrewder and more industrious than other men. He is told that his father is an unselfish individual who "helped develop the country." He is told that because his father has done this noble work he can now look down on everyone less rich than he. This privilege, the boy gathers from his mother, is the highest inspiration of which a citizen is capable.

So, as it turns out, our rich boy grows up in one of two ways. Either he learns a set of intensely soft, intensely selfish ideals at his mother's knee and spends his life busily adding to the fortune that his father made; or he learns no ideals at all, and assuming that aristocracy is a sort of drunken reel between two long lines of bribed policemen, spends his life and money in a riot of extravagance and petty vice.

Five Hundred of Richest

What a waste! Think of the hundreds of first-rate men who have come out of the British leisure class—statesmen, poets, painters, architects, soldiers, scientists, physicians, philosophers, empire builders—men who have made life easier and more beautiful by having lived. And then look at the American leisure class and note that it has produced—well, two Presidents out of twenty-seven! The greatest Americans have come almost invariably from the very poor class—Lincoln, Edison, Whitman, Ford, Mark Twain.

All that leisure—for nothing! All that wealth—it has begotten waste and destruction and dissipation and snobbery—nothing more. Three generations of chorus girls and racetrack touts and one generation of bootleggers have profited from it—that is all.

Is this to go on forever? Are the rich to breed 10,000 Jimmies until they become a race apart—or will they find that if they want to survive they must realize what really is the responsibility toward the country? Otherwise it will be brought home to them in the decay and failure of their own begotten sons.

(Copyright, 1924, by Metropolitan Newspaper Service, New York.)

"What Kind of Husbands Do 'Jimmies' Make?" *Baltimore American*, March 30, 1924, ME, p. 7. Syndicated by Metropolitan Newspaper Service and published with variant titles.

"Wait Till You Have Children of Your Own!"

By F. Scott Fitzgerald

The original younger generation (I mean, of course, the one that burst forth back in 1919 and got itself thoroughly talked over) used to be periodically squelched with that ominous refrain. Well, the original younger generation are parents now. They are looking at the new world which has established itself out of the confusion of the war, and trying to decide just how their children's education shall differ from their own.

When I say education I mean the whole bag of habits and ideals and prejudices that children receive from their parents between the ages of two and sixteen. I mean more than that—I mean what my own father meant when he said one day that he hoped my life would be different from his. He wanted me to have a better equipment than he had with which to face the world.

All parents want that for their children—except those so smug and self-satisfied that they hope their children will be exactly like themselves. For one parent who sits back at forty now and says to his offspring:

"Look upon this perfect man (or woman) that the Lord made as an example for you"—

There are three who believe the children should be an improvement on their parents, who want their children not to follow blindly in their steps but rather to profit by their mistakes.

Now, ideals, conventions, even truth itself, are continually changing things so that the milk of one generation may be the poison of the next. The young Americans of my time have seen one of these transformations with their own eyes, and for this reason they will not make the initial mistake of trying to teach their children too much. Before a man is thirty he has already accumulated, along with a little wisdom, a great quantity of dust and rubbish in his mind, and the difficulty is to let the children profit by what is wise without unloading the dust and rubbish on them too. We can only try to do better at it than the last generation did—when a generation succeeds in doing it completely, in handing down all its discoveries and none of its delusions, its children shall inherit the earth.

To begin with, my child will have to face conditions of which I am utterly unaware. He may live in a communist state or marry a girl from Mars or sit under an electric fan at the North Pole. Only one thing can I be sure of about the world in which he will live—it will not be as cheerful a world as the world into which I was born. Never had faith in the destiny of man reached such a height as during the nineties—seldom has it ebbed so low as it has now. When we see around us a great decay in ideals of conduct there is some fundamental cause behind it. It is impossible to be vicious in a vacuum. Something serious (which only professional evangelists, cheap novelists, and corrupt politicians profess to understand) is the matter with the world. It will be a strong heart that can fight its way upstream in these troubled waters and not be, like my generation, a bit cynical, a bit weary, and a bit sad. We have seen the war and its attendant ferocity, the hysteria both of the communists and, over here, of the "100% Americans," the cheating of the wounded veterans, the administration corruption, the prohibition scandal—what wonder if we are almost afraid to open the newspapers in the morning lest our eyes fall on some new rift in civilization, some new vileness in that dark chamber which we call the human heart!

On such a world our children are now opening their eyes. Not long ago I was in a room where lay a young mother whose first child had just been born. She was a young woman of exceptional culture and education who had always had the good things of this world and who can expect to have them until she dies. When she awakened from the ether she turned to the nurse with a question, and bending over her the nurse whispered:

"You have a beautiful little girl."

"A girl?" The young mother's eyes opened and then closed again. Suddenly she began to cry.

"All right," she said brokenly, "I'm glad it's a girl. And I hope she'll be a fool—that's the best thing a girl can be in this world, a beautiful little fool!"

Of course, despite everything, few of us are sick enough, or perhaps logical enough, for such pessimism. We do not want our daughters to be beautiful little fools nor our sons to be mere "healthy animals," despite the suffering that it might save them. More than that, we want them to have ideas above the bank book and the comfortable house. We want them to be decent, honorable, and, if I can no longer conscientiously add law-abiding, at least capable of voting against laws which they cannot obey.

I can imagine a young father born as I was in the middle nineties talking somewhat like this to his brand-new son:

"I don't want you to be like me," he says, standing over the baby's bed, "I want you to have time for the finer things in life. I want you to go into politics where not one man in ten has clean hands, and keep your hands clean. Or if you're a business man I want you to be a better kind of business man than I am. Why, my son, except for a few detective stories, I haven't read a book since I left college. My idea of amusement is to play golf or bridge with a lot of people just as dumb as I am, with a bottle of bootleg gin on the side so we won't know how dull we are. I don't know anything about science, or literature, or art, or architecture, or even economics. I believe everything I read in the papers, just like my janitor does. Except for my business I'm almost a half-wit, scarcely fit to vote—but I want you to be something better, and I'm going to give you a chance, so help me God."

Now, that isn't at all what his own father said to *him* way back in 1896. The older man probably talked something like this:

"I want you to be a success. I want you to work hard and make a lot of money. Don't let anybody cheat you, and don't cheat anybody else, or you'll get put in jail. Remember, you're an American"—(here substitute Englishman, Frenchman, or German, for the same speech was being made in many languages)—"and we're much better than any other race, so just remember that everything we don't believe right here in this nation is pretty sure to be wrong. I went to college and I read the papers, so I ought to know."

You recognize this? It is the philosophy of the nineteenth century, the philosophy of personal selfishness and national conceit that led to the great war and was indirectly responsible for the bloody deaths of many million young men.

At any rate, the new baby, our baby, starts out with something a little different. Having been in the war, and perhaps seen actual fighting, his father doesn't hate the Germans—he leaves that to the non-combatants—and maybe he remembers that life in Paris can be just as pleasant as life in Podunk, Indiana. He doesn't give a whoop whether his son sings the national anthem in school, because he knows that surface patriotism means less than nothing, and that Grover Cleveland Bergdoll's childish treble once piped out "My Country, 'Tis of Thee" at Teacher's command. This young father hasn't any un-natural faith in the schools anyhow—good as they are—because he knows the teachers are people just like him, not geniuses, but simply hard-working, half-educated young men and women who earn their bread by doing the best they can. He knows that the schools are of necessity a stereotyping agency in a somewhat stereotyped country. What the child will learn are the ideals of a busy shopkeeper, with side glances at the pictures of Abraham Lincoln and George Washington on the wall—those two romantic Presidents who are fast being made into illustrations for Sunday-school books by silly biographers and sloppy short-story writers.

No, the young father knows that his children are not likely to find ideals in school with which to face the modern world. If the child's soul is going to bear any imprint except a few outworn rubber stamps, he must get his inspiration at home. A school system is such a colossal undertaking that it must often be regulated by convenience. But the young father does not have to tell his children shoddy lies about life because of convenience. And I don't believe he will—the bitterest critics of this generation cannot accuse it of mock modesty. Its children will have at least that advantage over my contemporaries, who learned all the filthy words in the English language before they knew anything of the side of life they so grossly misrepresented.

Now I don't mean to give the impression that the young men and women of my generation are bulging with a hundred sure-fire ways of turning children into veritable Abraham Lincolns. On the contrary, they will be inclined to protect their children from the canned rubbish at large in the world. They know that the knowledge of one good book, Van Loon's "Story of Mankind" for example, is worth a list of a hundred "Children's Classics" compiled by some senile professor. And as they dread canned culture for their child so more than against anything else will they protect him from the canned inspiration that has become a national nuisance. The friendship of one older man of wisdom and character is a great boon—but such men are rare, there are not three to every city. And the substitute, the lectures by professional educationalists and boy-thrillers, represents, I think, a very real danger.

It is the danger of overstimulation. A boy or a girl that comes home every day from school with a new idea about beautifying the home or collecting old clothes for the Laplanders or making one noble sacrifice every week, is not a boy or girl whose brain will be anything but a cluttered bird's nest in a few years. I do not want my child's mind stimulated by every quack in the world, from paid patriots to moving-picture magnates who have rummaged among the ash heaps for shoddy ideas to give to the young. Eventually, of course, the child will grow tired both of the radio and of uplifting the neighbors, and there is no individual means of diversion to which I object—but the continual round of them dulls a child's enthusiasm and permanently injures his mind. He is unable to enjoy or even to understand everything that is not presented to him in canned, predigested form—canned music, canned inspiration, even canned play—until it is no wonder that when he is a man he will be ripe for canned opinions and canned ideals.

"But," objects the realist, "your children will grow up like mine into a world over which you have no control. If you forbid him all these things, will you not be setting up a ring of prohibitions around him— just as a short while since you objected to having about you?"

I'm going to try and answer that question, but first I want to discuss one important respect in which my child's attitude toward life will be different from my own.

It is simply this: whatever respect he may hold for the opinions of age will be taken from him. Unless my mind fails and I join the common conspiracy to teach children that their parents are better than they are, I shall teach my child to respect nothing because it is old, but only those things which he considers worthy of respect. I shall tell him that I know very little more than he knows about the purpose of life in this world, and I shall send him to school with the warning that the teacher is just as ignorant as I am. This is because *I want my children to feel alone*. I want them to take life seriously from the beginning with neither dependency nor a sense of humor, and I want them to know the truth—that they are lost in a strange world compared to which the mystery of all the caves and forests is as nothing. The Russian Jewish newsboy on the streets of New York has an enormous commercial advantage over our children, because he feels alone. He is aware of the vastness and mercilessness of life, and he gets his own knowledge of humanity for himself. Each time he falls down he is not picked up and set on his feet.

I cannot give my son that advantage without exposing him to the thousand dangers of a vagabond's life—but I can make him feel mentally alone, as every great man has been in his heart—alone in his convictions which he forms for himself, and in his character which expresses those convictions. Not only will I force no standards on my son but I will question what others tell him about life. A supreme confidence is one of a man's greatest assets, and we know from the story of our great men that it comes only through self-reliance—and nothing that can be told my son will be of any value to him beside what he finds out for himself. All I can do is watch the vultures who swarm outside with conventional lies for his ear. The best friend we ever have in our adolescence is the one who teaches us to question and to doubt—I would be that kind of friend to my son.

Here, then, are five ways in which my child's early world will be different from my own:

First—He will be less provincial, less patriotic. He will be taught that a citizen of the world is of more value to Podunk, Indiana, than is a citizen of Podunk, Indiana, to Podunk, Indiana. He will be taught to look closely at American ideals, to laugh at those that are absurd, to scorn those that are narrow and small, and give his best to those few in which he believes.

Second—He will know everything about his body from his head to his feet before he is ten years old. It is better that he should know this than that he should learn to read and write.

Third—He will be put as little as possible in the way of constant stimulation whether by men or by machines. Any enthusiasm he has will be questioned, and if it is mob enthusiasm—he who lynches negroes and he who weeps over Pollyanna is equally low at heart—it will be laughed out of him as something unworthy.

Fourth—He shall not respect age unless it is worthy in itself, but he shall look with suspicion on all that his elders say. If he does not agree with them he shall hold his own opinions rather than theirs, not only because he may prove to be right but because he must find out for himself that fire burns.

Fifth—He shall take life seriously and feel always alone: that no one is guiding him, no one directing him, and that he must form his own convictions and standards in a world where no one knows much more than another.

He'll have then, I hope with all my heart, these five things—a citizenship in the world, a knowledge of the body in which he is to live, a hatred of sham, a suspicion of authority, and a lonely heart. Their five opposites—patriotism, modesty, general enthusiasm, faith, and goodfellowship—I leave to the pious office boys of the last generation. They are not for our children.

That much I can do—further than that it depends on the capabilities of the boy—on his intelligence and his inherent honor. Let us suppose that, having these things, he came to me at fourteen and said:

"Father, show me a good great man."

I would have to look around in the living world and find someone worthy of his admiration.

Now no generation in the history of America has ever been so dull, so worthless, so devoid of ideas as that generation which is now between forty and sixty years old—the men who were young in the nineties. I do not, of course, refer to the exceptional people in that generation, but to the general run of "educated" men. They are, as a rule, ill-read, intolerant, pathetic in their mental and spiritual poverty, sharp in business, and bored at home. Culturally they are not only below their own fathers who were fed on Huxley, Spencer, Newman, Carlyle, Emerson, Darwin, and Lamb, but they are also below their much-abused sons who read Freud, Remy de Gourmont, Shaw Bertrand Russell, Nietzsche, and Anatole France. They were brought up on Anthony Hope and are slowly growing senile on J. S. Fletcher's detective stories and Foster's Bridge. They claim that such things "relax their minds," which means that they are too illiterate to enjoy anything else. To hear them talk, of course, you would think that they had each individually invented the wireless telegraph, the moving picture, and the telephone—in point of fact, they are almost barbarians.

Whom could my generation look up to in such a crowd? Whom, in fact, could we look up to at all when we were young? My own heroes were men my own age or a little older—men like Ted Coy, the Yale football star. I admired Richard Harding Davis in default of someone better, a certain obscure Jesuit priest, and, occasionally, Theodore Roosevelt. In Taft, McKinley, Bryan, Generals Miles and Shafter, Admirals Schley and Dewey, William Dean Howells, Remington, Carnegie, James J. Hill, Rockefeller, and John Drew, the popular figures of twenty years ago, a little boy could find little that was inspiring. There are good men in this list—notably Dewey and Hill, but they are not men to whom a little boy's heart can go out, not men like Stonewall Jackson, Father Damien, George Rogers Clark, Major André, Byron, Jeb Stuart, Garibaldi, Dickens, Roger Williams, or General Gordon. They were not men half as good as these. Not one of them sounded any high note of heroism, no clear and distinct call to something above and beyond life. Later, when I was grown, I learned to admire a few other Americans of that generation—Stanford White, E. H. Harriman, and Stephen Crane. Here were figures more romantic, men of great dreams, of high faith in their work, who looked beyond the petty ideals of the American nineties—Harriman with his transcontinental railroad, and White with his vision of a new architectural America. But in my lifetime these three men, whose free spirits were incapable of hypocrisy, moved under a cloud.

Now, ten years from to-day, I hope that if my son comes to me and says, "Father, show me a good man," I can point out something better for him to admire than shrewd politicians or paragons of thrift. Some of those who went to prison for their conscience' sake in 1917 are of my generation, and some who left legs and arms in France and came back to curse not the Germans but the "dollar-a-year men" who fought the war from easy chairs. There have been writers already in my time who have lifted up their voices fearlessly in scorn of sham and hypocrisy and corruption—Cummings, Otto Braun, Dos Passos, Wilson, Ferguson, Thomas Boyd. And in politics there have been young men like Cleveland and Bruce at Princeton, whose names were in the papers before they were twenty because they scrutinized rather than accepted blindly the institutions under which they lived. Oh, we shall have something to show our sons, I think—to point at and say—not, perhaps, "There is a perfect man," but "There is a man who has tried, who has faced life thinking that it could be fuller and freer than it is now and hoping that in some way he could help to make it so."

The women of my generation present a somewhat different problem —I mean the young women who were lately flappers and now have babies at their breasts. Personally I can no more imagine having fallen in love with an old-fashioned girl than with an Amazon—but I think that on the whole the young women of the well-to-do middle classes are somewhat below the men. I refer to the dependent woman, the ex-society girl. She was pretty busy in her adolescence, far too busy to take an education, and what she knows she has learned vicariously from a chance clever man or two that have come her way. Of a far better type are the working girls of the middle classes, the thousands of young women who are the power behind some stupid man in a thousand offices all over the United States. I don't mean that she will bear a race of heroes simply because she has struggled herself—on the contrary, she will probably overemphasize to the children the value of conformity and industry and commercial success—but she is a far higher type of woman than our colleges or our country clubs produce. Women learn best not from books or from their own dreams but from reality and from contact with first-class men. A man can live with a fool all his life untouched by her stupidity, but a smart woman married to a stupid man acquires eventually the man's stupidity and, what is worse, the man's narrow outlook on life.

And this brings on a statement with which many people will disagree violently, a statement which will seem reactionary and out of place here. I hope for the newest generation that it will not be so women-educated as the last. Our fathers were too busy to know much about us until we were fairly well grown, and in consequence such a condition came about that, as Booth Tarkington justly remarked, "All American children belonged to their mother's families." When I said the other day before some members of the Lucy Stone League that most American boys learned to lie at some lady teacher's knee, a shocked silence fell. Nevertheless I believe it to be true. It is not good for boys to be reared altogether by women as American children are. There is something inherent in the male mind that will lie to or impose upon a woman as it would never consider doing to a man.

"If the boys at school don't like you, come here to me," says the mother to her sons.

"If the boys at school don't like you, I want to know the reason why," says the father.

Properly the young boy needs to meet both these two attitudes at home, but my generation got only the first, and it made us soft; and we would still be soft, unpleasantly soft, if we had not had the two years' discipline of the war.

And so, if the young men whom I see every day are typical of their generation, we have by no means hauled down our flags and moderated our opinions and decided to bring up our children in the "good old way." The "good old way" is not nearly good enough for us. That we shall use every discovery of science in the preservation of our children's health goes without saying; but we shall do more than this—we shall give them a free start, not loading them up with our own ideas and experiences, nor advising them to live according to our lights. We were burned in the fire here and there, but—who knows?—fire may not burn our children, and if we warn them away from it they may end by never growing warm. We will not even inflict our cynicism on them as the sentimentality of our fathers was inflicted on us. The most we will urge is a little doubt, asking that the doubt be exercised on our ideas as well as on all the mortal things in this world. Already they are on their hearth, charming us with strange new promises in their eyes as they open them upon the world, with their freshness and beauty and the healthy quiet with which they sleep. We shall not ask much of them—love if it comes freely, a little politeness, that is all. They are free, they are little people already, and who are we to stand in their light? They must fight us down at the end, as each generation fights down the one before, the one that is cluttering up the earth with all those decayed notions which it calls its ideals. And if my child is a better man than I, he will come to me at the last and say, not "Father, you were right about life," but "Father, you were entirely wrong."

And when that time comes, as come it will, may I have the justice and the sense to say: "Good luck to you and good-by, for I owned this world of yours once, but I own it no longer. Go your way now strenuously into the fight, and leave me in peace, among all the warm wrong things that I have loved, for I am old, and my work is done."

" 'Wait Till You Have Children of Your Own!' " *Woman's Home Companion*, LI (July 1924), 13, 105.

What Became of Our Flappers and Sheiks?

A few years ago there were so many experts on the younger generation, like for instance, the lady who wrote "Dancing with the Darkies" (which I may say I have never seen done in my own city), and Madame Glynn who said that young ladies always checked their corsets at dances. So every time I went to a dance in those days I always inquired for the corset check-room because I wanted to see a lot of corsets all hung up in a row. I even asked young ladies, while entering a dance, if there was anything they would like to check, but they never handed me anything immoral—even when I shut my eyes and held out my hand in case they should be embarrassed.

Then came the kind of younger generation who were all dressed up in bell-bottom trousers. The excitement was at fever heat. The newspapers in my town were afraid that the bell-bottoms would seize the city hall, raise a pair of trousers on the flag-staff and kill all the he-men.

Personally it made me nervous to have bells or any sort of musical instruments attached to my trousers, but I had no objections to anyone else doing it if he liked.

If you want to read about any of these kinds you had better lay this down right now. This is about the young man who was once saddled with the ghastly name of "male flapper"—a name that is as depressing as "lady wrestler," and was about as popular with the young man as "Liberty Lads" was with the doughboys.

The midland cities have changed. Apartment houses have risen on the vacant lots where football teams composed of wealthy boys once played against football teams composed of "muckers." At fourteen the wealthy boy is no longer anxious to have enormous muscles and be Ted Coy of Yale, but to own a sport car and be Ben Lyons—or even Michael Arlen. The cheap literature of daring, of Nick Carter and Young Wild West, has vanished. It is a conquered world into which the post-war boy grows up; there are no outposts of civilization to grasp his imagination. He gets the impression that everything has been done. Instead of the Henty books he reads the moving picture magazines.

If by the time he is fifteen he hasn't a car of his own, some one else in his crowd is sure to have one—some one a little older or some one whose parents are too careless or too new to their money to think what having a car may mean. With a car one can be downtown, across a city, out of sight in fifteen minutes. So young Tommy gets his car and the fun begins. What could be more harmless than for Tommy to take Marjorie to the movies? Why Marjorie's mother and Tommy's mother have known each other all their lives. Besides, it's done—other children do it. So Tommy and Marjorie are licensed to drift where they will through the summer night.

The probabilities are that Tommy and Marjorie will never so much as kiss. He tells her how he once "picked up a chicken" and took her to ride, and Marjorie is impressed with his temerity. Sometimes there is a faint excitement, a faint glow between them. Usually—not always, but usually—there is nothing more.

Tommy becomes sixteen. He goes out every night now—to the movies, to a dance, to a gathering on a girl's porch. It seems to his parents that there is always something and that the something always sounds harmless and is always what the other boys are doing. In fact, what worries Tommy's parents is what he is *not* doing. He was bright, as a little boy, but now, because he never has time to work at night, his report cards from his local private school are invariably unsatisfactory. There remains a solution of course—the prep-school. Smiles of relief from the parents. The prep-school will do the trick. Nothing easier than passing it off on somebody else. It is discovered, however, that most of the stricter and more thorough prep-schools have an annoying habit of asking for the boy before fifteen—and refusing to take him any older. So he is sent instead to some small prep-school in New York state or New Jersey that is not so particular.

A year passes. The popular Tommy takes his preliminary examinations for college. The examinations are an absurd hodge-podge and as the preparations for them have failed to intrigue Tommy's interest he scratches through, say, one out of five. He is glad to be home for the summer. He has his car again, and with the other boys of his age, is beginning to go to dances at various country clubs. He finds this most amusing—an unbearably pleasant contrast to the childish restraint of his prep-school. In fact, when autumn comes he persuades his father to send him to one of those curious institutions that are springing up all over the east—the tutoring schools.

Now the tutoring school has neither the discipline of a prep-school nor any of the restraining force that lies in the modeled public opinion of a great university. Theoretically the fact that there is no football team gives the boy time to concentrate on cramming. Actually it gives him time to do what he likes. The masters are smarter and better-paid than the masters in the small prep-schools. In fact they are so smart and they explain everything so clearly that they completely cure Tommy of any faculty of working things out for himself. It is notorious that although the tutoring school boys generally get into college they seldom survive the first mid-year examinations.

Meanwhile the lack of athletic activities in the school drives Tommy to express his vitality in other ways. He smokes incessantly and experiments with alcohol. Some of the boys are twenty and twenty-one years old. They are dull and unimaginative or they would long since have passed their examinations, so, for stimulus and amusement they turn to —New York. And Tommy does too. Many of the boys have automobiles because their parents realize how bored they would otherwise be.

We are almost all newly rich in America, and the number of millionaires who have any definite idea of a modern education is so small as to be negligible. They are aware, however, that their sons require an astonishing lot of money to keep up with the "other boys." An Englishman goes through an Eton and Oxford that are not so different from what they were in his father's time. The Harvard graduate of 1870 could keep a pretty good tab on his Harvard son of 1900. But all that Mr. Thomas senior in San Francisco knows about his son's school is that it promises to get Tommy into college.

Tommy is now eighteen. He is handsomely dressed and an excellent dancer, and he knows three chorus girls in the Follies by their first names. He takes this side of life much more seriously than does the college man—he has no senior societies or upper class clubs to hold up a warning finger. His life is one long weekend.

Coming home for another summer Tommy resumes his country-club existence in a somewhat haughty manner. His home town, if it happens to be in the middle west, bores him now. With a rather pathetic wistfulness he still reads the moving-picture magazines and thinks naively that he would like to have a test taken for the screen. He sees in the newspaper that the younger generation has been debauched by the movies and corrupted by jazz music, and in a dim way he supposes that the newspapers are right. He finds that the only things which do not seem to have given his friends a shove downward are the pie-eating contest and the penny arcade. Mingled with such nonsense he finds the statement that the boy of today is a great deal less courteous than his older brother in the preceding generation. And this, despite Tommy's ease of manner and his apparent worldliness, is quite true. It is due in some measure to modern dancing—not, as our local Savonrolas think, to the steps that are danced, but to the "cutting in" system which has cut the ground from under the unattractive girl.

In the age of the program, two or three dances were always devoted to the fat girl or the female Ben Turpin because Tommy's father and her father were friends. It wasn't anything to look forward to, even then, but nowadays if Tommy should ask her to dance he would have to dance with her until the musicians packed up their sandpaper and went home.

Tommy has never learned courtesy. He has no faith in any conventions but his own. If you tell him that his manners or his dance are "common," are borrowed from the lower classes, he will laugh at you and be right. He knows that if he wants to see close dancing forbidden or steps censored he must go to the cheap dance halls, the amusement park pavillions or the cabarets in small cities where the bouncer and the policewoman are on the alert to enforce the properties and keep the patrons from being—"common."

He is now nineteen. By this time he has managed to pass off almost enough examinations to get into college. But his ambition to enter college is on the wane—at least it fails to inspire him to successful effort. Perhaps the war occurred when he was at tutoring school and in the attendant disorganization of the universities he came to feel that it was the natural thing to give up going or leave in mid-term or find one's educational status in a sort of bizarre jumble. Besides, he thinks that he has had all the college has to offer—except the curriculum. So he comes home at twenty, perhaps after a hectic half-year at New Haven or Princeton, having now assumed to himself all the privileges of aristocracy without any of its responsibilities. He is a complete parasite, polished without being cultured, and "fast" without being vicious. There is nothing effeminate about him. He is healthy, good looking, a bit vacuous—perfectly useless.

I like Tommy personally. He interests me. He is pleasant company. And if he is useless, he knows it and makes a joke of it, says he is "dumb" and blames himself. He is convinced that he wasn't smart enough to get through college. He prefers married women to flappers, who rather bore him. You couldn't call him a "male flapper" to his face because he would probably knock you down—golf and boxing are liable to be his two accomplishments. He is simply a boy who under different circumstances might have been what is known in the editorials as "a useful member of society." He might have done more than cornered the wheat or manufactured a new potato peeler. If the wilderness is conquered there is a whole world of science, theoretical and applied, calling out for recruits who have money and time to spare.

I must admit that personally I have passed on. I am not even part of the younger generation. I have reached the stage where I ask, "How is the food?" instead of "How is the music?" And I have learned my dance. Once I was always among those two or three couples who stand up at the overture and hesitate and look at other couples to see who will begin—and finally get off that world famous remark: "We don't want to give an exhibition!"

But that was back before the civil war when we used to do the good old lancers and the shimmee. Since then I have learned my dance. It is not much—in fact it is so out of date that I have been asked if it is something new—but I am going to stick to it.

And I can still watch the comedy from the chaperone's bench.

I have no solutions, although I am profoundly interested. Perhaps it is just as well that we cannot produce an aristocracy that is capable of surviving. Perhaps Tommy's ineffectuality is some indirect economic re-assertion of the principle of equality. Who knows? Perhaps he will turn about at thirty and reshape the world upon his own desire. It's little we can guess.

"What Became of Our Flappers and Sheiks?" *McCall's,* LIII (October 1925), 12, 30, 42, 66, 69. Tandem articles by F. Scott and Zelda Sayre Fitzgerald.

Girls Believe in Girls

Being Certain Impressions of the Flapper's Successor

Back in 1912 the Castles, by making modern dancing respectable, brought the nice girl into the cabaret and sat her down next to the distinctly not-nice girl. At that moment the Era of the Flapper was born. Some ten commandments crashed in the confusion of the war, and afterwards there was a demand not to be let down from its excitement. There were books that extended the possibilities of freedom and there was a generation educated entirely by women, and hence malleable, who simply flowed out to the new horizons of the prewar liberals. By about 1922 youth had been thoroughly converted, or, as some reactionaries said, perverted, and the fun went out of it—the "flapper movement" proper was over.

But had the movement ever been really unsentimental, a real facing of anything except a little questionable biological data? (It is, for instance, doubtful whether a protracted physical courtship is a normal or healthy introduction to marriage, particularly for men.) On the contrary, the young girl making a present of herself to a swain stuck pretty close to the fictional pattern. She was Thackeray's Beatrix Esmond who, in 1912, turned up again in Wells' Tono-Bungay under the name Beatrice Normandy, and was passionately emulated by a very select and daring crop of London débutantes. The fascinating Beatrice begot the ladies of Michael Arlen, and of almost everyone else who dealt in heroic English girls—but I think the adolescent group in Chicago, who about 1915 discovered the automobile, were more nearly a spontaneous apparition. Anyhow, by the end of the war the whole thing was so drippy with sentimentality that the sob sisters got their teeth into it and the crowd took it up, and with the crowd there ran a woman of forty-four, a bit out of breath, in whom the flapper was somewhat surprised to recognize her own mother.

It was finished—yesterday's fashion—heavens, how horrible! Marching with the advance guard was one thing, trailing along with the herd was another, and straightaway individualism was born, and with it the modern and somewhat disturbing cult of the heroine.

Before speaking of this, it is well to remember that a true generation, one which forms a clearly marked type and is stamped with a certain unanimity of conduct and opinion, doesn't appear every three or four years. Roughly speaking, the girls who were, or would have been, débutantes in 1917–19 were the nucleus of the wild generation. Their numbers were swollen by older and younger girls who were determined not to miss anything, for the wild ones seemed to be having a good time. It is dispersed now to the country club, the European casino, the stage, and even the home, and is passing its thirtieth birthday.

There may not be another such generation until there is a new war, or new limits are marked out for new youth to surge into and fill. For youth is not original—remove the automobile and the bottom drops out of the whole hilarious spectacle which has amused the nation for a decade. The monkey strapped to a bicycle is, after all, without significance. What is worth examining is a changing of the heart.

II

When I was very young, many older girls still kept theatrical scrapbooks and waited by the stage door after matinées to see Elsie Janis or Ethel Barrymore come out. Maybe the cult of the heroine is an accentuated and intensified development of that, but I do not think so. I think women have come to believe that they have nothing of value to learn from men. Generally speaking, the man of intelligence either runs alone or seeks amusement in stimulating circles—in any case, he is rarely available; the business man brings to social intercourse little more than what he reads in the papers, together with a passionate desire to be entertained; so that, in the thousand and one women's worlds that cover the land, the male voice is represented largely by the effeminate and the weak, the parasite and the failure.

That the first of these groups has increased in size since the war is notorious. Certain words describing certain types are in everyone's vocabulary. Scarcely a popular woman in a large city but hasn't one or two in tow who can be counted on to take her part, appreciate her clothes, keep the ball of gossip rolling—and, especially, to be available.

If a somewhat bizarre locality can be put in evidence, one finds in Los Angeles a host of often charming and almost always pretty women partnered by countless actors, profile boys, costume designers, hangers-on, and people's brothers—with the addition of a few exceptionally tough-skinned business men on Saturday and Sunday nights. At how many parties have I watched the attractive girls slip quietly away to talk and joke with each other in the washroom, bored and impatient with such a world of men. And in the country at large a parallel mood exists.

With the general confusion as to what men want—"Shall I be fast or shall I be straight? Shall I help him succeed or join him only after he has? Shall I settle down or shall I keep young? Shall I have one child or four?"—these problems, once confined to certain classes, being now every girl's problems—they have begun to turn for approval, not to men, but to each other. "Crushes" were once a boarding-school phenomenon—now any sort of courageous individualism makes a woman the center of a cult. Not only do Edna Millay, Helen Wills, Geraldine Farrar, and the Queen of Roumania have their disciples, but there are passionately admiring voices for Aimée Semple McPherson and even Ruth Snyder. What effect has this woman worship on the young girl herself?

She is quieter—lest other girls might think her rowdy—and, with the same idea in mind, she has grown increasingly polite. She wants to be considered simple and sincere, because among girls emphasis is put on these qualities. She drinks less, save in the bored South and Middle West, where it is still the fashion. She knows "something about music," but is less likely to be a virtuoso of the piano, because, while one played for men, one talks about it for women. She knows something about calories but nothing about cooking, and for the same reason.

Yet she would gladly take up these things were she a little surer they led to distinction. Distinction is everything—not merely the distinction of Clara Bow but the distinction of Mme. Curie. It is the old American idealism, but functioning well outside the no longer all-absorbing home—restlessly seeking women messiahs, but indifferent to the self-appointed stuffed chemises of public life and grown skeptical about the causes for which their elders have battled these twenty years—and so, by a curious reaction become conservative, become cagy, waiting to see.

On the Riviera last summer there were English girls who still believed in men; you could tell by the deliberate outdoor swagger of their walk, by what they laughed at so heartily, as if they were still apologizing for having been born girls, and were being "good chaps" for critical elder brothers. But as for the others—you could only tell the Americans from the French because they were pretty—the negligence with which they obviously took their men was almost shocking. Outside of material matters, man's highest and most approved incarnation was "a good old horse"—be he fiancé, husband, or lover. The merely masculine was considered by turns stuffy, dull, tyrannical, or merely ludicrous.

I remember a girl responding to a desirable middle-aged party's inquiry as to whether he could smoke a cigar with: "Please do. There's nothing I like so much as a good cigar," and I remember the suppressed roar of hilarity that circled the table. It was the voice of another age; it was burlesque. Naturally, one wanted and needed men, but wanting to please them, positively *coddling* them in that fashion—that was another matter.

The Prince, the Hero, no longer exists, or rather fails to put in an appearance, for society, with its confusion and its wide-open doors, no longer offers the stability of thirty years ago. In New York it has been difficult for years to arrange a numerical superiority of men over women at débutante balls. All the young girl can be sure of when she comes out into "the world" is that she will meet plenty of males competent to stimulate her biological urges—for the heterogeneous stag line can do that, if nothing more.

Her current attitude toward moral questions is that of the country at large—in other words, the identification of virtue with chastity no longer exists among girls over twenty, and to pretend it does is just one of those things you are welcome to do if it gives you comfort. There are those of an older and purer generation who would have liked the present observer to have devoted his entire article to this phenomenon —and, at the end, would have virtuously thrown the magazine out the window. For America is composed, not of two sorts of people, but of two frames of mind: the first engaged in doing what it would like to do; the second pretending that such things do not exist. It is obvious to the most casually honest glance that we have taken over, in its entirety, the French lightness about sexual matters in speech and in deed—with the difference that in America this lightness extends to the young girl.

She is quieter about her rules of conduct, much less blatant and boastful than was her flapper sister—and I am reminded that back in the days of unbelievable inhibitions the girls who really necked didn't talk about it. Difficult as it is to make generalities, it is apparent through the thinning smoke that most of the barriers are pretty definitely down. Men, being reduced in the great national matriarchy to love-making animals, need no longer be considered in their masterful, priestly, and retributive aspect, demanding accounts and passing judgments, for then they were merely "being stupid"—and who cares, anyhow? There are increasing thousands of girls who choose to go their way alone.

Besides, the contemporary girl has thrown a mantle of good taste over much that was previously offensive. Absorbing manners from both her prewar mother and her postwar sister, she has chosen something from each, and, wandering over Europe, she displays a poise and self-confidence that makes the English girl seem immature and the French girl rigid and harsh. At this moment, she is our finest and most repre-sentative product from the point of view of beauty, charm, and courage, and it seems positively disloyal to wonder if progress does finally culminate in her insouciant promenade along the narrow steel girder of our prosperity. Yet the question remains whether any type so exquisitely achieved, so perennially unworried, will accomplish anything at all.

III

It is not my question—I expect wonders of them, literally. It is the poor young man I worry about—in such time as all but professional worriers spare for such matters. From the international circus on the Riviera one picks out the perfect flower of every race—the dark little Greek with a head by Praxiteles, the sun-colored Neapolitan virgin, the rose-pink Briton, the svelte Parisian—and she turns out generally to be Miss Mary Meriwether of Paris, Michigan, or Athens, Georgia—triumphantly and gratifyingly ours. To them the world is not the romantic mystery it was to us; even the past throws no shadow, since they believe in nobody but themselves.

Such loveliness cannot lack a voice to express it, nor such courage a way to spend itself—and, turning the medal, one guesses that such intolerable success will drive the defeated and repressed ones to justify themselves passionately by achievement. Something dynamic and incalculable that has always been inherent in American life, even when it was reduced to the fretful whine of the frontier woman—something that failed to fulfill itself in either the sentimental Gibson girl or the rowdy flapper—seems to have broken through the egg at last, and come into its own.

"Girls Believe in Girls," *Liberty*, vii (February 8, 1930), 22–24.

Autobiographical

What I Think and Feel at 25

By F. Scott Fitzgerald

*Author of "This Side of Paradise," "Flappers and Philosophers,"
and "The Beautiful and Damned"*

The man stopped me on the street. He was ancient, but not a mariner. He had a long beard and a glittering eye. I think he was a friend of the family's, or something.

"Say, Fitzgerald," he said, "say! Will you tell me this: What in the blinkety-blank-blank has a—has a man of your age got to go saying these pessimistic things for? What's the idea?" I tried to laugh him off. He told me that he and my grandfather had been boys together. After that, I had no wish to corrupt him. So I tried to laugh him off.

"Ha-ha-ha!" I said determinedly. "Ha-ha-ha!" And then I added, "Ha-ha! Well, I'll see you later."

With this I attempted to pass him by, but he seized my arm firmly and showed symptoms of spending the afternoon in my company.

"When I was a boy—" he began, and then he drew the picture that people always draw of what excellent, happy, care-free souls they were at twenty-five. That is, he told me all the things he liked to *think* he thought in the misty past.

I allowed him to continue. I even made polite grunts at intervals to express my astonishment. For I will be doing it myself some day. I will concoct for my juniors a Scott Fitzgerald that, it's safe to say, none of my contemporaries would at present recognize. But they will be old themselves then; and they will respect my concoction as I shall respect theirs. . . .

"And now," the happy ancient was concluding; "you are young, you have good health, you have made money, you are exceptionally happily married, you have achieved considerable success while you are still young enough to enjoy it—will you tell an innocent old man just why you write those—"

I succumbed. I would tell him. I began:

"Well, you see, sir, it seems to me that as a man gets older he grows more vulner—"

But I got no further. As soon as I began to talk he hurriedly shook my hand and departed. He did not want to listen. He did not care why I thought what I thought. He had simply felt the need of giving a little speech, and I had been the victim. His receding form disappeared with a slight wobble around the next corner.

"All right, you old bore," I muttered; "*don't* listen, then. You wouldn't understand, anyhow." I took an awful kick at a curbstone, as a sort of proxy, and continued my walk.

Now, that's the first incident. The second was when a man came to me not long ago from a big newspaper syndicate, and said:

"Mr. Fitzgerald, there's a rumor around New York that you and— ah—you and Mrs. Fitzgerald are going to commit suicide at thirty because you hate and dread middle-age. I want to give you some publicity in this matter by getting it up as a story for the feature sections of five hundred and fourteen Sunday newspapers. In one corner of the page will be—"

"Don't!" I cried, "I know: In one corner will stand the doomed couple, she with an arsenic sundae, he with an Oriental dagger. Both of them will have their eyes fixed on a large clock, on the face of which will be a skull and crossbones. In the other corner will be a big calendar with the date marked in red."

"That's it!" cried the syndicate man enthusiastically. "You've grasped the idea. Now, what we—"

"Listen here!" I said severely. "There is nothing in that rumor. Nothing whatever. When I'm thirty I won't be *this* me—I'll be somebody else. I'll have a different body, because it said so in a book I read once, and I'll have a different attitude on everything. I'll even be married to a different person—"

"Ah!" he interrupted, with an eager light in his eye, and produced a notebook. "That's very interesting."

"No, no, no!" I cried hastily. "I mean my wife will be different."

"I see. You plan a divorce."

"No! I mean—"

"Well, it's all the same. Now, what we want, in order to fill out this story, is a lot of remarks about petting-parties. Do you think the—ah— petting-party is a serious menace to the Constitution? And, just to link it up, can we say that your suicide will be largely on account of past petting-parties?"

"See here!" I interrupted in despair. "Try to understand. I don't know what petting-parties have to do with the question. I have always dreaded age, because it invariably increases the vulner—"

But, as in the case of the family friend, I got no further. The syndicate man grasped my hand firmly. He shook it. Then he muttered something about interviewing a chorus girl who was reported to have an anklet of solid platinum, and hurried off.

That's the second incident. You see, I had managed to tell two different men that "age increased the vulner—" But they had not been interested. The old man had talked about himself and the syndicate man had talked about petting-parties. When I began to talk about the "vulner—" they both had sudden engagements.

So, with one hand on the Eighteenth Amendment and the other hand on the serious part of the Constitution, I have taken an oath that I will tell somebody my story.

As a man grows older it stands to reason that his vulnerability increases. Three years ago, for instance, I could be hurt in only one way —through myself. If my best friend's wife had her hair torn off by an electric washing-machine, I was grieved, of course. I would make my friend a long speech full of "old mans," and finish up with a paragraph from Washington's Farewell Address; but when I'd finished I could go to a good restaurant and enjoy my dinner as usual. If my second cousin's husband had an artery severed while having his nails manicured, I will not deny that it was a matter of considerable regret to me. But when I heard the news I did *not* faint and have to be taken home in a passing laundry wagon.

In fact I was pretty much invulnerable. I put up a conventional wail whenever a ship was sunk or a train got wrecked; but I don't suppose, if the whole city of Chicago had been wiped out, I'd have lost a night's sleep over it—unless something led me to believe that St. Paul was the next city on the list. Even then I could have moved my luggage over to Minneapolis and rested pretty comfortably all night.

But that was three years ago when I was still a young man. I was only twenty-two. When I said anything the book reviewers didn't like, they could say, "Gosh! That certainly is callow!" And that finished me. Label it "callow," and that was enough.

Well, now I'm twenty-five I'm not callow any longer—at least not so that I can notice it when I look in an ordinary mirror. Instead, I'm vulnerable. I'm vulnerable in every way.

For the benefit of revenue agents and moving-picture directors who may be reading this magazine I will explain that vulnerable means easily wounded. Well, that's it. I'm more easily wounded. I can not only be wounded in the chest, the feelings, the teeth, the bank account; but I can be wounded in the *dog*. Do I make myself clear? In the dog.

No, that isn't a new part of the body just discovered by the Rockefeller Institute. I mean a real dog. I mean if anyone gives my family dog to the dog-catcher he's hurting *me* almost as much as he's hurting the dog. He's hurting me *in* the dog. And if our doctor says to me tomorrow, "That child of yours isn't going to be a blonde after all," well, he's wounded me in a way I couldn't have been wounded in before, because I never before had a child to be wounded in. And if my daughter grows up and when she's sixteen elopes with some fellow from Zion City who believes the world is flat—I wouldn't write this except that she's only six months old and can't quite read yet, so it won't put any ideas in her head—why, then I'll be wounded again.

About being wounded through your wife I will not enter into, as it is a delicate subject. I will not say anything about my case. But I have private reasons for knowing that if anybody said to your wife one day that it was a shame she *would* wear yellow when it made her look so peaked, you would suffer violently, within six hours afterward, for what that person said.

"Attack him through his wife!" "Kidnap his child!" "Tie a tin can to his dog's tail!" How often do we hear those slogans in life, not to mention in the movies. And how they make me wince! Three years ago, you could have yelled them outside my window all through a summer night, and I wouldn't have batted an eye. The only thing that would have aroused me would have been: "Wait a minute. I think I can pot him from here."

I used to have about ten square feet of skin vulnerable to chills and fevers. Now I have about twenty. I have not personally enlarged— the twenty feet includes the skin of my family—but I might as well have, because if a chill or fever strikes any bit of that twenty feet of skin *I* begin to shiver.

And so I ooze gently into middle age; for the true middle-age is not the acquirement of years, but the acquirement of a family. The incomes of the childless have wonderful elasticity. Two people require a room and a bath; couple with child require the millionaire's suite on the sunny side of the hotel.

So let me start the religious part of this article by saying that if the Editor thought he was going to get something young and happy—yes, and callow—I have got to refer him to my daughter, if she will give dictation. If anybody thinks that I am callow they ought to see her—she's so callow it makes me laugh. It even makes her laugh, too, to think how callow she is. If any literary critics saw her they'd have a nervous breakdown right on the spot. But, on the other hand, anybody writing to me, an editor or anybody else, is writing to a middle-aged man.

Well, I'm twenty-five, and I have to admit that I'm pretty well satisfied with *some* of that time. That is to say, the first five years seemed to go all right—but the last twenty! They have been a matter of violently contrasted extremes. In fact, this has struck me so forcibly that from time to time I have kept charts, trying to figure out the years when I was closest to happy. Then I get mad and tear up the charts.

Skipping that long list of mistakes which passes for my boyhood I will say that I went away to preparatory school at fifteen, and that my two years there were wasted, were years of utter and profitless unhappiness. I was unhappy because I was cast into a situation where everybody thought I ought to behave just as they behaved—and I didn't have the courage to shut up and go my own way, anyhow.

For example, there was a rather dull boy at school named Percy, whose approval, I felt, for some unfathomable reason, I must have. So, for the sake of this negligible cipher, I started out to let as much of my mind as I had under mild cultivation sink back into a state of heavy underbrush. I spent hours in a damp gymnasium fooling around with a muggy basket-ball and working myself into a damp, muggy rage, when I wanted, instead, to go walking in the country.

And all this to please Percy. He thought it was the thing to do. If you didn't go through the damp business every day you were "morbid." That was his favorite word, and it had me frightened. I didn't want to be morbid. So I became muggy instead.

Besides, Percy was dull in classes; so I used to pretend to be dull also. When I wrote stories I wrote them secretly, and felt like a criminal.

If I gave birth to any idea that did not appeal to Percy's pleasant, vacant mind I discarded the idea at once and felt like apologizing.

Of course Percy never got into college. He went to work and I have scarcely seen him since, though I understand that he has since become an undertaker of considerable standing. The time I spent with him was wasted; but, worse than that, I did not enjoy the wasting of it. At least, he had nothing to give me, and I had not the faintest reasons for caring what he thought or said. But when I discovered this it was too late.

The worst of it is that this same business went on until I was twenty-two. That is, I'd be perfectly happy doing just what I wanted to do, when somebody would begin shaking his head and saying:

"Now see here, Fitzgerald, you mustn't go on doing that. It's—it's morbid."

And I was always properly awed by the word "morbid," so I quit what I wanted to do and what it was good for me to do, and did what some other fellow wanted me to do. Every once in a while, though, I used to tell somebody to go to the devil; otherwise I never would have done anything at all.

In officers' training camp during 1917 I started to write a novel. I would begin work at it every Saturday afternoon at one and work like mad until midnight. Then I would work at it from six Sunday morning until six Sunday night, when I had to report back to barracks. I was thoroughly enjoying myself.

After a month three friends came to me with scowling faces:

"See here, Fitzgerald, you ought to use the week-ends in getting some good rest and recreation. The way you use them is—is morbid!"

That word convinced me. It sent the usual shiver down my spine. The next week end I laid the novel aside, went into town with the others and danced all night at a party. But I began to worry about my novel. I worried so much that I returned to camp, not rested, but utterly miserable. I *was* morbid then. But I never went to town again. I finished the novel. It was rejected; but a year later I rewrote it and it was published under the title, "This Side of Paradise."

But before I rewrote it I had a list of "morbids," chalked up against people that, placed end to end, would have reached to the nearest lunatic asylum. It was morbid:

1st. To get engaged without enough money to marry
2d. To leave the advertising business after three months

3d. To want to write at all
4th. To think I could
5th. To write about "silly little boys and girls that nobody wants to read
     about"

And so on, until a year later, when I found to my surprise that everybody had been only kidding—they had believed all their lives that writing was the only thing for me, and had hardly been able to keep from telling me all the time.

But I am really not old enough to begin drawing morals out of my own life to elevate the young. I will save that pastime until I am sixty; and then, as I have said, I will concoct a Scott Fitzgerald who will make Benjamin Franklin look like a lucky devil who loafed into prominence. Even in the above account I have managed to sketch the outline of a small but neat halo. I take it all back. I am twenty-five years old. I wish I had ten million dollars, and never had to do another lick of work as long as I live.

But as I *do* have to keep at it, I might as well declare that the chief thing I've learned so far is: If you don't know much—well, nobody else knows much more. And nobody knows half as much about your own interests as *you* know.

If you believe in anything very strongly—including yourself—and if you go after that thing alone, you end up in jail, in heaven, in the headlines, or in the largest house in the block, according to what you started after. If you *don't* believe in anything very strongly—including yourself—you go along, and enough money is made out of you to buy an automobile for some other fellow's son, and you marry if you've got time, and if you do you have a lot of children, whether you have time or not, and finally you get tired and you die.

If you're in the second of those two classes you have the most fun before you're twenty-five. If you're in the first, you have it afterward.

You see, if you're in the first class you'll frequently be called a darn fool—or worse. That was as true in Philadelphia about 1727 as it is to-day. Anybody knows that a kid that walked around town munching a loaf of bread and not caring what anybody thought was a darn fool. It stands to reason! But there are a lot of darn fools who get their pictures in the schoolbooks—with their names under the pictures. And the sensible fellows, the ones that had time to laugh, well, their pictures are in there, too. But their *names* aren't—and the laughs look sort of frozen on their faces.

The particular sort of darn fool I mean ought to remember that he's *least* a darn fool when he's being *called* a darn fool. The main thing is to be your own kind of a darn fool.

(The above advice is of course only for darn fools *under* twenty-five. It may be all wrong for darn fools over twenty-five.)

I don't know why it is that when I start to write about being twenty-five I suddenly begin to write about darn fools. I do not see any connection. Now, if I were asked to write about darn fools, I would write about people who have their front teeth filled with gold, because a friend of mine did that the other day, and after being mistaken for a jewelry store three times in one hour he came up and asked me if I thought it showed too much. As I am a kind man, I told him I would not have noticed it if the sun hadn't been so strong on it. I asked him why he had it done.

"Well," he said, "the dentist told me a porcelain filling never lasted more than ten years."

"Ten years! Why, you may be dead in ten years."

"That's true."

"Of course it'll be nice that all the time you're in your coffin you'll never have to worry about your teeth."

And it occurred to me that about half the people in the world are always having their front teeth filled with gold. That is, they're figuring on twenty years from now. Well, when you're young it's all right figuring your success a long ways ahead—if you don't make it *too* long. But as for your pleasure—your front teeth!—it's better to figure on to-day.

And that's the second thing I learned while getting vulnerable and middle-aged. Let me recapitulate:

1st. I think that compared to what you know about your own business nobody else knows *any*thing. And if anybody knows more about it than you do, then it's *his* business and you're *his* man, not your own. And as soon as your business becomes *your* business you'll know more about it than anybody else.

2d. Never have your front teeth filled with gold.

And now I will stop pretending to be a pleasant young fellow and disclose my real nature. I will prove to you, if you have not found it out already, that I have a mean streak and nobody would like to have me for a son.

I do not like old people. They are always talking about their "experience"—and very few of them have any. In fact, most of them go on making the same mistakes at fifty and believing in the same white list of approved twenty-carat lies that they did at seventeen. And it all starts with my old friend vulnerability.

Take a woman of thirty. She is considered lucky if she has allied herself to a multitude of things; her husband, her children, her home, her servant. If she has three homes, eight children, and fourteen servants, she is considered luckier still. (This, of course, does not generally apply to more husbands).

Now, when she was young she worried only about herself; but now she must be worried by *any* trouble occurring to *any* of these people or things. She is ten times as vulnerable. Moreover, she can never break one of these ties or relieve herself of one of these burdens except at the cost of great pain and sorrow to herself. They are the things that break her, and yet they are the most precious things in life.

In consequence, everything which doesn't go to make her secure, or at least to give her a sense of security, startles and annoys her. She acquires only the useless knowledge found in cheap movies, cheap novels, and the cheap memoirs of titled foreigners.

By this time her husband also has become suspicious of anything gay or new. He seldom addresses her, except in a series of profound grunts, or to ask whether she has sent his shirts out to the laundry. At the family dinner on Sunday he occasionally gives her some fascinating statistics on party politics, some opinions from that morning's newspaper editorial.

But after thirty, both husband and wife know in their hearts that the game is up. Without a few cocktails social intercourse becomes a torment. It is no longer spontaneous; it is a convention by which they agree to shut their eyes to the fact that the other men and women they know are tired and dull and fat, and yet must be put up with as politely as they themselves are put up with in their turn.

I have seen many happy young couples—but I have seldom seen a happy home after husband and wife are thirty. Most homes can be divided into four classes:

1st. Where the husband is a pretty conceited guy who thinks that a dinky insurance business is a lot harder than raising babies, and that everybody ought to kow-tow to him at home. He is the kind whose sons usually get away from home as soon as they can walk.

2d. When the wife has got a sharp tongue and the martyr complex, and thinks she's the only woman in the world that ever had a child. This is probably the unhappiest home of all.

3d. Where the children are always being reminded how nice it was of the parents to bring them into the world, and how they ought to respect their parents for being born in 1870 instead of 1902.

4th. Where everything is for the children. Where the parents pay much more for the children's education than they can afford, and spoil them unreasonably. This usually ends by the children being ashamed of the parents.

And yet I think that marriage is the most satisfactory institution we have. I'm simply stating my belief that when Life has used us for its purposes it takes away all our attractive qualities and gives us, instead, ponderous but shallow convictions of our own wisdom and "experience."

Needless to say, as old people run the world, an enormous camouflage has been built up to hide the fact that only young people are attractive or important.

Having got in wrong with many of the readers of this article, I will now proceed to close. If you don't agree with me on any minor points you have a right to say: "Gosh! He certainly is callow!" and turn to something else. Personally I do not consider that I am callow, because I do not see how anybody of my age could be callow. For instance, I was reading an article in this magazine a few months ago by a fellow named Ring Lardner that says he is thirty-five, and it seemed to me how young and happy and care free he was in comparison with me.

Maybe he is vulnerable, too. He did not say so. Maybe when you get to be thirty-five you do not *know* any more how vulnerable you *are*. All I can say is that if he ever gets to be twenty-five again, which is very unlikely, maybe he will agree with me. The older I grow the more I get so I don't know anything. If I had been asked to do this article about five years ago it might have been worth reading.

"What I Think and Feel at 25," *American Magazine*, xciv (September 1922), 16, 17, 136–140.

A Short Autobiography

(With Acknowledgments to Nathan)

1913

The four defiant Canadian Club whiskeys at the Susquehanna in Hackensack.

1914

The Great Western Champagne at the Trent House in Trenton and the groggy ride back to Princeton.

1915

The Sparkling Burgundy at Bustanoby's. The raw whiskey in White Sulphur Springs, Montana, when I got up on a table and sang, "Won't you come up," to the cowmen. The Stingers at Tate's in Seattle listening to Ed Muldoon, "that clever chap."

1916

The apple brandy nipped at in the locker-room at the White Bear Yacht Club.

1917

A first Burgundy with Monsignor X at the Lafayette. Blackberry brandy and whiskey with Tom at the old Nassau Inn.

1918

The Bourbon smuggled to officers' rooms by bellboys at the Seelbach in Louisville.

1919

The Sazzarac Cocktails brought up from New Orleans to Montgomery to celebrate an important occasion.

1920

Red wine at Mollat's. Absinthe cocktails in a hermetically sealed apartment in the Royalton. Corn liquor by moonlight in a deserted aviation field in Alabama.

1921

Leaving our champagne in the Savoy Grill on the Fourth of July when a drunk brought up two obviously Piccadilly ladies. Yellow Chartreuse in the Via Balbini in Rome.

1922

Kaly's crème de cacao cocktails in St. Paul. My own first and last manufacture of gin.

1923

Oceans of Canadian ale with R. Lardner in Great Neck, Long Island.

1924

Champagne cocktails on the Minnewaska, and apologizing to the old lady we kept awake. Graves Kressman at Villa Marie in Valescure and consequent arguments about British politics with the nursery governess. Porto Blancs at a time of sadness. Mousseux bought by a Frenchman in a garden at twilight. Chambéry Fraise with the Seldes on their honeymoon. The local product ordered on the wise advice of a friendly priest at Orvieto, when we were asking for French wines.

1925

A dry white wine that "won't travel," made a little south of Sorrento, that I've never been able to trace. Plot coagulating—a sound of hoofs and bugles. The gorgeous Vin d'Arbois at La Reine Pédauque. Champagne cocktails in the Ritz sweatshop in Paris. Poor wines from Nicolas. Kirsch in a Burgundy inn against the rain with E. Hemingway.

1926

Uninteresting St. Estèphe in a desolate hole called Salies-de-Béarn. Sherry on the beach at La Garoupe. Gerald M.'s grenadine cocktail, the one flaw to make everything perfect in the world's most perfect house. Beer and weenies with Grace, Charlie, Ruth, and Ben at Antibes before the deluge.

1927

Delicious California "Burgundy-type" wine in one of the Ambassador bungalows in Los Angeles. The beer I made in Delaware that had a dark inescapable sediment. Cases of dim, cut, unsatisfactory whiskey in Delaware.

1928

The Pouilly with Bouillabaisse at Prunier's in a time of discouragement.

1929

A feeling that all liquor has been drunk and all it can do for one has been experienced, and yet—"*Garçon, un Chablis-Mouton 1902, et pour commencer, une petite carafe de vin rose. C'est ça—merci.*"

—*F. Scott Fitzgerald*

"A Short Autobiography (With Acknowledgments to Nathan)," *New Yorker*, v (May 25, 1929), 22–23.

Unclassified

THIS IS A MAGAZINE

A Group of Familiar Characters from the American Periodical World

By F. Scott Fitzgerald

The scene is the vast and soggy interior of a magazine—not powder or pistol, but paper and popular. Over the outer curtain careens a lady on horseback in five colours. With one hand she raises a cup of tea to her glossy lips while with the other she follows through on a recent mashie shot, meanwhile keeping one rich-tinted, astounding eye upon the twist of her service and its mate on the volume of pleasant poetry in her other hand. The rising of the curtain reveals the back-drop as a patch-work of magazine covers. The furniture includes a table on which lies a single periodical, to convey the abstraction 'Magazine', and around it your players sit on chairs plastered with advertisements. Each actor holds a placard bearing the name of the character represented. For example, the Edith Wharton Story holds a placard which reads "By Edith Wharton, in three parts."

Near (but not in!) the left hand stage box is stationed a gentleman in underwear holding a gigantic placard which announces that "THIS IS A MAGAZINE".

As the Curtain rises the audience discovers the Edith Wharton Story attempting a tête à tête *with a somewhat arrogant British Serial.*

THE EDITH WHARTON STORY (*a bit bitterly*): And before I could so much as shoot a saucy subtlety, there I was plumped down between an odious fable in broken Yiddish and this—this affair next to me.

'This affair' is a very vulgar and proletarian Baseball Yarn who sprawls colloquially in his chair.

THE BASEBALL YARN: Was you speakin' to me, lady?

(*On the lady's part a frigid and Jamesian silence. She looks, by the way, like a lady who has lived all her life in three-room apartments and had her nerves ruined by impulsive elevator boys.*)

THE BASEBALL YARN (*in brutal soliloquy*): If they could jes' stick a guy in a magazine where he could borrer one good chewterbacker!

A DETECTIVE STORY (*in a tense whisper*): There's one in my third paragraph. But be quiet and be careful not to break any retorts.

THE BASEBALL STORY (*facetiously*): Or make any, eh? Ha! Ha! Ha!

THE BRITISH SERIAL (*to The Edith Wharton Story*): I say, who's that little story over near the Editorial? Don't fancy I've seen her before since I've been running.

THE EDITH WHARTON STORY (*lowering her voice*): My Dear Man, she's a nobody. Seems to have no family—nothing but a past.

THE BRITISH SERIAL: She has a certain charm, but a deuced vulgar plot. (*He yawns.*)

THE BASEBALL YARN (*in a rude aside to the Detective Story*): The noble Duke looks a bit padded his own self. Say! Pipe the old grampa asleep on his advertisements.

THE DETECTIVE STORY: That's the Robert Chambers Serial. He's through this issue.

THE BASEBALL YARN: Kinda like that little thing next to him. New in here ain't she?

THE DETECTIVE STORY: New and scared.

THE BASEBALL YARN: Looks as if she was wrote with a soft pencil.

THE DETECTIVE STORY: Overdressed! Her illustrations cost more than she did.

(*Several chairs down, a little Love Poem leans tenderly across a story to another Love Poem.*)

THE FIRST LOVE POEM: I adore your form.

THE SECOND LOVE POEM: You've got a good figure yourself—in your second line. But your meter looks a little strained.

THE FIRST LOVE POEM: You are the caesura in the middle of all my lines. Alas! someone will cut you out and paste you on a mirror—or send you to his sweetheart with "Isn't this lovely!" scrawled across you—or passepartout you.

THE SECOND LOVE POEM (*coyly*): Now you just get right back to your own page.

(*At this point, the Robert Chambers Story awakens with a start, and walks rheumatically over to the Edith Wharton Story.*)

THE ROBERT CHAMBERS STORY (*asthmatically*): May I join you?

THE EDITH WHARTON STORY (*acidly*): You seemed well content to flirt with that sentimental little piece, behind the advertisements.

THE ROBERT CHAMBERS STORY: On the contrary, she bores me. Every character in her is born in wedlock. Still she's a relief from the Commercial yarns.

THE BRITISH SERIAL: You can be thankful you haven't got your feet between two smelly soap advertisements. (*He points to what appears to be a paralytic dwarf at his feet.*) Look! There's my Synopsis of Preceding Chapters all tangled up again.

THE ROBERT CHAMBERS STORY: Thank heavens, I'm published! I've had some annoying experiences in the last eight months. In one issue there was a Penrod Story next to me making so much noise that I couldn't hear my own love scenes.

THE EDITH WHARTON STORY (*cruelly*): Never mind. The shop-girls could fill them in with their eyes closed.

THE ROBERT CHAMBERS STORY (*sourly*): My dear lady, your climax is on crooked.

THE EDITH WHARTON STORY: At least I have one. They tell me you drag horribly.

THE BASEBALL YARN: Well, if the swells ain't scrappin' with each other!

THE EDITH WHARTON STORY: No one invited your comments.

THE BASEBALL YARN: Go on! You're full of dots!

THE EDITH WHARTON STORY: At least, I'm not full of mixed metaphors!

THE ROBERT CHAMBERS STORY: Weak repartee! Columnist's humor.

(*A new voice, very oratorical and sonorous, breaks in. It is—*)

THE POLITICAL ARTICLE: Come! There's nothing irreconcilable there. There's no knot so tight that there isn't a way out of the labyrinth.

THE LITTLE STORY WITHOUT A FAMILY (*timidly*): Dear folks, it's a sweet cosy world. So don't poison your little lungs with naughty, unkind words.

THE BRITISH SERIAL: Shades of those Porter women!

THE LITTLE STORY WITHOUT A FAMILY: You don't know what abuse is until you've been returned with "Join the Navy" stamped on your envelope.

THE BRITISH SERIAL: If I had been fished out of the waste-basket, I shouldn't boast about it!

THE BASEBALL YARN: Let her alone! She's a honest Gurl. I'll kick you one in the conclusion!

(*They rise and square off, eying each other menacingly. A contagious excitement springs up; the Basil King Revelation forgets its credulous queens and tears over; an Efficiency Article loses its head and runs wildly through the issue, and even the illustrations leap out of their borders, the half-tones vying democratically with the Ben Days, in reaching the scene. The excitement spreads to the advertisements. Mr. Madison Whims of Seattle falls into a jar of No-Hairo Cold Cream. A Health and Strength Giant arrives clinging to an earphone; a Short Story Course becomes covered with Rat Poison. The Circulation increases.*

In fact, for a minute everything is something awful! Just as the number's minutes seem as numbered as its pages, a stentorian voice proceeds from the Table of Contents, an efficient-looking gentleman with a megaphone who has been sitting unnoticed in the orchestra: "Places! A Reader!" A hush falls; everyone scurries back into position, just as a thick and impenetrable dark descends upon the stage through which emerge, as an emanation from limbo, the large glossy eyes of the cover girl, on horseback in five colours.

A voice comes out of the dark and, in the great quiet, it is like the voice of God.)

THE VOICE: Wonder if there's anything in this worth readin'. Sure is some queen on the cover!

AN INSERT JOKE (*laughing feebly*): Hee! Hee! Hee! (*It is the grotesque and horrible cackle of an old man.*)

The lights go on to show that the curtain is now down. In front of it sits a reader, a lone stage hand. He wears an expression of tremendous and triumphant boredom. He is reading the magazine.

"This is a Magazine," *Vanity Fair*, xv (December 1920), 71.

REMINISCENSES OF DONALD STEWART

By F. Scott Fitzgerald

(In the Manner of . . . .)

Sitting surrounded by my children and fortified by many tons of coal at $20 a ton, against the northern winter it pleases me to look back upon the days of my youth. Back and back, as the flames flicker, I seem to gaze upon those very first moments of my literary career and the years give up a certain name to be pondered upon—the name of a companion of my youth, now, like me, a white-beard grown old in the service of letters—his name, Donald Ogden Stewart.

How well do I remember our first meeting! It was at a dinner of Sidney Strong's at the University club. Donald Ogden Stewart said:

"How do you do?"

And quick as a flash I answered.

"Very well thank you."

With these first words we seemed to understand that there was a kinship between us. We were not monkeys, but MEN. There was no doubt about it. We could talk, we could laugh, we could shimmee—

Ah, the old days! Those quaint old fashioned dances like the shimmee—How different from the rough boisterous steps I see performed by the youngsters of today. But I depart from the subject, the old man's mind is feeble and it wanders.

The first thing he said to me, I think, was: "Let's commit a burglary!"

Oh the simple hearts of those days, the pleasures!

Then he wanted us to break the windows of an undertaker just established on Summit ave. I remember the smile of amusement that this quaint old idea aroused. But that was Don—innocent, trying always to see things for the best. After that, I remember him at a party. He caused to be thrown on a white screen, upside down, a picture of a religious revival in South Africa and in his naive and gullible way he thought, he believed, mind you, that this was the photograph of the reunion of a certain family well known in St. Paul. He believed it! And of course everybody was lauging at him. Nobody believed it was that family. Why, the people in the picture were upside down. It was absurd.

Then at another party he pretended that he was a ventriloquist. That's what he told everybody. And anybody who was at the party could see that he was not. All it took was common sense to see that he wasn't. The doll that he was supposed to have in his lap was not a doll. It was a real fellow. How he thought he'd get away with it I don't know. Everybody that came knew it wasn't a doll even when it moved its mouth and head. So they gave poor Don the laugh as usual and made a guy of him. He felt pretty cheap after that.

How cheerful was St. Paul while he was here. He made all the women feel beautiful and all the men feel witty. He went to the opening of a "one-building university" down in southern Minnesota, enrolled as a freshman, made the football team and was initiated into the Delta Omicron Psi fraternity. Then his vacation was over and he came back to St. Paul to his position—putting up telephone wires or tearing them down or something.

When the snow came he would throw snowballs against my window about midnight and we would stroll out Summit ave. wondering if we had the nerve to call on Father Barron and start a small hours discussion as to the ascetic ideals of the 13th century or whether, after all, we hadn't better break the undertaker's window to assert the sacrosenctity of Summit ave. against the invasions of mortuary commerce.

Sometimes, when the snow covered boulevard was deserted, we would give his favorite Colgate college cher: "Comes out like a ribbon, lies flat on the brush"—or he would speculate as to how he could inject his synthetic gin of humor into an imitation vermouth party that promised to be awfully dull.

It's not the same town without him—so say many of us. A scandal is only a scandal, but he could turn a Sunday school picnic into a public holiday. But we were all young then. And as I look around at my white haired compatriots I wonder that the old days have gone. Ah, that was away back before the arms conference, when Fatty Arbuckle was still respectable, when bobbed hair was considered daring. Sic transit. The author of "A Parody Outline of History" and I are old men. I realize at last that our work is behind us and our day is done.

"Reminiscenses of Donald Stewart," *St. Paul Daily News*, December 11, 1921, City Life Section, p. 6.

Weather Rotten

THE ST. PAUL DAILY DIRGE

Mortuary Edition

PRICE—A SWEET KISS.   ST. PAUL, MINNESOTA, FRIDAY, JANUARY 13, 1922.   VOL. I, NO. 1.

COTILLION IS SAD FAILURE

Frightful Orgy at University Club

The benedict's cotillion given Friday, the 13th, was the worst social failure of the year. In a sordid first fight started by Mr. William Motter four noses were broken and one removable bridge was bent out of all recognition.

The fight was said to have started because some remark derogatory to Yale was made before Mr. Motter.

The "Bad Luck Ball," as it was called by the vain, shallow and frivolous society people who were present, was opened by Gov. Preus, who did a tasty clog dance with Mrs. L. P. Ordway, Jr. (the Twin City correspondent for Town Topics). This was followed by a piano, zither and harp number rendered by Mrs. William Motter and Mrs. Samuel Ray, who is visiting here from her home in Jersey City, N. J.

Mr. Homer Sweeney, who with Mr. Clifford Corning was to have led the cotillion, unfortunately arrived in no condition to lead anything. In fact the only leading in which he participated was when he was led from the room by Mr. Eddie Saunders, whose feelings were naturally outraged by this performance.

Mr. Ted White, the well-known Harvard lacrosse player, wore a braided surtout of feathered duveteen and a diamond tiara. Mr. Alvah Warren was splendid in a Worth creation with slashed pockets and a pearl and cocoanut stomacher.

Mrs. C. O. Kalman was there, in rags as usual. Mrs. Samuel Ray wore a dress of pink gingham, a Woolworth creation, and a beautiful imitation diamond.

In fact the whole party was simply obnoxious. Nobody had any luck at all, and when it was over the two leaders were presented with large life-sized lemons in thanks for their wretched services.

It is hoped that these vain, frivolous peacocks who strut through the gorgeous vistas of the exclusive and corrupt St. Paul clubs will learn to conduct themselves in a more normal, wholesome way.

"It is disgusting," said Mr. T. J. Bunk, the well-known old settler. "In my day things were different. When we danced we did not do the toddle or any of the modern lascivious dances. We stuck to the good old lancers and the shimmee. In those days it was the proper thing to have biblical readings during the evening and the festivities always closed with a good rousing prayer. We did not have scotch and rye then or any of these immoral dishes like caviare and anchovy. A couple of doughnuts and a pint of moonshine apiece for everybody was all we needed. We were red-blooded, bulge-chest, two-fisted he men in those days, and don't you forget it."

ENTERTAINS FOR YALE PROFESSOR

LAWYER LANGUISHES IN LOCKUP.

Mr. Bennet Ordway, a young lawyer of the city, was arrested on the corner of Selby and Western Aves. for singing a tube of Peperoni tooth paste, when, for W. A. Fiott, the well-known druggist. Fortunately Mr. Ordway's theft was observed by Mr. Fiott's little assistant, Carl Schumacher, and the youth yelled lustily for aid during the night.

Flax Man Fears Fluke

Mr. Elmore Archer was thrown into a heavy gloom this evening when the news reached St. Paul that flax had fallen to 48 cents. He has sold his Deltwood home to Mr. Otto Finkel bums, the well-known farrier and will spend next summer at Bald Eagle lake. He has resigned from the White Bear Yacht club and been elected a member of the Phalen Boat Club. He is expected to go still lower. Mr Archer says he has ceased to care.

Business Rotten, Says Bootlegger

Mr. Chuck Kennedy, a well known bootlegger of this vicinity, gave out an interview to our reporter in which he says that business is no good.

Mr. Kennedy has just returned from the Canadian border with a truckload of Scotch whisky.

Boost St. Paul. Patronize local bootleggers!

NO STILLS IN STILLWATER, SAYS CONVICT

William Skinner, better known as "Hardboiled Billy," for years a notorious safe cracker and gunman, was released from Stillwater last night, after having served an eight-year term. He has lost faith in the state prison, perfectly white and has had trouble as he makes the warden ponder.

"The 13 happiest years of my life," he said, as he walked away with our reporter. "Nothing to worry about," Mr. Skinner will soon publish his book of prison verses "Bread and Water."

BIG BUSINESS MAN IS INTERESTED IN BODIES

Mr. Frederick Ettinger of this city is said to be interested in designing automobile bodies. Visit his shop some day in the cellar of the Manns building. He says that since the automobile crashed, business has been a failure. He is reported to have referred to friends' double skies as "spare."

GROWS EYELASHES OVER NIGHT

Matron Surprises Friends by Her Vivid Orbs.

Mrs. F. Scott Fitzgerald had always wanted eyes with long eyelashes and now she is not ashamed to go anywhere.

"There is a beauty parlor on every street in the town," said Mrs. Fitzgerald, "and it will remove them with success."—and settlement.

SELLS SECOND HAND AND THIRD HAND CARS FOR NEW

Mr. John Upham and partner, Mr. Paul Kalman, brought before Judge Eddie Saunders of the county probate court, were accused by the county prosecutor of registering old models of Knox and Hudsons cars and selling them to unsuspecting farmers as brand new, it's some was discovered because he found in return the gears slacked from the radiator of a car he had bought from Mr Birkmire. The farmer to whom he passed it on was found peeved out on the Stillwater Road shortly afterward.

MRS. ALEX McDONALD, MRS. JULE HANNAFORD AND MRS. WILLIAM GRAVES STROLLING ON 5TH ST.

Chilier in Chile, Newlyweds Wire

As we go to press the following telegram has been received, addressed to "The Benedict Bad Luck Ball." We print it here:

"VALPARAISO, Chile, New Year's Day—We are very happy. Sorry we cannot be with you tonight. All best luck to the party.
"MR. AND MRS. Donato Rossi."

Mr. and Mrs. T. DENISON ROSSI.
Mrs. T. Denison Rossi and husband expect to spend two months in Chile, after which they will return to St. Paul. They have rented the J. J. Hill home on Summit ave.

Saxophones

PHOTOGRAPH OF ANCIENT MUSICAL INSTRUMENT USED IN WARS OF THE ROSES.

Foley Fined for Fizz

Frederick Foley, H. D., is accused of selling gin permits. The class of Dr. Foley arrested Fri's last year for practicing without a license, takes up space but week in a different form. He was stabbing at the intersection of Victor & Robert Ave., making out gin prescriptions of which 10 were found under his busy income soul.

MRS. T. L. WANN, JR. IN DASHING BATHING SUIT.

"Times Are Tough," Says Labor Leader

"Times are punk," said Mr. Norman Irving in the last night when interfered in his most at little funeral we had.

Answers all, "It's all we can do to buy any children to wash next years. My wife and Mrs. John Ordway are opening a millinery shop on 5th st. In the spring and that may help some.

A jailor's god is low."

ENTERTAINS FOR YALE PROFESSOR

Mr. William Motter, the president of the Yale Alumni association of St. Paul and one of the most ardent Yale men in the city, entertained in his office this afternoon for Mr. William Leon Phelps, the Yale professor. The meeting was conducted by Mr. Motter leading the Yale men in Bright College Years. Mr. Motley has a son entering Yale this fall.

Princeton was represented on the present occasion by Mr. Theodore Driscoll.

PROMINENT PLUMBER IS PESSIMISTIC

"Things are terrible," said Mr. John C. Ordway, sitting in a luke-warm bath-tub in the Crane stairway "plumbing shop on Selby ave. "Bolshevism is the only thing that will survive. Crane fixtures are on the rocks and expect to fall before spring."

Mr. Ordway is a well-known graduate of the Union Theological seminary.

JAZZ JANITOR HAS GOOD XMAS

Mr. Daniel Calhoun, the popular janitor of the Lowry building, is reported to have had a successful Christmas. Tips from satisfied clients totaled up to more than $17 at the smiling janitor in low new overalls told our reporter this morning.

"Nothing doesn't fix the floor," he added gracefully. "So long!"

PORTRAIT OF MR. TED BROWN.

"WHY DIE?" FUR MAN DEMANDS

"I never expect to die" says Mr. John Manucci, formerly editor of the Twin City Reporter, and now in the fur business.

"How?" he was asked.

"Well," he answered, "I survived the Red Luck Ball given by the benedicts, and so die as looked. It'll nothing can harm me."

With that he struck our reporter a sharp blow on the ear and hurried off.

A NEW STATUE OF JOAN OF ARC JUST ERECTED BY FRENCH GOVERNMENT.

THE MOST DISGRACEFUL
THING I EVER DID

The Invasion of the Sanctuary

It was Christmas eve. In a fashionable church were gathered the great ones of the city in a pious swoon. For the hour bankers had put out of their weary minds the number of farmers on whom they must foreclose next day in order to make their twenty per cent. Real Estate men had ceased worrying what gaudy lies should embellish their prospectuses on the following Monday. Even fatigued flappers had turned to religion and were wondering if the man two pews ahead really looked like Valentino, or whether it was just the way his hair was cut in the back.

And at that moment, I, who had been suppering heavily in a house not two doors from the church, felt religion descend upon me also. A warm current seemed to run through my body. My sins were washed away and I felt, as my host strained a drop or so from the ultimate bottle, that my life was beginning all over again.

"Yes," I said softly to myself, drawing on my overshoes, "I will go to church. I will find some friend and, sitting next to him, we will sing the Christmas hymns."

The church was silent. The rector had mounted to the pulpit and was standing there motionless, conscious of the approving gaze of Mrs. T. T. Conquadine, the wife of the flour king, sitting in the front row.

I entered quietly and walked up the aisle toward him, searching the silent ranks of the faithful for some one whom I could call my friend. But no one hailed me. In all the church there was no sound but the metallic rasp of the buckles on my overshoes as I plodded toward the rector. At the very foot of the pulpit a kindly thought struck me—perhaps inspired by the faint odor of sanctity which exuded from the saintly man. I spoke.

"Don't mind me," I said, "go on with the sermon."

Then, perhaps unsteadied a bit by my emotion, I passed down the other aisle, followed by a sort of amazed awe, and so out into the street.

The papers had the extra out before midnight.

"The Most Disgraceful Thing I Ever Did," *Vanity Fair*, xxii (October 1923), 53. Unsigned—one of ten contributions on the same topic by ten authors. There were prizes for readers who identified the authors. Fitzgerald's confession recalls an escapade in St. Paul while he was a Princeton undergraduate.

SALESMANSHIP IN THE CHAMPS-ELYSÉES

To work for the Company Automobile is a *métier* exacting. There of them are many of the world who, wanting to purchase an automobile, enter and say "I want to purchase an automobile," whereupon this affair begins. Now one has at the outset the information that this man wishes well to purchase a car and has already decided on this mark—otherwise he would not have entered here. One can then, naturally, amuse one's self by for a moment mocking of him, giving him to wonder if of them there are after all. During this quarter of an hour one can discover much of the type with which one is dealing at the moment and thus in any further dealing one has provided himself with resources or even established a certain dominance of character, one on top of the other.

It there has been several days when an American entered and demanded me to make him see a car. I was engaged standing in a spot thinking of affairs of one's own; presently I demanded:

"What is it that it is?"

"A car."

"But what kind of car?" I demanded sharply.

"A six-cylinder touring car."

"We have not one here."

I had the man there, and for a moment he looked stupefied—but then he made:

"Can you have one here for me to see this afternoon?"

This fantastic request I only answered with a bitter and short laugh.

"And how much is it?" he continued. "As a matter of fact I'm pretty sure I want one, so I can write you a cheque."

This was becoming wearying. I drew in my breath and made: "Listen, monsieur, it is not the trouble to talk when I have told you I have now no car of that kind in the house. Nothing! Nothing! Nothing! It does not exist here. Look for yourself."

"When will you have?"

"How should I know? Perhaps in eight days. Perhaps in a month."

"I don't think you want to sell me a car," he said. "As a matter of fact they carry a make next door that I begin to think will do just as well."

He turned and went out suddenly and I stood looking after the impolite. But thinking to profit himself he is in the end deceived, because Mr. Legoupy, the seller next door, will no more sell him without making a proper study of his sincerity and his character and the extent of his desire for the car than I myself. The impolite will end himself by being able to get no car at all.

—*F. Scott Fitzgerald*

"Salesmanship in the Champs-Elysées," *New Yorker,* v (February 15, 1930), 20.

THE TRUE STORY OF APPOMATTOX

———

Columnist Discovers That It Was Grant Who Surrendered to Lee Instead Of Lee Surrendering to Grant

———

Circumstances Divulged For The First Time By Captain X

———

We have learned that when Grant had decided to surrender his milk-fed millions to Lee's starving remnants and the rendezvous was arranged at Appomattox Court House, Lee demanded that Grant put his submission into writing. Unfortunately Grant's pencil broke, and, removing his cigar from his mouth, he turned to General Lee and said with true military courtesy: "General, I have broken my pencil; will you lend me your sword to sharpen it with?" General Lee, always ready and willing to oblige, whipped forth his sword and tendered it to General Grant.

It was unfortunately just at this moment that the flashlight photographers and radio announcers got to work and the picture was erroneously given to the world that General Lee was surrendering his sword to General Grant.

The credulous public immediately accepted this story. The bells that were prepared to ring triumphantly in Loudoun county were stilled while the much inferior Yankee bells in Old North Church in Boston burst forth in a false pæan of triumph. To this day the legend persists, but we of the Welbourne *Journal* are able to present to the world for the first time the real TRUTH about this eighty-year-old slander that Virginia lost its single-handed war against the allied Eskimos north of the Mason and Dixon line.

"The True Story of Appomattox," Baltimore: 1934. A spoofing account of Appomattox specially printed for Fitzgerald as a gag. A clipping is in the Fitzgerald Papers, Princeton University. See Fitzgerald to Maxwell Perkins, July 30, 1934.

A BOOK OF ONE'S OWN

In this age of drastic compression, it is the ambition of all the publishers I know to get everything worth reading into one little book no bigger than a Reuben's sandwich. I've been playing with this idea off and on for a year, and finally worked out a new super-anthology that over a single weekend should make the conscientious reader as nearly omniscient as a man can be. It ought to make its fortunate publisher (and me) rather rich, I think. This is my prospectus:

AT LAST!

All you want to read in One Pocket-size Volume! A miracle of Book Making. Large Type—Thick Paper.

SOME OF THE SPLENDID CHAPTERS

Burton's Anatomy, Gone with the Wind, Steinbeck, Remnants of Modern Literature.

10,000 Words oft. mispronounced (Condensed), Nurses' Hand Book and Indian Sex Love (Orig. 6 vol.), Sheet Welding, Manual Univ. Hist. (Cond.), Mrs. Rorer's Cooking.

All You Want to Know in Swedish (Cond.), Soc. Register Western States, Gotha's Almanac, Macfadden's Body, Famous Operas, Tolstoi, Mike Gold, Marx (Leaflet edition).

Shakespeare (Laughs from), Plastic Age, Ten Atlantic Prize Novels condensed in one, Sears-Roebuck, Bradstreet, Tony Adverse.

Memoirs of a Statistician (Cond.), Cath. Index, Readers' Digest (Cond.), Sorrows of Grand Dukes (Compressed), Orph. Annie (Selects.), Scenario Writing, quick course, Elements of Brewing, Familiar Quots., Apostles' Creed.

Plato, Adam Smith, Tif Thayer, Bryce's Am. Comintern, Bladder and Intest.

Great Leaders: Nathan Bedford Forrest, Artemus Ward (Bill Nye), Washington, Voliva, Dante, Doc Dafoe, etc.

Audubon's Birds, Astrology (Simp.), Caesar & Virgil Trots, Ten Commandments.

Bible (Cond.), New Test. Stories, Moses, Abraham's Sac., Serm. on Mount, Noah's Ark, Dorian Gray.

Tales of Wayside Inn (Unexpurg.), Rover Boys (Summary), Shirley Temple Cutouts, Painting Thru Ages, Fish of Labrador.

Famous Clowns of Bygone Days, Unsolved Murders (Cond.), Margot Asquith, Al Capone, Donald Duck, Tank Corps, etc., etc., etc.

ONE HANDY VOLUME
Bound in Boards $2.00
Compressed Morocco $3.50

As an added inducement, the publisher might give with it a set of O. Henry or van Dyke in ten volumes. This gets the buyer both ways, for if he happens to have a bookshelf, then the set will fill it up. The book needs no shelf of its own, but it might be bound to look like a small radio. Then, if the purchaser has a radio that looks like a set of books—but I become too visionary; it is time for some practical man to take hold.

—*F. Scott Fitzgerald*

"A Book of One's Own," *New Yorker*, xiii (August 21, 1937), 19.

Constant Tras

Coiffeur

ANCIENNEMENT :
95, Avenue des Champs-Elysées
PARIS

For Mr. Constant Tras
The best barber in France. Also
cuts the hair of literary men—but
not as in the cartoons
F. Scot Fitgerald

Testimonial for barber (Paris, n.d.) The only known copy of this card is in
the Fitzgerald Papers, Princeton University Library.

Part Two

Miscellany about Fitzgerald

Interviews

"I'm Sick of the Sexless Animals Writers Have Been Giving Us"

FREDERICK JAMES SMITH

F. Scott Fitzgerald is the recognized spokesman of the younger generation—the dancing, flirting, frivoling, lightly philosophizing young America—since the publication of his now famous flapper tale, *This Side of Paradise*. Perhaps our elders were surprised to discover, as Mr. Fitzgerald relates, that the young folk, particularly the so-called gentler sex, were observing religion and morals slightly flippantly, that they had their own views on ethics, that they said damn and gotta and whatta and 'sall, that older viewpoints bored them and that they both smoked cigarets and admitted they were "just full of the devil."

All of which *is* the younger generation as Fitzgerald sees it. Indeed, the blond and youthful Fitzgerald, still in his twenties, is of, and a part of, it. He left Princeton in the class of '17 and, like certain young America, slipped into the world war *via* the training camp and an officership. We suspect he did it, much as the questioning hero of *This Side of Paradise*, because "it was the thing to do." He was a lieutenant in the 45th Infantry and later an aide to Brigadier General Ryan. It was in training camp that he first drafted *This Side of Paradise*.

"We all knew, of course, we were going to be killed," relates Fitzgerald with a smile, "and I, like everybody else, wanted to leave something for posterity." But the war ended and Fitzgerald tried writing advertising with a New York commercial firm. All the time he was endeavoring to write short stories and sell them, but every effort came back with a rejection slip. Finally, Fitzgerald resolved upon a desperate

Originally published as "Fitzgerald, Flappers and Fame," *Shadowland*, January 1921.

step. He would go back to his home in St. Paul and live a year with his parents, aiming consistently to "get over."

Then he sold his first story to *Smart Set* in June, 1918, receiving thirty dollars therefrom. He worked for three months rewriting *This Side of Paradise*—and sold it to Scribner's. Success came with a bang and now Fitzgerald is contributing to most of the leading magazines. At the present moment he is completing his second novel, to be ready shortly.

"I realize that *This Side of Paradise* was immature and callow, just as such critics as H. L. Mencken and others have said, altho they were kind enough to say I had possibilities. My new novel will, I hope, be more mature. It will be the story of two young married folk and it will show their gradual disintegration—broadly speaking, how they go to the devil. I have one ideal—to write honestly, as I see it.

"Of course, I know the sort of young folks I depict *are* as I paint them. I'm sick of the sexless animals writers have been giving us. I am tired, too, of hearing that the world war broke down the moral barriers of the younger generation. Indeed, except for leaving its touch of destruction here and there, I do not think the war left any real lasting effect. Why, it is almost forgotten right now.

"The younger generation has been changing all thru the last twenty years. The war had little or nothing to do with it. I put the change up to literature. Our skepticism or cynicism, if you wish to call it that, or, if you are older, our callow flippancy, is due to the way H. G. Wells and other intellectual leaders have been thinking and reflecting life. Our generation has grown up upon their work. So college-bred young people, here and in England, have made radical departures from the Victorian era.

"Girls, for instance, have found the accent shifted from chemical purity to breadth of viewpoint, intellectual charm and piquant cleverness. It is natural that they want to be interesting. And there is one fact that the younger generation could not overlook. All, or nearly all, the famous men and women of history—the kind who left a lasting mark—were, let us say, of broad moral views. Our generation has absorbed all this. Thus it is that we find the young woman of 1920 flirting, kissing, viewing life lightly, saying damn without a blush, playing along the danger line in an immature way—a sort of mental baby vamp. It is quite the same with the boys. They want to be like the interesting chaps they read about. Yes, I put it all up to the intellectuals like Wells.

"Personally, I prefer this sort of girl. Indeed, I married the heroine of my stories. I would not be interested in any other sort of woman."

We asked Fitzgerald about motion pictures. "I used to try scenarios in the old days," he laughed. "Invariably they came back. Now, however, I am being adapted to the screen. I suspect it must be difficult to mold my stuff into the conventional movie form with its creaky mid-Victorian sugar. Personally, when I go to the pictures, I like to see a pleasant flapper like Constance Talmadge or I want to see comedies like those of Chaplin's or Lloyd's. I'm not strong for the uplift stuff. It simply isn't life to me."

"Hugh Walpole Was the Man Who Started Me Writing Novels"

THOMAS A. BOYD

When I came to St. Paul I was interested most in meeting people who could tell me of the intimate side of Fitzgerald. Being charmed with *This Side of Paradise*, and with the remarkable promise it evinced I wanted to know something of the person who wrote it other than that which was appearing in the literary supplements and magazines. From numerous opinions of him given by people who know him and his family I conjectured that in some way he had ruffled the composure of his fellow townsmen. It might have been, I thought, that he refused to pronounce the name of the city of his birth in the provincial way. But he had done something, I was sure.

One of his friends of an earlier day, replying to a question I had asked, told me: "Yes. I know Scott very well. He is an awful snob." Another reported that at the present time he was sequestered in a New York apartment with $10,000 sunk in liquor and that he was bent on drinking it before he did anything else.

Still another related the story of how in New York, Fitzgerald became bored with his guests and called the fire department. When the

Originally published as "Literary Libels—Francis Scott Key Fitzgerald," St. Paul (Minn.) *Daily News*, March 5, 1922, March 12, 1922, March 19, 1922. This text is a shortened version of the original.

firemen arrived and asked where the fire was Scott pounded his stomach and dramatically announced: "The fire is right here. Inside me."

One or two admitted that "Scottie was a great boy" but further than that they would not pledge themselves. That all of these cheerfully thrown handsful of mud could be true I doubted. Further I was a little put out with my informants because, I reflected, I could have imagined more lurid stories than those myself.

Then one day someone told me that Fitzgerald was coming to St. Paul to spend the winter. He was to take a house at White Bear until the weather got cold and then he was to move into the city. Eager to meet him I awaited the opportunity with a great deal of interest.

But when the time came it was on one of those torrid days of late summertime when the collar around one's neck becomes a wriggling snake with a hot sticky belly.

Thoroughly disgusted, I was all for calling it a day when a close acquaintance walked into the office and said, "Scott Fitzgerald is out at White Bear. Let's go out and see him." Had the day been less stifling I would have been more impressed. As it was I managed only to answer that as no place in the world could be hotter than the office where I then was I would be glad to drive out with him to meet Mr. Fitzgerald.

We were soon on our way and as we rode past the small pumpkin-planted farms the various rumors that I had heard concerning Fitzgerald came to my mind. I judged that if they were true he would appear rather dissipated. No one could drink a thousand bottles of liquor in one year without having a red nose and blue-veined face. Not even Anton Dvorak. Nor could anyone, because he was bored with his guests, telephone a hurry call to the fire department and not show that he was a peculiar person. These thoughts, and others of more marvelous fabric, engaged me as we plowed through the necessary 10 miles of white smoky dust to reach White Bear.

"Now that we are here how are we going to find the house," my friend wanted to know and I was about to tell him that we might ask at the yacht club, when a Ford laundry delivery truck coughed past. We hailed the driver and explained our difficulty. "You wish to be directed to the home of Mr. Scott Fitzgerald the novelist," he answered in a high voice. "Well, if you'll just follow behind me I will take you there because I am delivering some laundry to them." We thanked him and drew our car in rear of his and in this way we reached a modestly proportioned house whose color, setting and architecture was admirably suited for a summer home.

Grasping a bottle of synthetic gin firmly around the neck I preceded my friend out of the car and up the path to the house. A voice answering the bell announced: "I'll be down in a minute." It was a strong boyish voice that could not have ascended from a liquor-parched throat. Another literary legend punctured.

Out on the enclosed porch, with the bottle of gin resting on a table beside us, we waited for the appearance of Mr. Fitzgerald. In a few minutes he came and, on seeing us, exclaimed to me: "Why, I thought you'd be wearing a frock coat and a long white beard."

I scanned him closely. His eyes were blue and clear; his jaw was squared at the end which perceptibly protruded; his nose was straight and his mouth, though sensitive looking, was regular in outline. His hair which was corn-colored, was wavy. His were the features that the average American mind never fails to associate with beauty. But there was a quality in the eye with which the average mind is unfamiliar.

"I thought you would be a baby with rouged lips, so I too am disappointed," I told him.

We resumed our seats while he visited the kitchen, returning in a few minutes with lemons, oranges and cracked ice. I was surprised that he only brought two glasses. "I suppose that's synthetic gin you've got there. Will you have lemon or orange." We named our choice and while squeezing the juice of an orange into a glass turned and said: "You like Mencken, don't you?"

"That would be like saying that I like the law of gravity," I replied, "but I suppose I would say yes.

"Speaking of Mencken," I resumed, "I thought I saw a Baltimore forefinger in *This Side of Paradise*. There is hardly a good book these days without it."

"Well!" he replied, "I don't think *Main Street* would have been written if Mencken hadn't been born. There are pages in that book that read just like the Repitition Generale, but that isn't true with *This Side of Paradise*. It was not until after I had got the proofs of my book back from the publishers that I learned of Mencken. I happened across the *Smart Set* one day and I thought 'Here's a man whose name I ought to know. I guess I'll stick it in the proof sheets.' But I've met Mencken since then and I'm glad I put his name in. Have you ever met?"

I sorrowfully replied that I had not, but that I meant to some day.

"Gee, he's great. He's the one man in America for whom I have a complete respect."

"But what is he like," I wanted to know.

"Well, he's like a good natured beer-drinking German whom you would imagine liking to sit around in his stocking feet."

"I can conceive of him being good-natured and liking to drink beer, if it is good beer, but somehow the shoeless feet won't fit in. I suppose it's because he plays the piano or else I have the orthodox complex. But he certainly has made many things possible for the younger generation."

"Yes, you bet he has. He even helped boost Floyd Dell's *Moon Calf* into success. There's a book which certainly touches the depths of banality. He hasn't even a pretense of style and his manner of dumping youthful history into the reader's lap with such a profound air of importance is simply disgusting. No, for once Mencken made a mistake."

At the time I was a Dell enthusiast so I took Fitzgerald's criticism with a gulp. I had nothing on the subject to offer in return and the conversation was as self-conscious as a fish out of water; my mind grasped at the first thought that entered my head.

"Sandburg," I said. "What do you think of Sandburg?"

And again my choice was horrific.

"Sandburg is probably an intelligent fellow. But to say that he is a poet is rot. The great city of Chicago felt a literary awakening and they looked around for a verse writer to call great, Sandburg was the only one in sight and immediately the legend of the great poet of the proletariat was built up to fit the shoulders of Sandburg."

But this time my position was not untenable.

"But, I don't agree with you there," I said. "Sandburg is a great poet. There are only two or three great poets in America and surely Sandburg is one of them."

"But he doesn't write any great lines. Tell me one of his verses that stick in your memory like Keats' "Ode to a Grecian Urn?""

"Well, there's 'Five Towns on the B. and O.' "

"All right, say it."

And I tried and failed. It may have been the fourth synthetic gin and orange juice concoction but my tongue would go no further than: "Hungry smoky shanties hanging to the slope."

"See there, you can't do it. And what kind of a poet is a man who can't make lines to stick in your head. Why even Vachel Lindsay—"

And he started off a verse from the "Chinese Nightingale."

"From that point of view probably you're right, but Sandburg works otherwise. He makes his poems so that in their entirety they are ravishing. They are a complete thing in themselves. You see in them lyricism. The whole drama of the human race unfolds when he recites one of his verses."

"Why he's not half as lyrical as the feet of Charlie Chaplin."

"Well, if you're going to drag in Charlie Chaplin's pathetic feet I can't discuss Sandburg with you any more. I should like to see Chaplin because I admire his work so much, but I detest the whole caboodle of the movies outside of him. Consequently, I am seldom aware when a picture of his is showing in town."

"But you might as well protest against a Cunarder or the income tax as to protest against the movies," said Fitzgerald. "The movies are here to stay."

"Yes, I suppose they are, but then so is *Uncle Tom's Cabin*. By the way, what do you think of Ben Hecht as a writer."

"Oh, I like the things of his that I've seen very much. I'm looking forward to his novel that's coming out this fall. *Erik Dorn*, I think is the name of it."

"*Erik Dorn*, yes. So am I looking out for it. I remember seeing one of Hecht's plays shown at a ragamuffin theater in Chicago. It was about a hungry bum who was spending the night on the sidewalk. Toward morning as he was passing a plate-glass window in a store he saw his reflection and exclaimed: 'Well, I'm a cock-eyed son-of-a-gun, if it ain't Jesus.' I thought it was good."

"That's funny. I've no doubt that Hecht will do wonders in fiction, but the author whose book I want to see most is John Dos Passos."

"Oh yes, I heard about his book. It's called *Three Soldiers*, isn't it?"

"That's it, and I've a hunch that it will be one of the best, if not the best book of the year," Fitzgerald said enthusiastically.

Three months later that proved to be a very wise prediction.

"I've got Charles Norris' new novel in the house. John Farrar of the *Bookman* sent it to me for review. Have you seen it?"

I replied that I had read the book and that I thought it very good.

"Well, the question of marriage is a rather important one and for one to write a novel, or what Norris would call an interpretative novel, of marriage, in which the author fails to take sides either for or against marriage and divorce, is quite an achievement. And then Norris makes his characters into real human beings. That's more than many fictionists do."

"Maybe you're right. But I can't see much in it. The grouping isn't clever and he has loaded his book with too many characters. It's too much like a brief."

"Norris can take care of himself. Tell me about your new novel. I've read the first installment of it in the *Metropolitan*."

"It's something after the manner of *Linda Condon*. Hergesheimer tried to show the effect on a woman after her once-legitimate beauty had passed. That is what I am trying to do with Gloria."

"But that isn't all, is it?"

"No that isn't all, but you wait and read it." He disappeared into the house and returned with the manuscript of *The Beautiful and Damned*. "Here it is."

It was written on ordinary sized paper and not typed. The pencil scrawl was in large letters and altogether it must have been two-feet thick. This thing must be almost 200,000 words, I thought. After I had finished reading the first chapter (He writes legibly), I remarked that the manuscript was not very much like the printed story in the *Metropolitan*.

"Look here," I said, "this is much better than the *Metropolitan* version. There were some excellent descriptive passages entirely left out in the part that I read."

"Well," he looked in rather a funny way, "they bought the rights to do anything they like with it when they paid for it."

"Of course it will appear as it was originally written when it comes out in book form, won't it?"

"Surely it will, I only hope—" and then he was silent.

"But good lord, if I were you I'd go around telling people that the original story was different from the *Metropolitan* story. Why, that *Metropolitan* story," I confessed, "was nothing but cheap sensationalism without any coherence at all."

As he offered no remark on the subject I turned the conversation. "What started you writing?"

"I've written ever since I can remember. I wrote short stories in school here, I wrote plays and poetry in prep school and I wrote plays and short stories for the Triangle and the 'Lit' at Princeton. But Hugh Walpole was the man who started me writing novels. One day I picked up one of his books while riding on a train from New York to Washington. After I had read about 100 pages I thought that 'if this fellow can get away with it as an author I can too.' His books seemed to me to be as bad as possible. The principal thing he did was to make unessentials seem important, but he was one of the near-best sellers. After that I dug in and wrote my first book.''

"Well, you are probably right about Walpole and you may be right about Floyd Dell, but I think you're wrong about Charlie Norris and I know you're wrong about Sandburg. The trouble is you don't get Sandburg. It's the same way with Sherwood Anderson. Now that Anderson has been boosted so long by really intelligent persons the pretenders are beginning to praise him and ascribe motives to his work of which I know he never dreamed. There's something to Sandburg, a lot. I wish I could tell you about it, but it's not clear enough in my mind.''

"I sure wish I could see it. If the man even wrote as well as Vachel Lindsay—you can remember Lindsay's stuff. 'Booth led boldly with a big brass drum.' ''

"But that's only cheap alliteration and it comes from a howling Methodist Y.M.C.A. proselyte to right-living. You can't seriously consider him.''

But just then another automobile horn sounded from the gravel path and we prepared to leave. St. Paul already was paying homage to success! The sight of the large automobile stopping in front of the Fitzgerald home was an inspirational sight, I reflected. People will go 10 miles to warm themselves in the warm rays thrown off by his glory. Oh, well, it were better that the singer of beauty be honored even at the cost of annihilation of the decalogue rather than that it be left to its own devices.

The Fitzgerald family gave up the summer place rather early and removed to one of the new apartment hotels here. After that we saw each other daily. Scott was at that time beginning a comedy for the stage and he felt that his work would be less interrupted if he rented an office in a down-town business building. His new novel *The Beautiful and Damned* had appeared in its last installment in a popular magazine and Fitzgerald had suggested that I should not read it until I could read the entire book.

He had been hard at work rewriting parts of the original story and changing it to advantage so that it would be ready for publication in book form by March 3. He had also written three or four short stories. Two of them he sold to popular magazines and the price he got for one, he told me, was $1,500. And there he worked nearly every day on his play. And yet people with the utmost seriousness report stories of

Fitzgerald's abandoned carousals that to hear them tell it happened every day.

Enthusiasm runs high in the nature of Fitzgerald. He is even enthusiastic in his dislikes and certainly he is whole-hearted over the things that he enjoys. To be with him for an hour is to have the blood in one's veins thawed and made fluent. His bright humor is as infectious as smallpox and as devastating to gloom. He has humor all right, someone may remark, but it is never shown when he is made the butt of it. Of course, it isn't. He is not enough of a dissimulator for that. What person honestly does enjoy being made the butt of a joke? I have searched far but the man still remains a bird of paradise. Some persons, when a joke is made at their expense, will smile, but the mouth will droop in one corner, like a courageous prize-fighter who has been struck on the nose. No, the entire psychology of the joke is against one's smiling at one's own expense. Where is the "sudden glory" of which Max Eastman speaks? How can one appreciate the "cracker" when it knocks out three of his front teeth?

At this time a man passed through St. Paul who had, years ago, written three or four good books, but since had almost completely stopped writing to devote his time to drink.

One day after we left him and were walking up the street Scott remarked:

"There goes one of the last survivors of the 'booze and inspiration' school. Bret Harte was one of the earliest ones and it was all right in his day, but the old school of writers who learned to drink and to write while reporting for a newspaper is dying out. Do you remember that story of how Harte, visiting Mark Twain in California, said one night that he had to write a story and get it to the publisher the next afternoon?"

I replied that I might have heard it but if I had I must have forgotten.

"Well, Bret Harte came to Mark Twain's home one afternoon for a visit and after he had been there a few hours he said that he had to write a story that night because he had promised the publishers of a magazine that he would have it for them in the morning. So Twain suggested that Harte could use his study, but Harte said, 'I've got plenty of time. Let's talk a while.'

"They killed most of the afternoon talking and after dinner Twain again suggested that Harte go up to his study and start to work. But again Harte was not ready. 'There's no rush. Let's talk a while longer.'

"After a while it got to be 1 o'clock and Twain becoming sleepy, told Harte that he was going to bed and asked him whether he wanted anything before he started to work.

" 'Well,' said Harte. 'If you'll have a fire made in the study and a quart of whiskey sent up I'll be all right.'

"So Twain went to bed and Harte to the study. About 5 o'clock in the morning a servant was called and another fire was made in the room and another bottle of whiskey was brought in. At 9 o'clock Harte came downstairs to breakfast with the story of 6,000 words, completed.

"But that gang is not to be met any more. I can't think of how he could have done it. For me, narcotics are deadening to work. I can understand any one drinking coffee to get a stimulating effect, but whiskey—oh, no."

"*This Side of Paradise* doesn't read as if it were written on coffee," I remarked.

"And it wasn't. You'll laugh, but it was written on coca cola. Coca cola bubbles up and fizzes inside enough to keep me awake."

Imagine Amory Blaine being born of a coca cola mother! But it is exuberant and sparkling enough to have been at that.

Fitzgerald's apartment was perhaps 20 minutes walk from his office and, when there was not too much snow on the ground, he would walk rather than take the street car. From this, many people got the idea that he positively refused to ride on the street car and many of them began to uphold him in what they considered another of his eccentricities.

His writing is never thought out. He creates his characters and they are likely to lead him into almost any situation. His phrasing is done in the same way. It is rare that he searches for a word. Most of the time words come to his mind and then spill themselves in a riotous frenzy of song and color all over the page. Some days he writes as many as 7,000 or 8,000 words; and then, with a small *Roget's Thesaurus*, he carefully goes over his work, substituting synonyms for any unusual words that appear more than once in seven or eight consecutive pages. Bernard Shaw has said that no one should write until he can supply at least five synonyms for any word that comes into his mind. Mr. Shaw says that he is able to do that, but it is not an entirely wild speculation to venture that if anyone entered the Shaw study sometimes he might see a well thumbed *Thesaurus* lying around.

Fitzgerald is extraordinarily curious. To that quality in him is due the responsibility for a number of the legends that have been built up around him. To illustrate:

We had gone into a cigar store to roll dice for a package of cigarettes. Fitzgerald rolled the dice first and the highest combination that turned was three of sixes. I must have been standing on a four-leafed clover because when I threw the dice I was apportioned four treys. But Fitzgerald did not notice. A blind man, feeling his way along with walking stick, had come in the door and Fitzgerald was watching him as if he were a unique fact. "You lose," I called. "I've got four treys," but he did not hear. So I paid the cigar man for both packages and we went out into the street. I noticed that Fitzgerald was acting queerly as we stepped on the sidewalk. He seemed quite unsteady on his feet and, as I looked up, I saw that he had closed his eyes. Silently, I watched him walk down the crowded street, feeling his way along by tapping against the sides of the buildings with his walking stick. A young woman, passing in company with a man, exclaimed, "Oh look at that poor boy. How sad it must be to be blind." But Fitzgerald walked on, his eyes shut. He had almost experienced the sensations of a blind man for an entire block on a crowded street when unluckily, two middle aged women passed us by and passing, one said to the other: "Oh look at that." And then Fitzgerald opened his eyes.

I told you he was curious. When he discovered that the woman's ejaculation had been caused by the sight of a bargain window in a department store he was furious.

"It's perhaps just as well that no one recognized you else you would be reported to have blind staggers." I said to him.

"Didn't I walk very well—as well as the blind man?" His voice was truculent.

"No you didn't. It is remarkable that you didn't knock your brains out. There were a number of times when I started to take hold of your arm to keep some passerby from knocking you down."

At that he seemed rather downcast, but he almost immediately cheered up, thinking, no doubt, that he could sell his experiences to some popular magazine.

"Our American Women Are Leeches"

MARGUERITE MOOERS MARSHALL

"New York is going crazy! When I was here a year ago I thought we'd seen the end of night life. But now it's going on as it never was before Prohibition. I'm confident that you can find anything here that you find in Paris. Everybody is drinking harder—that's sure. Possessing liquor is a proof of respectability, of social position. You can't go anywhere without having your host bring out his bottle and offer you a drink. He displays his liquor as he used to display his new car or his wife's jewels. Prohibition, it seems to me, is having simply a ruinous effect on young men."

It is a young man himself who is speaking—no clergyman, no social reformer, but a "regular" young man. Most of you know his name— F. Scott Fitzgerald, who wrote *This Side of Paradise*, a book that managed to be both brilliant and popular, when he was just out of Princeton, two years ago; whose second novel, *The Beautiful and Damned*, is newly published. (A reader of both suggests that, in view of the first tale, the second could have been called, consistently, "Next Stop Is Hell!")

The frank Mr. Fitzgerald undoubtedly set the fashion of holding the mirror up to the flapper. Some of us, in two years, have grown a bit weary of studying her reflection. So we welcome the fact that, in his second novel, Mr. Fitzgerald turns his attention to other representatives of his generation—to the "younger marrieds," in the locution of the society columns. They out-flap the flapper! With youth, health, beauty, love, friends, money, pleasure, his Anthony and Gloria, typifying the prosperous, newly married couple in New York, are hopelessly, irretrievably "damned," broken in body and spirit; one an accomplished, the other an incipient dipsomaniac, before the end of the story.

"But why?" I asked the young novelist, when I met him at the Plaza Hotel, where he and his wife are staying for a few days. Their home is in St. Paul, Minn. "In some ways your pair were a special case. But we all know scores of young men and women here in New York who marry

Originally published as "F. Scott Fitzgerald, Novelist, Shocked By 'Younger Marrieds' and Prohibition," New York *Evening World*, April 1, 1922.

under the happiest auspices, and who, in a few years, manage to throw away all their chances of lifelong happiness and security together. What is the matter with our young married couples?"

"First of all, I think it's the way everybody is drinking," replied the blue-eyed, frank-faced, fastidiously dressed author. His stories are world-weary, but he himself is as clean and fresh and boyish as if he'd never had an idea or a disillusion. Then he gave the candid, impartial impression of New York life of the present quoted at the beginning of this interview.

"There's the philosophy of ever so many young people to-day," he went on, thoughtfully. "They don't believe in the old standards and authorities, and they're not intelligent enough, many of them, to put a code of morals and conduct in place of the sanctions that have been destroyed for them. They drift. Their attitude toward life might be summed up: 'This is ALL. Then what does it matter? We don't care! Let's GO!'"

A little nervous movement of Mr. Fitzgerald's cigarette finished the sentence.

The young wife in his book remarks, even before entering the state of matrimony, that she does not want to have responsibility and a lot of children to take care of. "Evidently," observes her creator, with a nuance of sarcasm, "she did not doubt that on her lips all things were good." So I asked him how far he considered the young married woman to blame for the "damnation" of her own life and that of her husband.

"She's very largely to blame," he responded promptly. "Our American women are leeches. They're an utterly useless fourth generation trading on the accomplishment of their pioneer great-grandmothers. They simply dominate the American man. You should see the dowagers trailing around this hotel with their dependent males! No Englishman would endure one-eighth of what an American takes from his wife.

"I've often asked myself the question, 'To what is a woman entitled from life?' The answer, obviously, is, 'All she can get!' And when she marries she gets the whole thing. She makes a man love her, then proceeds to hog all his emotions, to get all the money out of him she can, to keep him at her beck and call. She makes a monkey of him, in many cases, and he has to stand it unless he wants a continuous verbal battle."

Mr. Fitzgerald took another whiff of his cigarette.

"What chance have they, these men and women of my generation who come from families with some money!" he exclaimed. "I'm not blaming them. What chance has the young man, unless he has to work for his living? If he were born in England there would at least be a tradition behind him and a background. Here he is born in a Middle Western town. His grandfather, perhaps, was a farm laborer. He—the third generation—is brought up to be absolutely helpless. He is sent to a fine private school, near New York, and before he's through he knows everything every boy ever knew and every chorus girl in town. His idea of happiness is to have one of them on the back seat of a limousine. Then his family resolves that he must go to Yale. He goes there to raise hell. When he's through—if he gets through—he's absolutely ruined.

"He ought to do something. But what can he do? Suppose he thinks that he might try to help govern his country." But what he would think next is so perfectly summed up in *The Beautiful and Damned* that I shall quote it word for word:

"He tried to imagine himself in Congress, rooting around in the litter of that incredible pigsty, with the narrow and porcine brows he saw pictured sometimes, those glorified proletarians babbling blandly to the Nation the ideas of high school seniors! Little men with copy-book ambitions who by mediocrity had thought to emerge from mediocrity into the lustreless and unromantic heaven of a government by the people—and the best, the dozen shrewd men at the top, egotistic and cynical, were content to lead this choir of white ties and wire collar-buttons in a discordant and amazing hymn, compounded of a vague confusion between wealth as a reward of virtue and wealth as a proof of vice, and continued cheers for God, the Constitution and the Rocky Mountains!"

"Nevertheless," I said, "all our younger married set cannot be 'damned.' Surely you can suggest some way in which they may be 'saved?' "

"Work!" at once exclaimed Mr. Fitzgerald, his blue eyes earnest. "Work is the one salvation for all of us—even if we must work to forget there's nothing worth while to work for, even if the work we turn out— books, for example—doesn't satisfy us. The young man must work. His wife must work"—

"How?" I interrupted. "At bringing up an old-fashioned family?"

Scott Fitzgerald IS a boy, and married happily, and not too long.

"I think," he confided, ingenuously, "that just being in love, really in love—doing it well, you know—is work enough for a woman. If she keeps her house the way it should be kept and makes herself look pretty when her husband comes home in the evening and loves him and helps him with his work and encourages him—oh, I think that's the sort of work that will save her. It's not so easy, you know, being in love and making it go."

Evidently the younger generation, whatever the vagaries of its head, still believes in keeping its heart in the same old place!

"Home Is the Place
To Do the Things You Want To Do"

An Interview With Mr. and Mrs. F. Scott Fitzgerald

"So this is to be all about me?" asked Mrs. Scott Fitzgerald vivaciously. "I've never been interviewed before!"

She leaned far back into the plastic depths of an overstuffed chair, querying expectantly, "Now what do we do? Is it going to be very formal? Scott, please come into the living room and help me be interviewed."

Obediently, Scott Fitzgerald left his study—scene of the creation of those brilliant tales to which American Flappers thrill en masse. Tall, blond, broad-shouldered, he towers above his petite wife, whose blue eyes and yellow hair match his own.

"My stories?" Mrs. Fitzgerald said, "Oh, yes, I've written three. I mean, I'm writing them now. Heretofore, I've done several magazine articles. I like to write. Do you know, I thought my husband should write a perfectly good ending to one of the tales, and he wouldn't! He called them 'lopsided' too! Said that they began at the end."

She waved a gayly protesting white hand at her husband's efforts to explain that they were "good."

Originally published as "What a 'Flapper Novelist' Thinks of His Wife," Baltimore *Sun*, October 7, 1923. Reprinted by permission of the Sun-papers, Baltimore, Md. This text is a slightly shortened version of the original.

"Writing has its advantages," she continued. "Just think: I buy ever so many of Scott's presents that way. And buy ever so many other things on the theoretical proceeds of stories I'm going to write some day.

"Spending money is fun, isn't it?—Oh, yes, I wrote them in long hand. Typewriters are an unknown institution here at Great Neck."

Thus is necessitated the explanation that the abode of this charming and brilliant young couple among the newer lights of the modern literary world is a charming country house at Great Neck, Long Island.

Speaking "in domestic vein," which isn't the usual thing for her, Mrs. Fitzgerald remarked upon the absence of the butler. "He must be taking his saxophone lessons. Yes, today is the day. My great disappointment is that I've never heard him play; just infrequent tootings from afar.

"Yes. I love Scott's books and heroines. I like the ones that are like me! That's why I love Rosalind in *This Side of Paradise*. You see, I always read everything he writes. It spoils the fun, the surprise, I mean, a bit. Sometimes I act as official critic.

"But Rosalind! I like girls like that," she continued, shaking a curly crop of honey-yellow bobbed hair. "I like their courage, their recklessness and spend-thriftness. Rosalind was the original American flapper.

"Three or four years ago girls of her type were pioneers. They did what they wanted to, were unconventional, perhaps, just because they wanted to, for self-expression. Now they do it because it's the thing—everyone does.

"When Scott and I were first introduced, he was in a southern military camp during the war, commencing to write *This Side of Paradise*. He said that he was working on an episode in the book about a girl named Eleanor who was a trifle like me. But as the episode was woven into completeness, our acquaintance grew, and he decided that Eleanor wasn't like me at all. But, he wrote some more chapters about Rosalind."

Rosalind is a character symbolic, in a measure, of the present restless generation of young women—a daring young person, infinitely entertaining, with opinions and a frankness that would precipitate mid-Victorian damsels into mild fainting bouts.

This same charm is possessed by the original of Rosalind, Zelda Sayre Fitzgerald.

"Her youth was spent in going to proms," Scott Fitzgerald explains with evident and wholly understandable pride, "and she lived in Montgomery, Ala. That's a mighty long way from New York, as measured by carfare, especially when the man in question is working—or trying to—on the munificent salary of $35 a week. That was before I started to write—oh, yes." This in answer to the mute question expressed in an inquiringly uplifted eyebrow.

Asked to use his much-lauded gift for description in composing a word picture of his wife, he replied laconically and readily. "She is the most charming person in the world."

"Thank you, dear," was the gracious response.

Asked to continue the description thus commenced so auspiciously, he said: "That's all. I refuse to amplify. Excepting—she's perfect."

The last was given with an ardor worthy of one of his best heroes—Amory Blaine, for instance.

"But you don't think that," came the protest from the overstuffed arm chair, "You think I'm a lazy woman."

"No," judicially, "I like it. I think you're perfect. You're always ready to listen to my manuscripts at any hour of the day or night. You're charming—beautiful. You do, I believe, clean the ice box once a week."

"Zelda's Book" is a fat scrap book—a memory book filled with souvenirs of the "high lights."

Well-filled programs, plentifully x'ed, place cards, telegrams, notes, pictures are there.

"We were married on April Fools' Day, 1920," Mrs. Fitzgerald continued, "then came a trip abroad—I loved England and hated Italy—then came Patricia Scott Fitzgerald, known popularly as 'Scotty,' 1922, then Great Neck, L. I., 1923. In the interim were lots of short stories from my husband's pen and two books, *This Side of Paradise* and *The Beautiful and the Damned.* Montgomery, Ala.—in the scrap book!

"Here's a telegram from Montgomery," Zelda Sayre Fitzgerald . . . read " 'Hurry back to Montgomery, as town is shot to pieces since you left. No pep, no one to give the gossips a source of conversation. Country Club is intending firing chaperone, as there is no further need for her. Knitting parties prevail. For the sake of saving dear, old Montgomery, hurry back home.'

"Oh, yes, I can draw. Scott says I don't know much about it, but that I draw well. And I play golf.

"I've a hearty liking for jazz music, especially Irving Berlin's," she continued. "It's most artistic. One of the first principles of dancing is abandon, and this is a quality that jazz music possesses. It's complex. It will, I believe, occupy a great place in American art."

Here her husband turned on the phonograph and Mrs. Fitzgerald replied that she "didn't care especially" for dancing—an unexpected admission.

At this juncture her husband decided to take a hand in the matter of interviewing. He propounded a series of questions with startling rapidity.

"Whom do you consider the most interesting character in fiction?"

After a considerable discussion no less a person than Becky Sharpe was decided upon.

"Only I do wish she'd been pretty," the interviewer remarked wistfully.

"What would your ideal day constitute?"

"Peaches for breakfast," was the prompt response. "There, that's a good start, isn't it? Let me see. Then golf. Then a swim. Then just being lazy. Not eating or reading but being quiet and hearing pleasant sounds—rather a total vacuity. The evening? A large, brilliant gathering, I believe."

"Am I ambitious?" she echoed the next question. "Not especially, but I've plenty of hope. I don't want to belong to clubs. No committees. I'm not a 'joiner.' Just be myself and enjoy living."

"Do you like to study?"

This question asked, her husband eyed her merrily, as though expecting an outburst.

It was forthcoming.

"You know I don't. Never did. But my ancestors made up for any lack of brilliance of mine in that line."

Coming from a long line of distinguished Southern ancestry, Mrs. Fitzgerald's grandfathers were both in the United States Senate.

"Do you like large or small families?"

"Large ones. Yes, quite large. The reason is that then children have a chance to be what they want to be—not oppressed by too much 'looking after' nor influenced by ordinary life in any way.

"Children shouldn't bother their parents, nor parents their children. If possible to establish friendly relations, mutual understanding, between them, it's an excellent thing; but if this isn't possible, it seems worse to bring them together too much. Let children work out their own ideas as to duty to their parents, immortality and choosing a career."

"What do you want your daughter to do, Mrs. Fitzgerald, when she grows up?" Scott Fitzgerald inquired in his best reportorial manner, "not that you'll try to make her, of course, but—"

"Not great and serious and melancholy and inhospitable, but rich and happy and artistic. I don't mean that money means happiness, necessarily. But having things, just things, objects, makes a woman happy. The right kind of perfume, the smart pair of shoes. They are great comforts to the feminine soul."

"Women care for 'things,' clothes, furniture, for themselves," her husband interjected, "and men, in so far as they contribute to their vanity."

"About Patricia, 'Scotty,' " her mother continued, "I'd rather have her be a Marilyn Miller than a Pavlowa. And I do want her to be rich."

Outside, in a shady corner of the side lawn, the very young lady in question played happily, quite oblivious of the fact that her career was being decided upon, in theory, indoors. She is a quite remarkable young woman, for she is at most times silent. She isn't, her parents stated, a loquacious person at all. But she is a very pretty one.

"What would you do if you had to earn your own living?" the catechism was continued.

"I've studied ballet. I'd try to get a place in the Follies. Or the movies. If I wasn't successful, I'd try to write."

Speaking of home life in general, and that of the Scott Fitzgeralds in particular, she declared that "Home is the place to do the things you want to do. Here, we eat just when we want to. Breakfast and luncheon are extremely moveable feasts. It's terrible to allow conventional habits to gain a hold on a whole household; to eat, sleep and live by clock ticks."

Her favorite among her husband's writings are the episodes of Rosalind in *This Side of Paradise*, the last half of *The Beautiful and Damned*, the short story "The Off Shore Pirate," and the play, "The Vegetable."

"All Women Over Thirty-Five Should Be Murdered"

B. F. WILSON

The press decries a superabundance and mushroom-growth of Young Intellectuals. A suffering public has had so many masterpieces of literature written by twenty-year-old hands of late that the age of our well-known authors is being carefully suppressed by wary publishers.

However, there are one or two exceptions where youth becomes a matter of minor importance. F. Scott Fitzgerald, author of *This Side of Paradise, The Beautiful and Damned, Tales of the Jazz Age*, etc., is a particularly noteworthy exception. Inasmuch as he is strictly responsible for the introduction into this country of a new and devastating type of girl whose movements, thoughts and actions—to say nothing of deeds—have become matters of international importance, the editor decided that anything Mr. Fitzgerald might have to say on the subject would be worth hearing.

So I hied myself down to Great Neck, Long Island. There in the cool of the afternoon, I visited with the famous young author and his family.

He made me feel completely at home from the moment I entered the house. He had just awakened from a nap and I caught him as he came into the library to fetch a book. A quiet dressing-gown covered a more distracting pair of pajamas. His blond hair was tousled like the head of a sleepy kid, and he seemed a bit non-plussed at my somewhat abrupt appearance.

He called loudly for the bride. Parking me with the comic supplement of the Sunday paper, he disappeared into the upper regions of the house. When he reentered the library he was clad in the conventional knickerbockers of the country gentleman; but the tousled-haired boy was still there.

"Didn't you feel desperate when you saw the result of your handiwork?" I asked him. "And aren't you glad that the flapper craze is passing?"

"But I don't think it is," he protested. "The flapper is going stronger

Originally published as "F. Scott Fitzgerald Says: 'All Women Over Thirty-Five Should Be Murdered,' " *Metropolitan Magazine*, November 1923. This text is a slightly shortened version of the original.

than ever; she gets wilder all the time. She keeps on doing the things she has done before, and adding to them all the time. She is continuously seeking for something new to increase her store of experience. She still is looking for new conventions to break—for new thrills, for sensations to add zest to life, and she is growing more and more terrible."

"You know we've often wondered how she came into existence," I interrupted. "Just how she arrived and where from. Quite a few people attribute her to you. They claim she sprang from your books and stories. Is it true?"

He smiled a bit ruefully.

"Did you ever read Thackeray's *Henry Esmond?*" he asked. "Well, Beatrice was the first flapper. She lived for thrills; she turned over two kingdoms to indulge a whim and to see just how much power she possessed over the Young Pretender. She lived to embroil herself in one intrigue after another. Sensation was the breath of life to her, and inasmuch as the ladies of her century were still in the obscure stage of subservience to the male, she was a distinct shock to the middle classes and the court reporter.

"She was the first woman to test openly her power over men. She was the first to manifest a desire for independence.

"Much later, the suffragette type came into existence. You know how she clamored for independence. She was a horrible person. A woman of thwarted desires endeavoring to satisfy her restlessness by demanding from men that which they had refused to surrender by persuasion. She couldn't attract men; therefore she decided to fight them."

He ran restless fingers through his hair as he warmed to his subject.

"Just before the war, a new type of girl had appeared in England. You remember Stephen McKenna's books, don't you? Well, most of his heroines were flappers. Then there was an outbreak of new heroines in English life and letters. They wanted independence. They loved danger, and were excitement-mad, and faintly neurotic. They realized that men were adamant to the suffragette type, therefore they stopped bombing Prime Ministers. But they showed their independent spirit in other ways. They discussed subjects, which had hitherto been considered taboo for women; they lived independently of their families; they were to be seen everywhere unchaperoned. In short, having decided that unto each person life was an individual law, they did as they pleased. When their actions began to arouse comment, they increased their daring.

"When the war came on they had a new outlet for their energy. Of course by this time, this type had drifted into America. I had no idea of originating an American flapper when I first began to write. I simply took girls whom I knew very well and, because they interested me as unique human beings, I used them for my heroines.

"I lived out West. In Chicago and St. Paul, for instance, the girls of my acquaintance seemed utterly different from any girls I had ever read about. Of course money was the direct reason. In the Middle West there was wealth without background, tradition, or manners, in the broad sense of the word. Naturally, with this new and powerful resource in their hands to do with as they desired, many of the younger girls could use their leisure and exuberant vitality only in some form of excess.

"Then Freud came into existence. He has had the widest influence on the younger generation. You cannot begin to conceive how far his theories have spread in America. I remember a girl—one of the nicest girls I ever knew. She had never heard of Freud, but she had begun to ask questions. We talked one evening, and she informed me that whether by hearing other girls talk, or by analyzing her own unhappiness, she had discovered herself to be a victim of suppressed instinct."

He waved his hand in an emphatic gesture.

"Why, Freud at third-hand ran over this country like wildfire. He gave the wealthy young girls something new in the way of sensationalism. They decided that they were all victims of repressed desires, and began to cut loose. When the war was over and the young men came back, the best and smartest of them disillusioned at the fiasco of their ideals, they subconsciously helped the independence of the girls along."

"Well, don't you think the young girl of today is beginning to tire of all this sensationalism?" I asked.

"Not at all," he replied emphatically. "I think she is going on and on, carrying the younger men with her—until there will be some sort of catastrophe which may or may not face her in another direction. Look at all the unhappy girls you see—look at the number of wretched marriages. Look at the increase in divorce—look at the increase in extranupital affairs. Of course she is an awe-inspiring young person. I thoroughly dislike her as a rule—unless she is very pretty and has authentic charm—or on the other hand, unless she is intelligent enough to conduct herself with sense and discretion. Most of them are so messy with their amours."

He smiled at his own intensity of feeling—but we knew he meant what he said.

"By 1915, the best send-off a girl who visited in St. Paul could possibly have was that she bore the reputation of being a violent petter, and had driven innumerable men to distraction. And, as I have said before, I think she is growing wilder all the time."

He looked me straight in the eye.

"Be perfectly frank, now," he said. "Don't you think men are much nicer than women? Don't you find them more open and aboveboard, more truthful and more sincere? Wouldn't you a whole lot rather be with a bunch of men than with a group of women?"

I had to confess to the impeachment.

"I know that after a few moments of inane conversation with most girls I get so bored that unless I have a few drinks I have to leave the room."

As if in answer to his argument, a beautiful young woman appeared in the doorway. Instantly a wide smile lit up his features. He introduced me to his wife.

"Zelda," he explained. "I was on my customary thesis of the superiority of men over women." He turned towards me. "She agrees with me entirely. We always have the house full of my friends, and when I ask her if she wouldn't like to have some girls down for a week-end she declines with thanks."

"Why, Scotty, aren't you horrid?" she protested in a soft Southern drawl. "You know, I have a lot of girls down here all the time. But just the same, I must admit," she confessed smiling to me, "that I have a better time when Scotty's friends are here."

"He's just a crank on the subject of women," she continued. "He says all women over thirty-five should be murdered."

The husband protested.

"I mean the women who, without any of the prerogatives of youth and beauty, demand continual slavery from their men," he said warmly. "You know the type. There are thousands of them. They sit back complacently and watch their husbands slave for them; and, without furnishing any of the pleasantries of life for their husbands, they demand the sort of continual attention that a charming fiancée might get. They make tame-cats of them. They are harridans and shrews who continually nag and scold until the men are driven idiotic.

"I have one of them in my new play, 'The Vegetable.' Of course she isn't as fully developed as the kind I mean, but you would know her instantly."

"I Am a Pessimist,
A Communist (With Nietschean Overtones),
Have No Hobbies Except Conversation
—And I Am Trying to Repress That"

CHARLES C. BALDWIN

If I were given to prophecying I should certainly predict, once his mania for writing ephemeral short stories is done with, a great and glorious future for F. Scott Fitzgerald; and I should base that prediction upon the irony, the beauty, the wit of *This Side of Paradise* and *The Beautiful and Damned*. These are two books unique in American literature, though imitated a thousand times. They are the young man showing his oats, reaping his whirlwind, muddled, worried, triumphant and moody, with his gay colors and gray castles tumbled in a heap. They have form, ease and variety. They are utterly fearless, shirking no conclusions, true to their characters.

If a chap is a bounder, selfish and conceited, soon or later his friends will find it out. Fitzgerald knows this. But that does not blind him to the fact that the chap may be immensely interesting and, in his way, tragic and likable. The chap may be generous; the cad may be a pose— as it was with Byron. Or the loss may be a woman's, some woman who has put her trust in him. But not always. Sometimes the loss is ours. If I remember right, Sidney Carton was a sot, but his is the only name one regrets and recalls when *A Tale of Two Cities* is done with—as, in the course of the years, most books are done with, becoming only memories, half and more than half forgotten.

But it is not so much his characters that matter, to Fitzgerald and in his books, as what is done with them. In *This Side of Paradise* they are given their heads, in *The Beautiful and Damned* rope. Yet when they threaten to run away or hang themselves, Fitzgerald does not wring his hands and say, "I told you so." Nor does he stand idly by and shrug

Originally published as "F. Scott Fitzgerald," *The Men Who Make Our Novels*. New York: Dodd, Mead, 1924. Reprinted by permission of Dodd, Mead. This text is a shortened version of the original.

his shoulders, murmuring, "The funeral is theirs." He lets them play their piece out to the end; and they become, even for the dullest, tragic comedians, dangling helplessly on the threads of destiny and time. Rightly understood, they are heroic—and Fitzgerald understands them absolutely.

'My third novel," he says, "is just finished and quite different from the other two in that it is an attempt at form and refrains carefully from trying to 'hit anything off.' Five years ago the new American novels needed comment by the author because they were facing a public that had had very little but trash for a hundred years—that is to say, the exceptions were few and far between and most of them were commercial failures. But now that there is an intelligent body of opinion guided by such men as Mencken, Edmund Wilson and Van Wyck Brooks, comment should be unnecessary; and the writer, if he has any aspirations toward art, should try to convey the feel of his scenes, places and people directly—as Conrad does, as a few Americans (notably Willa Cather) are already trying to do."

That incorrigible gossip, Burton Rascoe, in the New York *Tribune*, tells of a luncheon with Edmund Wilson during which Wilson remarked that Fitzgerald mispronounces more words than any other educated person he (Wilson) has ever known; going on to say that when Fitzgerald is with Ring Lardner, Lardner is forever correcting Fitzgerald's pronunciation. However, no harm is done as Fitzgerald never remembers the correction from one moment to the next.

Fitzgerald is free from all feeling for words. He uses them or abuses them as suits his fancy. He coins them anew. They are divorced from their past, made over, becoming utterly modern tramps as are so many of Fitzgerald's best liked characters, and somehow individual—awhile, Ralph Henry Barber, Sarycuse, Compton MacKenzie, Van Wyke Brooks, Nietchean, Gertrude Stein, traveling. . . .

But don't let that worry you: The man's an artist just the same.

"When, in St. Paul and about twelve," says Fitzgerald, "I wrote all through class in school in the back of my geography and first year Latin and on the margin of themes, declensions and mathematic problems. Two years later the family decided the only way to force me to study was to send me to a boarding school. This was a mistake. It took my mind off my writing. I decided to play football, to smoke, to go to college, to do all sorts of irrelevant things that had nothing to do with the proper mixture of description and dialogue in the short story.

"But in school I went off on a new tack. I saw a musical comedy called 'The Quaker Girl' and from that day forth my desk bulged with Gilbert and Sullivan librettos and dozens of notebooks containing the germs of dozens of musical comedies.

"Near the end of my last school year I came across a musical comedy score lying on top of the piano. It was a show called 'His Honor the Sultan' presented by the Triangle Club of Princeton University. That was enough for me. The University question was settled. I was bound for Princeton.

"I spent my entire freshman year writing an operetta for the Triangle Club. I failed in algebra, trigonometry, coordinate geometry and hygiene, but the Triangle Club accepted my show, and by tutoring all through a stuffy August I managed to come back a sophomore and act in it as a chorus girl. A little later I left college to spend the rest of the year recuperating in the West.

"The next year, 1916–17, found me back in college, but by this time I had decided that poetry was the only thing, so with my head ringing with the meters of Swinburne and the matters of Rupert Brooke, I spent the spring doing sonnets, ballads and rondels. I had read somewhere that every great poet had written great poetry before he was twenty-one. I had only a year and, besides, war was impending. I must publish a book of startling verse before I was engulfed.

"By autumn I was in an infantry officer's training camp with poetry in the discard and a brand new ambition—I was writing an immoral novel. Every evening, concealing my pad behind Small Problems for Infantry, I wrote on a somewhat edited history of me and my imagination. And then I was detected and the game was up. I could write no more during study period.

"This was a distinct complication. I had only three months to live— in those days all infantry officers thought they had only three months to live—and I had left no mark in the world. But such consuming ambition was not to be thwarted. Every Saturday at one o'clock I hurried up to the Officer's Club, and there, in a corner of a room full of smoke, conversation and rattling newspapers, I wrote a one-hundred-and-twenty-thousand word novel on the consecutive week-ends of three months. There was no revising; there was no time for it. As I finished each chapter I sent it to a typist in Princeton.

"I went to my regiment happy. I had written a novel. The war could now go on. I forgot paragraphs and pentameters, similes and syllogisms.

I got to be a first lieutenant, got my orders over seas—then the pub-lishers wrote that though *The Romantic Egotist* was original they could not publish it. Six months after this I arrived in New York and pre-sented my card to the office boys of seven city editors asking to be taken on as a reporter. I had just turned twenty-two, the war was over, and I was going to trail murderers by day and do short stories by night. But the newspapers sent their office boys out to tell me they didn't need me. They decided definitely and irrevocably by the sound of my name on a calling card that I was absolutely unfitted for a reporter. Instead I be-came an advertising man at ninety dollars a month, writing the slogans that while away the weary hours in rural trolley cars. After hours I wrote stories—from March to June. There were nineteen all together; the quickest written in an hour and a half, the slowest in three days. No one bought them, no one sent personal letters. I had one-hundred-and-twenty-two rejection slips pinned in a frieze about my room. I wrote movies. I wrote song sketches. I wrote jokes. Near the end of June I sold one story for thirty dollars.

"On the Fourth of July, utterly disgusted with myself and all the edi-tors, I went to St. Paul and informed family and friends that I had given up my position and had come home to write a novel. By this time I knew that I had a novel to write, and all through two hot months I wrote and revised and compiled and boiled down. On September 15 *This Side of Paradise* was accepted by special delivery.

"In the next two months I wrote eight stories and sold nine. The ninth story was accepted by the same magazine that had rejected it four months before. In November, I sold my first story to the *Saturday Eve-ning Post*. By February I had sold them half a dozen. Then my novel came out. Then I got married. Then I wrote *The Beautiful and Damned*. Now I spend my time wondering how it all happened.

"I am a pessimist, a communist (with Nietschean overtones), have no hobbies except conversation—and I am trying to repress that. My en-thusiasms at present include Stravinski, Otto Braun, Mencken, Conrad, Joyce, the early Gertrude Stein, Chaplin and all books about that period which lies between the V and XV centuries."

"America Is the Place Where Everybody Is Always Going to Have a Good Time Tomorrow"

MURIEL BABCOCK

The flapper generation was ruined by the war.

The preflapper group has still a chance to do something, to make itself heard.

The postwar generation is pretty feeble.

The youth of today—an unknown quantity.

Thus F. Scott Fitzgerald, in town to write for the movies, who once in the long ago (1920) told a very much surprised and somewhat shocked world about what the younger generation was doing in its spare time, who wrote frankly of sad young men and beautiful young women, of their thoughts, feelings, moods, their gin and necking parties.

F. Scott Fitzgerald is still writing about these same people. His generation. The prewar, the preflapper group, he calls them, as they are moving and living today.

"It is a mistake to call my generation the flapper group," he said. "They were preflapper. They belonged to the period before the newspaperman and American war hero on the Italian front."

Then he was persuaded to talk about himself—about the books he had read; about the books that he thought were the best books ever written. He was asked to name his list of "10 best books."

But he wouldn't. He said:

"I'm 30 now. I've been reading since I was 14—that is, books have been influencing me since I was 14. So I will try to name, one for each two years during the past 16 years, the books I have read that have been the greatest influence on my mind."

He found a pencil (He always uses a pencil instead of a typewriter when he writes) and wrote down, after much crossing out and revising, the following table:

At 14, *The Varmint*—Owen Johnson.

Originally published in an unidentified Los Angeles newspaper as "F. Scott Fitzgerald Upholds His Own Generation," 1927. Located in one of Fitzgerald's scrapbooks.

At 16, *The Lord of the World*—Robert Hugh Benson.
At 18, *The Picture of Dorian Gray*—Oscar Wilde
At 20, *Sinister Street*—Compton MacKenzie
At 22, *Tono Bungay*—H. G. Wells
At 24, *The Genealogy of Morals*—Friedrich Neitzsche
At 26, *The Brothers Karamazov*—Fyodor Dostoievski
At 28, *Ludendorf's Memoirs*.
At 30, *The Decline of the West*—Oswald Spengler.

He talked about American literature. He thought that Theodore Dreiser is the greatest living American author.

"*An American Tragedy*," he said, "is without doubt the greatest American book that has appeared in years."

But, being a young writer, he is most concerned and interested in the work of other young writers, chiefly John Dos Passos, Ernest Hemingway and E. E. Cummings.

Then Mrs. Fitzgerald came into the room. She is blonde, with bobbed hair, and you remember, southern—from Montgomery, Ala. She has a southern drawl that makes you think of white houses with tall columns on the front porch, and of hot black fields where the negroes sang blue songs that were first hummed on the Congo, and of bob whites calling in the spring time, when the rows of young cotton plants stretch out like long green ribbons.

She knows a great deal about books, too. She sat down, talked for a few minutes, compared the style of a certain much lauded young woman writer to the twisted, inverted style of the late Henry James, and went out again.

And the author of *The Great Gatsby* lit another cigarette from his 15-cent package for himself and one for a newspaperman, and went on talking. He didn't have anything to say about the present day flappers in America, because he hadn't seen many lately. He and Mrs. Fitzgerald have been in Europe for the past three years. They got back three weeks ago, visited the old home of Mrs. Fitzgerald in Montgomery, Ala., and then came west, to Los Angeles.

"I was shocked when I returned to America," he said. "I had been, you know, three years in Paris. I saw shows on the New York stage which would have shocked the French.

"Everything in New York seems mouldy, rotten. We went to the night clubs. It was like going to a big mining camp in the boom days.

". . . I got a sensation of horror. There were these fat men smoking fat cigars, and big butter and egg men, and half nude women. There was nothing fine about it all. It was vulgarity without the faintest trace of redeeming wit.

"Coming from Paris to New York was like plunging from a moral world to a state of moral anarchy.

"It gave me a fear that everyone had gone crazy—that everything was being done for nothing; that human lives were being exploited for nothing.

"And it's not the fault of prohibition. Prohibition is just a crazy symptom of a crazy race. I don't know what it is. Perhaps America just came too late—too late to be anything in our own right, but just part of the history and tradition of Europe.

"The country seems like warmed-over hash—warmed over from the day before. America is the place where everybody is always going to have a good time tomorrow.

"There is nothing, no tradition, no background, that you can summon when you say you are an American, as you can if you could say you were an Englishman, or even a Frenchman.

"It perhaps was different, in the days of Washington and Hamilton and Tom Paine—but it is not so now!"

But almost immediately after these gloomy observations, Mr. Fitzgerald became cheerful. The subject of his new novel was mentioned. He really can't help being cheerful and pleasant, it seems, despite the fact that he has just finished reading *The Decline of the West*, and the further fact that he named a book by Nietzsche among the books that had influenced him most.

He was all excited about his new novel, which won't appear for some months yet. He thinks it is the best thing that he has done.

"I keep myself pure in regard to my novels," he said, seriously. "I have written only three of them. Each one takes two or three years. Of course, there are my short stories—but, then, you have to live—"

"The Next Fifteen Years Will Show
How Much Resistance There Is in The American Race"

HARRY SALPETER

F. Scott Fitzgerald is a Nietzschean, F. Scott Fitzgerald is a Spenglerian, F. Scott Fitzgerald is in a state of cosmic despair. From within his slightly shuttered eyes, F. Scott Fitzgerald looks out upon a world which is doomed, in his sight, to destruction; from his unbearded lips comes conviction of America that is as final as the sentence is harsh. Summation of the evidence and conviction came in such a rush of words, in such a tumbling of phrase upon phrase that neither objection nor appeal was possible. It was a rush of words which only powerful feeling could dictate. Here was I interviewing the author of *This Side of Paradise,* the voice and embodiment of the jazz age, its product and its beneficiary, a popular novelist, a movie scenarist, a dweller in the gilded palaces, a master of servants, only to find F. Scott Fitzgerald, himself, shorn of these associations, forecasting doom, death and damnation to his generation, in the spirit, if not in the rhetoric, of your typical spittoon philosopher. In a pleasant corner of the Plaza tea garden he sounded like an intellectual Samson prophesying the crumbling of its marble columns. He looks like a candid, serious youth. His blue eyes, fair hair and clear-cut profile, no less than his reputation, give the lie to the mind of F. Scott Fitzgerald.

I had caught Fitzgerald at the Plaza, his midway stop between Hollywood where, after much travail, he had completed a scenario for Constance Talmadge, and Brandywine Hundred, Del., an address which tickles him. There he will make his home for the next two years and there he will complete his next novel. This, he said, had been vaguely suggested by the Loeb-Leopold case and in the tragic moments of this novel will be mirrored some of the cosmic despair under the burden of which Fitzgerald manages, somehow, to maintain a resilient step.

And after this novel—on which he has already worked three years— is completed?

Originally published as "Fitzgerald, Spenglerian," New York *World,* April 3, 1927.

Why, what is there left to do? Go to pieces. Or write another novel. A writer is good only for writing and showing off. Then people find him out or he runs out of money and then he goes and writes another novel.

* * *

Fitzgerald has been "a hot Nietzschean" ever since he read *Thus Spake Zarathustra*. To-day, Oswald Spengler's *Decline of the West* is his "bedbook." What have Nietzsche and Spengler in common? "Spengler stands on the shoulders of Nietzsche and Nietzsche on those of Goethe." This civilization has nothing more to produce. "We threw up our fine types in the eighteenth century, when we had Beethoven and Goethe. The race had a mind then." All that there is left to do is to go into a period of universal hibernation and begin all over again at the sheep-grazing stage. He said:

Spenglerism signals the death of this civilization. We are in a period paralleling Rome 185 years after Christ, Greece just before Alexander, the Mohammedan world about 1200. There is now no mind of the race, there is now no great old man of the tribe, there are no longer any feet to sit at. People have to stage sham battles in their own minds.

Mussolini, the last slap in the face of liberalism, is an omen for America. America is ready for an Alexander, a Trajan or a Constantine. The idea that we're the greatest people in the world because we have the most money in the world is ridiculous. Wait until this wave of prosperity is over! Wait ten or fifteen years! Wait until the next war on the Pacific, or against some European combination! Then we shall have to fight for our race and not under the leadership of a Calvin Coolidge.

The next fifteen years will show how much resistance there is in the American race. The only thing that can make it worth while to be an American is a life and death struggle, a national testing. After that it may be possible for a man to say 'I'm an American' as a man might say 'I'm a Frenchman' or 'I'm a German,' or, until recently, when the colonies made cowards of them all, 'I'm an Englishman.' The good American is the best in the world, as an individual. But taken collectively, he is a mass product without common sense or guts or dignity.

At present writing, this descendant of the author of "The Star-Spangled Banner" is not proud to be an American. "I have never said I was an American." That descendant can say: "Better that an entire Division should have been wiped out than that Otto Braun should have been killed." Braun, a German boy, at the age of nineteen or twenty, gave such evidences of genius that he was regarded as a Goethe in the budding. He was killed in the Argonne during the advance of the 77th Division.

Yet the man who is not proud to be an American is an American, if descent, on one side, from landholders on grant who came in 1630 means anything. On one side, said Fitzgerald, he comes from straight 1850 potato-famine Irish who prospered with the rising Middle West; and, on the other, from sometimes prosperous, sometimes indigent, but always proud, Maryland stock, who threw off, among other freaks, Philip Key, the manufacturer who made, without charge, all the buttons on the Continental uniforms, and Francis Scott Key.

* * *

We talked about the American in Paris, to which city Fitzgerald sometimes goes in quest of refuge from America.

The best of America drifts to Paris. The American in Paris is the best American. It is more fun for an intelligent person to live in an intelligent country. France has the only two things toward which we drift as we grow older—intelligence and good manners.

And why isn't it any fun to be an American?

Because it's too big to get your hands on. Because it's a woman's country. Because its very nice and its various local necessities have made it impossible for an American to have a real credo. After all, an American is condemned to saying "I don't like this." He has never had time—and I mean time, the kind of inspired hush that people make for themselves in which to want to be or to do on the scale and with all the arrogant assumptions with which great races make great dreams. There has never been an American tragedy. There have only been great failures. That is why the story of Aaron Burr—let alone that of Jefferson Davis—opens up things that we who accept the United States as an established unit hardly dare to think about.

Fitzgerald is distrait. He can't call himself a liberal. Finding liberalism "mushy and ineffectual," he is compelled to turn to the Mussolini-

Ludendorff idea. He does and does not want Mussolini. "If you're against Mussolini you're for the cesspool that Italy was before him; if you're for Mussolini you're for Caesarism." To call one's self a Communist is no solution either. Fitzgerald's hope for the Nation lies in the birth of a hero who will be of age when America's testing comes. It is possible that an American woman may be big enough of soul to bear and nurture such a hero; it is more likely that he will come out of the immigrant class, in the guise of an east-side newsboy. "His mother will be a good woman, in the sense that Otto Braun's mother was; she knew that he was a hero. But when this American hero is born one knows that he will not be brought up by the reading of liberal magazines, nor educated by women teachers." The father, said Fitzgerald, doesn't matter. Behind Fitzgerald's pessimism there is mysticism.

"Flappers Are Just Girls With a Splendid Talent for Life"

MARGARET REID

The term "flapper" has become a generalization, meaning almost any *femme* between fifteen and twenty-five. Some five years ago it was a thing of distinction—indicating a neat bit of femininity, collegiate age, who rolled her stockings, chain-smoked, had a heavy "line," mixed and drank a mean highball and radiated "It."

The manner in which the title has come into such general usage is a little involved, but quite simple. A young man wrote a book. His heroine was one of the n. bits of f. referred to above. "Flapper" was her official classification. The man's book took the country by, as they say, storm. Girls—all the girls—read it. They read about the flapper's deportment, methods and career. And with a nice simultaneousness they became, as nearly as their varied capabilities permitted, flappers. Thus the frequency of the term today. I hope you get my point.

Originally published as "Has the Flapper Changed? F. Scott Fitzgerald Discusses the Cinema Descendents of the Type He Has Made So Well Known," *Motion Picture*, July 1927. Reprinted by permission of *Motion Picture Magazine*, a Macfadden-Bartell publication.

The young man responsible for it all, after making clear—in his book—the folly of flappers' ways, married the young person who had been the prototype for the character and started in to enjoy the royalties. The young man was F. Scott Fitzgerald, the book was *This Side of Paradise,* and the flapper's name was Zelda. So about six years later they came to Hollywood and Mr. Fitzgerald wrote a screen story for Constance Talmadge. Only people don't call him Mr. Fitzgerald. They call him "Scotty."

But we don't seem to be getting anywhere. The purpose of this discursion was to hear Mr. F. Scott (or Scotch) Fitzgerald's opinion of the cinema descendants of his original brain-daughter, the Flapper.

It was with an admirable attempt to realize the seriousness of my mission that I went to his bungalow at the Ambassador. Consider, tho! By all literary standards he should have been a middle-aged gentleman with too much waist-line, too little hair and steel-rimmed spectacles. And I knew, from pictures in *Vanity Fair* and hysterical first-hand reports, that instead he was probably the best-looking thing ever turned out of Princeton. Or even (in crescendo) Harvard—or Yale. Only it was Princeton. Add "It," and the charming, vibrant, brilliant mind his work projects. My interest was perhaps a bit more than professional.

There was a large tray on the floor at the door of his suite when I reached it. On the tray were bottles of Canada Dry, some oranges, a bowl of cracked ice and—three very, very empty Bourbon bottles. There was also a card. I paused before ringing the bell and bent down to read the inscription—"With Mr. Van Vechten's kindest regards to Scott and Zelda Fitzgerald." I looked for any further message on the other side, but there was none, so I rang the bell.

It was answered by a young man of medium height. With Prince-of-Wales hair and eyes that are, I am sure, green. His features are chisled finely. His mouth draws your attention. It is sensitive, taut and faintly contemptuous, and even in the flashing smile does not lose the indication of intense pride.

Behind him was Mrs. Fitzgerald, the Rosalind of *This Side of Paradise.* Slim, pretty like a rather young boy; with one of those schoolgirl complexions and clear gray eyes; her hair as short as possible, slicked back. And dressed as only New Yorkers intangibly radiate smartness.

The two of them might have stepped, sophisticated and charming, from the pages of any of the Fitzgerald books.

They greeted me and discovered the tray hilariously.

"Carl Van Vechten's going-away gift," the First Flapper of the Land explained in her indolent, Alabama drawl. "He left this morning after a week's stay. Said he came here for a little peace and rest, and he disrupted the entire colony."

In the big, dimly lit room, Mrs. Fitzgerald sank sighing into a chair. She had just come from a Black Bottom lesson. F. Scott moved restlessly from chair to chair. He had just come from a studio conference and I think he'd rather have been at the Horse Show. He was also a trifle disconcerted by the impending interview. In one he had given to an avid press-lady the day before, he had said all his bright remarks. And he couldn't think up any more in such a short time.

"What, tho, were his opinions of screen flappers? As flappers? As compared to his Original Flappers?"

"Well, I can only," he began, lighting a cigaret, putting it out and crossing to another chair, "speak about the immediate present. I know nothing of their evolution. You see, we've been living on the Riviera for three years. In that time the only movies we've seen have been a few of the very old pictures, or the Westerns they show over there. I might," his face brightening, "tell you what I think of Tom Mix."

"Scotty!" his wife cautioned quickly.

"Oh, well. . . ."

Having exhausted all the available chairs in the room, he returned to the first one and began all over again.

"Have flappers changed since you first gave them the light of publicity? For better? For worse?"

"Only in the superficial matter of clothes, hair-cut, and wise-cracks. Fundamentally they are the same. The girls I wrote about were not a type—they were a generation. Free spirits—evolved thru the war chaos and a final inevitable escape from restraint and inhibitions. If there is a difference, it is that the flappers today are perhaps less defiant, since their freedom is taken for granted and they are sure of it. In my day"— stroking his hoary beard—"they had just made their escape from dull and blind conventionality. Subconsciously there was a hint of belligerence in their attitude, because of the opposition they met—but overcame.

"On the screen, of course, is represented every phase of flapper life. But just as the screen exaggerates action, so it exaggerates type. The girl who, in real life, uses a smart, wise-cracking line is portrayed on the screen as a hard-boiled baby. The type, one of the most dangerous, whose forte is naïveté, approximates a dumb-dora when she reaches the screen. The exotic girl becomes bizarre. But the actresses who do flappers really well understand them thoroly enough to accentuate their characteristics without distorting them."

"How about Clara Bow?" I suggested, starting in practically alphabetical order.

"Clara Bow is the quintessence of what the term 'flapper' signifies as a definite description. Pretty, impudent, superbly assured, as worldly wise, briefly clad and 'hard-berled' as possible. There were hundreds of them—her prototypes. Now, completing the circle, there are thousands more—patterning themselves after her.

"Colleen Moore represents the young collegiate—the carefree, lovable child who rules bewildered but adoring parents with an iron hand. Who beats her brothers and beaus on the tennis-courts, dances like a professional and has infallible methods for getting her own way. All deliciously celluloid—but why not? The public notoriously prefer glamor to realism. Pictures like Miss Moore's flapper epics present a glamorous dream of youth and gaiety and swift, tapping feet. Youth—actual youth—is essentially crude. But the movies idealize it, even as Gershwin idealizes jazz in the Rapsody in Blue.

"Constance Talmadge is the epitome of young sophistication. She is the deft princess of lingerie—and love—plus humor. She is Fifth Avenue and diamonds and Catalya orchids and Europe every year. She is sparkling and witty and as gracefully familiar with the new books as with the new dances. I have an idea that Connie appeals every bit as strongly to the girls in the audience as to the men. Her dash—her *zest* for things—is compelling. She is the flapper *de luxe*.

"I happened to see a preview the other night, at a neighborhood movie house near here. It was Milton Sills' latest, I am told. There was a little girl in it—playing a tough baby-vamp. I found that her name was Alice White. She was a fine example of the European influence on our flappers. Gradually, due mostly to imported pictures, the vogue for 'pose' is fading.

"European actresses were the first to disregard personal appearance in emotional episodes. Disarranged hair—the wrong profile to the camera—were of no account during a scene. Their abandonment to emotion precluded all thought of beauty. Pola Negri brought it to this country. It was adopted by some. But the flappers seem to have been a bit nervous as to the results. It was, perhaps, safer to be cute than character. This little White girl, however, appears to have a flair for this total lack of studied effect. She is the flapper impulsive—child of the moment—wildly eager for every drop of life. She represents—not the American flapper—but the European.

"Joan Crawford is doubtless the best example of the dramatic flapper. The girl you see at the smartest night clubs—gowned to the apex of sophistication—toying iced glasses, with a remote, faintly bitter expression—dancing deliciously—laughing a great deal with wide, hurt eyes. It takes girls of actual talent to get away with this in real life. When they do perfect the thing, they have a lot of fun with it.

"Then, inevitably, there is the quality that is infallible in any era, any town, any time. Femininity, *ne plus ultra*. Unless it is a very definite part of a girl, it is insignificant, and she might as well take up exoticism. But sufficiently apparent, it is always irresistible. I suppose she isn't technically a flapper—but because she *is* Femininity, one really should cite Vilma Banky. Soft and gentle and gracious and sweet—all the lacy adjectives apply to her. This type is reticent and unassuming —but just notice the quality of orchids on her shoulder as she precedes her reverential escort into the theater.

"It's rather futile to analyze flappers. They are just girls—all sorts of girls. Their one common trait being that they are young things with a splendid talent for life."

F. Scott Fitzgerald

CHARLES G. SHAW

F. Scott Fitzgerald, the son of Edward and Mary Fitzgerald, was born in St. Paul, Minnesota, on the twenty-fourth of September, 1896. He is a mixture of Irish and Maryland English. Francis Scott Key Fitzgerald is his full name, Francis Scott Key having been a brother of his great-grandfather.

Originally published as "F. Scott Fitzgerald," *The Low-Down*. New York: Henry Holt, 1928. © 1956 by Charles G. Shaw. Reprinted by permission of Holt, Rinehart and Winston, Inc.

The Newman School of Hackensack, N. J. and, later, Princeton University (which he left in 1917 to join the army) served as his educational fields, though in point of fact he is actually self-educated.

He is essentially romantic, egoistic and somewhat vain.

This Side of Paradise was his first novel, published in 1920, the year of his marriage to Zelda Sayre of Montgomery, Alabama.

Among his favored gastronomic interests are *petite marmite*, sole *meuniere*, duck with orange sauce, mushroom soup, and partridge with currant jelly. He looks with small favor, however, upon bird's nest pudding or Algerian *kous-kous*.

As a youth, he yearned to be a famous football star and "king of the world" (neither of which desires has left him since). He is congenitally shy but the fact is efficiently concealed.

His early habits of reckless extravagance were an outgrowth of trying to keep up with others whose incomes were many times his own.

He has written one play, "The Vegetable"—a comedy.

His suits, in hue, are usually of green or mauve and are made by Davies & Son, of 19–20 Hanover Street, London, W. I., while his shirts come from the shop of Hilditch & Key, also of London. His ties and pocket handkerchiefs are all brightly-colored.

He ordinarily rises about eleven o'clock and does most of his work from 5 P.M. to 3:30 A.M. He is left-handed in everything save writing. He will frequently talk to himself.

Belts refuse to hold up his trousers.

He believes that happiness consists of the performances of all the natural functions, with one exception—that of growing old. Sunday, Washington, D. C., cold weather, Bohemians, the managing type of American woman, avarice, and dullness are his principal dislikes.

From childhood he had intended to be a writer and entered Princeton with the plan of writing the Triangle Club musical comedies.

He is a member of the Cottage Club of Princeton.

His best-beloved beverages are Pouilly, Mersault, Arbois, and Pilsner, and his favorite literary piece—Spengler's *Decline of the West*.

Chaplin's "The Pilgrim" is his pet motion-picture, and "The Playboy of the Western World" his favorite play.

He has almost always lived in the country and made spasmodic excursions into town, the French Riviera and New York City being his idea of the world's most frolicsome resorts.

When away from home, he usually carries a package of bromides.

The chief early influences on his life he believes to have been the Roman Catholic Church, John Peale Bishop's friendly tutelage in English poetry, the wealthy middle-west, his marriage, the works of Compton Mackenzie, Samuel Butler, H. G. Wells, and H. L. Mencken, together with certain friendships.

During the war he served as (1): First Lieutenant of Infantry and (2): *Aide de Camp* to Brigadier General J. A. Ryan in various training camps.

He dances only under pressure, and prefers, at a party, to talk or listen to the chatter of others. While drinking, he is able to stand almost any company, but prefers that of Celts, and when on gaiety bent, will never set out with any liquor on his person but ultimately purchase a bottle at some dubious drug-store, which he will convince himself is pre-war stock.

He has always relished planning a trip or embarking upon a new piece of work.

He has spent three years in France and Italy and possesses a remarkable (and blood-curdling) collection of stereoptical slides of the war, amassed while in Europe. He would hate to live the rest of his life in Italy.

Currently, his favorite author is André Gide.

When writing, he is usually nervous and irritable and will engulf, during his labors, innumerable cups of Coca-Cola. He writes entirely in pencil and makes from two to four drafts, depending upon the class of work involved. While so engaged, he will consume about half a carton of Chesterfield cigarettes.

He will contract a hangover from work as well as from play.

For popular music he hands the first prize to Vincent Youmans.

Foyot's and La Reine Pedauque are his best-liked Parisian haunts, while in Rome he favors the Castello dei Cesari. In Cannes it is the Cafe des Allies and in New York the Meadowbrook and Caesar's.

His preference in women is a not-too-light blonde, who is intelligent, unopinionated and responsive.

He likes watching college football games and, for diversion, reading detective stories. Swimming is his chief outdoor exercise.

He is able to speak a rather bad French.

Scandal touching upon his friends, everything about the late war, discovering new men and books of promise, Princeton, and people with extraordinary personal charm are his greatest interests in life.

He parts his hair in the middle and his eyes are light green.

After a certain number of highballs, in some curious fashion, he will appear to have shrunk to about two-thirds his ordinary size.

He is always ready to laugh at himself.

Of an evening's outing, he has, time and again, purchased a newsboy's complete supply of morning papers, and tipped taxi-drivers to the extent of paying the fare several times over.

He is able to put away, in a single session, a lay-out of gins, wines, whiskies, and liqueurs.

His headquarters in New York is the Plaza.

As to politics, he is an autocrat in theory but a socialist in practice, and with respect to the Younger Generation, he says, he feels like an old man.

Though by nature not at all Rabelaisian, he enjoys acting so when with people who are easily shocked.

"In Ideals I Am Somewhat of a Communist"

WALLING KEITH

F. Scott Fitzgerald, fiction writer and author of several novels, and Mrs. Fitzgerald, the former Miss Zelda Sayre, daughter of Judge A. D. Sayre here, arrived in Montgomery yesterday to spend the Winter. Their 10-year-old daughter, Scottie, will arrive Saturday.

At the Greystone Hotel where the Fitzgeralds are stopping until their home they have leased for the Winter on Felder Avenue is fitted, Mr. Fitzgerald expressed delight in finding that Montgomery "showed less signs of depression" than any American city that he has recently visited.

"The people here don't seem to recognize the existence of a depression," he declared, telling of his amazement at finding poor business conditions the chief topic of conversation everywhere he went after his return from Europe.

Originally published as "Scott Fitzgeralds to Spend Winter Here Writing Books," Montgomery (Ala.) *Advertiser*, October 8, 1931. Reprinted by permission of the Montgomery *Advertiser*. This text is a shortened version of the original.

"In the East, even at places where people seek recreation and at parties where one goes to forget the day's work, it seemed that I hardly became acquainted with members of the party before they were talking of the depression. I'm going to like it here in Montgomery, I know. It's a relief to spend a few hours in a city where I'm not met with talk of depression."

In a conversation in which he discussed prohibition, national politics, current literature and writers, Communism and baseball, Mr. Fitzgerald touched upon the South and its typical cities.

"You see, I'm not a stranger to Montgomery at all," he explained, "having been stationed here during the war and marrying a Montgomery girl, I have felt the warmness of the city's hospitality."

Mr. Fitzgerald, who said he was a Jeffersonian Democrat at heart and somewhat of a Communist in ideals, declared that the prohibition law was not only a foolish gesture but that it was a hindrance to the machine of government.

"Understand now, I'm purely a fiction writer and do not profess to be an earnest student of political science," he smiled, "but I believe strongly that such a law as one prohibiting liquor is foolish, and all the writers, keenly interested in human welfare whom I know, laugh at the prohibition law."

"Not only is the question a laughable one," he said, "but it has done more to prevent perfect coordination among the members of both major political parties than any one thing."

"This is now new. All of my writer friends think and say the same thing," he added hastily.

"Another great difference I have found since my few hours in Montgomery," he said, "is the seemingly lack of fear of communistic activity or thought here. It seems foolish for an American to be afraid of any communistic revolution in this country, right now, but I heard so many conjectures of possible reactions here, while in Eastern cities, that at times I felt myself becoming concerned with the question.

"In ideals I am somewhat of a communist. That is, as much as other persons who belong to what we call 'the arts group'; but communism as I see it has no place in the United States," he laughed, "and the American people will not stand for its teachings."

Mr. Fitzgerald, who counts among his friends many writers of national and international note, expressed a fondness for Alabama and showed interest in Southern writers.

Ernest Hemingway, whom he saw in New York several days ago, is finishing a new novel, Mr. Fitzgerald said. Ring Lardner, the humorist, a friend of Fitzgerald's whom he visited before coming to Montgomery, is seriously ill.

The novel on which Mr. Fitzgerald is now working will be his first one in four years. He is a regular contributor of short stories to *The Saturday Evening Post* and other magazines.

"The American People Are Just Beginning to Wake Up to the Fact That Success Comes Hard"

BALTIMORE SUN

F. Scott Fitzgerald, of *This Side of Paradise* fame, let it be known here last night that the Fitzgeralds are about to become a two-novelist family.

From the bed she has occupied in the Johns Hopkins Hospital for the last six weeks, Mrs. Fitzgerald, who was Miss Zelda Sayre, of Montgomery, Ala., has sent her first novel to a publisher, he said.

The completion of Mrs. Fitzgerald's first novel—autobiographical at her husband's suggestion—was not the only news Mr. Fitzgerald had to impart. He said he had been looking about for a place so that he and Mrs. Fitzgerald and their 10-year-old daughter, Frances, might make their permanent home in the vicinity of Baltimore.

Mr. Fitzgerald, whose name has not appeared upon a new book since his *All the Sad Young Men* was published in 1926, was almost as happy about his wife's novel as he was about the fact that physicians have told him she should be able to leave the hospital in two weeks.

Mrs. Fitzgerald has been a semi-invalid for the last two years.

"She was training for the Russian ballet, but she had started too late; the strain was too hard for her," Mr. Fitzgerald said. "Then, Diaghilev died, and shortly after that Mrs. Fitzgerald had a complete nervous breakdown."

Originally published as "Scott Fitzgerald Seeking Home Here," Baltimore *Sun*, May 8, 1932. Reprinted by permission of the Sunpapers, Baltimore, Md.

Her illness halted Mr. Fitzgerald's work on a new novel which had engaged him for two years. Now that she is recovering, he has returned to the novel, whose first chapter is four years old. He would divulge nothing of its nature, however.

"I hate to talk about an unfinished novel," he said. "These things change so while you're working on them."

While the novel has been gathering dust he has been busy writing short stories, approximately fifty having come from his pen. One, soon to be published, is called "Family in the Wind" and is based on his experiences in the tornadoes that recently swept part of Alabama.

He spoke enthusiastically of it, as if he considered it one of his best. Of others recently published he was highly critical. With a tinge of surprise in his voice he admitted that "quite a few people seemed to like" one of them—"Babylon Revisited."

Mrs. Fitzgerald also has written successful short stories. Most of them have appeared in *College Humor* and *Scribner's*. Mr. Fitzgerald said he preferred not to make public the title of her novel.

Sitting in his room at the Rennert Hotel he discussed modern literary trends since the day when he left Princeton University to fight with the American Expeditionary Forces and returned to . . . write *This Side of Paradise, Flappers and Philosophers, The Beautiful and Damned, Tales of the Jazz Age, The Vegetable,* a play, *The Great Gatsby* and *All the Sad Young Men,* a collection of short stories.

"We were a serious generation," he said. "The things I wrote about in *This Side of Paradise* we took as something new, something strange. Last night I attended a fraternity party at the Hopkins. It made me feel old. This generation is lighter than ours. What was new to us is the accepted thing to them."

Mr. Fitzgerald is 35 and looks much younger. If his writing has changed measurably in recent years, "as I suppose it has," he has not been aware of it, he said. He spoke with admiration of Ernest Hemingway, William Faulkner, Thornton Wilder, John Dos Passos and others in the new generation of writers whose names were unknown when his novels of flapperdom and other phenomena of the post-war generation were creating a furor.

"No, I can't see that there's been any pronounced political or economic swing in the novel recently," he said. "A few have shown a tendency in that direction, inspired by the depression, but the majority retain their highly individualistic attitude. I think it's a good thing that we're getting over our boom-years period when we pictured life and success as easy, but I think it's a mistake for the novelist to sacrifice his detached viewpoint.

"The American people are just beginning to wake up to the fact that success comes hard. It's been easy in the past. But it's a mistake to think that the increasing concern of novelists with their characters' economic struggles is a new thing in American literature. We had it before the war in Jack London, in Edna Ferber and Fannie Hurst, and in Ida Tarbell with her story of the Standard Oil."

One of the results of the depression is that "young writers just starting out now have only one chance in a hundred of getting a hearing; the publishers not only have cut rates, but also are interested only in big names," Mr. Fitzgerald said.

Seven years ago the Fitzgeralds bade the United States adieu and sailed to make their permanent home in France. Deaths in their families and the depression have brought them back.

"Off there in a little village we had such a horrible feeling of insecurity," Mr. Fitzgerald said. "We had so little information from home, and we kept hearing these reports about business conditions until we didn't know but that any moment the United States would go smash and we'd be cut adrift.

"I'm very much interested in the state of the nation. Personally,—I think it's entirely too big ever to be managed properly. I think it ought to be cut up in six independent political sections. Recently I wired a certain Southern university to hire an economist to work out the six divisions for me, but the university replied that it had no department of economics."

"This Is a Very Cautious Generation in a World So Full of Alarm"

ED. G. THOMAS

This seems to be the "Oh, yeah" generation, in the opinion of F. Scott Fitzgerald, one of America's most widely read novelists and short story writers.

When I interviewed him at Asheville, N. C., where he is visiting, I asked him about the "flapper," because it was his books and stories of "flaming youth" and the "jazz age" that made him famous soon after he left Princeton.

"The flapper," he said, "is now a very hesitant mother. She seems to rush into extremes; not with abandon, but nevertheless with a certain swing between extremes. She is still in the same state of uncertainty that she was in during the days she was a flapper.

"The protest against old customs that taught her courage has made her want to take definite lines, but like all of us nowadays in turbulent times she is caught up into a vast uncertainty.

"That same courage that made her a hell-raiser at one time is the anchor around which she now swings. Brought up in a world in which men with courage were fighting, she learned to admire courage, and you can never take that admiration of it away from her. Courage is perhaps a small point to swing a life around, but in the last analysis it's a great point to swing a life around. So the women of my generation live on courage."

Mr. Fitzgerald believes the exact way of young people in the future seems uncertain, because "they have inherited the uncertainty of their elders.

"This generation will be exactly like the generation of one hundred years ago, brought up in the aftermath of the Napoleonic Wars. In peace, something works, something functions. There is something to fight against or to agree with. These children of today have nothing

Originally published as "Our 'Oh Yeah' Generation," Atlanta (Ga.) *Journal*, August 25, 1935. Reprinted by permission of the Atlanta *Journal*. This text is a slightly shortened version of the original.

certain to fight against or to agree with. Although they try to follow the wishes of their parents, they see the father fumbling in affairs he does not know the end of, and see the mother in the same sort of predicament. No class really knows what to do, what to say. Mother doesn't know whether to tell daughter to sacrifice everything for love. The indecision in both the masculine and the feminine world has baffled youth. There is no 'court of last appeals.' "

The author added, however, that "This is not to say that the new generation is more or less spiritual than any other."

Mr. Fitzgerald's work, largely about young people, has been much read by young people.

"This generation has lost faith in its elders unusually early," he lamentingly observed. "They now have a negative philosophy, which they get from this uncertainty of their elders and of the times. They are not at the moment idealists. Too much has happened. They have been preached to, lied to. Most generations grow up with idealism, but the expression, 'Oh, yeah!' comes closer to expressing the feeling of the present younger generation than anything else I can think of. They are, like all mankind, essentially spiritual, but just simply haven't found leadership they can honestly accept. The spiritual line-up has not been competently restated for this generation. In other words, nobody knows what 'no can do' means."

"This is a very cautious generation in a world so full of alarm," Mr. Fitzgerald declared.

"There is a self-protective force—a will to survive—that asserts itself when the morale is low. It takes the form of caution. This is a cautious generation. I think the young folk are taking no chances. So there is a balance which evens things up. The younger folk are not much better or not much worse than their forebears. The very fact of having to fumble in a mist, while it is not conducive to much original thinking, does make people walk slowly. And when they marry and have children I shall not be surprised if the names the younger generation gives its children are Prudence and Faith—perhaps even Hope."

Asked if he thought young people now prefer any special kind of literature, he said: "I have a 13-year-old daughter, Frances. I know things she doesn't like, codes of which she doesn't approve, but it's hard to learn just what she likes. Even in the very young I find utter disillusionment. Here one finds the negative philosophy being expressed."

I asked Mr. Fitzgerald about modern literature. In his opinion the three greatest literary "talents" that have come to the front in America so far in the 1930s have been southerners—Thomas Wolfe, of Asheville; William Faulkner, of Mississippi, and Erskine Caldwell, of Georgia.

The quality of the American novel has fallen off during the last five years, according to this distinguished, affable and very likable writer. He also finds that writing on the whole was better during the 1920's than it has been so far during the 1930s.

This can be explained in part by the depression, according to Mr. Fitzgerald.

"In times of turbulence writing is not usually so good as it is in more peaceful times," he pointed out. "Poetry and fiction are best written in tranquil times. We must remember, too, that there are two kinds of tranquility. One is the genuine kind; the other is the sort that comes when we have finished a task and are utterly worn out, and is not genuine at all.

"In years of turbulence everything, including writing, comes too quickly, too hastily, and this is not productive of the best literature. On the other hand, the times immediately following turbulence occasionally produce a great flowering of literature."

Illustrating his remarks from the period in history known as The Renaissance he said: "During the time of trouble, there was no flowering by writers and painters. Then followed good work. During any time of turbulence, the main thing is to live. The bare necessities of life are considered first."

Therefore as more genuinely tranquil times come, we may expect more in the way of good literature to crop out, predicted Mr. Fitzgerald, who believes that the south's lead in new literary talent so far in the 1930's probably indicates that Dixie has led in the emergence from the depression.

He has written scores of short stories for magazines, including sixty-five published in the *Saturday Evening Post*. His latest short story in the *Post* was "Zone of Accident."

"There's a history behind 'Zone of Accident,' " he explained.

Three years ago when suffering from influenza he was taken to Johns Hopkins Hospital, Baltimore, Md., where Mr. Fitzgerald, his wife and daughter live.

"I began to consider those two weeks just so much wasted time. I was observant of things going around me in the hospital, however, and realized after I left the place that I had been accumulating material for some writing and hadn't known it at the time. So followed 'Interne,' a short story with a hospital as its scene."

Mr. Fitzgerald then decided that he wanted to write more of medicos, nurses, accident rooms and treatment of the ailing.

For fifteen consecutive nights he trekked to the emergency room of the hospital in which he had once been a patient. He hoped to gather material, to observe goings-on, for more work on hospitals. He stayed hours at a time. But the accident case he had hoped to learn from just didn't come in at the right time. "The wrecks and emergency cases always occurred just after I left," he complained.

But he wrote "Zone of Accident," didn't like it, and since it was his own work, decided he would do what he pleased with it—dump it into a desk drawer. A little while ago he happened to re-read it, decided it was better than he had at first thought, made some revisions, and it was published in the *Post* in July.

He has done some writing since coming to Asheville, but prefers not to talk of it or of his plans for future work.

"The Less the Parents of Today Try to Tell Their Children, the More Effective They Can Be in Making Them Believe in a Few Old Truths"

ANTHONY BUTTITTA

Six generations have passed in review since 1914, F. Scott Fitzgerald, one of America's most brilliant and distinctive novelists declared here today in an exclusive interview at the Grove Park Inn where for the past two months he has been working on his new novel which will be released by Scribner's sometime in 1936.

The subject of generations, and the influence of one generation upon another, has always fascinated Mr. Fitzgerald. This interest was

Originally published as "Fitzgerald's Six Generations," Raleigh (N. C.) *News and Observer*, September 1, 1935. Reprinted by permission of the Raleigh *News and Observer*. This text is a shortened version of the original.

definitely noticed in his last work, *Taps at Reveille,* a collection of short stories, including two youth studies, "Basil" and "Josephine." His latest novel, *Tender Is the Night,* was well received by both the reading public and the critics.

The six generations as listed and analysed by Mr. Fitzgerald are: Pre-War, The War, Post-War, Boom, Shock and Hard-Times. It is interesting to note that he builds the first three around the war and its effects, and the last three around the rise and fall of our contemporary economic and financial structure.

Mr. Fitzgerald said that the Pre-War generation was one full of inhibitions. It was attached strongly to the Victorian tradition and manner of living. In spite of fancying themselves modern, those of the Pre-War period were fundamentally moral in both ideas and actions. The novel which represents this era and its thought is H. G. Wells' *Anna Veronica.*

Enough has been said of the War generation, according to Mr. Fitzgerald, but the best that has been said about it was Ernest Hemingway's remark "that the words duty, honor and courage lost all reality, and only somethings which seemed to have any dignity were names of places, streams and rivers." This was true first of men and eventually was also true of women. Hemingway has pictured this "lost" generation in *Farewell to Arms.*

The Post-War generation is an utterly disrupted one. Youth suffered with interrupted educations. Mr. Fitzgerald finds this generation essentially weak, and much inclined to be looking to the two older groups for guidance, without being certain of which to follow as a standard. There is no vitality in this group, and it is best described in fiction by books like *The Plastic Age* and *Flaming Youth.*

Many years are included in the Boom Era. The members of this generation, according to the novelist, "are brassy, metalic and in their ethics unsympathetic. Their best quality is a scorn of weakness, and their worst quality is a sort of inhumanity." They do not hold their heads as high as they used to, for their action has been conditioned by parental optimists who once boomed forth "Maybe in five years, I'll own—the company!" Peter Arno's *Hullaballo* typifies this generation for Mr. Fitzgerald.

The Shock generation is that of the war repeated. It has the same qualities and is a generation of daring. It is prematurely old, too. The Youth of this generation could not live without an education. It is not a happy one, but will prove itself more worthy of respect than the two generations which preceded it. The Shock group is not unlike the generation which grew up under defeat in the South after the Civil War. The blow gave it dignity. William Faulkner's *Pylon* is a somewhat morbid representation of the spirit of the Shock era.

The youngest generation is that of Hard-Times. "The less the parents of today try to tell their children, the more effective they can be in making them believe in a few old truths," Mr. Fitzgerald declared emphatically. "This generation should be held close to whatever elements of character we have been able to find and develop in ourselves." Mr. Fitzgerald says the book of this period has yet to be written.

"A Writer Like Me Must Have an Utter Confidence, an Utter Faith in His Star"

MICHEL MOK

Asheville, N. C., Sept. 25—Long ago, when he was young, cock-sure, drunk with sudden success, F. Scott Fitzgerald told a newspaper man that no one should live beyond thirty.

That was in 1921, shortly after his first novel, *This Side of Paradise*, had burst into the literary heavens like a Roman candle.

The poet-prophet of the post-war neurotics observed his fortieth birthday yesterday. . . . He spent the day as he spends all his days— trying to come back from the other side of Paradise, the hell of despondency in which he has agonized for the last couple of years.

He had no company except his nurse—a soft spoken, Southern, maternal young woman—and this reporter. With the girl he bantered in conventional nurse-and-patient fashion. With his visitor he chatted bravely, as an actor, consumed with fear that his name will never be in lights again, might discuss his next starring role.

He kidded no one. There obviously was as little hope in his heart as

Originally published as "The Other Side of Paradise," New York *Post*, September 25, 1936. Reprinted by permission of the New York *Post*. © 1936, New York Post Corporation. This text is a shortened version of the original.

there was sunshine in the dripping skies, covered with clouds that veiled the view of Sunset Mountain.

Physically he was suffering the aftermath of an accident eight weeks ago, when he broke his right shoulder in a dive from a fifteen-foot springboard.

But whatever pain the fracture might still cause him, it did not account for his jittery jumping off and onto his bed, his restless pacing, his trembling hands, his twitching face with its pitiful expression of a cruelly beaten child.

Nor could it be held responsible for his frequent trips to a highboy, in a drawer of which lay a bottle. Each time he poured a drink into the measuring glass on his bedside table, he would look appealingly at the nurse and ask, "Just one ounce?"

Each time the nurse cast down her eyes without replying.

Fitzgerald, for that matter, did not attempt to make his injury an excuse for his thirst.

"A series of things happened to papa," he said, with mock brightness. "So papa got depressed and started drinking a little."

What the "things" were he refused to explain.

"One blow after another," he said, "and finally something snapped."

Before coming to North Carolina, however, his visitor had learned something of Fitzgerald's recent history from friends in Baltimore, where he lived until last July.

The author's wife, Zelda, had been ill for some years. There was talk, said his friends, of an attempt at suicide on her part one evening when the couple were taking a walk in the country outside Baltimore. Mrs. Fitzgerald, so the story went, threw herself on the tracks before an oncoming express train. Fitzgerald, himself in poor health, rushed after her and narrowly saved her life.

There were other difficulties. Mrs. Fitzgerald finally was taken to a sanitarium near this city, and her husband soon followed her, taking a room in the rock-built Park Grove Inn, one of the largest and most famous resort hotels in America.

But the causes of Fitzgerald's breakdown are of less importance than its effects on the writer. In a piece entitled "Pasting It Together," one of three autobiographical articles published in *Esquire*, which appeared in the March issue of that magazine, Fitzgerald described himself as "a cracked plate."

Yesterday, toward the end of a long, rambling, disjointed talk, he put it in different words, not nearly as poetic but no less moving for that reason.

"A writer like me," he said, "must have an utter confidence, an utter faith in his star. It's an almost mystical feeling, a feeling of nothing-can-happen-to-me, nothing-can-harm-me, nothing-can-touch-me.

"Thomas Wolfe has it. Ernest Hemingway has it. I once had it. But through a series of blows, many of them my own fault, something happened to that sense of immunity and I lost my grip."

In illustration, he told a story about his father:

"As a boy, my father lived in Montgomery County, Maryland. Our family has been mixed up quite a bit in American history. My great-grandfather's brother was Francis Scott Key, who wrote 'The Star-Spangled Banner'; I was named for him. My father's aunt was Mrs. Suratt, who was hanged after the assassination of Lincoln because Booth had planned the deed in her house—you remember that three men and a woman were executed.

"As a youngster of nine, my father rowed spies across the river. When he was twelve he felt that life was finished for him. As soon as he could, he went West, as far away from the scenes of the Civil War as possible. He started a wicker-furniture factory in St. Paul. A financial panic in the nineties struck him and he failed.

"We came back East and my father got a job as a soap salesman in Buffalo. He worked at this for some years. One afternoon—I was ten or eleven—the phone rang and my mother answered it. I didn't understand what she said but I felt that disaster had come to us. My mother, a little while before, had given me a quarter to go swimming. I gave the money back to her. I knew something terrible had happened and I thought she could not spare the money now.

"Then I began to pray, 'Dear God,' I prayed, 'please don't let us go to the poorhouse; please don't let us go to the poorhouse.' A little while later my father came home. I had been right. He had lost his job.

"That morning he had gone out a comparatively young man, a man full of strength, full of confidence. He came home that evening, an old man, a completely broken man. He had lost his essential drive, his immaculateness of purpose. He was a failure the rest of his days."

Fitzgerald rubbed his eyes, his mouth, quickly walked up and down the room.

"Oh," he said, "I remember something else. I remember that when my father came home my mother said to me, 'Scott, say something to your father.'

"I didn't know what to say. I went up to him and asked, 'Father, who do you think will be the next President?' He looked out of the window. He didn't move a muscle. Then he said: 'I think Taft will.'

"My father lost his grip and I lost my grip. But now I'm trying to get back. I started by writing those pieces for *Esquire*. Perhaps they were a mistake. Too much de profundis. My best friend, a great American writer—he's the man I call my artistic conscience in one of the *Esquire* articles—wrote me a furious letter. He said I was stupid to write that gloomy personal stuff."

"What are your plans at the moment, Mr. Fitzgerald? What are you working on now?"

"Oh, all sorts of things. But let's not talk about plans. When you talk about plans, you take something away from them."

Fitzgerald left the room.

"Despair, despair, despair," said the nurse. "Despair day and night. Try not to talk about his work or his future. He does work, but only very little—maybe three, four hours a week."

Soon he returned. "We must celebrate the author's birthday," he said gayly. "We must kill the fatted calf or, at any rate, cut the candled cake."

He took another drink. "Much against your better judgment, my dear," he smiled at the girl.

Heeding the nurse's advice, the visitor turned the talk to the writer's early days and Fitzgerald told how *This Side of Paradise* came to be written.

"I wrote it when I was in the army," he said. "I was nineteen. I rewrote the whole book a year later. The title was changed, too. Originally, it was called 'The Romantic Egotist.' "

"Isn't *This Side of Paradise* a beautiful title? I'm good at titles, you know. I've published four novels and four volumes of short-stories. All my novels have good titles—*The Great Gatsby, The Beautiful and Damned* and *Tender Is the Night*. That's my latest book. I worked on it four years.

"Yes, I wrote *This Side of Paradise* in the army. I didn't go overseas —my army experience consisted mostly of falling in love with a girl in each city I happened to be in.

"I almost went across. They actually marched us onto a transport and then marched us right off again. Influenza epidemic or something. That was about a week before the armistice.

"We were quartered at Camp Mills, in Long Island. I sneaked out of bounds into New York—there was a girl concerned, no doubt—and

I missed the train back to Camp Sheridan, Ala., where we had been trained.

"So this is what I did. Went to the Pennsylvania station and commandeered an engine and a cab to take me to Washington to join the troops. I told the railroad people I had confidential war papers for President Wilson. Couldn't wait a minute. Couldn't be intrusted to the mails. They fell for my bluff. I'm sure it's the only time in the history of the United States Army that a lieutenant has commandeered a locomotive. I caught up with the regiment in Washington. No, I wasn't punished."

"But how about *This Side of Paradise?*"

"That's right—I'm wandering. After we were mustered out I went to New York. Scribner's turned my book down. Then I tried to get a job on a newspaper. I went to every newspaper office with the scores and lyrics of the Triangle shows of the two or three previous years under my arm—I had been one of the big boys in the Triangle Club at Princeton and I thought that would help. The office boys were not impressed."

One day, Fitzgerald ran into an advertising man who told him to stay away from the newspaper business. He helped him to get a job with the Barron Collier agency, and for some months Fitzgerald wrote slogans for street car cards.

"I remember," he said, "the hit I made with a slogan I wrote for the Muscatine Steam Laundry in Muscatine, Iowa—'We keep you clean in Muscatine.' I got a raise for that. 'It's perhaps a bit imaginative,' said the boss, 'but still it's plain that there's a future for you in this business. Pretty soon this office won't be big enough to hold you.' "

And so it turned out. It didn't take Fitzgerald long to get bored to the point of pain, and he quit. He went to St. Paul, where his parents again were living, and proposed that his mother give him the third floor of her home for a while and keep him in cigarettes.

"She did, and there in three months I completely rewrote my book. Scribner's took the revised manuscript in 1919, and they brought it out in the spring of 1920."

In *This Side of Paradise*, Fitzgerald had one of his principal characters take a crack at the popular authors of the period—some of whom are popular still—in these words:

"Fifty thousand dollars a year! My God, look at them, look at them—Edna Ferber, Gouverneur Morris, Fannie Hurst, Mary Roberts Rinehart—not producing among 'em one story or novel that will last ten years.

This man Cobb—I don't think he's either clever or amusing—and what's more, I don't think many people do, except the editors. He's just groggy with advertising. And—oh, Harold Bell Wright and Zane Grey, Ernest Poole and Dorothy Canfield try, but they are hindered by their absolute lack of any sense of humor."

And the lad wound up by saying it was no wonder that such English writers as Wells, Conrad, Galsworthy, Shaw and Bennett depended on America for over half their sales.

What does Fitzgerald think of the literary situation in this country today?

"It has improved a lot," he said. "The whole thing broke with 'Main Street.' Ernest Hemingway, I think, is the greatest living writer of English. He took that place when Kipling died. Next comes Thomas Wolfe and then Faulkner and Dos Passos.

"Erskine Caldwell and a few others have come up just a bit after our generation, and they haven't done quite so well. We were products of prosperity. The best art is produced in times of riches. The men who came some years after us didn't have the chance we had."

Has he changed his mind on questions of economics? Amory Blaine, the hero of *This Side of Paradise*, predicted the success of the Bolshevik experiment in Russia, foresaw eventual government ownership of all industries in this country.

"Oh, but I made an awful boner," said Fitzgerald. "Do you remember I said publicity would destroy Lenin? That was a fine prophecy. He became a saint.

"My views? Well, in a pinch, they'd still be pretty much toward the left."

Then the reporter asked him how he felt now about the jazz-mad, gin-mad generation whose feverish doings he chronicled in *This Side of Paradise*. How had they done? How did they stand up in the world?

"Why should I bother myself about them?" he asked. "Haven't I enough worries of my own? You know as well as I do what has happened to them.

"Some became brokers and threw themselves out of windows. Others became bankers and shot themselves. Still others became newspaper reporters. And a few became successful authors."

His face twitched.

"Successful authors!" he cried. "Oh, my God, successful authors!"

He stumbled over to the highboy and poured himself another drink.

Reviews

Apprentice Work Done at Princeton

"Shadow Laurels" (play), *Nassau Literary Magazine*, April 1915

. . . Mr. Fitzgerald's drama "Shadow-Laurels" (a piquant title) succeeds well for the most part in conveying the intended atmosphere of sordid and suffocating despair, an atmosphere so different from the "lies, sunlight, and salvation" of our sturdy Anglo-Saxon civilization. This implied contrast—if we read aright—between a French world of ideas plus impotence and an American world of sterile thought plus success is very suggestive. If the three men "like blind rats dying in a sewer" fail to see all of truth, neither is it altogether summed up in "the barren optimistic sophistries of comfortable moles." And this much and more should be apparent to the careful reader in spite of a somewhat Maeterlinckian mystery of atmosphere.

—L. Wardlaw Miles, *Daily Princetonian*, April 17

*

"The Ordeal" (short story), *Nassau Literary Magazine*, June 1915

. . . The interior conflict of the novice is well portrayed and the nameless dread induced by malign powers physically apparent in the ray of the waxen taper, is handled with restraint. . . . We might suggest, however, that Mr. Fitzgerald devote more care to the niceties of speech, especially in a story of this type, where style is of the utmost importance.

—Cortlandt Van Winkle, *Daily Princetonian*, June 9

*

"The Debutante" (play), *Nassau Literary Magazine*, January 1917

. . . Mr. Fitzgerald's deft and saucy satire reveals a quite uncanny discernment of the springs whereby a wayward debutante may shift the moving toyshop of her heart. The plot is lightly but firmly conceived; the air of light comedy is evenly sustained; the characters are sharply struck off and discriminated from each other. The people are unlikeable enough, yet we admire the skill of Helen's counterplay and the arch, if feline, naughtiness of her younger sister Cecilia. The latter's mock ennui and sophistication in the closing lines is wholly delicious.

—H. S. Murch, *Daily Princetonian,* January 19
*

"The Spire and the Gargoyle" (short story) and "Rain Before Dawn" (poem), *Nassau Literary Magazine,* February 1917

. . . Mr. Fitzgerald leads off in this number of the *Lit.* He is good at the Princeton background. My last visit to Princeton included just such an evening as he suggests with his "late-burning scholastic light" and "dripping fog." The first pages struck me as very good. Then I came to " 'Well, it's over,' he whispered to himself—'all over!' " There leapt back at me my own love for succinct and repetitive tragic phrases, when I was younger. It sounds typical, on paper, of "the boy"—and yet I wonder if a somewhat more profane ejaculation would not have been nearer the truth? And from that point the story became for me somewhat of an attempt at "fine writing." The beginning of "Part Two" confirmed this feeling, where the author is rather out of his depth among significances, even though such an excellent description sparkles out as "Perhaps because the 'bus on which he rode was resplendent in its shining new coat of green paint, and the stick-of-candy glamor of it had gone into his disposition." But there is also an extravagance of figurative speech which defeats its object. With such an instrument one must use a very deft surgeon's hand or the body of the phrase stiffens to a corpse (Perhaps a case in point!). Mr. Fitzgerald says that the preceptor's face was "latticed with enormous spectacles," again refers to these spectacles as "his two 'Mirrors of Shalott,' " and finally shows the boy and the gargoyle conversing in a restaurant *"knit together by the toast* and the sense of exile." The italics, of course, are mine. The author will see at once what I mean. The symbolism of "The Spire, and the Gargoyle" is hardly precise enough in relation to the "boy," is somewhat blurred. Therefore I doubt its real significance. Mr. Fitzgerald has an instinct for style but very little for proportion. His poem, "Rain before Dawn" has a number of virtues but is disarticulated. The total effect is confused. There is promise, however, in his work.

—William Rose Benét, *Daily Princetonian,* February 24
*

"Tarquin of Cheepside" (short story), *Nassau Literary Magazine*, April 1917

. . . The two stories "Tarquin of Cheapside" (I am sure I may be forgiven for not writing "Cheepside") and "Bring out Your Dead," calumniate, respectively, Shakespeare and Marlowe. Marlowe's finish "in a tavern brawl" is so familiar to us all that we are in no danger of being shocked by this fresh account. Mr. Knight simply makes us very sorry for Marlowe, all over again. . . . In all these stories of a dead age, one feels the psychologizing too modern—the phrasing of it, at least, for there is nothing particularly new in the states of mind. Mr. Fitzgerald has done the trick—for it is a trick, pure and simple—better on the whole than Mr. Knight; but then he has not had so many people dealing with his incident before him. "Tarquin of Cheapside" is strikingly well-written. If one does not believe the plot, that is because most of us made up our minds long ago as to what manner of man Shakespeare was and was not. We may have made up our minds wrongly; Mr. Fitzgerald's little hypothetical adventure may be plausible. But I think most people will laugh and say "Fie!" Personally, I am very glad that Mr. Fitzgerald wrote it. I got a new thrill out of it. I think it is as delightful as it is funny, to show Shakespeare up, at this stage of the game, as that sort of hero. Mr. Fitzgerald's story has the noble element of surprise that Mr. Knight's lacks. But Mr. Knight's story has its own poignancy.
—Katherine Fullerton Gerould, *Daily Princetonian*, April 24

*

"The Pierian Springs and the Last Straw" (short story) and "The Cameo Frame" (poem), *Nassau Literary Magazine*, October 1917

. . . *The Nassau Literary Monthly*, in the person of Mr. F. Scott Fitzgerald, has been and gone and went and done it. Williams College has been shown up, and there is nothing to do but close down the college and sit in sackcloth and ashes, a-repenting of our sins. The dreadful *exposé* occurs in a story in the October number of the Princeton magazine, entitled "The Pierian Springs and the Last Straw," though what the Pierian Springs have to do with the last straw, or whether the straw is intended for convenience in drinking out of the springs, or not, goodness knows, and Mr. Fitzgerald doesn't say. The story is about a talented author, who is also a Regular Devil, and who used to be member of the board of this staid and respectable Williams journal. Mr. Fitzgerald says so.

The name of the distinguished author and regular devil is George

Rombert. This is how Mr. Fitzgerald describes him: "A Romeo and a mesogamist, a combination of Byron, Don Juan, and Bernard Shaw, with a touch of Havelock Ellis for good measure. He was about thirty, had been engaged seven times, and drank ever so much more than was good for him. . . ."

You know that kind of characterization. Why Mr. Fitzgerald doesn't add the Kaiser, Herr von Bernstorff and the Crown Prince, and make it complete, I can't imagine. At any rate, the story is so explicit as to Uncle George's deep purple character that the merest numbskull can feel fairly certain that he is not a Methodist clergyman.

Then there is a girl. A Girl, to be quite explicit; and her methods are those of the movie vamp, simple and direct, and entirely uninspired by the fear of God. Let Uncle George tell the whole sad story himself:

"When she wanted a boy there was no preliminary scouting among other girls for information, no sending out of tentative approaches meant to be retailed to him. There was just direct attack by every faculty and gift that she possessed. She had no divergence of method—she just made you conscious to the highest degree that she was a girl. . . . We had the most frantic correspondence—each wrote ridiculous letters and sent ridiculous telegrams, told all our acquaintances about our flaming affair and—well, you've been to college. All this is banal."

Mr. Fitzgerald hits the nail squarely in that last sentence. It is—very. But why does he wish Uncle George on to the *Williams Literary Monthly*. He avers that he once saw a picture of the naughty but dreadfully clever Uncle George—imagine a regular devil named Uncle George!—"at Williams in the center of the Literary Magazine picture."

"Half a thought in my brain," Uncle George is made to say in another place, "would have sent me to Williamstown or the Manhattan bar."

Very probably. Very probably indeed. They are both very excellent places of their kind.

Mr. Fitzgerald is a very clever young man, and he has written some extraordinarily good verse, which Mr. Alfred Noyes printed in his recent *Book of Princeton Verse*. But why does Mr. Fitzgerald dismount from Pegasus to attack the short story? Not to mention the *Williams Lit.*

—John Bakeless, *Williams Literary Magazine*, November

This Side of Paradise: A Youth in the Saddle

BURTON RASCOE

If you have not already done so, make a note of the name, F. Scott Fitzgerald. It is borne by a 23-year-old novelist who will, unless I am much mistaken, be much heard of hereafter. His first novel *This Side of Paradise* gives him, I think, a fair claim to membership in that small squad of contemporary American fictionists who are producing literature. It is sincere, it is honest, it is intelligent, it is handled in an individual manner, it bears the impress, it seems to me, of genius. It is the only adequate study that we have had of the contemporary American in adolescence and young manhood.

Beside it Tarkington's *Seventeen*, Johnson's *Stover at Yale*, and Samuel Merwin's yarns are amusing and superficial sketches. Here are not the obviously ridiculous episodes of youth, the maturely callow reflections upon callow sentiments; but the truth about prep school boys and American collegians by a young man who has just emerged from their experiences.

Ten years from now, it seems safe to say, Mr. Fitzgerald could not have written this book. He may—I think he will—write better books; but, ten years from now, he could not, probably, give so sincere a record of the activities, the reactions, the reflections, and the problems of the adolescent and immature. At 35 the episodes herein related would have taken on a more romantic cast; nostalgia would have empurpled the grayest fact; the skepticism of age would have discounted the relevance of important points; and caution would have killed its charming frankness.

It is a novel which is, curiously, important largely through its apparent defects—its bland egotism, its conceited extravagance, its immaturity of thought. The hero is frequently a prig, a snob, an ass, and—may I whisper it?—something of a cad; but a youth is all these things rather than the amiable baby Mr. Tarkington pictures him as being. Moreover, at 17 a youth has despite the evidence of Mr. Tarkington, begun to think —funny things, true enough—but to think, to have ideas, worries, am-

Originally published as "A Youth in the Saddle," Chicago *Daily Tribune*, April 3, 1920. Reprinted by permission of the Chicago *Tribune*.

bitions—unless he is fated for a life of utter stupidity and automatic action.

In form the novel shows traces of various happy influences. It opens in a manner somewhat reminiscent of Joseph Hergesheimer; the boy's mother is a bit like Linda's mother in *Linda Condon* and she is handled in somewhat the same deft, unflinching fashion. Then the influence of Joyce's *Portrait of the Artist as a Young Man* is seen in the effects obtained in condensation, the elimination of detail and needless links in narrative, and the use of episodic material—a snatch of dialogue, a bit of sure and rapid characterization, a passage of introspection. And the younger English novelists have given him the key to the literary treasure of early manhood. But all these influences he has made his own and he has developed out of them a peculiarly individual method of presentation. When a one-act playlet with stage directions serves his purpose better than a chapter of prose narrative, he uses it. When a poem is written by the youth at the inspiration of a pretty girl, he gives us the poem. When his mood is that of exalted reflection, he records in italics his musings of the moment. That these poems are rather bad and that the "exalted reflections" are rather rhetorical matters not; they serve reality. Everything is grist for his mill and the product is excellent.

This Side of Paradise: Two Undergraduate Views

I. DAVID W. BAILEY (HARVARD)

HE: I'm afraid of you. I'm always afraid of a girl—until I've kissed her.

SHE: (Emphatically) My dear boy, the war is over.

HE: So I'll always be afraid of you.

SHE: (Rather sadly) I suppose you will.

(A slight hesitation on both their parts.)

HE: (After due consideration) Listen. This is a frightful thing to ask.

SHE: (Knowing what's coming) After five minutes.

HE: But will you—kiss me? Or are you afraid?

SHE: I'm never afraid—but your reasons are so poor.

HE: Rosalind, I really WANT to kiss you.

Originally published as "A Novel About Flappers For Philosophers," *Harvard Crimson*, May 1, 1920.

SHE: So do I.

(They kiss—definitely and thoroughly)

HE: (After a breathless second) Well, is your curiosity satisfied?

SHE: Is your's?

HE: No, it's only aroused.

(He looks it.)

SHE: (Dreamily) I've kissed dozens of men. I suppose I'll kiss dozens more.

HE: (Abstractedly) Yes, I suppose you could—like that.

SHE: Most people like the way I kiss.

HE: (Remembering himself) Good Lord, yes. Kiss me once more, Rosalind.

That's only a sample from Mr. Fitzgerald's first novel—and the rest is just as good as that, and better. Small wonder the book has taken the bookstalls by storm, that it has been hailed as a truly American novel, bewildering, brilliant. The story is a little slice carved out of real life, running over with youth and jazz and sentiment and romance and virile American humor—everything in short that is dear to a Princeton man (Mr. Fitzgerald himself), or a Yale man, or a Harvard man, or just any kind of a man. The author calls it a book about flappers for philosophers, which amounts to the same thing.

The title page of *This Side of Paradise* is appropriately graced with quotations from Rupert Brooke and Oscar Wilde. The wrapper is suitably decorated by a charming young debutante with an enormous fan and by a typical "slicker," whom we suspect of being the artist's conception of a Princeton man, with his bow-tie neatly tucked under at the corners, leaning thoughtfully over her armchair.

The story itself tells the history of one Amory Blaine, son of a highly emotional mother, pampered and petted in his childhood, brought through his boyish years by relatives in the Twin Cities, prepared at an expensive eastern school and sent to Princeton. Mere narrative, however interesting, is lost sight of, however, in the presence of Isabelle, Clara, Rosalind, and Eleanor, and a host of other young ladies who in turn serve as objects of Amory's infatuation. And such a quartet as they make.

Isabelle, with her wide and starry eyes, that "proclaimed the ingenue," was the heroine of the first great episode in Amory's varied career among women-folk. She proved to him the power of young contralto voices on sink-down sofas, but she didn't last—dear me, no. Amory made the "Prince," became a half-celebrity at Nassau, "slid smoothly into Cottage"—and met Clara.

Clara was a distant cousin or something, and a charming young widow. She and Amory read Browning together. He even would have proposed to her, but she headed him off in time and he remembered her as the only girl he ever knew with whom he could understand how another man might be preferred.

With the coming of the war many of the old friendships were broken up, and upon his return to America in 1919 Amory found only Alec Connage and Tom D'Invilliers, the former a son of the idle rich, the latter a promising young scribbler. Alec's sister, Rosalind, the charming debutante figuring in the little drama quoted above, quickly became the object of the only deep and abiding love that Amory ever experienced. That, too, was put behind, though, and the next target for despondent Amory's affections was the rollicking figure of Old King Cole over the Knickerbocker Bar.

Alcohol served to dull the poignancy of his pain and tide his soul over until the day he met Eleanor Savage—Eleanor, whom he found seated a-top of a haystack, singing verses from Verlaine to an extemporaneous tune. She had discovered him first, reciting "Ulalume," and a kindred feeling was at once aroused by their romantic meeting. To see the outcome of his friendship for Eleanor and the result of the clash within him of the artist striving for unbridled expression and the orthodox but disgraced puritan turning to the refuge of conventionality one must read the book.

And to read *This Side of Paradise* once is to read it twice and to quote it endlessly.

II. R. F. MCPARTLIN (DARTMOUTH)

Dartmouth students have a not peculiar antipathy for the collegiate life commonly given us in the modern novel or movie. Rightly so, for nothing is more horrible than Paramount's conception of a football hero, Selznick's idea of a famous stroke oar, or even Booth Tarkington's laughable picture of an undergraduate Bolshevist. But now comes the

Originally published as "Princeton Scene of Novel—'This Side of Paradise' is True-to-Life Novel," *The Dartmouth*, April 24, 1920. Reprinted by permission of *The Dartmouth*.

first book which is "regular." *This Side of Paradise* fulfills the demands of readers who know undergraduate life at first-hand, and who wish to have it described in an entertaining yet always faithful manner.

F. Scott Fitzgerald, a 1917 man at Princeton, is the author. The first half of the story, if a series of episodes such as this may be classed under that head, is woven almost entirely about Dartmouth's erstwhile "big" opponent. Yet many of the incidents might well have taken place in Hanover, so truly collegiate are they.

The book abounds in slang, much of it wholly individual to Princeton, but every word has its Dartmouth synonym. "Petting," promising title of one episode, is locally known by the less euphemistic "mugging." A "slicker," transferred from New Jersey to New Hampshire, becomes a "smooth bird." "Goopher," "simple,"—much of the Dartmouth dictionary may be used in working out the translation of the story for the non-college reader.

Sticking to the same slang, we might say that there are some among our undergraduates who will find some parts of the book a trifle damp. But we must take in consideration that Amory Blaine, the hero, is essentially literary, even if he is a member of the staff of *The Daily Princetonian*, parallel of *The Dartmouth*. Amory breaks into poetry every now and then, but his stuff is pretty readable, and anyway, you can skip it, if you don't like it.

This Side of Paradise should be read by every Dartmouth undergraduate, if for no other reason than the tremendous insight it gives him into life at another, and somewhat different college. It is a story that will point out at least one big lack locally—a novel of Dartmouth—and one that may well prompt some potential fiction writer, now an undergraduate, to prepare for the production of such a novel a few years from now.

This Side of Paradise: With College Men

NEW YORK TIMES BOOK REVIEW

The glorious spirit of abounding youth glows throughout this fascinating tale. Amory, the "romantic egotist," is essentially American, and as we follow him through his career at Princeton, with its riotous gayety, its superficial vices, and its punctilious sense of honor which will tolerate nothing less than the standard set up by itself, we know that he is doing just what hundreds of thousands of other young men are doing in colleges all over the country. As a picture of the daily existence of what we call loosely "college men," this book is as nearly perfect as such a work could be. The philosophy of Amory, which finds expression in ponderous observations, lightened occasionally by verse that one thinks could have evolved only in the cloistered atmosphere of his age-old alma mater, is that of any other youth in his teens in whom intellectual ambition is ever seeking an outlet. Amory's love affairs, too, are racy of the soil, while the girls, whose ideas of the modern development of their sex seem to embrace a rather frequent use of the word "Damn," and of being kissed by young men whom they have no thought of marrying, quite obviously belong to Amory's world. Through it all there is the spirit of innocence in so far as actual wrongdoing is implied, and one cannot but feel that the sexes are well-matched according to the author's presentment. Amory Blaine has a well-to-do father and a mother who lives the somewhat idle, luxurious life of a matron who has never known the pinch of even economy, much less of poverty, and the boy is the creature of his environment. One knows always that he will be safe at the end. So he is, for he does his bit in the war, finds afterward that his money has all gone and goes to work writing advertisements for an agency. Also, he has his supreme love affair, with Rosalind Connage, which is broken off because the nervous temperaments of both would not permit happiness. At least, so the girl thinks. So Amory goes on the biggest spree noted in the book—a spree which is colorfully described as taking in everything in the alcoholic line from the Knicker-

Originally published as "With College Men," *New York Times Book Review*, May 9, 1920. © 1920, The New York Times Company. Reprinted by permission.

bocker "Old King Cole" bar to an out-of-the-way drinking den where Amory is "beaten up" artistically and thoroughly. The whole story is disconnected, more or less, but loses none of its charm on that account. It could have been written only by an artist who knows how to balance his values, plus a delightful literary style.

This Side of Paradise: Books More or Less Amusing

H. L. MENCKEN

The best American novel that I have seen of late is also the product of a neophyte, to wit, F. Scott Fitzgerald. . . . In *This Side of Paradise* he offers a truly amazing first novel—original in structure, extremely sophisticated in manner, and adorned with a brilliancy that is as rare in American writing as honesty is in American statecraft. The young American novelist usually reveals himself as a naïve, sentimental and somewhat disgusting ignoramus—a believer in Great Causes, a snuffler and eye-roller, a spouter of stale philosophies out of Kensington drawing-rooms, the doggeries of French hackdrivers, and the lower floor of the Munich Hofbräuhaus. Nine times out of ten one finds him shocked by the discovery that women are not the complete angels that they pretend to be, and full of the theory that all of the miners in West Virginia would become instantly non-luetic, intelligent and happy if Congress would only pass half a dozen simple laws. In brief, a fellow viewing human existence through a knot-hole in the floor of a Socialist local. Fitzgerald is nothing of the sort. On the contrary he is a highly civilized and rather waggish fellow—a youngster not without sentiment, and one even cursed with a touch or two of pretty sentimentality, but still one who is many cuts above the general of the land. More, an artist—an apt and delicate weaver of words, a clever hand, a sound workman. The first half of the story is far better than the second half. It is not that Fitzgerald's manner runs thin, but that his hero begins to elude him. What, after such a youth, is to be done with the fellow? The author's solution is anything but felicitous. He simply drops his

Originally published as "Books More or Less Amusing," *Smart Set*, August 1920. This text is a shortened version of the original.

Amory Blaine as Mark Twain dropped Huckleberry Finn, but for a less cogent reason. But down to and including the episode of the love affair with Rosalind the thing is capital, especially the first chapters. Not since Frank Norris's day has there been a more adept slapping in of preliminaries.

This Side of Paradise: The Dangerous Teens

SAN FRANCISCO CHRONICLE

F. Scott Fitzgerald's *This Side of Paradise* has a very troublesome sort of power, uneven and shaky, like a child pulling out the stops of a great pipe organ. This epic of youth embodies a real attempt to say something—it is said sometimes morbidly, sometimes shrilly, sometimes foolishly. It combines a certain precosity of language with such gaucherie as "latter of the three" and "whom I admit is." Its struggle toward expression of the nightmare of adolescence has innumerable faults and a haunting touch of talent.

As a presentation of the dreams and ways of our generation of young men and girls, we are rescued from the sense of depravity which makes the "yellow nineties" shine as clear sunshine in comparison by the doubt whether color quite so lurid could be the right paint for any very large group of people still in their teens. Amory Blaine, egoist, poseur, whose progress through youth is the theme of the book, encounters a bewildering procession of sensually beautiful young girls, who have vaguely hinted "pasts" at the age of 16 and a half, who invariably kiss Amory first and talk to him afterward, and behind whom stretches so indefinite a number of passionate episodes that one wonders when they had time for them all, unless they began in their kiddy-koops. One of these sirens (none of whom are older than 19 years), "whispered 'Damn' as no other girl was ever able to whisper it." These young people are bound to be sophisticated at all costs, but their desperate disillusionment has an atmosphere of hectic unreality. It is all ridiculous and tantalizing, morbid and mad—a debauch of the imagination which sug-

Originally published as "The Dangerous Teens," San Francisco *Chronicle*, August 22, 1920. Reprinted by permission of the San Francisco *Chronicle*.

gests to the psychologically curious that the author's preoccupation with evilly alluring debutantes who drink a great deal and kiss a great deal more is akin to St. Anthony's tempting visions, indicating, not that he depicts a social condition which he knows, but that he projects a purely subjective phantasy. If this were all, it would not be worth calling attention to. But throughout the intensities of life at Princeton and in New York, whose episodes are punctuated with heavily embossed poems, runs a faculty for making the most absurd abnormalities compellingly vivid. There is indication in the closing chapter, when Amory Blaine has lost his money and is tramping the road to Princeton, that he will awaken from his subjective absorption and look upon the world with a new keenness of apprehension. When he has done this, he will be worth a real novel. Meanwhile, whatever its very glaring shortcomings of conception and execution, *This Side of Paradise* is of interest—not as an accurate delineation of social conditions among our gilded youth, but as a "psychological document" adumbrating the murky adolescence of its author, who, we suspect, is not yet quite as old as his hero at the end of the volume. If he is really not a case of arrested development, he will almost certainly, when he grows up, write something worth reading for its own sake, which will be less like an additional chapter to G. Stanley Hall's *Adolescence* or a psychopathological case record.

Incidentally, he may then be less supercillious about Edgar Lee Masters, whom he dismisses rather loftily with a reference to his "conscientious, if slender, artistry."

This Side of Paradise

LONDON TIMES LITERARY SUPPLEMENT

This Side of Paradise, by F. Scott Fitzgerald, will interest readers less for its own sake than as evidence of the intellectual and moral reaction that has set in among the more advanced American circles. As a novel, it is rather tiresome; its values are less human than literary, and its characters, men and women alike, with hardly an exception, a set of exasper-

Originally published as "*This Side of Paradise*," *Times Literary Supplement*, June 23, 1921. Reprinted by permission of the London *Times*.

ating *poseurs*, whose conversation, devoted largely to minute self-analysis, is artificial beyond belief. Consider, for example, the following fragment of a conversation that is supposed to take place between a boy of fifteen and his mother:

"Are you quite well now, Beatrice?"

"Quite well—as well as I will ever be. I am not understood, Amory. I know that can't express it to you, Amory, but—I am not understood."

Amory was quite moved. He put his arm round his mother, rubbing his head gently against her shoulder.

"Poor Beatrice—poor Beatrice."

"Tell me about *you*, Amory. Did you have two horrible years?"

Amory considered lying, and then decided against it.

"No, Beatrice. I enjoyed it. I adapted myself to the bourgeoisie. I became conventional."

Is such dialogue credible, even in America, where black cats are doubtless blacker and egoists more fantastically self-absorbed than in our less precocious European countries? Or take the following exchange of compliments between two young people who have just made each other's acquaintance (it will be noticed that the author switches away from narrative into drama without the slightest warning or apology):

SHE: Most people like the way I kiss.

HE (remembering himself): Good Lord, yes. Kiss me once more, Rosalind.

SHE: No—my curiosity is generally satisfied at one.

HE (discouraged): Is that a rule?

SHE: I make rules to fit the cases.

HE: You and I are somewhat alike—except that I'm years older in experience.

SHE: How old are you?

HE: Almost twenty-three. You?

SHE: Nineteen—just.

HE: I suppose you're the product of a fashionable school.

SHE: No—I'm fairly raw material. I was expelled from Spence—I've forgotten why.

HE: What's your general trend?

SHE: Oh, I'm bright, quite selfish, emotional when aroused, fond of admiration.

And so on. It is idle to take such people seriously. But a pose can be amusing, and though we cannot laugh and weep with Rosalind and Amory (as their creator, we suspect, would really like us to do) we can often laugh at them. In their very unreality, moreover, they foreshadow an anti-Puritan phase, which may be destined to outgrow its purely literary beginnings and become a vital force in the development of American culture. They never have existed, never will exist, yet in their way they are representative—an omen of liberation.

Flappers and Philosophers

LOS ANGELES TIMES

The youthful perpetrator of *This Side of Paradise*, a first novel referred to by one critic as "a masterly monograph on life in its osculatory aspects," has now produced a group of short stories which bid fair to attract as much attention as did the novel, which reached the umpty-teenth edition in record time.

Mr. Fitzgerald, who is still in what his heroine would call early middle age, being 24, is an original limb, seeing life through his own eyes and expressing his thoughts thereon in his own way. His specialty is the all-devouring flapper, half woman and half vixen, full of pertness and self-esteem, all aflame with the instinct for the perpetuation of the race, but quite able to take care of herself in all circumstances.

The first story in the book, "The Offshore Pirate," is a jolly fairy tale beginning thus:

'This unlikely story begins on a sea that was a blue dream, as colorful as blue silk stockings, and beneath a sky as blue as the irises of children's eyes. From the western part of the sky, the sun was shying little gold disks—at the sea—if you gazed intently you could see them skip from wave tip to wave tip until they joined a broad collar of golden coin that was collecting half a mile out and would eventually be a dazzling sunset. About half way between the Florida shore and the

Originally published as an untitled review, Los Angeles *Times*, January 9, 1921.

golden collar a white steam yacht, very young and graceful, was riding anchor, and under a blue-and-white awning aft a yellow-haired girl reclined in a wicker settee reading 'The Revolt of the Angels' by Anatole France.

'She was about 19, slender and supple, with a spoiled, alluring mouth and quick gray eyes full of radiant curiosity. Her feet, stocking-less and adorned rather than clad in blue satin slippers which swung nonchalantly from her toes, were perched on the arm of a settee op-posite the one she occupied. And as she read she intermittently re-galed herself by a faint application to her tongue of a half-lemon that she held in her hand. The other half, sucked dry, lay on the deck at her feet and rocked very gently to and fro at the almost impercepti-ble motion of the tide.'

If such a beginning does not pique the reader's curiosity, Scott Fitz-gerald is not for him. If it does, why spoil the tale by telling more of it here?

In more serious vein is "The Ice Palace," which pictures the effect upon Sally Carrol, southerner, of northern ways, and northern temper-ment, reaching the climax when she becomes lost in the ice palace and feels the life slowly squeezed out of her body by the cold. Though the story has life and feeling, it strikes one as being merely a story, not a transcript from life. In other of these stories we have the same feeling at times; the author does not always conceal the mechanics of his master-pieces, so we consider them now and then rather as clever literary pro-ductions than accounts of actual happenings. But they are clever enough to amuse and entertain even at their worst.

"Head and Shoulders" is the whimsical account of an infant prodigy who at the age of 17, went to Yale to study for his master's degree, and then, "just as nonchalantly as though Horace Tarbox had been Mr. Beef, the butcher, or Mr. Hat, the haberdasher, life reached in, seized him, handled him, stretched him, and unrolled him like a piece of Irish lace on a Saturday afternoon bargain counter." It was Horace's meeting with Marcia Meadow, a show girl who "sang a song about the 'Blunder-ing Blimp' in the first act and did a shaky, shivery, celebrated dance in the last," that was his undoing. Just how Marcia and life together undid him you must read Mr. Fitzgerald's story to find out. All youths about to throw ambition to the winds in order to marry the pretty girl with whom they are now in love should read this story and ponder it well. Of course, it won't deter them—nothing will, unless they meet another pretty girl in time—but it will show them just what hash they may make of their lives.

In "The Cut Glass Bowl" the victims of an implacable fate are depicted, a couple hopelessly struggling against odds, but doomed to defeat. The story is a little forced, suggesting now and then that it is the implacable author, after all, who is responsible for the tragic and sordid series of events that spoiled the lives of the characters and that life is not to be held responsible.

"Bernice Bobs Her Hair" is one of the most successful stories of the book, dealing as it does with sub-debs and the equally obnoxious youth who fill their horizon. It is your flapper that Mr. Fitzgerald does best, not because he loves her, but because he is able to see quite through her. Her cold calculation, her barreness of soul, her technique and her make-up are all as clear as day to him. Yet seeing her as she is, he finds her still amusing if not tantalizing. Three other stories, "Benediction," "Dalrymple Goes Wrong" and "The Four Fists" complete the collection. What next?

The Beautiful and Damned: The Flapper's Tragedy

HENRY SEIDEL CANBY

This is a pathetic story. It is the bitter cry of the children who have grown up in their pleasant vices and found them no longer pleasant, but only expensive habits. Mr. Fitzgerald's flapper has grown harder as she has grown older. The paint that was so piquant begins to fleck off, the pursuit of pleasure grows feverish. His college dilettantes come to the crossroads and, finding that the only lesson to be learned from life is that there is no lesson to be learned from life, chuck what ideals they had, cut their unsuccessful friends, and go after material success. Or they become still more dilettantish and end in perfect futility. Getting drunk on Saturday nights becomes a necessity. Without money the

Originally published as "The Flapper's Tragedy," New York *Post*, March 4, 1922. Reprinted by permission of the New York *Post*. © 1922, New York Post Corporation.

world is unendurable. Gloria, the beautiful girl, loses her only spiritual virtue, the clean instinct for splendid physical living. Anthony, the would-be connoisseur, becomes an alcoholic. His brilliant group of friends find their own particular damnations.

In other words, Scott Fitzgerald, rather surprisingly, has written a tragedy, an almost uncompromising tragedy, which is more than their critics have led us to expect from one of the younger generation. He has felt the implications of a rudderless society steering gayly for nowhere and has followed them down the rapids to final catastrophe. Not, of course, in any Puritan fashion nor with an Ibsen view of the sins of the race, but simply because his story led him that way; and defiantly scoffing at lessons, joyously dwelling upon the life that leads his friends to perdition, he follows. I admire him for it; and if *This Side of Paradise* showed in certain passages and in the essential energy of the whole that he had glimpses of a genius for sheer writing, this book proves that he has the artist's conscience and enough intellect to learn how to control the life that fascinates him.

He has not yet learned that lesson, a lesson which even those who believe, as he pretends to believe, that life is meaningless, must learn. He has chosen to wallow in naturalism, to be a romantic unrestrained, and he must pay the price. The scenes of debauchery in this book will be very much censured, by some on moral grounds, by others (more justly, I think) on artistic; his verbose excursions into philosophy and literary criticism will be mentioned without favor. And it will be his own fault. Following what he believes to be popular taste, he has decided to gratify curiosity as to what they do on Broadway after midnight with the fullest detail, and to supply scenes at riotous country-house week-ends regardless of taste and proportion. Following his own desire, he has reported his own reactions to life and its problems in general with a fulness only justifiable in a young man's diary. Like a reporter with a moving-picture camera, he has squirmed into hallways and hid behind café tables until the result is an endless film of racy pictures, relieved by aesthetic vaporings. "Give 'em all the truth," has been his motto, and therefore from one point of view *The Beautiful and Damned* is not so much a novel as an irresponsible social document, veracious, in its way, as photographs are always veracious in their way, but often untruthful, as photographs are often untruthful, and with about the same relation to the scope and significance of life that is possessed by a society drama in the films.

Thanks to these excesses, Mr. Fitzgerald will miss his due meed of praise for some very outstanding accomplishments, and his book will be talked about for what is least valuable in it. Readers who spend their time counting the number of cocktails drunk in each chapter are not in the proper mood to appreciate subtler claims upon their attention. They will miss in their pursuit of sensationalism the evidences of great and growing artistic power which this book undoubtedly displays. No finer study of the relations between boy husband and girl wife has been given us in American fiction. If Anthony Patch, the hero, is a nullity, scarcely worth following after the graceful sketch of his first steps in connoisseurship, Gloria is an original creation, frightening in her truth. And when he is not showing off in pseudo-wit, or trying to shock the bourgeoisie, or discovering profound truths of philosophy which get muddled before he can grasp them, how this novelist can write!

Of course, like Mr. Hergesheimer's *Cytherea*, this novel is another picture of a society upset by modernism. And like Mr. Hergesheimer, Mr. Fitzgerald is too much in the whirl, too much in love with its abandoned irresponsibility, to understand it, and to be detached while still sympathetic. But if *The Beautiful and Damned* is a less competent book than *Cytherea*, and if its author is far more deeply involved in the life he tries to see as from without, nevertheless the mute witness of the story to tragedy is more impressive, simply because it is the youngest generation, yesterday's children, who are dancing and suffering there. Of course, it is only the flapper fringe of them that he depicts, but in that margin are involved the more sensitive spirits, those richer in life as well as in gayety, the feelers and some of the thinkers, young men and young women who visibly embody the charm and the inspiration of youth. Fitzgerald has written of them as a man would write who watches a cabaret dance through rosy films of exhilaration, but his knowledge of their hearts is nevertheless poignant, and he is never too intoxicated with the excitement of living to miss the tragedy waiting behind. It is a pathetic story, which seems to say, "Here we are, we youngsters, and this is how we can drink and suffer and wonder and pretend to have no hope. What do you make of us?"

The answer is that we are a little disgusted, a little touched, and profoundly interested. When Mr. Fitzgerald himself grows up, in art as well as in philosophy, he may tell us more, and more wisely. He will write better novels, but he will probably never give us better documents of distraught and abandoned but intensely living youth.

The Beautiful and Damned:
Mr. Fitzgerald Sees the Flapper Through

JOHN PEALE BISHOP

However barren may have been the wise and their old wisdoms, Scott Fitzgerald, at the time when he was writing *This Side of Paradise*, found ample comfort in the doings of feckless and brave-hearted young. Amory Blaine, like another Playboy, went romancing through a foolish world, kissing innumerable girls between 9 o'clock and midnight, drinking wittily with his fellows from midnight until the milkman brought up the dawn, discarding old loves and dead beliefs like a brisk young snake, who every month might slough off his dry shell for a new, shining green skin. Even the breaking of his heart was a sound to be listened to and enjoyed like the rest. Mr. Fitzgerald has in the meanwhile lost none of his alertness in observing the manners and speech of his contemporaries, but he no longer finds any great pleasure in the American scene. Life it seems is now meaningless; the beautiful are damned; the glamour he once saw was only a gauze curtain lowered before the stage to conceal the fact that those twilight nymphs were, after all, only middle-aged chorus ladies.

Anthony Patch, who succeeds Amory Blaine as a figure through whom Mr. Fitzgerald may write of himself, is when *The Beautiful and Damned* opens 25, and it is already two years "since irony, the Holy Ghost of this later day," has, theoretically at least, descended upon him. Irony was the final polish of the shoe, the ultimate dab of the clothes brush, a sort of intellectual 'There!'—yet at the brink of this story he has as yet gone no further than the conscious stage."

Since the younger generation, as they are commonly called, began finding publishers and appearing on lecture platforms, this word irony has been heard with such frequency that I have begun to wonder just what these young men mean by it. Mr. Fitzgerald invokes it, and Stephen Vincent Benét inscribes it on all his gay banners, and even Donald Ogden Stewart is frequently heard to murmur it between whacks

Originally published as "Mr. Fitzgerald Sees the Flapper Through," New York *Herald*, March 5, 1922. Reprinted by permission of the New York **Sun** Corporation.

with his buffoon's bladder. And I am a little confused, for clearly they do not mean that faculty which allows one to smile appreciatively when Tragedy enters wearing a propitious mask and speaking equivocal phrases. Their irony is not that good counsellor of Anatole France, who, in smiling, renders life a thing to be loved the more, who rails neither at love nor beauty, who teaches us to mock liars and fools, which we should, without her, be feeble enough to hate. As I say, I am a little uncertain just what these young men mean when they hold themselves to speak ironically. For they have not that superb detachment which would allow them to expose the littleness of their characters without ever seeming themselves to rush in with a measuring rod, their mockery is not dispassionately gay, they cannot allow circumstances to slaughter their heroes without applying a dagger or two with their own hands.

II

With Mr. Fitzgerald, if one is to judge by his latest book, he means to say that Anthony has found out that life is purposeless, beauty in no way allied with the truth, all effort, even of the intellect, unreasonable. Anthony is, when he is presented to us, a man "aware that there could be no honor and yet had honor, who knew the sophistry of courage and yet was brave." Later, it is true, he turns out to be an arrant coward on occasion and disports himself most dishonorably. Of irony he never either in the beginning nor at the end achieves more than a passing glimpse.

As a matter of fact, Anthony Comstock Patch is a rather futile young man with a pallid skin and dark polished hair, shy enough in his extreme youth to have spent his time among many books without deriving from them either erudition or richness of mind. It is his inherent laziness rather than a fine skepticism which prevents him from ever accomplishing more than a single precious essay toward his volume on the Renaissance Popes. It is his uxoriousness which makes of him a pathetic adjunct to the more vivid Gloria, the thinness of his zest for life which makes him turn, more and more thirstily, toward alcohol. Sophisticated, he is constantly under the illusion that he is rather superior in intellect and character to the persons about him; disillusioned, he is at the mercy of circumstances.

In 1913 he is living in an apartment in the Fifties of New York trying to prove that an American can live idly and gracefully on seven thousand a year. He is awakened each morning by a frayed English servant with the exquisitely appropriate name of Bounds; he arises to bathe in his mirrored and crimson carpeted bathroom; he arranges his impeccable toilet and saunters forth to savor life effortlessly. He pays hasty and unwilling visits to his grandfather, Adam J. Patch, once known as a financier who had risen by none too creditable means, now as a reformer employing a retinue of paid moralists. He loafs and invites his soul with two friends—Maury Noble, imperturbably feline, self-consciously superior, animated by an undisguised boredom, and Richard Caramel, a bulgy young novelist, with one brown and one topaz eye, who is destined before he is 30 to have written a number of utterly silly novels which he will believe to be wise.

Comes then into his life one Gloria—as Mr. Fitzgerald with a recently acquired fondness for the D. W. Griffith order of words might well say—"Coast to Coast Gloria," she of the bobbed hair and the many sounding kisses, with lips carmined and sweetly profane, with an enduring taste for gumdrops and swiftly passing fancies for attractive young men. She is Rosalind of *This Side of Paradise* seen through slightly older and less romantic eyes; she is the girl of "The Off Shore Pirate" portrayed at full-length with a more careful treatment of light and shade and more conscious accumulation of detail. Born in Kansas City, Mo., of a Bilphist mother and father engaged in the celluloid business, she has been brought to her twenty-third year in surroundings of inescapable vulgarity. She has the wit to perceive that there is something tawdry in her prettiness; she has not the innate perception of form which would have allowed her to become beautiful. It has obviously been within Mr. Fitzgerald's intention to give her a touch of that immemorial loveliness which is in Donna Rita despite her peasant origin, a suggestion of that power to drive young men wild which was Zuleika Dobson's for all her rococo vulgarity. He has allowed her a sensitiveness to sensuous impressions, a more delicate perception than might be expected from a flapper with a past so monotonous in its promiscuity. Gloria has the hard and solitary will of a child and a child's petulance and vanity. Spoiled, contemptuous, willful, she feels pathetically that somewhere her beauty might have had its due; here she must take whatever adulation comes her way, nor as if the admirer be second-rate or worse. The book belongs to her as the earlier volume belonged to Amory Blaine. Not because she is the more vivid character than Anthony but because she is more vividly imagined, more consistently presented. There is something about him that suggests that he has been made out of too many and too discordant bits of observation, like the philosophy of William Blake, which, as T. S. Eliot says, was made out of the odds and ends he happened to find in his pocket.

At their first contact Anthony is stirred from his carefully composed calm and for a while Mr. Fitzgerald returns to his earlier moods to manage their meetings with romance.

"Oh, for him there was no doubt. He had arisen and paced the floor in sheer ecstasy. That such a girl should be; should poise curled in a corner of the couch like a swallow newly landed from a clean, swift flight, watching him with inscrutable eyes. He would stop his pacing and, half shy each time at first, drop his arm around her and find her kiss.

"She was fascinating, he told her. He had never met any one like her before. He besought her jauntily but earnestly to send him away; he didn't want to fall in love. He wasn't coming to see her any more —already she had haunted too many of his ways.

"What delicious romance! His true reaction was neither fear nor sorrow—only this deep delight in being with her that colored the banality of his words and made the mawkish seem sad and the posturing seem wise."

III

They marry and Mr. Fitzgerald takes up his theme in earnest. He is prepared to show that this disintegration of a young man who, for all his lack of illusion, cannot bear the contact with life, of a girl who for all her hardness of heart cannot gracefully survive the passing of her first youth.

The middle portions of the book are at once too long and too hurried. That is, incidents are presented diverting in themselves which have no bearing on the theme. And in those places where the material presented is essential to the story, the deductions made are too violent, the transitions too abrupt. One is hardly prepared that Anthony should, even under the influence of Gloria, his own idleness and a diminishing income, turn so quickly from his pleasant nonchalance to so consistent a dipsomania. Gloria's beauty fades out and her nerves wear thin at a strangely early age.

Yet, taken as a whole, it seems to me that the book represents both in plan and execution an advance on *This Side of Paradise.* If, stylistically speaking, it is not so well-written, neither is it so carelessly written. The minor characters are admirably foreshortened; the criticism applied to them seems at times unfortunately Menckenian, the art through which they are shown often comes too close to burlesque. The alcoholic interludes are, if frequent, agreeably heady. The humor with which the quarrels of Gloria and Anthony are touched, the satiric description of army life in a Southern conscript camp, Anthony's adventures in bond-selling are excellently done, with skill and a fine zest and whips adroitly applied.

In order to arrive at those qualities in Scott Fitzgerald which are valuable it may not be unprofitable to compare him with an Englishman like Aldous Huxley. Both are of an age and both have a gift of wit and phantasy, an eye for the absurdities of their contemporaries. Huxley has erudition, a rich knowledge of contemporary literature, taste even when dealing with the indecencies of life, the attitude of the philosopher even in contemplating a sow and her litter of pigs. But he is exceedingly weary, his grace is that of a man well-bred but tired. Whereas Fitzgerald is at the moment of announcing the meaninglessness of life magnificently alive. His ideas are too often treated like paper crackers, things to make a gay and pretty noise with and then be cast aside; he is frequently at the mercy of words with which he has only a nodding acquaintance; his aesthetics are faulty; his literary taste is at times extremely bad. The chapter labeled "Symposium," pictorially good, does not seem clearly thought out or burdened with wisdom. The episode entitled "Flash Back in Paradise" might, except for its wit, have been conceived in the mind of a scenario writer. But these are flaws of vulgarity in one who is awkward with his own vigor.

The Beautiful and Damned:
Reveals One Phase of Jazz-Vampire Period

PHILADELPHIA PUBLIC LEDGER

It would be hard to say how many times the main and principal themes of *The Beautiful and Damned* have been used by American novelists in the last ten years. It owes something to Robert W. Chambers and to Owen Johnson and a very great deal to the sex and saxophone era, the jazz-vampire period of the last three or four years.

Originally published as " 'The Beautiful and Damned' Reveals One Phase of Jazz-Vampire Period in Gilded Panorama of Reckless Life," Philadelphia *Public Ledger*, March 11, 1922.

Anthony Patch is a F. Scott Fitzgerald dilettante parasite on the county of his grandfather, Adam Patch. The grandfather had insisted that this grandson be named Anthony Comstock Patch, and that illuminates the kind of mind and outlook on his fellow beings that grandfather owned. Anthony toiled not nor did he spin. He graduated from Harvard, loafed about New York, had a part-time valet, a little income of his own, a cozy apartment where he often entertained Gertrude, the theatre usheress, and thought that some day he might write a history of the Middle Ages. He had two dissolute friends, one a "newspaper person" named Noble, an idler like himself, who lived in Philadelphia, but did his plain and fancy loafing in New York.

Comes into the picture Gloria Gilbert, the beautiful, cool, collected, selfish Gloria, late of Kansas City. Gloria comes seeking something. There is "Sighlight and Moonlight," and Anthony and Gloria get married. The tale of the courtship, while short, is colorfully and hectically done. They go to Los Angeles on the honeymoon, and thereafter for some years they continue to go to Los Angeles.

Then begins the dissection of the lives of two very ordinary, frivolous, excitement-seeking people. Gloria is selfish, and has always been petted. Anthony is equally selfish, and has always pampered himself. They get on each other's nerves. Anthony pads through cold halls to get Gloria "dinky-water" at midnight. She notes that he is something of a coward, as all men are. They drift and bump in a series of society eddies, waiting for old Adam's money, counting on dead men's shoes.

Fitzgerald set about the painting in multi-color of a panorama of one of the weary, queer, reckless, noisy, worthless and troublesome cross-sections of American life. The idea was to devastate it with satire and overwhelm that part of America that lives in theatres, cafes, cabarets, summer resorts and winter colonies with considerable scorn. He is dealing with the homeless, unanchored, dangerous folks with no background or fading pasts. He has ended by making vice, loose living, sex, red liquor and twelve-cylinder cars much less hateful than he intended, or maybe not. Certainly, he spares no intimate touch of bedroom, lingerie, sex contacts, perfume, alcohol and other excitants.

You are likely to get the idea from the tale of Anthony and Gloria that the author knows a good many things that he ought not to know, or that if he does know them he had done better to keep them to himself. A seasoned author with the proper values of crude colors and chile pepper in mind would hardly have splashed them so prodigally. He tells much that might have been better guessed at of Gloria's boudoir manners, of the texture of sheets, of Gloria's little ways when she was drunk and of dirty glasses and soiled laundry.

To be quite frank about it, the book stinks with the smell of dead cigarette butts, bootleg whisky and dirty clothing. And yet Gloria never "goes wrong," even if the listless, piffling Anthony does falter from the straight and narrow sexually while at Camp Hooker, where he served as a "buck private" during the war.

Waiting for the soft gaiters of Adam Patch the marriage drifts into petty disasters from the beginning. Anthony is a solemn coot most of the time, always drinking just a little more and dependent upon mixed company and excitement. But always he is in love with Gloria. He is jealous, after a fashion, of one Bloeckmann, a pushful, capable Semite of a motion-picture magnate. The newly-weds take a small New York apartment in winter, and stumble away like babes in wood into Connecticut, and someone wishes an old gray house on them. Here they bore each other to death, using up what little money Anthony has and waiting for old Adam to die.

They stage a "party" one night. There is much liquor and Tana, the moron of a Jap, who does the Patch housework, plays on his flute while the mixed company of drunks tries to dance. Out of the summer night appears old Adam who takes one look, departs and the next day makes a new will leaving all the cause of prohibition, general reform and suppression and naming his "secretary" Shuttleworth, a reformed prize fighter, to administer the estate. Then Adam dies, finally and completely. The dead man's shoes go somewhere else.

There is a fight to break the will, a long, wearying fight. Meanwhile Anthony tries to go to work as a salesman and comes home very drunk. Every little while he sells another bond. He drinks bootleg whisky and "hangs out" in the backroom of a saloon. The war takes him to camp, where he meets "Prissie." He comes back after the armistice. Gloria is drinking more and more. The suit still drags.

There is genuine tragedy in the breaking of Gloria. She tries at last to get into the movies. Hopeless. In the first light of dawn she looks at herself in the glass.

"The eyes were different. Why they were different! And then suddenly she knew how tired her eyes were. 'Oh my pretty face,' she whispered, passionately grieving. 'Oh my pretty face. Oh I don't want to live without my pretty face! Oh what's happened!' "

There is nothing ordinary about the story. It will be one of the most read.

The Beautiful and Damned

CARL VAN DOREN

The sense of sin rarely sleeps long in an American novelist; sooner or later it wakes and comes to the surface. Even F. Scott Fitzgerald, grown reflective, takes one of his gilded couples in *The Beautiful and Damned* past the age of radiance into a tawdry state for which the sin of futility is to blame. His Anthony Patch and his Gloria Gilbert cannot have their fling forever, waiting for a grandfather's millions. The bright beauty of Gloria fades a little, the brilliance of Anthony cracks: drink and the devil of idleness do for them. With an edifying irony Mr. Fitzgerald traces the dingy process, but he makes it very clear that edification is not—or is not yet—his forte. Compared, for instance, with the pitiful descent of Hurstwood in Theodore Dreiser's *Sister Carrie* the descent of Anthony Patch has the look of being argued out, of being made on a machine. Though at the end he has got to the foot of his ladder, he must have got there by falling unobserved past certain sections where the rungs were out. Nor does it increase the reality of the fall to allow him a penultimate hour of madness and an ultimate hour of victory, his millions in his hand. All that happens to him carries less of dramatic conviction than the single episode in the career of his wife when she finds, after long believing she could at any moment rehabilitate their fortunes on the screen, that instead she can play nothing better than the part of "a very haughty rich widow."

Of such flashes of drama there are only a few in the book. Its excellence lies in its rendering not of the ordinary moral universe but of that detached, largely invented region where glittering youth plays at wit and love. To youth like this the rest of the world seems to exist, as it seems to children, to thwart gay purposes. Why will old men not die and leave their money to those who know how to spend it exquisitely? Why does experience with its heavy feet come glowering over the green fields where Corydon romps with Amaryllis or into the cool shade where every gallant has his dainty marquise in a perpetual *fête champetre*? Must the beautiful be damned? Because such questions are insistent

Originally published as "The Roving Critic," *The Nation*, March 15, 1922. Reprinted by permission of *The Nation*.

Anthony and Gloria and their friends play madly, as if there were much to be done before wisdom catches them and spoils their rapture. They have, of course, their own young wisdom: they are full of careless speculation which gives edge and point to the story; they have a smart cynicism which often blinds it. But it is in their unclouded days that they delight, when wit heightens love and love warms wit. Then they flutter across the continent in a perpetual honeymoon. Then poverty touches them only as a jest, and languor not at all. They have beauty and health and fresh, contagious passion and merry eloquence. They are of the fellowship of Alcibiades and Lalage, of Mercutio and Rosalind.

If it was haste and insolence which hurt *This Side of Paradise*, what hurts *The Beautiful and Damned* is deliberate seriousness—or rather, a seriousness not deliberated quite enough. Bound to bring some sort of instruction in, Mr. Fitzgerald pushes his characters downhill as if gravitation needed help. He must have lost some of his interest in them as they went down; at least he imparts interest less and less as they advance; his imagination flames only while they are at the summit. Few current writers can represent young love in its incandescence as he can, but his knowledge—so far as this novel goes to show—does not extend with the same accuracy to the seedy side of life which he has felt he must explore. He has trusted, one suspects, his doctrine rather more than his gusto. For this reason, too, he has, without adding much to the body of his style, sacrificed—or lost—some of the poetry which illuminated the earlier narrative and which illuminates the higher places of this one with a light never present unless there is genius not far off. Why did he have to mix good poetry with indifferent moralism? Moralists are plenty but poets few. It is encouraging, however, to see signs of increasing power in his work.

The Beautiful and Damned: This Side of Innocence

GILBERT SELDES

The impression Mr. Fitzgerald's work makes on his elders is so intense that one is grateful for the omission of the name of the Deity from his new title. To his contemporaries, "interested only in ourselves and Art," his revelations are of quite secondary importance and he has neither the critical intelligence nor the profound vision which might make him an imposing figure. His elders, naturally, do not require these things of him, since they have other sources of supply, and they are the best judges of his immediate significance. To them he presents a picture of the world which is no longer theirs, and even when they doubt his supreme truthfulness they can safely go behind the book to the author and say that this is what the younger generation would like us to think.

It cannot, of course, continue indefinitely, because even about so bright and cheerful a talent as Mr. Fitzgerald's the shadows of the prison house are bound to close. Especially since he had been considered as a revealer and an artist he has had to grow quickly, and he can say (I speak not of his private life with which I am unacquainted, but of his fiction) "my grief lies onward and my joy behind." The golden lads and girls of *This Side of Paradise* are in the new novel, but they are far more than Amory Blaine and Rosalind aware of their kinship in the dust with the world's chimney-sweepers. It is not only because of the tragedy into which Gloria and Anthony Patch are somewhat hastily precipitated. Tragedy, and particularly in our own time a rather meaningless tragedy, are quite the natural thing for young people to deal in; it was surprising and creditable to him that Mr. Fitzgerald's first book held so steadily to a gay worldliness. Nor is it Mr. Fitzgerald's increasingly detailed naturalism which marks the change in him. The new thing is his overburden of sentiment and his really alarming seriousness. Sentiment, to be sure, has been surreptitiously conveyed, and so made more poignant, and, when it doesn't come off, more objectionable, by being presented always with scepticism. (This is, I believe,

Originally published under the pseudonym "Vivian Shaw" as "This Side of Innocence," *The Dial*, April 1922.

the real nature of the author's noted irony.) It is very strange that Mr. Fitzgerald should render emotion directly, that is without sentimentality, so that the early love of Anthony and Gloria has the credible, somewhat incomprehensible atmosphere of any love affair to any outsider; so, too, the quite successful episode of Anthony and Geraldine, the attractive although virginal usher. It is whenever he approaches either the mind or the soul of his characters that Mr. Fitzgerald becomes romantic. The first state culminates in the testament of Maury Noble, which reads like a résumé of *The Education of Henry Adams* filtered through a particularly thick page of *The Smart Set*. The second stage sets in heavily when the author finds his catastrophe approaching too rapidly and tries to conceal his failure to foreshorten by forcing the dramatic pace over into melodrama.

I do not know whether this change in Mr. Fitzgerald is due to alien influence; nor, when I mention the most impressive of his teachers, do I wish to suggest that he is in any sense plagiarizing. The pell-mell of ideas, or rather of the names of ideas, in the book is startling, and more startling is the incipient philosophy of the author; but the book is important not for these. It is important because it presents a definite American milieu and because it has pretentions as a work of art; the degree of success (the degree, that is, of importance) comes out in comparison with the work of another American novelist: Mrs. Edith Wharton. It is not essential for my purpose to know whether Mr. Fitzgerald has read *The House of Mirth* and *The Custom of the Country*, since I wish to make a comparison, not an accusation.

Lily Bart's tragedy and that of Anthony Patch are similar in direction and Undine Spragg is an older sister of Gloria Gilbert. Lily dies undefiled, to be sure, and Anthony lives ignominiously; that difference is beyond criticism. But where the comparison injures Mr. Fitzgerald is in the treatment of the gradual disintegration of the physical lives of the two characters, for Mrs. Wharton, with a fraction of the detail, has given the effect of the lapse of time, has kept Lily's character active and growing before us, and has given us, all the while, the result of Lily's poverty upon her; Mr. Fitzgerald has clearly intended us to see that as the strain of life grew more tense, Anthony became incapable of that devotion to abstractions which made him so entertaining before, but as Anthony had somehow ceased to exist long before he got to camp, the remaining scenes are impotent. As for Gloria and Undine, the methods used are singularly alike and the younger writer comes out of the comparison rather well. His half-chapter of preparing the stage for Gloria's entrance is remarkable; he gives her general effect circuitously so that when she appears it matters very little whether he can stop to describe her, which he actually never does, adding touches to the created character as his story proceeds. The Gilberts are not in the same country as the Spraggs; literally, since Apex City, or wherever it was for the Spraggs, came effectively on the scene, while the background of the Gilberts is pure conversation. But the careful treatment of Gloria in the beginning brings its own reward to the author; as Anthony recedes, Gloria becomes more and more vivid. She is, at first, a presence; Undine (Mrs. Wharton understands irony) has a soul. In the second half of the book Gloria slowly acquires being. If Mr. Fitzgerald had followed his subject to the bitter end, instead of to an end which is merely bitter, the triumph of Gloria would have been inevitable.

The failure to carry Gloria through, his seeing her as a flapper and not as a woman, marks the precise point at which Mr. Fitzgerald now rests—this side of innocence, considerably this side of the mad and innocent truth. He is this side, too, of a full respect for the medium he works in; his irrelevance destroys his design. I have nothing against his sudden descents into the dialogue of the printed play, if that is the most effective way of presenting his scene, although I wish he did not do this whenever he has a crowd to handle and something in itself insignificant to tell. His interludes are usually trivial and never contribute to the one thing they can create, his atmosphere. But I do wish that Mr. Fitzgerald would stop incorporating into his novels his wingéd words and his unrelated episodes as they are published from time to time. It indicates a carelessness about structure and effect which one who has so much to gain from the novel ought to find displeasing.

The Beautiful and Damned: Friend Husband's Latest

ZELDA SAYRE

I note on the table beside my bed this morning a new book with an orange jacket entitled *The Beautiful and Damned*. It is a strange book, which has for me an uncanny fascination. It has been lying on that table for two years. I have been asked to analyze it carefully in the light of my brilliant critical insight, my tremendous erudition and my vast impressive partiality. Here I go!

To begin with, every one must buy this book for the following aesthetic reasons: First, because I know where there is the cutest cloth-of-gold dress for only $300 in a store on Forty-second Street, and also if enough people buy it where there is a platinum ring with a complete circlet, and also if loads of people buy it my husband needs a new winter overcoat, although the one he has has done well enough for the last three years.

Now, as to the other advantages of the book—its value as a manual of etiquette is incalculable. Where could you get a better example how not to behave than from the adventures of Gloria? And as a handy cocktail mixer nothing better has been said or written since John Roach Straton's last sermon.

It is a wonderful book to have around in case of emergency. No one should ever set out in pursuit of unholy excitement without a special vest-pocket edition dangling from a string around his neck.

For this book tells exactly, and with compelling lucidity, just what to do when cast off by a grandfather, or when sitting around a station platform at 4 A.M., or when spilling champagne in a fashionable restaurant, or when told that one is too old for the movies. Any of these things might come into any one's life at any minute.

Just turn the pages of the book slowly at any of the above-mentioned trying times until your own case strikes your eye and proceed according to directions. Then for the ladies of the family there are such helpful lines as: "I like gray because then you have to wear a lot of paint."

Originally published as "Friend Husband's Latest," New York *Tribune*, April 2, 1922. © 1922, New York Herald Tribune Inc. Reprinted by permission of W. C. C. Publishing Company, Inc.

Also what to do with your husband's old shoes—Gloria takes Anthony's shoes to bed with her and finds it a very satisfactory way of disposing of them. The dietary suggestion, "tomato sandwiches and lemonade for breakfast," will be found an excellent cure for obesity.

Now, let us turn to the interior decorating department of the book. Therein can be observed complete directions for remodeling your bathroom, along modern and more interesting lines, with plans for a bookrack by the tub, and a detailed description of what pictures have been found suitable for bathroom walls after years of careful research by Mr. Fitzgerald.

The book itself, with its plain green back, is admirably constructed for being read in a tub—wetting will not spoil the pages; in fact, if one finds it growing dry simply dip the book briskly in warm water. The bright yellow jacket is particularly adapted to being carried on Fifth Avenue while wearing a blue or henna-colored suit, and the size is adaptable to being read in hotel lobbies while waiting to keep dates for luncheon.

It seems to me that on one page I recognized a portion of an old diary of mine which mysteriously disappeared shortly after my marriage, and also scraps of letters which, though considerably edited, sound to me vaguely familiar. In fact, Mr. Fitzgerald—I believe that is how he spells his name—seems to believe that plagiarism begins at home.

I find myself completely fascinated by the character of the heroine. She is a girl approximately ten years older than I am, for she seems to have been born about 1890—though I regret to remark that on finishing the book I feel no confidence as to her age, since her birthday is in one place given as occurring in February and in another place May and in the third place in September. But there is a certain inconsistency in this quite in accord with the lady's character.

What I was about to remark is that I would like to meet the lady. There seems to have been a certain rouge she used which had a quite remarkable effect. And the strange variations in the color of her hair from cover to cover range entirely through the spectrum—I find myself doubting that all the changes were of human origin; also the name of the unguent used in the last chapter is not given. I find these aesthetic deficiencies very trying. But don't let that deter you from buying the book. In every other way the book is absolutely perfect.

The other things I didn't like in the book—I mean the unimportant things—were the literary references and the attempt to convey a profound air of erudition. It reminds me in its more soggy moments of the essays I used to get up in school at the last minute by looking up strange names in the *Encyclopaedia Britannica.*

I think the heroine is most amusing. I have an intense distaste for the melancholy aroused in the masculine mind by such characters as Jenny Gerhardt, Antonia and Tess (of the D'Urbervilles). Their tragedies, redolent of the soil, leave me unmoved. If they were capable of dramatizing themselves they would no longer be symbolic, and if they weren't—and they aren't—they would be dull, stupid and boring, as they inevitably are in life.

The book ends on a tragic note; in fact a note which will fill any woman with horror, or, for that matter, will fill any furrier with horror, for Gloria, with thirty million to spend, buys a sable coat instead of a kolinsky coat. This is a tragedy unequaled in the entire work of Hardy. Thus the book closes on a note of tremendous depression and Mr. Fitzgerald's subtle manner of having Gloria's deterioration turn on her taste in coats has scarcely been equaled by Henry James.

The Beautiful and Damned

MARY M. COLUM

Mr. Scott Fitzgerald could never utter the names of Mr. H. G. Wells and Edward Fitzgerald in the same breath: none of his young heroes could ever come up to seek his fortune in Chicago armed with one treasured book, that book being a Wells—at least he could not do it with the approval of the author. Mr. Fitzgerald's heroes would probably bring a Swinburne, and the poems that they would know by heart would be "The Hounds of Spring" and "Dolores." They would, perhaps, be a little more commonplace than Mr. Floyd Dell's young hero [in *The Briary Bush*], but how intelligent they would be, and how well they would compare with young gentlemen of the same denomination in other countries! This is one of Mr. Fitzgerald's real merits: his chief

Originally published as "Certificated, Mostly," *The Freeman,* April 26, 1922. This text is a shortened version of the original.

merit, however, is that with him there has stepped into the ranks of the young novelists a satirist; so rare an apparition in this—indeed, in any—country, that he ought to be rocked and dandled and nursed into maturity, or given any treatment whatever that will ensure his free development. He uses his weapon so stumblingly yet that it is hard to know how strong or how finely-tempered it may be. For instance, when he causes his hero to be called "Anthony Comstock Patch" at the request of a reforming, uplifting grandfather, he is indulging in a sort of buffoonery that is not above the level of the popularly called satire of the afternoon columnists: if Thackeray had so dealt with one of his characters, he would have made it seem as if the gods from all time had decided upon this piece of mockery. Again, when he satirizes the hypocrisies of people during the war, he is simply flogging a dead horse, besides taking up what is now a popular occupation. A genuine satirist would never berate unpopular things; and, of all unpopular things, war-behaviour is now the most unpopular.

The story of this book deals with the married life of two young people, of that class which in Europe is called the middle class, but which in America is nearly always called the upper. These two have grown up without any of the discipline which is the training for life invented by the aristocracy, or the prudent worldly-wisdom which is the substitute invented by the *petite bourgeoisie:* they are peculiarly the product of a commercial civilization. The book deals with a life in America which has had few serious interpreters, and Mr. Fitzgerald has done it with impressive ability. The story of these two young people and their life in various places, including their amazing existence in that uncivilized form of shelter peculiar to New York, the two-room-and-bath apartment, is told with real conviction. They have no occupation and no responsibilities, and tragedy overtakes them—in so far as tragedy can overtake the tender-minded and the undisciplined; for tragedy, like happiness, is the privilege of the strong. Mr. Fitzgerald's character-drawing is, in the main, somewhat amateurish, and he uses his people indifferently to express opinions quite unrelated to their characters. A certain easy grasp of conventional technique is his, especially in showing the interplay of the characters on each others' lives. His best and most consistent piece of character-drawing is that of Bloeckman, whose evolution is indicated with great subtlety. A novelist, and particularly a novelist who is a satirist, has to be on the outside as well as on the inside of his characters, and Mr. Fitzgerald has not the faculty of standing away from his principal characters: with Bloeckman he has done this, and also with the gentleman who appears for a moment to teach salesmanship. Everything in this salesmanship episode is done excellently and the satirist's touch is revealed in all of it. *The Beautiful and Damned* is indeed an achievement for so young a writer. It is one which, however, would seem less striking in England where they have had the highly intelligent commonplace for so long, or in France where they are the greatest masters of the highly intelligent commonplace in the world. Mr. Fitzgerald is yet young enough to achieve the feat of stepping down the peaks of his intelligence into that region where the great adventurers among the arts sought for "roots of relish sweet, and honey wild, and manna-dew"; though I must own that one does not find too many signs of it.

The Beautiful and Damned

HENRY BESTON

Graduating from Harvard in the Class of 1909, Anthony Patch goes to New York and assumes a position there as heir-presumptive to the millions of his grandfather, Adam Patch, a senile apostle of the "uplift." Eleven years of drifting and wasting follow; a modern marriage, insecurely founded on an immensity of kissing, breaks down into faithlessness and boredom; and finally Patch, followed at no great distance by his wife, lurches downhill from occasional drunkenness to habitual and bewildered sottishness. Two final pages, in which a kind of ironic "happy ending" lies concealed are to be found, but they do not convince; the tail refuses to wag the dog.

In spite of the synopsis, however, the book is not a tragedy of character. Who remembers a name or even a real individuality among the *jeuness dorée* of *This Side of Paradise?* The Anthony of the present volume is a type; carefully studied and carefully observed, to be sure, but a type, nevertheless, and not a person; Gloria, his wife, though more

Originally published as an untitled review, *Atlantic Monthly*, June 1922. Reprinted with the permission of the Atlantic Monthly Corporation.

individualized than Anthony, is likewise a type of the kind of being into which civilization is making some women; Muriel Kane is a type rendered with the care, accuracy, and mechanism with which a phonograph record produces a voice; Mrs. Gilbert is a Western type, Bloeckman a metropolitan. Certain personages are mere clichés—Anthony's uplifter grandfather, for instance.

And the story—what is it but an account, half ironic, half photographic, of a sordid race downhill? Yet the book is alive, very much alive.

Wherein, then, lies its secret vitality? It dwells, one imagines, in the shrewd, complete, and quite unequaled picture it renders of the life of the day and the manners and customs of a class. The topic of the hour, its favorite slang phrase, the kind of human being in which the moment dwells incarnate, all are to be found here at their best and freshest. And what a crew they are—these young men without the slightest sense of social obligation, these young women who live for their own enjoyment of their beauty, these loafers, drunkards, climbers, and rich wastrels of a great metropolis! Now it is the rich, wandering, unattached, hotel-dwelling girl whom Mr. Fitzgerald depicts; now the type of young, alert, well-dressed Jew who has made his way into a certain social world (a remarkable study this); now the flapper type as it exists among the populace. And not only are these types keenly chosen, skillfully described, and endowed with the minute's most appropriate language, but also are they housed in the world of daily experience, the world of the movie, the electric sign, the smell of taxicabs, the sport suit, the jazz orchestra, and the prohibition evader. One wearies of the egotistic Gloria and becomes disgusted with the swineries of Anthony; but the picture and the good talk carry the reader brilliantly through to the end.

Those who expected great things from the promise of the first novel will probably be disappointed. The present endeavor marks no advance in either method or philosophy of life. But the picture of the time is there; a really amazing picture. It represents no mean achievement.

Tales of the Jazz Age: The Fitzgerald Legend

WOODWARD BOYD

Those self-styled "mellowed" critics, who in the antebellum days were accustomed to being called naughty-naughty now and then by the hordes of lady journalists then running the literary affairs of the nation; those unhappy men who now sit pulling their mustaches, Van Dyke beards, rubbing their bald heads nervously over the appalling vista of unmentionable subjects that they must mention if they are not to bask forever on that dreary Waikiki where the bathing girls are all angular club women; those intellectually once gay old dogs, have one and all hit upon the very ingenious and moderately successful plan of pretending that their rocking chairs are a-rocking to and fro on Parnassus, and that, looking down through the dizzy distance, they are amused and diverted by the efforts of the "dis-illusioned" young.

Of the younger ironists, they have appropriately ironical things to say about the irony of the younger ironists essaying irony. And for the "dis-illusioned" who seemed to have caused them the greatest expenditure of nervous energy, they have that gentle, "mellow" compassion of the world-worn soul who has gone through the process and come out on the bright, sweet side.

Of all the disillusioned young, F. Scott Fitzgerald has caused the greatest wear and tear on these wistful yearners toward broad-mindedness. What to do about this young man was a great problem until the "What will the baby do next!" idea occurred to these amiable gentlemen. That at once did away with the necessity for going to greater lengths of disillusionment—the plan they had formerly followed and, of course, out of the question if it were indeed possible.

This attitude of—well, let us say—mind has saved these worthies many a sad bump. For instance, the Fitzgerald pen records "For most men the years between 35 and 65 are taken up with a gradual withdrawal from life, a retreat, first from a front with many shelters, those myriad amusements and curiosities of youth, to a line with less, when we peel down our ambitions to one ambition, our recreations to one

Originally published as "The Fitzgerald Legend," St. Paul *Daily News,* December 10, 1922.

recreation, our friends to a few to whom we are anesthetic; ending up at last in a solitary, desolate strong point that is not strong, where the shells now whistle abominably, now are but half heard as, by turns frightened and tired, we sit waiting for death."

Most of these critics are sojourning peacefully in these same years between 35 and 65. They call it sailing adventurously, and are emphatically not waiting for death. They would therefore be somewhat hurt by paragraphs like this if they had not made up their minds once and for all that F. Scott Fitzgerald is so frightfully disillusioned in the younger manner that it's really laughable.

The legend that has grown up around F. Scott Fitzgerald in consequence is as grotesque as most literary legends. Disillusioned, cynical, and so young, too.

I would like to shoot a few arrows through this legend, and I will begin by saying that Mr. Fitzgerald is about as disillusioned as a little crappie nibbling at the end of a worm before he has encountered the hook. He not only believes that the moon is made of green cheese, but he imagines the world and the solar system are composed of some similar delightful material. He believes anything and everything and is enchanted and ecstatic because there are so many interesting things to believe. And his beliefs are so whole-hearted, so convincing that he carries his audience along with him. You can imagine him as a small boy sitting before a fire in the woods, with 10 other spell-bound, hair-raised youths, rolling his eyes and thumping his palm with his fist, "—and then, and then, the Injuns tore out his arm and swapped him across the face with the bloody end of it—and then." But the hoary-haired critics call him morbid.

And cynical. Cynic, a morose, surly, or sarcastic person, says my dictionary. A flat contradiction of the essential nature of Fitzgerald, which is gay, light-hearted, and pervaded with the gusto of an incorrigible love of life which betrays him again and again when he is swimming in the most decadent of waters. And if he is not the only member of the younger intellegentzia with a genuine sense of humor, he is very near it.

Fitzgerald no more believes that life is meaningless than he believes in prohibition. Yet his novel *The Beautiful and Damned* could be interpreted either as a variation on the now popular futility theme, or a tract to back up the slogan of the Woman's Christian Temperance union. And yet, I do not mean to say that I think *The Beautiful and Damned* was either an insincere or a muddled novel. It was remarkably sincere in its incidents; its scenes were vivid, real scenes, faithful reproductions from life. But over it did not brood that somber, wondering spirit reputed to such persons as Thomas Hardy, and Theodore Dreiser, but rather the spirit of, "Gee whiz, kids, this is going to be slick! What won't happen to this Anthony Patch, this Gloria Gilbert. Oh Golly!"

And about the Fitzgerald youth. He is young, certainly, but not so young as to look absurd in long trousers. When his first novel appeared he was 23 or 24 years old, the same age that Dickens was when *Pickwick Papers* was published, a little older than was Dos Passos at the time of the publication of *Three Soldiers*, a few months younger than John Keats was when he had published all the poems he was to write. Yet Keats, Dickens, Dos Passos, and hundreds of others who wrote things before they were 25 are not judged as "infant phenomenons" while Scott Fitzgerald, in spite of the fact that he is only two years younger than Ben Hecht, whom no one ever dreams of calling childish, still suffers under this absurd handicap. I call these facts to the attention, not of intelligent people who never supposed that Fitzgerald was cynical, disillusioned or babbling "goo-goo" at the world, but to those hordes lately restored to self-confidence through the great success of *If Winter Comes?*

His new book, *Tales of the Jazz Age*, a collection of short stories, is a better assemblage, on the whole, than *Flappers and Philosophers*.

The table of contents is written in the intimate and chatty manner which so well illustrates the undisillusioned, uncynical enjoyment which is one of Fitzgerald's most marked characteristics. Here he is essentially the happy father exhibiting his children. And with his ebullitions goes that rare talent for convincing his audience that his enthusiasms are genuine and worthwhile enthusiasms which is the prime ingredient of the Fitzgerald genius.

Read the table of contents and see if you can refrain from reading the book afterward. It lures you into re-reading even stories that you have read before in magazines. It is a pity that these little author's chats at the beginning of a volume are not used by every writer. Any book of modern short stories would be improved by such a commentary in the table of contents as has been used in *Tales of the Jazz Age*. You can open the book and tell in a few moments whether you like the author's manner, his subject matter and his morals, and you can also titillate yourself with that subtle feeling of intimacy with the author generally roused only by feature interviews in popular magazines.

"My Last Flappers," he heads the first group of stories in the spirit of melancholy joy which a young man is supposed to exhibit when he kisses his bachelor days goodbye. Among this group is the story, so famous in St. Paul, of "The Camel's Back"—a story fictitiously located in Toledo, but which really happened, if all good citizens and perusers of paragraphs should know, in this very town.

"The Jelly Bean" exhibits the growth of Fitzgerald since his last volume of short stories was published. This seems to me to be one of the most well-constructed stories that he has ever done. It is the same kind of thing that he attempted in his earlier short stories, holding all the vitality of them yet showing a surer touch, a more definite mastery of his tools. This story leads one to believe in the legend that O. Henry wrote hundreds of stories and tore them up just to teach himself how to write them. "The Jelly Bean" leaves you feeling that its author has learned all there is to learn about how to write that kind of a story.

I did not read "The Lees of Happiness" because I read it when it appeared in a magazine and wept over it. This is very unlike anything else he has ever done and is vaguely reminiscent of a certain sentimental woman who writes for the magazines, but whose name I cannot remember for the life of me.

The funny stories in the volume are the sort to make you hysterical with laughter if they appeal to you at all.

"This don't pretend to be literature" is the prelude to the nonsense story that closes the volume. "This is just a tale for red-blooded folks who want a story and not just a lot of 'psychological' stuff, or 'analysis.' Boy, you'll love it! Read it here, see it in the movies, play it on the phonograph, run it through the sewing machine."

I thought that the best story in the book was one called "O Russet Witch." The style moves along with the fluid crispness of a hurrying stream through the woods in autumn and it is a more delightful piece of work to me than the one which Fitzgerald confesses in the table of contents to prefering, "The Diamond as Big as the Ritz." They are both done in somewhat the same manner and are called by their author "Fantasies."

Other stories in the volume are "May Day," "Tarquin of Cheapside," an imaginative and exciting description of the circumstances in which Shakespeare might have written the "Rape of Lucrece," and "The Curious Case of Benjamin Button." There are also two short humorous plays—"Mr. Icky" and "Procelain and Pink."

The Vegetable: Scott Fitzgerald's Play

JOHN F. CARTER, JR.

I have no quarrel with the theatrical managers who rejected this play; as drama and as literature it is thoroughly and ostentatiously vulgar.

When I accuse Mr. Fitzgerald of vulgarity in *The Vegetable* I do not mean merely that it is written about vulgar people and that their language and idiom and environment are vulgar. I mean that the conception, treatment, and technique are distinctly cheap. I mean that the play is devoid of ideas and beauty; that it lacks sincerity, simplicity, and intellectual ruggedness.

Mr. Fitzgerald's literary career has been a disappointment. His sensational *This Side of Paradise* reminded one of Compton Mackenzie's *Sinister Street* both in subject and style. But it possessed a poignancy, a youthful passion, that caused us to hope that Mr. Fitzgerald might produce some vivid and original literature. Since then he has gracefully slipped along the pages of the popular magazines to a portentous psychological novel, *The Beautiful and Damned,* until he seems to have come to a dead stop with *The Vegetable,* his first published play.

This play is laboriously and glibly ironic. It is based on the idea of mental limitations. It is the story of Jerry Frost, a railway clerk of zero mentality, whose boyhood dream was to be a postman and who had vague desires to be the President of the United States. He drinks some synthetic gin purveyed to him, with threadbare buffoonery, by a bootlegger named Snooks. (In passing it may be said that Snooks is the only character sufficiently convincing to persuade one that he was drawn from the life.) Then Jerry has a nagging wife named Charlotte. Her nagging is obviously only introduced for dramatic effect, and as a character she is infinitely inferior to Sinclair Lewis's study of Zilla Riesling in a similar role in *Babbitt.* Charlotte's younger sister, Doris, and her fiancé, Fish, a young undertaker from Dubuque, Ia., together with Jerry's valetudinarian father, Dada, complete the cast. Jerry drinks the gin and falls asleep.

Originally published as "Scott Fitzgerald's Play," New York *Post,* June 23, 1923. Reprinted by permission of the New York *Post.* © 1923, New York Post Corporation.

In the second act he dreams that he is President, and presumably conveys Mr. Fitzgerald's idea of the naïve mental conceptions of a $3,000 a year railway clerk as to what the life of the President is like. At the White House everything is white—trees, clothes, even cigars. Barrie did that sort of thing charmingly and well in "A Kiss for Cinderella." Fitzgerald lays it on as thick as possible, with burlesque Senators, Judge Fossile of the Supreme Court, and a cheap parody army officer named General Pushing. It is possible that the burlesque of the Government and the White House may shock the public's sense of *lèse-majesté* enough to make this act a drawing card. In print it is worse than tedious.

In the last act Jerry, who disappeared on the night of the gin-drinking, returns in the rôle of postman, thus satisfying his boyhood desire, as the dream satisfied the Presidency complex! Mr. Fitzgerald blandly omits to give any explanation as to how, when, where, or why Jerry Frost became a postman. However, his wife, who has really worried over his disappearance, looks forward to a reunited life with "the best postman in the world."

The prose of *The Vegetable* is a fair imitation of Ring Lardner, the spirit an obvious act of deference to Mencken's virulent contempt for the American people. In consequence it is trashy and betrays a smugness of viewpoint that shows that one more of our bright young men has succumbed to the glamour of the self-advertising business.

The Vegetable

LISLE BELL

The writer of satire, if he hopes to be genuinely effective, wisely refrains from digging his spurs into his own mount. Even if he thinks it a spavined nag, instead of a worthy Pegasus, nothing is gained—and sometimes a great deal is lost—by advertising the fact. In other words, satire must trust its medium. Nothing is more fatal than an attitude of ill-concealed disparagement towards the means by which one rides into

Originally published as an untitled review, *The Freeman*, July 11, 1923.

the tournament of ideas. His failure to be guided by this principle weakens Mr. Fitzgerald when he attempts a satirical comedy in *The Vegetable*. The opportunity for an adroit thrust was in his grasp, but it is evident that the author rather looks down upon the dramatic form in which he has chosen to work. He patronizes it, and he patronizes the reader the moment he feels that the scene is becoming the least bit credible. As a consequence, the characters have about as much vitality as wax figures; his comedy becomes a comic strip, and the irony vanishes in thin air.

The Vegetable
In Performance, Atlantic City, November 20, 1923

PHILADELPHIA EVENING BULLETIN

F. Scott Fitzgerald made his debut as a playwright at the Apollo Theatre here last evening with *The Vegetable,* a comedy based on his book of that name. The apostle of the flappers has abandoned his theme of the deadly young female species and turned his satirical realism to X-raying the great American home of a humble white collar worker, with little gray matter above the white.

In the first act, with the artful aid of Ernest Truex at his best and funniest, he skilfully shows, or rather, shows up, the more or less happy, more or less turbulent home of Jerry Frost, railroad clerk, and his nagging wife, Charlotte. Nothing much happens, except that Jerry, after a deal of verbal buffeting from his spouse and her sister, is visited by his tough but genial bootlegger, and on the wings of synthetic gin soars far above the cares of family life.

The second act, supposed to show Jerry's gin-fizzled dream of himself in the White House as President, does little else than demonstrate that Mr. Fitzgerald would better stick to his modernist realism and leave fantasy to those of lighter touch and whim.

The third act comes back to that horror of amateur interior-

Originally published as "New Comedy at Shore," Philadelphia *Evening Bulletin,* November 20, 1923. Copyright, 1923, by Bulletin Co. Reprinted by permission.

decorating which to Jerry is home, and his sitting room. It develops that Jerry, after his bad dreams of realizing his boyhood ambition to become President, has fled from his home to bring to actual realization his later ambition, always stifled by his wife, to be a postman. He comes back after two weeks to a wife reduced to tearful contrition for her past nagging and a happy ending is achieved but not until Mr. Fitzgerald has revealed that he is as little at home with tender and old-fashioned sentiment as he is with fantasy.

However the comedy has many bright moments of keen mockery of our foibles and inanities. Minna Gombel, as the wife; Ruth Hammon as Doris, the one lone Fitzgerald flapper of the piece, and Malcolm Williams as Snooks, the irresistible bootlegger, all do their best to emphasize Mr. Fitzgerald's strong points, though they can't quite lift that second act out of the bog.

The Great Gatsby:
F. Scott Fitzgerald's Latest a Dud

NEW YORK WORLD

F. Scott Fitzgerald's new novel confirms the belief that there should be a consolidation of reviewers of average books and the selectors of scenarios. *The Great Gatsby* is another one of the thousands of modern novels which must be approached with the point of view of the average tired person toward the movie-around-the-corner, a deadened intellect, a thankful resigning of the attention, and an aftermath of wonder that such things are produced.

Mr. Fitzgerald shows the average wealthy American couple. The husband is a college-hero athlete, the wife an attractive nonentity. Each develops a love affair until between them they roll up a bill for one death by accident, one murder and one suicide. Gatsby is the wife's embryo lover, presumably a swindler on a swagger scale, burning with a steady devotion. But there is no important development of his char-

Originally published as "F. Scott Fitzgerald's Latest a Dud," New York *World*, April 12, 1925.

acter and many other titles would be equally appropriate. In fact with the telling of the plot *The Great Gatsby* is, in newspaper parlance, covered.

The Great Gatsby: Up to the Minute

ISABEL PATERSON

For a reviewer with a conscience, here is a nice problem—to give Scott Fitzgerald's new novel its just due without seeming to overpraise it, or, contrariwise, to say plainly that it is neither profound nor durable, without producing the impression that it is insignificant (which it is not).

This is like announcing a decision on points, when the public has been expecting a knock out. The former method of winning is quite as honorable, but not so showy. *This Side of Paradise* was put over with a punch of a very special kind. But *The Great Gatsby* is the first convincing testimony that Mr. Fitzgerald is also an artist.

The reason why *This Side of Paradise* created such a furore was not its intrinsic literary worth, but its rare combination of precocity and true originality. The universal difficulty for beginning novelists is to use what they know. Fiction must be shaped to a pattern. Life appears to be formless, incoherent, fantastically irrelevant. In the individual experience episodes don't seem to hang together; cause and effect are not even on speaking terms; apparently things just happen. The technical tricks of foreshortening for perspective, of working to scale, of selecting and composing, and, above all, of using documentary facts simply as a painter employs a model for his imaginative figure paintings, these things are usually learned by a long process of trial and error. For this reason youth has seldom been articulate of its own emotions and ideas. The young are busy drawing from casts, from "the antique," learning the craft. By the time they have skill enough to work from the life—the first fine, careless rapture has faded. It has to be done from memory.

Originally published as "Up to the Minute," *New York Herald Tribune Book Review*, April 19, 1925. © 1925, New York Herald Tribune Inc. Reprinted by permission of W. C. C. Publishing Company, Inc.

Mr. Fitzgerald managed somehow to pour his glowing youth on the page before it could escape forever. His natural facility was so extraordinary that he could get along with a minimum of conscious technique. Even the inevitable crudities and banalities of his first novel were a part of its authenticity. They were genuine echoes of the gaucheries of his age and environment. The smart, swaggering, callow cubs of 1915 (was it?) were like that; such were their amusements, catchwords, standards and point of view.

It was really a sociological document. Not even a personal confession, in the main, but a snapshot of one aspect of the crowd mind.

So is *The Great Gatsby* in a sense. But it is first and foremost a novel, which its predecessor wasn't. It is beautifully and delicately balanced; its shapeliness is the more praiseworthy for the extreme fragility of the material. It is an almost perfectly fulfilled intention. There is not one accidental phrase in it, nor yet one obvious or blatant line.

And to work at all with such people, such types and backgrounds, is something of a feat. They are the froth of society, drifting sand, along the shore. Can one twist ropes of sand? Decidedly not; but one may take the sand and fuse it in the warmth of fancy, and with skill enough one may blow it into enchanting bubbles of iridescent glass.

The Great Gatsby is just such an imponderable and fascinating trifle. Gatsby himself is the archetype of the species of ephemerides who occupy the whole tale. He was a man from nowhere, without roots or background, absolutely self-made in the image of an obscure and undefined ideal. You could not exactly call him an impostor; he was himself an artist of sorts, trying to remold himself. His stage was a Long Island summer colony, where he came in contact with the realities of his dream and was broken by them. That he was a bootlegger, a crook, maybe a killer (all on the grand scale) is part of the irony of things; for it wasn't his sins he paid for, but his aspirations. He was an incurable romanticist (I would draw a distinction between that and a romantic, as between sentimentality and sentiment), and his mistake was to accept life at its face value.

There, too, is the chief weakness of Mr. Fitzgerald as a novelist. In reproducing surfaces his virtuosity is amazing. He gets the exact tone, the note, the shade of the season and place he is working on; he is more contemporary than any newspaper, and yet he is (by the present token) an artist. But he has not, yet, gone below that glittering surface except by a kind of happy accident, and then he is rather bewildered by the results of his own intuition. Observe how he explains the duration and intensity of Gatsby's passion for Daisy Buchanan. He says it was because of Daisy's superior social status, because she was a daughter of wealth—Gatsby "hadn't realized how extraordinary a 'nice' girl could be"; and the revelation dazzled him, made him Daisy's slave forever. Pooh, there is no explanation of love. Daisy might have been a cash girl or a mill hand, and made as deep a mark—it is Carmen and Don Jose over again. There isn't any why about that sort of thing.

Again, Mr. Fitzgerald identifies, the strange rout who came of Gatsby's incredible parties as "the East," in contrast to a more solid, integrated society of the Middle West. But these drunken spenders and migratory merrymakers exist proportionately everywhere; there are more of them in and around New York because there is more of New York, and they congregate chiefly where there is easy money—like midges dancing over a pool. And they come from all quarters. They are not even peculiar to this age; they made up the guests at Trimalchio's supper, and Lucian satirized them.

But Gatsby hasn't the robust vitality of the vulgar Trimalchio. He and his group remain types. What has never been alive cannot very well go on living; so this is a book of the season only, but so peculiarly of the season, that it is in its small way unique.

The Great Gatsby

H. L. MENCKEN

Scott Fitzgerald's new novel, *The Great Gatsby*, is in form no more than a glorified anecdote, and not too probable at that. The scene is the Long Island that hangs precariously on the edges of the New York City ash dumps—the Long Island of gaudy villas and bawdy house parties. The theme is the old one of a romantic and preposterous love —the ancient *fidelis ad urnum* motif reduced to a macabre humor. The principal personage is a bounder typical of those parts—a fellow who seems to know everyone and yet remains unknown to all—a young

Originally published as "As H. L. M. Sees It," Baltimore *Evening Sun*, May 2, 1925. Reprinted by permission of the Sunpapers, Baltimore, Md.

man with a great deal of mysterious money, the tastes of a movie actor and, under it all, the simple sentimentality of a somewhat sclerotic fat woman.

This clown Fitzgerald rushes to his death in nine short chapters. The other performers in the Totentanz are of a like, or even worse quality. One of them is a rich man who carries on a grotesque intrigue with the wife of a garage keeper. Another is a woman golfer who wins championships by cheating. A third, a sort of chorus to the tragic farce, is a bond salesman—symbol of the New America! Fitzgerald clears them all off at last by a triple butchery. The garage keeper's wife, rushing out upon the road to escape her husband's third degree, is run down and killed by the wife of her lover. The garage keeper, misled by the lover, kills the lover of the lover's wife—the Great Gatsby himself. Another bullet, and the garage keeper is also reduced to offal. Choragus fades away. The crooked lady golfer departs. The lover of the garage keeper's wife goes back to his own consort. The immense house of the Great Gatsby stands idle, its bedrooms given over to the bat and the owl, its cocktail shakers dry. The curtain lurches down.

This story is obviously unimportant, and though, as I shall show, it has its place in the Fitzgerald canon, it is certainly not to be put on the same shelf with, say, *This Side of Paradise*. What ails it, fundamentally, is the plain fact that it is simply a story—that Fitzgerald seems to be far more interested in maintaining its suspense than in getting under the skins of its people. It is not that they are false; it is that they are taken too much for granted. Only Gatsby himself genuinely lives and breathes. The rest are mere marionettes—often astonishingly lifelike, but nevertheless not quite alive.

What gives the story distinction is something quite different from the management of the action or the handling of the characters; it is the charm and beauty of the writing. In Fitzgerald's first days it seemed almost unimaginable that he would ever show such qualities. His writing, then, was extraordinarily slipshod—at times almost illiterate. He seemed to be devoid of any feeling for the color and savor of words. He could see people clearly and he could devise capital situations, but as writer qua writer he was apparently little more than a bright college boy. The critics of the Republic were not slow to discern the fact. They praised *This Side of Paradise* as a story, as a social document, but they were almost unanimous in denouncing it as a piece of writing.

It is vastly to Fitzgerald's credit that he appears to have taken their caveats seriously and pondered them to good effect. In *The Great Gatsby* the highly agreeable fruits of that pondering are visible. The story, for all its basic triviality, has a fine texture, a careful and brilliant finish. The obvious phrase is simply not in it. The sentences roll along smoothly, sparklingly, variously. There is evidence in every line of hard and intelligent effort. It is a quite new Fitzgerald who emerges from this little book, and the qualities that he shows are dignified and solid. *This Side of Paradise*, after all, might have been merely a lucky accident. But *The Great Gatsby*, a far inferior story at bottom, is plainly the product of a sound and stable talent, conjured into being by hard work.

I make much of this improvement because it is of an order not often witnessed in American writers, and seldom indeed in those who start off with a popular success. The usual progression, indeed, is in the opposite direction. Every year first books of great promise are published —and every year a great deal of stale drivel is printed by the promising authors of year before last. The rewards of literary success in this country are so vast that, when they come early, they are not unnaturally somewhat demoralizing. The average author yields to them readily. Having struck the bull's eye once, he is too proud to learn new tricks. Above all, he is too proud to tackle hard work. The result is a gradual degeneration of whatever talent he had at the beginning. He begins to imitate himself. He peters out.

There is certainly no sign of petering out in Fitzgerald. After his first experimenting he plainly sat himself down calmly to consider his deficiencies. They were many and serious. He was, first of all, too facile. He could write entertainingly without giving thought to form and organization. He was, secondly, somewhat amateurish. The materials and methods of his craft, I venture, rather puzzled him. He used them ineptly. His books showed brilliancy in conception, but they were crude and even ignorant in detail. They suggested, only too often, the improvisations of a pianist playing furiously by ear but unable to read notes.

These are the defects that he has now got rid of. *The Great Gatsby*, I seem to recall, was announced a long while ago. It was probably several years on the stocks. It shows, on every page, the results of that laborious effort. Writing it, I take it, was painful. The author wrote, tore up, rewrote, tore up again. There are pages so artfully contrived that one can no more imagine improvising them than one can imagine improvising a fugue. They are full of little delicacies, charming turns of phrase, penetrating second thoughts. In other words, they are easy and excellent reading—which is what always comes out of hard writing.

Thus Fitzgerald, the stylist, arises to challenge Fitzgerald, the social historian; but I doubt that the latter ever quite succumbs to the former. The thing that chiefly interests the basic Fitzgerald is still the florid show of modern American life—and especially the devil's dance that goes on at the top. He is unconcerned about the sweatings and sufferings of the nether herd; what engrosses him is the high carnival of those who have too much money to spend and too much time for the spending of it. Their idiotic pursuit of sensation, their almost incredible stupidity and triviality, their glittering swinishness—these are the things that go into his notebook.

In *The Great Gatsby*, though he does not go below the surface, he depicts this rattle and hullabaloo with great gusto and, I believe, with sharp accuracy. The Long Island he sets before us is no fanciful Alsatia; it actually exists. More, it is worth any social historian's study, for its influence upon the rest of the country is immense and profound. What is vogue among the profiteers of Manhattan and their harlots today is imitated by the flappers of the Bible Belt country clubs weeks after next. The whole tone of American society, once so highly formalized and so suspicious of change, is now taken largely from frail ladies who were slinging hash a year ago.

Fitzgerald showed the end products of the new dispensation in *This Side of Paradise*. In *The Beautiful and Damned* he cut a bit lower. In *The Great Gatsby* he comes near the bottom. Social leader and jail bird, grand lady and kept woman, are here almost indistinguishable. We are in an atmosphere grown increasingly levantine. The Paris of the Second Empire pales to a sort of snobbish chautauqua; the New York of Ward McAllister becomes the scene of a convention of Gold Star Mothers. To find a parallel for the grossness and debauchery that now reign in New York one must go back to the Constantinople of Basil I.

The Great Gatsby: An Admirable Novel

WILLIAM ROSE BENÉT

The book finished, we find again, at the top of page three, the introductory remark: "No—Gatsby turned out all right at the end; it was what preyed on Gatsby, what foul dust floated in the wake of his dreams that temporarily closed out my interest in the abortive sorrows and short-winded elations of men."

Scott Fitzgerald's new novel is a remarkable analysis of this "foul dust." And his analysis leads him, at the end of the book, to the conclusion that all of us "beat on, boats against the current, borne back ceaselessly into the past." There is depth of philosophy in this.

The writer—for the story is told in the first person, but in a first person who is not exactly the author, but rather one of the number of personalities that compose the actual author—the hypothecated chronicler of Gatsby is one in whose tolerance all sorts and conditions of men confided. So he came to Gatsby, and the history of Gatsby, obscured by the "foul dust" aforementioned, "fair sickened" him of human nature.

The Great Gatsby is a disillusioned novel, and a mature novel. It is a novel with pace, from the first word to the last, and also a novel of admirable "control." Scott Fitzgerald started his literary career with enormous facility. His high spirits were infectious. The queer charm, color, wonder, and drama of a young and reckless world beat constantly upon his senses, stimulated a young and intensely romantic mind to a mixture of realism and extravaganza shaken up like a cocktail. Some people are born with a knack, whether for cutting figure eights, curving an in-sheet, picking out tunes on the piano, or revealing some peculiar charm of their intelligence on the typewritten page. Scott Fitzgerald was born with a knack for writing. What they call "a natural gift." And another gift of the fairies at his christening was a reckless confidence in himself. And he was quite intoxicated with the joy of life and rather engagingly savage toward an elder world. He was out "to get the world by the neck" and put words on paper in the patterns

Originally published as "An Admirable Novel," *Saturday Review of Literature,* May 9, 1925. Reprinted by permission of the *Saturday Review.*

his exuberant fancy suggested. He didn't worry much about what had gone before Fitzgerald in literature. He dreamed gorgeously of what there was in Fitzgerald to "tell the world."

And all these elements contributed to the amazing performance of *This Side of Paradise*, amazing in its excitement and gusto, amazing in phrase and epithet, amazing no less for all sorts of thoroughly bad writing pitched in with the good, for preposterous carelessness, and amazing as well as for the sheer pace of the narrative and the fresh quality of its oddly pervasive poetry. Short stories of flappers and philosophers displayed the same vitality and flourished much the same faults. *Tales of the Jazz Age* inhabited the same glamour. *The Beautiful and Damned*, while still in the mirage, furnished a more valuable document concerning the younger generation of the first quarter of the Twentieth Century. But brilliant, irrefutably brilliant as were certain passages of the novels and tales of which the "boy wonder" of our time was so lavish, arresting as were certain gleams of insight, intensely promising as were certain observed facilities, there remained in general, glamour, glamour everywhere, and, after the glamour faded, little for the mind to hold except an impression of this kinetic glamour.

There ensued a play, in which the present writer found the first act (as read) excellent and the rest as satire somehow stricken with palsy, granted the cleverness of the original idea. There ensued a magazine phase in which, as was perfectly natural, most of the stories were negligible, though a few showed flashes. But one could discern the demands of the "market" blunting and dulling the blade of that bright sword wildly whirled. One began to believe that Fitzgerald was coming into line with the purveyors of the staple product. And suddenly one wanted him back in the phase when he was writing so well and, at the same time, writing so very badly. Today he was writing, for the most part, on an even level of magazine acceptability, and on an even level of what seemed perilously like absolute staleness of mind toward anything really creative.

But *The Great Gatsby* comes suddenly to knock all that surmise into a cocked hat. *The Great Gatsby* reveals thoroughly matured craftsmanship. It has structure. It has high occasions of felicitous, almost magic, phrase. And most of all, it is out of the mirage. For the first time Fitzgerald surveys the Babylonian captivity of this era unblinded by the bright lights. He gives you the bright lights in full measure, the affluence, the waste, but also the nakedness of the scaffolding that scrawls skeletons upon the sky when the gold and blue and red and green have faded, the ugly passion, the spiritual meagreness, the empty shell of luxury, the old irony of "fair-weather friends."

Gatsby remains. The mystery of Gatsby is a mystery saliently characteristic of this age in America. And Gatsby is only another modern instance of the eternal "fortunate youth." His actual age does not matter, in either sense. For all the cleverness of his hinted nefarious proceedings, he is the coney caught. For he is a man with a dream at the mercy of the foul dust that sometimes seems only to exist in order to swarm against the dream, whose midge-dance blots it from the sky. It is a strange dream, Gatsby's,—but he was a man who had hope. He was a child. He believed in a childish thing.

It is because Fitzgerald makes so acid on your tongue the taste of the defeat of Gatsby's childishness that his book, in our opinion, "acquires merit." And there are parts of the book, notably the second chapter, that, in our opinion, could not have been better written. There are astonishing feats that no one but Fitzgerald could have brought off, notably the catalogue of guests in Chapter IV. And Tom Buchanan, the "great, big hulking specimen," is an American university product of almost unbearable reality.

Yet one feels that, though irony has entered into Fitzgerald's soul, the sense of mere wonder is still stronger. And, of course, there is plenty of entertainment in the story. It arises in part from the almost photographic reproduction of the actions, gestures, speech of the types Fitzgerald has chosen in their moments of stress. Picayune souls for the most part, and Gatsby heroic among them only because he is partly a crazy man with a dream. But what does all that matter with the actual narration so vivid and graphic? As for the drama of the accident and Gatsby's end, it is the kind of thing newspapers carry every day, except that here is a novelist who has gone behind the curt paragraphs and made the real people love and breathe in all their sordidness. They are actual, rich and poor, cultivated and uncultivated, seen for a moment or two only or followed throughout the story. They are memorable individuals of today—not types.

Perhaps you have gathered that we like the book! We do. It has some miscues, but they seem to us negligible. It is written with concision and precision and mastery of material.

The Great Gatsby: Fitzgerald on the March

CARL VAN VECHTEN

What will be the future of F. Scott Fitzgerald? This query has been futilely repeated whenever a new book from his pen has appeared, since the initial interrogation which greeted the publication of that sophomoric masterpiece, *This Side of Paradise.* It will be asked more earnestly than before by prescient readers of *The Great Gatsby,* who will recognize therein a quality which has only recently made its debut in the writings of this brilliant young author, the quality vaguely referred to as mysticism. Moreover this is a fine yarn, exhilaratingly spun.

Mr. Fitzgerald is a born story-teller; his words, phrases, and sentences carry the eye easily through to the end of his books. Further, his work is imbued with that rare and beneficent essence we hail as charm. He is by no means lacking in power, as several passages in the current opus abundantly testify, and he commands a quite uncanny gift for hitting off character or presenting a concept in a striking and memorable manner. The writer he most resembles, curiously enough, despite the dissimilarity in their choice of material and point of attack, is Booth Tarkington, but there exists at present in the work of Mr. Fitzgerald a potential brutality, a stark sense of reality, set off in his case by an ironic polish, that suggests a comparison with the Frank Norris of *Vandover and the Brute,* or *McTeague.*

Up to date, Mr. Fitzgerald has occupied himself almost exclusively with the aspects and operations of the coeval flapper and cake-eater. No one else, perhaps, has delineated these mundane creatures quite as skilfully as he, and his achievement in this direction has been awarded authoritative recognition. He controls, moreover, the necessary magic to make his most vapid and rotterish characters interesting and even, on occasion, charming, in spite of (or possibly because of) the fact that they are almost invariably presented in advanced stages of intoxication. More cocktails and champagne are consumed in the novels of Scott Fitzgerald than a toper like Paul Verlaine could drink in a lifetime.

Originally published as "Fitzgerald on the March," *The Nation,* May 20, 1925. Reprinted by permission of *The Nation.*

The Beautiful and Damned, indeed, is an epic of inebriation beside which *L'Assommoir* fades into Victorian insipidity.

In *The Great Gatsby* there are several of Mr. Fitzgerald's typical flappers who behave in the manner he has conceived as typical of contemporary flapperdom. There is again a gargantuan drinking-party, conceived in a rowdy, hilarious, and highly titillating spirit. There is also, in this novel, as I have indicated above, something else. There is the character of Jay Gatsby.

This character, and the theme of the book in general, would have appealed to Henry James. In fact, it did appeal to Henry James. In one way or another this motif is woven into the tapestry of a score or more of his stories. In "Daisy Miller" you may find it complete. It is the theme of a soiled or rather cheap personality transfigured and rendered pathetically appealing through the possession of a passionate idealism. Although the comparison may be still further stressed, owing to the fact that Mr. Fitzgerald has chosen, as James so frequently chose, to see his story through the eyes of a spectator, it will be readily apparent that what he has done he has done in his own way, and that seems to me, in this instance, to be a particularly good way. The figure of Jay Gatsby, who invented an entirely fictitious career for himself out of material derived from inferior romances, emerges life-sized and lifelike. His dog-like fidelity not only to his ideal but to his fictions, his incredibly cheap and curiously imitative imagination, awaken for him not only our interest and suffrage, but also a certain liking, as they awaken it in the narrator, Nick Carraway.

When I read "Absolution" in the *American Mercury* I realized that there were many potential qualities inherent in Scott Fitzgerald which hitherto had not been too apparent. *The Great Gatsby* confirms this earlier impression. What Mr. Fitzgerald may do in the future, therefore, I am convinced, depends to an embarassing extent on the nature of his own ambitions.

The Great Gatsby

JOHN M. KENNY, JR.

One has a feeling of exasperation after reading a novel of Scott Fitzgerald's that is not easy to overcome. His very real talent for writing sparkles throughout the book, on scattered pages, as does the sheer beauty of isolated phrases and the vividness of some of his description. The occasional insights into character stand out as very green oases on an all too arid desert of waste paper.

Fitzgerald's development as a writer has not been all that was expected of him, after his sudden burst into literary fame and financial fortune with *This Side of Paradise*. In the first three-quarters of the earlier book, he wrote well and entertainingly as the interpreter of the new jazz age that followed on the heels of the Armistice. Amory, the flappers, and would-be philosophers he loved and drank with, had not been pictured before—and everyone but Princeton graduates read and enjoyed the tale. Then came *The Beautiful and Damned*— a very weak novel without point or promise. Now he has written *The Great Gatsby*—a singular improvement over his last novel, but an improvement which fails to realize the hopes held out in his first success. Taken alone, *The Great Gatsby* is a mediocre novel. In the light of his former books, it marks an important stepping-stone toward a literary excellence which Scott Fitzgerald ought some day to achieve.

The Great Gatsby wasn't great at all—just a sordid, cheap, little crook whose gawdy palace on the Sound with its Saturday night parties, his glittering motor cars, speed boats, and his tawdry friends would classify him as what is called, in the Broadway vernacular, "a butter and egg man." For Fitzgerald he provides a convenient, if hackneyed, background upon which to weave his tale. Throughout the first half of the book the author shadows his leading character in mystery, but when in the latter part he unfolds his life story we fail to find the brains, the cleverness, and the glamor that countless melodramatic writers have taught us to expect of these romantic crooks.

The other characters in the book are of flimsy material, and when the author sets a real warm human emotion in their frail bodies the strain is too great, and they are left a smoking sacrifice on the altar of Fitzgerald's development of character insight. One feels he might better have pictured the unnatural types one has been taught to expect from him.

It is not beyond probability that Mr. Fitzgerald may have had one eye cocked on the movie lots while writing this last novel. The movie type of wild Bacchanalian revel, with the drunken ladies in the swimming-pool and garden fêtes that just drip expensiveness, are done to perfection—and who knows but that they will offer some soulful Hollywood director a chance to display his art? But for a writer in whom there is the spark at least of real distinction to be so palpably under suspicion of catering to Hollywood is a grievous thing.

The Great Gatsby: Bagdad-on-Subway

THOMAS CALDECOT CHUBB

In a short career, even now amounting to only five years, Scott Fitzgerald has already found time to do a great many things. He has written the most brilliant novel of the younger generation. He has written one of the two best novels of the younger generation. He has written probably the worst play of any generation. He has scattered very close of half a hundred short stories in all the better-paying receptacles for facile fiction. He has told—and presumably based the telling on his own experience—how it is possible to live on $30,000 a year. Latterly he has been responsible for *The Great Gatsby*, a fable in the form of a realistic novel, an Arabian Night's tale of the environs of what O. Henry used to call Bagdad-on-Subway, a hasheesh dream for a romantic-minded inhabitant of Nassau County, and incidently his most attractive book.

The publishers assure us that Jay Gatsby would only be possible in this age and generation. We beg respectfully to inform them that he would be possible in any age and generation and impossible in all of them. We beg to inform them that there is something of Jay Gatsby in

Originally published as "Bagdad-on-Subway," *The Forum*, August 1925.

every man, woman, or child that ever existed. But also we beg to inform them that their particular Jay Gatsby of West Egg, Long Island, and Oggsford, England, is a figment of the imagination. Just as that illustrious nature myth Jurgen—so the critics tell us—never left his pawnshop, so Jay Gatsby is James Gatz' dream of himself after he had poured down half a dozen synthetic drinks.

Here is a fragment of the story. Seventeen years old James Gatz is wandering out on the shore of Lake Superior. Up to the shore steams the yacht of Dan Cody, gambler and financier. Inventing the name of Jay Gatsby as he rows out to it, Gatz warns Cody that it would be dangerous to leave his yacht there. Cody is struck with him, makes him his steward, secretary and often jailer. Then, having given young Gatz a taste for extravagance, dies.

While he is still poor as an Irishman on Sunday morning, Gatz, now Gatsby, meets Dorothy Fay, a belle of Louisville. Since he is a soldier and it is during the war, she entertains him. Gatz, who is not unused to women, finds that she is just as amenable as any other. But she represents the dazzling security of a "nice" girl, and he falls in love with her. When he comes back from the war hoping to marry her, he finds that she has given up waiting for him and has married Ted Buchanan, ex-football star. Out of the bitterness of her marriage to Ted the great Gatsby is born.

All this, however, is merely background. The story takes place at West Egg, Long Island, where the enormously wealthy Gatsby, "big Bootlegger," so it is rumored, and friend of Meyer Wolfsheim, "the man who fixed the world series in 1919" and incidentally who was dining with the gambler Rosenthal the night that he was shot, has bought an enormous mansion simply to be able to gaze at the green light that flashes from the end of Daisy Buchanan's pier. And when the story does take place it is at once a tragedy and an extraordinarily convincing love tale and an extravaganza that is better than Michael Arlen because there is more control to it. Curiously enough in this day of studies it is actually a story, so I will not disclose it. It is the story of the green light.

Scott Fitzgerald is intellectually hard. He does not carry any baggage of sentimentality. He knows a great deal. And so he is not afraid of the sentimental because he realizes that it is part of the life he is considering. Gatsby is a sentimentalist. Daisy Buchanan is a sentimentalist. Ted Buchanan is a sentimentalist. Even the cool Jordan Baker, who is as cleanly drawn a feminine character as there is in modern fiction, and

Nick Carraway the teller of the story have hearts that, even if only at moments, beat erratically under the glazed ice of their suave understanding of everything. To recommend this book on the ground of technical excellence is of course superfluous. I recommend it as a study of these sentimentalists by one whose heart does not ever beat erratically. In *The Great Gatsby* Scott Fitzgerald has every bit of the brilliance that we associate with hard surfaces.

The Great Gatsby: Spring Flight

GILBERT SELDES

There has never been any question of the talents of F. Scott Fitzgerald; there has been, justifiably until the publication of *The Great Gatsby*, a grave question as to what he was going to do with his gifts. The question has been answered in one of the finest of contemporary novels. Fitzgerald has more than matured; he has mastered his talents and gone soaring in a beautiful flight, leaving behind him everything dubious and tricky in his earlier work, and leaving even farther behind all the men of his own generation and most of his elders.

In all justice, let it be said that the talents are still his. The book is even more interesting, superficially, than his others; it has an intense life, it must be read, the first time, breathlessly; it is vivid, glittering and entertaining. Scenes of incredible difficulty are rendered with what seems an effortless precision, crowds and conversation and action and retrospects—everything comes naturally and persuasively. The minor people and events are threads of colour and strength, holding the principal things together. The technical virtuosity is extraordinary.

All this was true of Fitzgerald's first two novels, and even of those deplorable short stories which one feared were going to ruin him. *The Great Gatsby* adds many things, and two above all: the novel is composed as an artistic structure, and it exposes, again for the first time, an interesting temperament. "The vast juvenile intrigue" of *This Side of Paradise* is just as good subject-matter as the intensely private intrigue of *The Great Gatsby*; but Fitzgerald racing over the country, jotting down whatever was current in college circles, is not nearly as significant

Originally published as "Spring Flight," *The Dial*, August 1925.

as Fitzgerald regarding a tiny section of life and reporting it with irony and pity and a consuming passion. *The Great Gatsby* is passionate as *Some Do Not* is passionate, with such an abundance of feeling for the characters (feeling their integral reality, not hating or loving them objectively) that the most trivial of the actors in the drama are endowed with vitality. The concentration of the book is so intense that the principal characters exist almost as essences, as biting acids that find themselves in the same golden cup and have no choice but to act upon each other. And the milieux which are brought into such violent contact with each other are as full of character, and as immitigably compelled to struggle and to debase one another.

The book is written as a series of scenes, the method which Fitzgerald derived from Henry James through Mrs. Wharton, and these scenes are reported by a narrator who was obviously intended to be much more significant than he is. The author's appetite for life is so violent that he found the personality of the narrator an obstacle, and simply ignored it once his actual people were in motion, but the narrator helps to give the feeling of an intense unit which the various characters around Gatsby form. Gatsby himself remains a mystery; you know him, but not by knowing about him, and even at the end you can guess, if you like, that he was a forger or a dealer in stolen bonds, or a rather mean type of bootlegger. He had dedicated himself to the accomplishment of a supreme object, to restore to himself an illusion he had lost; he set about it, in a pathetic American way, by becoming incredibly rich and spending his wealth in incredible ways, so that he might win back the girl he loved; and a "foul dust floated in the wake of his dreams." Adultery and drunkenness and thievery and murder make up this dust, but Gatsby's story remains poignant and beautiful.

This means that Fitzgerald has ceased to content himself with a satiric report on the outside of American life and has with considerable irony attacked the spirit underneath, and so has begun to report on life in its most general terms. His tactile apprehension remains so fine that his people and his settings are specifically of Long Island; but now he meditates upon their fate, and they become universal also. He has now something of extreme importance to say; and it is good fortune for us that he knows how to say it.

The scenes are austere in their composition. There is one, the tawdry afternoon of the satyr, Tom Buchanan, and his cheap and "vital" mistress, which is alive by the strength of the lapses of time; another, the meeting between Gatsby and his love, takes place literally behind closed doors, the narrator telling us only the beginning and the end. The variety of treatment, the intermingling of dialogue and narrative, the use of a snatch of significant detail instead of a big scene, make the whole a superb impressionistic painting, vivid in colour, and sparkling with meaning. And the major composition is as just as the treatment of detail. There is a brief curve before Gatsby himself enters; a longer one in which he begins his movement toward Daisy; then a succession of carefully spaced shorter and longer movements until the climax is reached. The plot works out not like a puzzle with odd bits falling into place, but like a tragedy, with every part functioning in the completed organism.

Even now, with *The Great Gatsby* before me, I cannot find in the earlier Fitzgerald the artistic integrity and the passionate feeling which this book possesses. And perhaps analyzing the one and praising the other, both fail to convey the sense of elation which one has in reading his new novel. Would it be better to say that even *The Great Gatsby* is full of faults, and that that doesn't matter in the slightest degree? The cadences borrowed from Conrad, the occasional smartness, the frequently startling, but ineffective adjective—at last they do not signify. Because for the most part you know that Fitzgerald has consciously put these bad and half-bad things behind him, that he trusts them no more to make him the white-headed boy of *The Saturday Evening Post*, and that he has recognized both his capacities and his obligations as a novelist.

The Great Gatsby

L. P. HARTLEY

Mr. Scott Fitzgerald deserves a good shaking. Here is an unmistakable talent unashamed of making itself a motley to the view. *The Great Gatsby* is an absurd story, whether considered as romance, melodrama, or plain record of New York high life. An adventurer of shady anteced-

Originally published as "New Fiction," *Saturday Review* (London), February 20, 1926. This text is a shortened version of the original.

ents builds a palace at a New York seaside resort, entertains on a scale which Lucullus would have marvelled at but could not have approved, and spends untold sums of money, all to catch the eye of his one time sweetheart, who lives on an island opposite, unhappily but very successfully married. At last, after super-human feats of ostentation and display, the fly walks into the web. A train of disasters follows, comparable in quantity and quality with the scale of the Great Gatsby's prodigies of hospitality. Coincidence leaps to the helm and throws a mistress under a motor-car. The car does not stop, which, all things considered, is the most natural thing that happens in the book. An injured husband finds the Great Gatsby in suicidal mood sitting on a raft in his artificial lake and (apparently) forestalls him; anyhow they are both discovered dead. The elder Gatsby is unearthed and gives a pathetic account of his son's early years. All the characters behave as if they were entitled to grieve over a great sorrow, and the book closes with the airs of tragedy. Mr. Fitzgerald seems to have lost sight of O. Henry and hitched his wagon to Mr. Arlen's star. It is a great pity, for even in this book, in the dialogue, in many descriptive passages, there are flashes of wit and insight, felicities of phrase and a sense of beauty. His imagination is febrile and his emotion over-strained; but how good, of its kind, is his description of Gatsby's smile, which:

> faced—or seemed to face—the whole eternal world for an instant, and then concentrated on *you* with an irresistible prejudice in your favour. It understood you just as far as you wanted to be understood, believed in you as you would like to believe in yourself, and assured you that it had precisely the impression of you that, at your best, you hoped to convey.

The Great Gatsby is evidently not a satire; but one would like to think that Mr. Fitzgerald's heart is not in it, that it is a piece of mere naughtiness.

The Great Gatsby and *All the Sad Young Men*

CONRAD AIKEN

F. Scott Fitzgerald has enjoyed a spectacular career as a writer of short stories for American magazines; and in these, as well as in *This Side of Paradise*, his first novel, he showed (mixed with much magazine shoddy) enough ability to make one fearful lest he should allow himself to be manipulated. In his latest collection of stories, *All the Sad Young Men*, he appears still all too manipulable; though in one or two of the stories he also makes it evident that his conscience is not yet wholly dead. "Absolution" is an attempt at a close psychological study of hysteria which has good things in it but as a whole is somewhat forced: one feels that Mr. Fitzgerald is not speaking his own language. In this, and in "The Rich Boy," he fails to detach, and to make clear, his effect—so much so that one suspects him of not seeing it too clearly himself.

In *The Great Gatsby*, however, Mr. Fitzgerald has written a highly coloured and brilliant little novel which, by grace of one cardinal virtue, quite escapes the company of most contemporary American fiction—it has excellence of form. It is not great, it is not large, it is not strikingly subtle, but it is well-imagined and shaped, it moves swiftly and neatly, its scene is admirably seized and admirably matched with the theme, and its hard bright tone is entirely original. Technically, it appears to owe much to the influence of the cinema; and perhaps also something to Henry James—a peculiar conjunction, but not so peculiar if one reflects on the flash-back and close-ups and paralleled themes of that "little experiment on the style of Gyp," *The Awkward Age*. Mr. Fitzgerald's publishers call *The Great Gatsby* a satire. This is deceptive. It is only incidentally a satire, it is only in the setting that it is satirical, and in the tone provided by the minor characters. The story itself, and the main figure, are tragic, and it is precisely the fantastic vulgarity of the scene which gives to the excellence of Gatsby's soul its finest bouquet, and to his tragic fate its sharpest edge. All of Mr. Fitzgerald's people are real—but Gatsby comes close to being superb. He is betrayed to

Originally published as an untitled review, *New Criterion*, October 1926. This text is a shortened version of the original. Reprinted by permission of the author.

us slowly and skilfully, and with a keen tenderness which in the end makes his tragedy a deeply moving one. By so much, therefore, *The Great Gatsby* is better than a mere satire of manners, and better than Mr. Fitzgerald's usual sort of superficial cleverness. If only he can refrain altogether in future from the sham romanticism and sham sophistication which the magazines demand of him, and give another turn of the screw to the care with which he writes, he may well become a first-rate novelist. How deeply does he feel? That is the question, . . .

All the Sad Young Men: The Boy Grows Older

HARRY HANSEN

Six years ago F. Scott Fitzgerald blazed across the literary horizon with *This Side of Paradise* and captured the startled attention of all the sad young men and all the glad young women. His seniors immediately predicted his quick demise. For several years F. Scott hovered between brisk fun, irony and tragedy, and then came *The Great Gatsby*, which proved him a competent painter of the American scene. And now he presents *All the Sad Young Men*, a collection of short stories published within the last year in various colored magazines, green, blue, red and yellow, and giving excellent proof of his ability to write well in half a dozen manners. It is a joy to read these tales. They lack sameness; they are ironical, and sad, and jolly good fun by turns; they scintillate. Moreover, they show F. Scott Fitzgerald keeping step with his generation. He is of our own time and we are glad that he is.

His most ambitious effort is "Absolution," a tale of a little boy and a priest, which shows a close study of human motives. The confusion in little Rudolph's mind was nothing to the confusion in the mind of the priest, and both were victims of a repression of the life forces. To expect the bewildered priest to guide the bewildered boy meant tragedy. But my favorite story is "The Rich Boy," which is a whole biography in small compass. Young Anson Hunter is one of these young men that Fitzgerald understands so well and that he loves to portray— reminding you of Anthony in *The Beautiful and Damned*. Life is

Originally published as "The Boy Grows Older," Chicago *Daily News*, March 3, 1926. Reprinted by permission of the Chicago *Daily News*.

largely a matter of sensual satisfactions to Anson and things come so easy to him that he loses the ability and desire to act decisively at "the psychological moment" in a love affair. An ironical touch is Anson Hunter's interference in the love affair of his uncle's wife—for the sake of his pride in the name he bears—in the face of his own loose code of living. "Winter Dreams," the story of a boy who made his way and who loves a capricious rich girl but cannot dominate her, opens in the conventional manner, but the ending is anything but conventional, for F. Scott makes no concessions to the expected. The picture of Judy Jones grown careworn and commonplace under a bullying husband shatters his dream of her perpetual youth, a dream that every man holds in his heart until the last. "Baby Party" is not so successful, but shows the author writing a sketch of suburban family life much in the manner of George Ade's stories in *In Babel*. I do not mean his *Fables in Slang*: *In Babel* is made up of light, understanding sketches of everyday people which were adequate for their day—the turn of the century; Fitzgerald sees a bit farther, just as he sees farther than Tarkington, and not quite so far as Ernest Hemingway. In his best jazz manner, reminding you of "Head and Shoulders" and "The Camel's Back," is "Rags Martin-Jones and the Prince of Wales," a story built around one of those satiated girls who are fed up on men and jewels. The girl who flings pearls about, who calls for her bath—"ice cold and half full of almond cream"—who calls to her lover: "Orchids; for the love of heaven! Four dozen, so I can choose four!" Nobody else can do these glad young women and these sad young men so well as F. Scott Fitzgerald.

All the Sad Young Men: Art's Bread and Butter

WILLIAM ROSE BENÉT

With *The Great Gatsby*, it is generally agreed, Mr. Fitzgerald came into his full maturity as a novelist. His natural gifts were displayed therein in abundance, but their exercise was controlled and chastened. He had learned form and the value of reticence. He had come to closer grips

Originally published as "Art's Bread and Butter," *Saturday Review of Literature*, April 3, 1926. This text is a slightly shortened version of the original. Reprinted by permission of the *Saturday Review*.

with life. The vorpal blade of youth, dulled by slashings, had been ground to a new cutting edge.

Mr. Fitzgerald followed *This Side of Paradise* with another brilliant but uneven performance, *The Beautiful and Damned*. He then essayed a play, "The Vegetable." And meanwhile he had burst into two volumes of short stories, *Flappers and Philosophers* and *Tales of the Jazz Age*. *The Great Gatsby* was a sixth book, as we make the count.

Well, Mr. Fitzgerald had his own day at being the "boy wonder," and now, certainly, after *The Great Gatsby*, he must be judged entirely as a mature artist. We know what he can do at his top. The Younger Generation stuff lies among the toys of yesterday.

Here then is a third volume of short stories, mostly gathered from a variety of our popular magazines. This is a winnowing. Mr. Fitzgerald has published many more short stories than these, in *The Saturday Evening Post*, *The Red Book*, *Liberty*, and so on.

What is one to expect? Well, if one has any acquaintance with the problem of "living by one's pen" in America, with the present status of the magazine short story, with the relationship that ordinary periodical publication bears to what a writer is actually capable of achieving in fiction, one is a proven fool if expectation be set too high. Mr. Fitzgerald determined to "make a living by writing." He has made it. And in spite of all the compromises to which one must come with the Market, he has succeeded in producing at least one book, *The Great Gatsby*, that is undeniable achievement. Meanwhile, here, in *All the Sad Young Men* (Mr. Fitzgerald is always fortunate with his titles) is evidence of his almost uncanny facility for magazine writing.

"The Rich Boy" leads off. It was over-advertised in *The Red Book*, even as, in our opinion, Julian Street's "Mr. Bisbee's Princess" was over-advertised. It isn't bad in spots. Mr. Fitzgerald draws a recognizable type. He refuses to tie a machine-made plot to his character sketch. But such a character, being essentially empty, yields little that seems salient. We found too little pith, after all, in this study of a stuffed shirt. It is sincere, but it failed to touch our emotions.

"Winter Dreams" is better. It is youthful in conception, but it achieves a sharper irony than that in "The Rich Boy." "The Baby Party" is simply an entertaining little magazine story. And then we come to "Absolution."

Despite the shadow of Sherwood Anderson in the background, "Absolution" is almost first-rate. Three-quarters of it, at least, is masterly. Then the author falters. He doesn't know quite what to do with his absorbing juxtaposition of Father Schwartz and Rudolph Miller; and while he doesn't exactly throw his story away, he seems to us to fall back on Anderson. For all that, this tale is memorable.

And right after it fox-trots "Rags Martin-Jones," with a revival of the Jazz Age type of thing. Lively O. Henry, at that. A brilliant bit of bunk. Then "The Adjuster," a "significant" magazine story, that is yet a shade better than most "significant" magazine stories. It has a peculiar pathos one remembers. "Hot and Cold Blood" and "The Sensible Thing" are lesser work. "Gretchen's Forty Winks" furnished us much amusement. That is the lot.

A young writer who is earning his living at literature must work fast and put his books close together. Mr. Fitzgerald has elected so to live. His ingenuity at evolving marketable ideas is extraordinary. But one naturally feels, behind most of the writing in this book, the pressure of living conditions rather than the demand of the spirit. As a writer of short stories the author more displays his astonishing facility than the compulsions of his true nature. He is keeping his hand in and paying the rent. And the performance is energetic with a certain gallantry. But now that he has written *The Great Gatsby* we are, perhaps, exorbitant in our demands.

All the Sad Young Men: One of the Wistful Young Men

FRANCES NEWMAN

Mr. Fitzgerald's complete name, as a great many of his admirers doubtless know, is Francis Scott Key Fitzgerald. And as a great many of his admirers doubtless also know, he is a descendent—just how remote I do not remember—of the Francis Scott Key who wrote the flamboyant verses which were fitted to a soaring melody called "Anacreon in Heaven," and which became the national anthem of these United States. But even with that tall sign-post to guide me, I had read Mr.

Originally published as "One of the Wistful Young Men," *New York Herald Tribune Book Review*, April 25, 1926. © 1926, New York Herald Tribune Inc. Reprinted by permission of W. C. C. Publishing Company, Inc.

Fitzgerald's sixth book before I realized that Mr. Fitzgerald is really a poet himself, and that only the twentieth century could have forced him into the more profitable medium of prose.

"All the Sad Young Men" is a poet's title, like all the titles Mr. Fitzgerald has invented or borrowed from other poets' verses. And the prose in which its nine stories are written, like all Mr. Fitzgerald's prose, has the virtues and the defects of prose written by a man who was born to write verse. His noticeable phrases are always phrases which might be the more noticeable phrases of a fairly modern poem—never the phrases of calm cynics like Anatole France and Norman Douglas, who were born to write prose because they were born with a sense of humor. In "The Rich Boy" and in "Winter Dreams" and in "Absolution," the deserts of uninspired prose between the flashing phrases are as long as the deserts of uninspired verse between "The Isles of Greece" and "The Bridge of Sighs" and "Belgium's Capital" in "Childe Harold." This also would have been an intentionally prose fiction if Byron had waited a hundred years to enjoy being born in the Younger Generation which believed that for the first time in history children were younger than their parents.

But the peculiarities of his prose are not the only quality which proves that Mr. Fitzgerald is a poet. In his three novels, and in all of his better stories, there is an odd aspiring wistfulness which I do not suppose Monsieur France or Mr. Douglas ever felt, and which is just enough like James Branch Cabell's feeling for the unattainably beautiful to explain Mr. Cabell's otherwise inexplicable taste for Mr. Fitzgerald's fictions. In "The Rich Boy," the aspiring wistfulness is for the one type of man to whom Mr. Fitzgerald seems to look up with a very touching admiration—the man who was born in New York's East '60s, or East '70s a little less than thirty years ago, whose family were "rich before 1880," who had an English governess and "acquired an accent that is peculiar to fashionable people in the City of New York," whom upper class men passed on the streets of New Haven and "knew without being told that he was a rich boy and had gone to one of the best schools."

In "Winter Dreams" and in "Rags Martin-Jones and the Pr-nce of W-les," Mr. Fitzgerald wistfully describes his ideal woman. She is about twenty years old, her face is like 7 o'clock on a wedding morning, she has $75,000,000, she is like a slender enameled doll wrapped in cloth of gold, her golden slippers have heels striped with layers of real gold and real silver, she is finished as though the long lifetime of some worker in fragility had been used to make her so, and men send her four dozen orchids that she may choose four. And, of course, she is very rude.

"Hot Blood and Cold Blood" is just a story about a nice young man, who couldn't help lending his money to people or giving his seats in street cars to tired women. "Gretchen's Forty Winks" is a magazine story about a young man who got on well in the advertising business, and in it and in "The Sensible Thing," Mr. Fitzgerald says again all that he thinks need be said about Southern girls. "The Baby Party" is hardly worth cutting down good trees to reprint, but "Absolution," I think, must be a story which meant something definite to its author when he was writing it. The Catholic Church is in its very blood, and in its less magnificent manner, and with its less magnificent soul, it shows an American Catholic boyhood as clearly as James Joyce showed an Irish Catholic boyhood in the earlier chapters of A *Portrait of the Artist as a Young Man.*

Take them all in all, these nine stories, and they show the relation between Mr. Fitzgerald's aspirations and the aspirations of the great Gatsby. They show why Mr. Fitzgerald is admired by just the reviewers who admire him. They show that he is still the man who once wrote a story about a diamond as big as the Ritz. Not a diamond as big as bristling Gibraltar, or as big as the shining Jungfrau, or as big as the Cathedral in Chartres. Precisely as big as the Ritz in New York.

Tender Is the Night:
In the Second Era of Demoralization

HENRY SEIDEL CANBY

It is clear enough now that Scott Fitzgerald's *This Side of Paradise* (1920) was a pioneer book. Sketchy, a little incoherent, youthful, it was nevertheless the introduction in fiction to that "younger generation," demoralized by war or the repercussions of war, which was later called the "lost" generation, and is now said to be "recovered," al-

Originally published as "In the Second Era of Demoralization," *Saturday Review of Literature,* April 14, 1934. Reprinted by permission of the *Saturday Review.*

though upon evidence not entirely convincing. What he has to say about life in the second era of demoralization is naturally interesting.

It is interesting and in the opening chapters of the novel brilliant. In theme, in setting, in characterization, and in the difficult art of narrative writing, there is the promise of a book of first importance. The hero of this novel, Dr. Driver, has "recovered," and has furthermore achieved that simplicity of perfectly sophisticated culture which makes his natural charm irresistible. Of the two heroines, one, a "baby star" of the movies, is also happily compounded of charm (innocent this time) and hardness. She has been brought up to be economically a boy. The other, Dr. Driver's wife, is, like him, a product of conditioning by civilized pleasure-seeking, but she has been once literally "lost"; an incestuous attack upon her in girlhood has split her personality, and it is her husband who has brought her back. Both women are "men's women," and the description of their type is admirable of its kind. What could be done with this subtly varied triangle is obvious. For if the lovely Nicole should come to feel that her dependence upon her husband for mental health was in its own way a slavery, so that once healed, rebellion was inevitable; or if the fresh and innocent Rosemary should step from the screen into this intensely difficult relationship and shatter both its charm and its permanence; why then a plot of unusual quality would be sure to unfold itself. And it does, and its background of the Riviera, the clinic in Zurich, and night-and-bar life is vivid, and their flotsam of cosmopolitans is described with so much more originality, with such a firmer dry point, than the Paris-Mediterranean novels of the baser sort, that one gladly admits the skill of this first witness to the new generation. But not the art—or at least not the sustained art. Alas, this promising novel is promising only in its first brilliant chapters. Part way through the author loses his grip upon the theme. The central figures change, the focus of the plot shifts, the story rambles, the style drops to the commonplace and even the awkward and ungrammatical. What begins as a study of a subtle relationship ends as the accelerating decline into nothingness of Dr. Driver—not for no reason, but for too many reasons, no one of which is dominant. This book may be life with its veil over causality, but it is not art which should pierce that veil.

And here is a writer capable of paragraphs that one reads twice for their incisiveness, their wit, or their wisdom, letting his story shamble through episodes, shifting his stance as if he wearied of a theme that required concentration, tossing clever but irrelevant digressions into a plot already growing confused because its focus is constantly changing, and making a novel which is too good and, in spite of all these strictures, too interesting, to escape the criticism which consistent mediocrity might escape. Any second-rate English society novelist could have written this story better than Scott Fitzgerald, though not one of them could have touched its best chapters. Is it laziness, indifference, a lack of standards, or imperfect education that results in this constant botching of the first-rate by American novelists?

Tender Is the Night

JOHN CHAMBERLAIN

I

As one who would rather have written *The Great Gatsby* than any other American novel published in the Twenties, we approached F. Scott Fitzgerald's *Tender Is the Night* with anticipation and trepidation. *The Great Gatsby* was so perfect in its feeling and its symbolism, such a magnificent evocation of the spirit of a whole decade, so great an improvement over Mr. Fitzgerald's second novel, *The Beautiful and Damned* (which might have been, as Jerome Hill once called it, "an American 'Madame Bovary,'" were it not for its diffuse quality), that one could hardly see Mr. Fitzgerald striking the same high level twice in succession. As the years went by, recurrent surges of gossip had it that Mr. Fitzgerald was unable to bring his unfinished post-*Gatsby* novel to any satisfactory conclusion. He had been a child of boom America; had the lean years after 1929 sapped his artistic vitality by stealing from him his field of reference?

After having read *Tender Is the Night*, we now know that the gossip was—just gossip. Mr. Fitzgerald has not forgotten his craftsmanship, his marvelous sense of what might be called social climate, his sheer writing ability. Judged purely as prose, *Tender Is the Night* is a con-

Originally published as "Books of The Times," New York *Times*, April 13 and 16, 1934. © 1934, by The New York Times Company. Reprinted by permission.

tinually pleasurable performance. From a technical point of view, it is not as perfect a novel as *The Great Gatsby,* but once the reader has gotten past the single barrier to complete appreciation of the book, it proves to be an exciting and psychologically apt study in the disintegration of a marriage.

Seemingly, Mr. Fitzgerald begins well. He introduces us to a fledgling film actress, Rosemary Hoyt, a girl with the dew still on her, who is taken up by Richard and Nicole Diver during a summer stay at the Riviera. For some eighty pages or more we constantly expect Rosemary to develop, to become more and more important in the story. And then suddenly, we realize that this innocent and as yet entirely plastic girl is introduced merely as a catalytic agent. When Dick Diver, who is a psychiatrist without a practice, falls in love with Rosemary, his marriage to Nicole commences to founder. But, Rosemary, having started a chain of developments, is dismissed almost completely from the novel, and the reader pauses, at page 100, in rueful bewilderment.

In the critical terminology of Kenneth Burke, Mr. Fitzgerald has violated a "categorical expectancy." He has caused the arrows of attention to point toward Rosemary. Then, like a broken field runner reversing his field, he shifts suddenly, and those who have been chasing him fall figuratively on their noses as Mr. Fitzgerald is off on a new tack.

At this point one could almost guarantee that *Tender Is the Night* is going to be a failure. But, as a matter of fact, the novel does not really begin until Rosemary is more or less out of the way. What follows is a study of a love affair and a marriage between doctor and mental patient that is as successful a bit of writing as it must have been difficult to create in dramatic terms. Mr. Fitzgerald set himself an incredibly confused problem, but he draws the lines clearly as he works the problem out in terms of two human beings.

Tender Is the Night is not, as might be thought, a story of post-war degeneracy. The story has nothing much to do with the famous "lost generation," although many playboy Americans figure on the periphery as Mr. Fitzgerald's drama moves through Europe, from the Riviera to Paris, and thence to Switzerland and Rome. Nicole Warren could have been psychologically violated by the attack by her father in any decade. She might not have found psychiatrists to take her case before Jung commenced practicing and before Freud commenced writing, but that is not germane to the "lost generation." Dick Diver himself is a brilliant young man; Nicole saves herself by transferring her outraged affection for her father to the young psychiatrist with his "cat's face" and his air of being a good, solid bulwark for distress.

What follows is dimly prefigured in the first hundred pages of the book, when Rosemary is seemingly the star attraction. We know that some horror lurks behind the facade of happiness that Dick and Nicole present to the world. But it is not until Mr. Fitzgerald suddenly cuts back to Nicole's years at the Swiss neurological hospital that we know much about the circumstances. And, given the circumstances, it is a foregone conclusion that Nicole will remain in love with Dr. Diver only so long as she needs him. The fact that she is in love with him is predicated on sickness; when she ultimately comes to feel that she can stand by herself, her love for him collapses. Mr. Fitzgerald, in nervous scenes of great skill, traces the forces leading to this collapse. And Dr. Diver is ruined in the process. We see him, at the end, pursuing a meaningless career as a general practitioner in upper New York State, where he had lived as a boy. Any love he may have had for Rosemary, the precipitant of the solution, has been smothered by events. And when he ceased to be Nicole's physician, he ceased also to be her lover. He has been mentally corrupted, too, by living for many years on Nicole's money, and by absence from active work as a psychiatrist taking many and all cases.

Beyond the story, there is Mr. Fitzgerald's ability to catch the "essence of a continent," the flavor of a period, the fragrance of a night and a snatch of old song, in a phrase. A comparison of *Tender Is the Night* as it ran in *Scribner's Magazine* and as it appears in book form gives a measure of the author's artistic conscience. He has made many deft excisions, many sound reallocations of conversation. If, with Rosemary, he presents nothing much beyond an unformed girl, that must lie within the conception of his novel. Rosemary was evidently intended to be meaningless in herself, an unknown quantity projecting itself into a situation that merely required leverage, any leverage, to start its development toward a predictable end. The story is the story of the Divers, husband and wife, how they came together, and how they parted. As such it is a skillfully done dramatic sequence. By the time the end is reached, the false start is forgotten.

II

The critical reception of F. Scott Fitzgerald's *Tender Is the Night* might serve as the basis for one of those cartoons on "Why Men Go Mad." No two reviews were alike; no two had the same tone. Some seemed to think that Mr. Fitzgerald was writing about his usual jazz age boys and girls; others that he had a "timeless" problem on his hands. And some seemed to think that Doctor Diver's collapse was insufficiently documented.

With this we can't agree. It seemed to us that Mr. Fitzgerald proceeded accurately, step by step, with just enough documentation to keep the drama from being misty, but without destroying the suggestiveness that added to the horror lurking behind the surface. Consider Doctor Diver's predicament in being married to a woman with a "split personality" deriving from a brutal misadventure in adolescence. He had married Nicole against his better judgment, partially because she brought him memories of home after years spent abroad. He was drawn into accepting her money, for reasons that living up to a certain income and "cushioning" existence were bound up with the cure. His husband-physician relationship to Nicole, involving constant companionship, cut him off from his practice, and he thought wistfully at times of how the German psychiatrists were getting ahead of him.

With all these factors preparing the ground, it would merely take the sight of an uncomplicated girl (Rosemary) to jar him into active unrest. And when Nicole, subconsciously jealous of Rosemary, comes to a new phase of her disease, and attempts to throw the car off the road when Dick is driving with her and the two children, it is enough to give any one the jitters. Weakness indeed! The wonder to us is that Dick didn't collapse long before Mr. Fitzgerald causes him to break down. And when he does collapse, his youth is gone, it is too late to catch up with the Germans who have been studying new cases for years. This seems to us to be a sufficient exercise in cause-and-effect. Compared to the motivation in Faulkner, it is logic personified.

Tender Is the Night

CLIFTON FADIMAN

In Mr. Fitzgerald's case, at any rate, money is the root of all novels. In *This Side of Paradise*, the world of super-wealth was viewed through the glass of undergraduate gaiety, sentiment, and satire. With *The Great Gatsby*, the goodtime note was dropped, to be replaced by a darker accent of tragic questioning. The questions have become sharper, bitterer in *Tender Is the Night*, but the world of luxurious living remains his only world. It has even become a trifle narrower—a Fitzgerald contraction, so to speak. This universe he both loves and despises; he sees through it and is confused by it. It is the contradictoriness of this emotional attitude that gives his novels their special quality, and is also in part responsible for some of their weaknesses.

Tender Is the Night is a definitely post-war, pre-depression story, and as such it has (in addition to its other virtues) a certain archeological value. It is built up on a dependable triangular base. Rosemary Hoyt, eighteen, a successful film star, and virgin, encounters on the bright Riviera sands the fabulous Divers. Nicole Diver, when we first meet her, is the last cry in beauty, charm, and income. Her husband, Dick, combines the best features of the Admirable Crichton, the Chevalier Bayard, and Ronald Colman. He is also a brilliant psychiatrist, though Mr. Fitzgerald is not overconvincing in his portrayal of this side of the favorite of the gods. Rosemary, fascinated by Dick, attaches herself wistfully to the Divers, travels with them, and meets their expatriate acquaintances, whom you will find amusing or disagreeable, according to your prejudices. I found them disagreeable; Mr. Fitzgerald finds them both. I'm a little tired, for example, of sexual-invertduets. They're becoming as stock as a mortgage-forecloser in an old melodrama.

Around page 150, the story begins to move, instead of merely glitter, and thenceforward the pace never slackens and Mr. Fitzgerald's beautifully burnished prose takes on added lustre. We explore Nicole's past life and learn that, as a girl, she had been saved from gathering madness by the love and patience of Dick. This courtship section is, I think, Mr. Fitzgerald's finest work to date. It is simple, skillful, and moving.

The tale now moves forward again. Rosemary reenters, misunderstanding between the Divers grows, Nicole's old schizophrenia shows its restless head, the magnificence of Dick's personality begins to develop cracks, and soon the breakup of the whole group is precipitated. The story becomes an anatomy of moral disintegration. Within four years, we see Rosemary transformed into the vapid, high-grade courtesan any good practicing cynic could easily have previsioned in her; Nicole flies to the arms of Barban, a gallant Gaul who likes to fight duels and has an adventurously scarred face; and Dick, abandoning his medical career, has sunk into muscular exhibitionism, alcoholism, neurotic sensuality, and a very unaristocratic tendency to pick scraps with gendarmes. The life that began so gaily, so musically, under the Riviera sun has withered to dust and ashes.

Mr. Fitzgerald's attitude toward his world changes as the story progresses. In the beginning, he apparently finds in the Divers and their friends the best values life can offer—the virtues of a serenely confident, graceful aristocracy, so civilized that it has passed even beyond snobbery. But there is apparently some fatal flaw in the codes by which these people live, for they collapse at the first touch of conflict and opposition. In the end, Mr. Fitzgerald is clearly the bitter commentator; he seems to be as much disillusioned with his characters as if he had never created them in the first place. One imagines him saying, with deep, angry irony, "Look, here is the best there is, and it turns out pretty second-rate—but show me something better!"

The actual decay of these super-civilized people (so civilized, indeed, that at times they seem to be edging over into barbarism) is traced with masterly narrative skill, but the primary causes of the decay are not made clear. (Nicole's mental instability and Dick's infatuation for Rosemary are only the detonators.) Dick's rapid acceptance of his failure, for instance, is not convincing; there must have been some fundamental weakness in his early youth to account for his defeatism, his willingness to shatter the marvellous strength he had so carefully built up. The events of the narrative, tragic as they are, are insufficient to motivate his downfall. It is the failure to reach far, far back into his characters' lives that helps to prevent this novel from being the first-rate work of fiction we have been expecting from F. Scott Fitzgerald. Perhaps, if he were less torn by a half-unwilling love for the bright world his creatures inhabit, he might perceive in them a certain basic weakness of will—and, more particularly, of intelligence. For no intelligence has any chance at healthful exercise when it is a function of a code, whether it be the collegiate code of "smoothness" or the Riviera-American code of would-be Renaissance aristocracy.

It is an open secret that Mr. Fitzgerald's gifts are bewilderingly varied. He has wit, grace, astonishing narrative skill. He is a careful and—in his non-commercial moments—a conscientious writer. His prose has polish and yet also bone and muscle. But he has not yet achieved an organized attitude toward his material. He is certainly not objective; he is both contemptuous of and in love with his characters. If his understanding of them should harden, mature, and if finally he should outgrow them, or at least apply his ready, quick intelligence to the complex relations between his highly specialized world and the rest of humanity (as Proust did), then we might see in him a completely first-rate American novelist.

A small but not trifling postscript: The atmosphere generated by the characters is one of such infallible worldly wisdom that the accidental, tiny errors cropping up here and there are doubly unsettling. Not to mention such blunders in French as *saland* for *salaud*, we find Anthiel for Antheil, Suppe for (von) Suppé, Marie Brizzard for Marie Brizard, Cherry Rochet for Cherry Rocher, Fernet Blanco for Fernet-Branca, *mousseaux* for *mousseux*, Krapaelin for Kraepelin, Wasserman for Wassermann (syphilis), schizzoid for schizoid, schizophrêne for schizophrene, *Privat docent* for *Privat-dozent*, Interlacken for Interlaken, etc. It would be picayune indeed to list these proofreader's oversights were it not that the inhabitants of Mr. Fitzgerald's world, who pride themselves on their impeccability, should never arouse in the reader's mind the slightest suspicion of their competence in fields—such as liquor, resort geography, and mental disease—that are staked out as their very own. It is perfection or nothing, as in a set by Mr. Belasco.

Tender Is the Night:
Scott Fitzgerald's Return to the Novel

J. DONALD ADAMS

Eight years have elapsed since the publication of Mr. Fitzgerald's last novel. Because *The Great Gatsby* seemed a manifesto of growth and because its author is now approaching middle age, the appearance of his new book is an interesting event of the Spring season. But bad news is best blurted out at once: *Tender Is the Night* is a disappointment. Though it displays Mr. Fitzgerald's most engaging qualities, it makes his weaknesses appear ineradicable, for they are present in equal measure and in undiminished form. One looked, too, for more deepening of tone, for a firmer grasp of life. His new book is clever and brilliantly surfaced, but it is not the work of a wise and mature novelist.

If Mr. Fitzgerald had never written *The Great Gatsby* the complaint would be unjust and uncalled for. But that book gave ground for belief that he might come to be remembered as something other than a symbol of articulate youth of the gin and jazz era. Within its sharply restricted scope *The Great Gatsby* embodied perfectly certain aspects of the days of the Big Boom. Jay Gatsby and his way of life were utterly the product of those feverish years, and Fitzgerald, in the mood of romantic realism, caught precisely the atmosphere and tempo of the time. In the figure of Gatsby himself he produced a figure at once individual and emblematic. It was not a full-bodied novel, but it was a distinct achievement, not easily forgotten.

Tender Is the Night is a more ambitious performance; it is, indeed, only fair to Mr. Fitzgerald to bear in mind that his central theme offers difficulties of the most subtle and complex kind. Essentially, he has written the story of the disintegration of a marriage and, at the same time, of the moral disintegration, in quite different ways, of the man and the woman. Dr. Richard Diver we meet as a brilliant young psychiatrist; we see the last of him as a shabby general practitioner, moving

Originally published as "Scott Fitzgerald's Return to the Novel," *New York Times Book Review*, April 15, 1934. © 1934, by The New York Times Company. Reprinted by permission.

from town to town in up-State New York. Nicole brought to their marriage great wealth and the problem of her split personality; she was the victim, when Diver met her, of a psychosis induced by an unnatural relationship with her father. Her mental derangement, apparently cured by transference of her love to Diver, becomes recurrent; we leave her as she transfers her affections to another man. Dr. Diver's own disintegration takes place as the result of his inability to adjust himself to the presence of wealth not his own and to the dual nature of his relation to Nicole, as husband and physician.

Mr. Fitzgerald has been at some pains about his abnormal psychology; one wishes he had been as careful about the normal reactions of his people. Nicole herself never becomes a fully realized person; she is the carefully documented figure in a case history—and that is all. Dr. Diver alone of the principals carries the conviction of character, and even in his case the wrecking of his morale seems contrived rather than the product of his inability to withstand the pressure to which he is subjected. The third figure of primary interest is a young movie star, on whom interest is centered for almost the first half of the book. Rosemary Hoyt's love for Dr. Diver, and its eventual reciprocation, vanish in thin air for both of them. She contributes to Nicole's growing dissatisfaction with her marriage, and she serves to emphasize Diver's devotion to his wife. But she is an inanimate magnet, an incredible blend of innocence and guile in whose reality it is impossible to believe.

If the novel is unsatisfying in its treatment of the human relationships with which it is centrally occupied, it comes off better in its handling of the numerous minor figures and of the background against which the story is projected. Most of the action takes place along the Riviera, at a Swiss mountain clinic for the treatment of nervous disorders and in Paris. In his treatment of the people by whom the Divers are surrounded, in spite of lapses into melodrama and the introduction of bizarre incidents which heighten the air of artificiality that pervades the novel, Mr. Fitzgerald conveys deftly and satirically the atmosphere of futility in which his playboys and playgirls waste away their lives.

Tender Is the Night

PETER QUENNELL

Mr. Scott Fitzgerald is wildly uneven. After *The Great Gatsby*, a book which, when it was published several years ago, aroused an intellectual furore and was acclaimed by critics as diverse as Mencken, T. S. Eliot and Gertrude Stein, Mr. Fitzgerald's new novel seems wordy and shapeless. It is very long and its narrative method is far from direct. A hundred-and-fifty pages are occupied by Mr. Fitzgerald in his description of a Mediterranean beach, and of the smart Europeanised Americans who congregate there, as observed through the personality of a famous but innocent film actress, Rosemary Hoyt; and it is not until the hundred-and-forty-eighth page that the novelist supplies us with a key to some of the less easily explicable aspects of the foregoing chapters, letting it appear—quite abruptly—that Nicole, the wife of the engaging young student of mental disorders with whom Rosemary has fallen in love, is herself on the borderline of madness, and that behind the calm facade of their affluent household lurked a secret and atrocious preoccupation.

The second half of the book is vivid and memorable. Elsewhere, the delicacy and acuteness that, in *The Great Gatsby*, distinguished Mr. Fitzgerald's choice of epithets and informed his delineation of contemporary characters have degenerated into a rather irritating type of *chic*. His imagery is elaborate and euphuistic; in his former novel he scored bull's-eyes with the accuracy of a crack marksman in the booth at a country fair, and in his present novel he has everything except his objective, drilling holes just as it pleases him, making the splinters fly, but very seldom getting down to the main business. His incidental commentary is often shrewd. Mr. Fitzgerald knows his modern Americans; he has a firm grasp of their foibles and their slang; he is the prophet of a generation which, though it has passed away, has left a distinct mark on contemporary American literature.

Originally published as an untitled review, *New Statesman and Nation*, April 28, 1934. Reprinted by permission of the *New Statesman*.

Tender Is the Night: A New Fitzgerald

PRINCETON ALUMNI WEEKLY

F. Scott Fitzgerald '17, the recording secretary of the Jazz Age, has moved into a new phase. That is clear, whatever conclusions may be reached as to other aspects of his new novel, *Tender Is the Night.* The style is different, the dialogue is different and the general mood of the author is different. Mr. Fitzgerald has moved still farther into the ranks of the impressionists, and the adroit way in which he uses that technique has excited the admiration of nearly all reviewers—including those who differ sharply with him on questions of structure.

Tender Is the Night lacks unity in the ordinary sense of the word; the debate of the reviewers is concerned with whether or not Mr. Fitzgerald has achieved a unity less conventional but not less serviceable. In any event, judged by usual standards, the book consists largely of a series of two major lines: the developmental psychology of the marriage of a psychiatrist and his patient; and the problem of values produced in a money economy. The story is enlivened by many bits of exciting melodrama. Princeton readers do not need to be told that Scott Fitzgerald knows how to tell a story. The strange goings-on of wealthy expatriated Americans make engrossing readings when told by Mr. Fitzgerald, quite aside from their connection with the story of Dr. Richard Diver and his wife Nicole.

Diver is seen through the eyes of Rosemary Hoyt, a dazzled young movie star, during the first part of the book, but later on the tragedy of his moral and intellectual disintegration is reported from his own point of view. He is a psychiatrist, and a circumstantial account of psychiatric practice is, to the layman at least, one of the most fascinating things in the book. Incidentally, able psychologists say the description of the genesis and treatment of his chief patient's disorder is in thorough accord with psychiatric tradition.

Tender Is the Night:
You Can't Duck Hurricane Under a Beach Umbrella

PHILIP RAHV

F. Scott Fitzgerald made a name for himself in the literature of the past decade as the voice and chronicler of the jazz age. This, in a sense, was his strength, as he showed himself capable of quickly responding to features of American life that other writers assimilated rather slowly; but it also proved to be his greatest defect, since he failed to place what he saw in its social setting. He himself was swept away by the waste and extravagance of the people he described, and he identified himself with them. Hence the critics who, at his appearance on the literary scene, saw in him a major talent in post-war American literature, soon realized that here was another creative promise petering out. The fever of the boom days settled in his bones. In the end he surrendered to the standards of the *Saturday Evening Post*.

In these days, however, even Fitzgerald cannot escape realizing how near the collapse of his class really is. In his new work he no longer writes of expensive blondes and yachting parties, lavish surroundings and insane love-affairs from the same angle of vision as in the past. These things are still there, but the author's enthusiasm for them has faded, giving way to the sweat of exhaustion. The rich expatriates who trail their weary lives across the pages of the novel breathe the thin air of a crazy last autumn. The author is still in love with his characters, but he no longer entertains any illusions concerning their survival. Morally, spiritually, and even physically they are dying in hospitals for the mentally diseased, in swanky Paris hotels and on the Riviera beaches. Yet, having immersed himself in the atmosphere of corruption, Fitzgerald's eye discerns a certain grace even in their last contortions. The morbid romance of death sways his mind, and signs are not wanting that instead of severing the cords that bind him to their degradation, he prefers to stick out with them to the end. Even while perceiving their doom, he still

Originally published as "You Can't Duck Hurricane Under a Beach Umbrella," *Daily Worker*, May 5, 1934. Reprinted by permission of the *Daily World*, successor to the *Daily Worker* since July 16, 1968.

continues to console and caress them with soft words uttered in the furry voice of a family doctor pledged to keep the fatal diagnosis from his patients.

A number of things happen in *Tender Is the Night*. First, let us introduce Mr. Warren, a Chicago millionaire who rapes his sixteen-year-old daughter Nicole. This non-plebeian act drives the girl out of her mind, and she is sent to a sanatorium in Switzerland, where she is partially cured and where she meets Dick Diver, a young American psychologist who marries her. Nicole is extremely wealthy and the Divers lead a model parasitic life, flitting from one European high spot to another, accompanied by a varied assortment of neurotics and alcoholics. Wherever they go they are intent on smashing things up. Dick Diver's strength and charm fall apart in the insufferable atmosphere of sophisticated brutality. In the course of time he realizes his role as a live commodity bought by the Warren family to act as husband-doctor to their crazy daughter. And Nicole, sensing Dick's growing despair, flies from him to the arms of Tommy Barban, the stylized young barbarian who is potentially an ideal leader of a Nazi storm-troop.

When the plot is thus bluntly stated, stripped of its delicate introspective wording, of its tortuous style that varnishes rather than reveals the essential facts, we can easily see that the book is a fearful indictment of the moneyed aristocracy. But Fitzgerald's form blunts this essence, transforming it into a mere opportunity for endless psychologizing. And on account of it many a reader will let himself float on the novel's tender surface, without gauging the horror underneath.

The reviewer is inclined to think that in creating the figure of Dick Diver, Fitzgerald has created—perhaps unconsciously—the image of a life closely corresponding to his own. The truth is that Nicole can be understood as a symbol of the entire crazy social system to which Fitzgerald has long been playing Dick Diver.

And lastly, a not too private postscript to the author. Dear Mr. Fitzgerald, you can't hide from a hurricane under a beach umbrella.

Tender Is the Night: The Worm i' the Bud

WILLIAM TROY

To label Mr. Fitzgerald's new novel a study in psychological degeneration is not strictly accurate, for such degeneration presupposes an ante-
rior dignity or perfection of character, and none of the characters in
this book is made sufficiently measurable at the beginning to give to his
later downhill course anything more than a mildly pathetic interest.
None of them is even what one might call, in the loosest sense, mature.
Richard Diver, young American war veteran turned psychiatrist, is too
perfect a specimen of the Yale man of his generation to seem quite
plausible as a surgeon of souls. Nicole recovers from her schizophrenia,
the effect of an incestuous assault in childhood, only to acquire the
neuroses of the frivolous, luxurious and empty-pated society to which
she is restored. And Rosemary Hoyt, that incredible flower of the Hollywood studios, begins and ends, as hardly more than a glamorous moron.
Yet the effect of the novel as a whole is quite as depressing as that of
any authentic study in moral and psychological degeneration. The
vague depression that hovers over the opening chapters increases in
intensity as the book moves on to its sordid termination. It increases, as
a matter of fact, in an exact ratio to the growth of our confusion as to
the precise reason for the hero's disintegration. Is it that once Nicole
is cured of her disease she no longer has need of his kind of love—the
old story of the physician unable to heal himself? Is it that her money
has acted like a virus to destroy his personality and with it his life-
work? Or is it simply that he is a man of weak character, unable to resist temptation and concealing the fact from himself through immer-
sion in alcohol? All these causes are indicated, and any one of them
might be made sufficient, but the author's own unwillingness to choose
between them, his own uncertainty communicated to the reader, continues to the last. And the result is depressing in the way that confusion
in a work of literature is always depressing.

Glamor is here as elsewhere one of the most frequently used words in
Mr. Fitzgerald's vocabulary, and because this very abstract word so ob-

Originally published as "The Worm i' the Bud," *The Nation*, May 9, 1934.
Reprinted by permission of *The Nation*.

viously sums up much important feeling, constituting perhaps a key to Mr. Fitzgerald's sensibility, it may be worth while to submit it to that process of "dissociation" which Rémy de Gourmont recommended for cases of this kind. Now the word glamor, in Mr. Fitzgerald's writing, is usually applied to people or things or ways of living represented as being, in some total and general sense, attractive. It stands for a whole imponderable compound of desirable qualities—youth, beauty, gaiety, romantic charm. Daisy in *The Great Gatsby* possessed glamor, and so do the two heroines in the present book. But it should be noted that in the case of each of these exquisite creatures to the possession of glamor is added another and more palpably attractive possession—money. In *The Great Gatsby*, the narrator, fumbling for an exact description of Daisy, is told by Gatsby himself, "Her voice is full of money."

> That was it. . . . It was full of money—that was the inexhaustible charm that rose and fell in it, the jingle of it, the cymbals' song of it. . . . High in a white palace the king's daughter, the gold girl. . . .

And now again, in this new book, we find Nicole's lover reminding her, "You've got too much money. That's the crux of the matter." In other words, for Mr. Fitzgerald's heroes youth and wealth, romance and luxury, love and money become somehow identified in the imagination. "Glamor" becomes a compound of glittering opposites. And because it consists for them in a confusion of essentially irreconcilable elements their surrender to it leads, in the end, either to inglorious death in Long Island swimming pools or to slow deterioration on foreign sands.

This conflict, since that is what it really amounts to, is probably the thing that makes Mr. Fitzgerald an artist, the very distinguished artist that he revealed himself to be in *The Great Gatsby*. But the time has come when we must demand a more clean-cut recognition of its elements and a more single-minded effort toward its resolution. The biographer of Gatsby, weary of his riotous excursions into the human heart, returned to the Middle West wanting the whole world to be "in uniform and at a sort of moral attention forever." But Dick Diver turns out to be Jay Gatsby all over again, another poor boy with a "heightened sensitivity to the promises of life" betrayed by his own inability to make the right distinctions. And the repetition of the pattern turns out to be merely depressing. It is time now for Mr. Fitzgerald, with his remarkable technical mastery of his craft, to give us a character who is not the victim of adolescent confusion, who is strong enough to turn deaf ears to the jingling cymbals of the golden girl.

Tender Is the Night: Breakdown

MALCOLM COWLEY

Tender Is the Night is a good novel that puzzles you and ends by making you a little angry because it isn't a great novel also. It doesn't give the feeling of being complete in itself.

The theme of it is stated in a conversation among the three principal characters. "What did this to him?" Rosemary asks. They are talking about Abe North, an American composer who became prominent shortly after the War. He was shy and very talented; often he came to stay with Dick and Nicole Diver in their villa near the Cap d'Antibes and they scarcely knew he was there—"sometimes he'd be in the library with a muted piano, making love to it by the hour." But for years now he hadn't been working; his eyes had a hurt look; he got drunk every day as if trying to escape from nobody knew what. And Rosemary wondered, "Why does he have to drink?"

> Nicole shook her head right and left, disclaiming responsibility for the matter: "So many smart men go to pieces nowadays."
>
> "And when haven't they?" Dick asked. "Smart men play close to the line because they have to—some of them can't stand it, so they quit."
>
> "It must lie deeper than that. . . . Artists like—well, like Fernand don't seem to have to wallow in alcohol. Why is it just Americans who dissipate?"
>
> There were so many answers to this question that Dick decided to leave it in the air, to buzz victoriously in Nicole's ears.

The question remains victoriously buzzing in the reader's ear long after the story has ended. Fitzgerald tries to answer it, but obliquely. He tells us why Dr. Richard Diver went to pieces—because he married a rich woman and became so dependent on her money that his own work seemed unimportant and he no longer had a purpose in living; that is the principal reason, although he is also shaken by his love for Rosemary and by Nicole's recurrent fits of insanity, during one of which she came near killing not only her husband and herself but also their two children. Dick's case seems clear enough—but what about Abe North, whose wife was poor and sane and devoted? What about the other nice people who ended as lunatics or drunkards? Fitzgerald is continually suggesting and reiterating these questions that he leaves in the air.

The Divers and their friends are, in reality, the characters he has always written about, and written well. They are the richer members of his own generation, the young women who learned to smoke and pet in 1917 and the Yale and Princeton men who attended their coming-out parties in new uniforms. In his early books, especially in *This Side of Paradise*, he celebrated the youth of these people in a tone of unmixed pride—"Here we are," he seemed to be saying, "the children of the conquerors, the free and beautiful and very wicked youngsters who are setting the standards for a nation." Later, when he described their business careers and their life in great country houses on the north shore of Long Island, his admiration began to be mixed with irony and disillusionment. In the present novel, which chronicles their years of exile, the admiration has almost completely vanished; the prevailing tone is one of disillusionment mixed with nostalgia. "We had good times together," Fitzgerald seems to say, "but that was a long time ago." Dick Diver is now an unsuccessful drunken country doctor, divorced and living somewhere in central New York State. Rosemary is an empty and selfish movie star; Abe North is dead, killed brawling in a speakeasy—all the kind and sensitive people of their circle have gone to pieces, and there remain only the "wooden and onanistic" women like Nicole's sister, only the *arrivistes* like Albert McKisco and the cultivated savages like Tommy Barban. A whole class has flourished and decayed and suddenly broken into fragments.

Here is a magnificent subject for a novel. The trouble is that Fitzgerald has never completely decided what kind of novel he wanted to write—whether it should center round a single hero or deal with a whole group. Both types of approach are present, the individual and the collective, and they interfere with each other. We are conscious of a divided purpose that perhaps goes back to a division in the author himself.

Fitzgerald has always been the poet of the American upper bourgeoisie; he has been the only writer able to invest their lives with glamor. Yet he has never been sure that he owed his loyalty to the class about which he was writing. It is as if he had a double personality. Part of him is a guest at the ball given by the people in the big house; part of him has been a little boy peeping in through the window and being thrilled by the music and the beautifully dressed women—a romantic but hard-headed little boy who stops every once in a while to wonder how much it all cost and where the money came from. (Fitzgerald says, "There is a streak of vulgarity in me that I try to cultivate.") In his early books, this divided personality was wholly an advantage: it enabled him to portray American society from the inside, and yet at the same time to surround it with an atmosphere of magic and romance that exists only in the eyes of people watching at the carriage entrance as the guests arrive in limousines. Since those days, however, the division has been emphasized and has become a liability. The little boy outside the window has grown mature and cold-eyed: from an enraptured spectator he has developed into a social historian. At the same time, part of Fitzgerald remains inside, among the dancers. And now that the ball is ending in tragedy, he doesn't know how to describe it—whether as a guest, a participant, in which case he will be writing a purely psychological novel; or whether from the detached point of view of a social historian.

There is another reason, too, for the technical faults of *Tender Is the Night*. Fitzgerald has been working on it at intervals for the last nine years, ever since he published *The Great Gatsby* in 1925. During these years his attitude has inevitably changed, as has that of every other sensitive writer. Yet no matter how much he revised his early chapters, he could not make them wholly agree with those written later—for once a chapter has assumed what seems to be a final shape, it undergoes a process of crystalization; it can no longer be remolded. The result is that several of his characters are self-contradictory: they don't merely change as living creatures change; they transform themselves into different people.

If I didn't like the book so much, I wouldn't have spoken at such length about its shortcomings. It has virtues that deserve more space than I can give them here. Especially it has a richness of meaning and emotion—one feels that every scene is selected among many possible scenes and that every event has pressure behind it. There is nothing false or borrowed in the book: everything is observed at first hand. Some of the minor figures—especially Gausse, the hotel keeper who was once a bus boy in London, and Lady Caroline Sibley-Biers, who carries her English bad manners to the point of viciousness—are more vivid than Rosemary or Dick; and the encounter between Gausse and Lady Caroline is one of those enormous episodes in which two social castes are depicted melodramatically, farcically and yet convincingly in a brief conversation and one gesture.

Fitzgerald says that this book is his farewell to the members of his own generation; I hope he changes his mind. He has in him at least one great novel about them, and it is a novel that I want to read.

Tender Is the Night

JOURNAL OF NERVOUS AND MENTAL DISEASE

In *Tender Is the Night* Mr. Fitzgerald draws a detailed and fascinating picture of the circumstantial and effective involvements attending inner dynamic developments in the lives of a young American couple living abroad. As one grasps fully the scope of the author's aim, and his discernment in face of the balance of psychotic cause and effect, the rich endowment of the book in regard to conscious mastery of authentic experience and exceptional descriptive powers becomes increasingly evident.

For the psychiatrist and psychoanalyst the book is of special value as a probing story of some of the major dynamic interlockings in marriage which, conditioned by set economic and psychobiological situations, have their innumerable counterparts in differences of degree rather than of kind. After her mother's death Nicole Warren suffers intercourse with the father. The psychotic effects, accruing during adolescence and

Originally published as an untitled review, *Journal of Nervous and Mental Disease*, July 1935. Reprinted by permission of *Journal of Nervous and Mental Disease.*

her early maturity, develop into a severe schizophrenia. The father, a capitalist "builder" of the middle west, presents the customary ignorance and adaptative weakness before demands of natural knowledge and discipline common to persons recapitulating psychobiological end-results derived from repeated conditionings of anal and acquisitive in-going trends. Anxious to be rid of responsibility for the daughter, and afraid of knowledge of the consequences of his act, Warren leaves her in a Zurich psychiatric hospital.

Richard Diver, an American physician studying psychiatry abroad, makes the girl's acquaintance through correspondence during the war. She improves greatly by means of this affective outlet; and after their meeting later they marry—Diver being, at the time he makes the step, both cognizant of the unconscious implications of the transference and prepared to fully incorporate in his creative energic organization the demands of her further cure with the work already planned for himself. In the following years there are two children, and, settled in a secluded spot on the Riviera, Diver's chief efforts are devoted to strengthening Nicole against the psychotic relapses of her illness. As, through Diver's care and constant attendance, she gains gradually to a firmer hold on reality, Diver himself slowly begins to slip: it would appear in the time scale of the novel that in proportion as Nicole's improvement becomes more definite and complete, Diver, superficially at first, but later more deeply and pragmatically, is aware of the accruing effects of his own integration.

The slipping of his own hold on the exigencies of creative advancement is increasingly manifest in various ways: his work, laid out definitely at first, is now sporadic, becoming more and more elusive; his partnership with a friend in a clinic, begun earnestly at first, falls through; and, concomitant with an extra-marital affair, there is a gradual emergence of destructive attitudes in all his contacts and orientations. As the story unfolds to the point where they separate finally several factors are clearly drawn as of important bearing on these new dynamic patternings. There is the extent of his wife's wealth, and the proprietary attitude of her narcissistic sister. Both facts, seemingly inconsequential at first, are shown clearly to have deep psychological cumulative effects, projecting their roots beneath all his plans and activities. At another level, his wife, aware of her husband's slow disintegration, realizes at the same time her increasing freedom from affective dependence on him, a situation which as described here clearly evidences the progressive comparative values in ego development between them.

Around the figures of Diver and his wife are grouped certain other characters, all of which in some degree have a bearing on the emotional relations between them. There is the old friend, the defeated composer North, whose dissolution is marked by the progressions of an acute alcoholism; Rosemary Spears, the young movie star through whom the first perspective of the Divers is cast and whose affair with Diver is one of the first objective signs of his disintegration; Barban, the Don Juanesque type who goes back and forth waiting for the couple's separation, casting himself as Nicole's second protector; and Franz, the one-time fellow-worker whose undeviating activity somehow stands as symbol for a way of life opposite to that which may be abstracted from the histories here mainly described. These characters, round whom the component parts of the history center, are in each instance deeply realized and completely drawn. They present a compact handling of detail making for very clear impressions of the post-war decade with all its aspects of manners, disintegration, and individual loss. Mr. Fitzgerald has written a book which is extremely valuable both as an understanding and sensitive record of human life, and as an accurate and fully prepared chronicle of European life circa 1917–1930. Its content and fine treatment in these respects, as in many others which present space limitations make it impossible to discuss fully, together with the author's insight and skill, constitute an achievement which no student of the psychobiological sources of human behavior, and of its particular social correlates extant today, can afford not to read.

Taps at Reveille:
F. Scott Fitzgerald, Looking Backward

ELIZABETH HART

The eighteen stories that comprise this collection have been chosen by Fitzgerald himself as the cream of his shorter writing for a decade. If you exclude a group of tinkling cymbals ("Majesty," "One Interne," "Two Wrongs") that might have been played by any of a dozen pat performers for the big-circulation magazines and that have no significant bearing on the main-stream of the author's work, the book falls into a pattern that gives you a pretty good idea of the course of his development during those seismic years.

It is not a straight and steady course, and a hasty reader may get the impression that it has been one-sided: Fitzgerald writing better and better about the same old things, strengthening and disciplining his lovely prose only to plagiarize himself, bringing an increasing maturity of style to subject matter that clings desperately to the knee-skirts of the jazz age. Indeed, there is plenty of evidence in *Taps at Reveille* to support the charge that Fitzgerald has become the prisoner of his own past, a literary Peter Pan who refused to grow up with the feverish, glamorous youth he immortalized. Nevertheless, when one has finished the book and reflected upon its contents as a whole, a different judgment will probably be rendered. The title is not meaningless. It symbolizes very neatly what Fitzgerald has actually done in these pages—worked an old phase thoroughly out of his system and begun to feel around for a new one.

The catharsis, it is admitted, takes up considerable of the volume's space. Here again are the golden girls, moving to dance-music and the throb of their own pulses within an enchanted circle of beauty, youth and wealth; and their partners, all the sad young men, whose sadness is as graceful and decorative as themselves—a sort of charming luxury, a little more dispensable than a roadster or membership in a good fra-

Originally published as "F. Scott Fitzgerald, Looking Backward," *New York Herald Tribune Book Review*, March 31, 1935. © 1935, New York Herald Tribune Inc. Reprinted by permission of W. C. C. Publishing Company, Inc.

ternity at Yale. Here are the raptures and qualms, the sweetness and disillusionment of the Great Kissing Era; and the Biltmore at tea-time, the old haunting tunes, the bewitched whirl of the holidays. But their presentation has a definitely valedictory tone. "The Last of the Belles," though nostalgic, is also a farewell to nostalgia for the "lost midsummer world of my twenties." "In "Josephine" and "A Short Trip Home" Fitzgerald wallows in memories of flaming youth in its late 'teens, much as a man who is about to go on the wagon indulges in a final bender. In "Basil," the longest story in the book, he proceeds to unburden himself of the years from fourteen to sixteen and, incidentally, does a very fine job. "Basil" has its flaws—chiefly an over-neat rounding off of the five separate episodes that compose it—but it is one of the best interpretations we have had yet of that age "between thirteen, boyhood's majority, and seventeen, when one is a sort of counterfeit man . . . a time when youth fluctuates hourly between one world and another." It is sympathetic without sentimentality, humorous without the condescension that makes Booth Tarkington a little hard to take even when he is handing out the richest laughs. Fitzgerald is much fairer to Basil than Tarkington was to either Penrod or Willie Baxter—with the result that he creates a recognizable boy.

The remainder of the collection represents the transitional Fitzgerald—please remember that I am not speaking in rigidly chronological terms, I do not know or care the precise order in which these stories were written. "The Fiend" is a brief, dispassionate study of the relationship between a degenerate, who is serving life-imprisonment for a peculiarly frightful murder, and the man whose wife and son were the prisoner's victims. It is excellently done. "Night at Chancellorsville" and "Family in the Wind" do not come off so well: the former is flimsy and wears its mimetic dress rather self-consciously: the latter is honest and shot through with effective description but confused of purpose. As a matter of fact, while all three are interesting as experiments with material that Fitzgerald has never, to my knowledge, used before, he does not seem quite at home in any of them. On the other hand, "Babylon Revisited," where he is working on more familiar terrain, is a superb story, firm, sure, vibrant. Again the past crops up—this time the boom days of American stock-market millionaires in Paris—but it is seen in the light of the present and seen astringently, it functions as the crazy, distorted roots of today's sober bloom. This would seem to indicate that Fitzgerald's future lies in writing about those people of certain means and background whom he knows and understands best, but writing about them realistically, interpreting them in full relation to the contemporary scene.

Taps at Reveille: Scott Fitzgerald's Tales

EDITH H. WALTON

According to his publishers, Mr. Fitzgerald has chosen for inclusion in this volume the best short stories that he has written during the past decade. It is a curious and rather disturbing admission, coming as it does from a writer of Scott Fitzgerald's stature. The characteristic seal of his brilliance stamps the entire book, but it is a brilliance which splutters off too frequently into mere razzle-dazzle. One wishes for more evidence that he has changed and matured since the days of *Flappers and Philosophers* and *Tales of the Jazz Age.*

Most in key with those earlier books are the three stories grouped under the heading, "Josephine." With a kind of deadly accuracy, Mr. Fitzgerald describes a specimen of the predatory young who makes Mr. Tarkington's Lola Platt seem like a milk-and-water baby. Josephine is sixteen—beautiful, ruthless and fickle. Whether or not he is earmarked as somebody else's property she goes out and gets her man with an appalling directness. Proms and tea-dances are her natural habitat, and she takes a certain pride in being considered fast. She dates—more, perhaps, than Mr. Fitzgerald realizes—but her wiles and adventures are undeniably comic.

Better, and poignant as well as amusing, is the longer sequence of stories which deals with a pre-war boy in his middle teens. Though his method is different from Booth Tarkington's, Mr. Fitzgerald approaches at times the same startling veracity. Basil Duke Lee is a bright, sensitive, likable boy, constantly betrayed by a fatal tendency to brag and boss. He knows his failing, especially after the minor hell of his first year at boarding school, but again and again he is impelled to ruin an

Originally published as "Scott Fitzgerald's Tales," *New York Times Book Review*, March 31, 1935. © 1935, The New York Times Company. Reprinted by permission.

initial good impression. Two of the Basil stories—"He Thinks He's Wonderful" and "The Perfect Life"—are small masterpieces of humor and perception, and Mr. Fitzgerald is always miraculously adept at describing adolescent love affairs and adolescent swagger.

A full half of *Taps at Reveille* is given over to these tales of youth. The remaining stories vary greatly in mood and merit. "Crazy Sunday," which has Hollywood for a setting, is clever but contrived; "Majesty," for all its irony, has a strangely hollow ring; "One Interne" is entertaining, but gets nowhere and has no real characterization. Even "The Last of the Belles," with its undertone of regret for youth and bright gayety, fails to make a point which one can regard as valid. Far better is "A Short Trip Home," a ghost story which yet can be considered as definitely realistic.

Three of the stories point toward directions which Mr. Fitzgerald might profitably take. "A Trip to Chancellorsville," in which a trainload of light ladies is catapulted unawares into the realities of the Civil War, is restrained irony at its best. "Family in the Wind," the story of a Southern town ravaged by tornadoes and of a drink-ridden doctor who stumbles on salvation, strikes a new and healthy note. "Babylon Revisited," which seems oddly linked in spirit to Mr. Fitzgerald's latest novel, *Tender Is the Night*, is probably the most mature and substantial story in the book. A rueful, though incompleted, farewell to the jazz age, its setting is Paris and its tone one of anguish for past follies.

It has become a dreadful commonplace to say that Mr. Fitzgerald's material is rarely worthy of his talents. Unfortunately, however, the platitude represents truth. Scott Fitzgerald's mastery of style—swift, sure, polished, firm—is so complete that even his most trivial efforts are dignified by his technical competence. All his writing has a glamourous gloss upon it; it is always entertaining; it is always beautifully executed.

Only when one seeks to discover what he has really said, what his stories really amount to, is one conscious of a certain emptiness. *Taps at Reveille* will bore no one, and offend no trained intelligence, but when one remembers how fine a writer Mr. Fitzgerald could still be, it simply is not good enough.

Taps at Reveille: The Perfect Life

WILLIAM TROY

Although it is one of the most obvious statements that can be made of any novelist, it has never exactly been pointed out about Scott Fitzgerald that what he is principally concerned with in all his novels and tales is character. "She was a fine girl—one of the best," remarks the hero of one of the stories in this collection, of the wife who has abandoned him to follow her own career. "She had character." All the important personages in the book have character or are trying to have character, or have irretrievably lost their character. Whether the emphasis is on achievement or struggle or failure the theme is one and the same. Whatever may be their age or sex or background all of them are sooner or later confronted, like the adolescent Basil Lee, with the vision of "the perfect life." This rambunctious Middle Western schoolboy, whose inner gyrations occupy the first story in the volume, is the father of the chastened hero of "Babylon Revisited," which is the last. Of course neither Basil nor his feminine counterpart, the precociously scandalous Josephine, is presented in any earnestly moralistic fashion; their adolescent crises are more often a source of amusement than of edification; but what gives to their histories a direction and finally a meaning is their common effort at some sort of personal regeneration. In the other stories, which deal with people adult at least in years, the theme is naturally treated with a more becoming gravity. "Babylon Revisited," one of the best of them, deals with the not quite successful attempt of a reformed survivor of the Paris pleasure front of the twenties to wrest custody of his child from skeptical relatives. "The Last of the Belles," as the title may suggest, is the record of a young Northerner's gradual recovery from the narcotic influences of the romantic South. In the somewhat melodramatic "Family in the Wind" a middle-aged country doctor emerges triumphantly from a long season with the bottle. The gin-colored twilight of Hollywood film-colony receptions supplies the atmosphere for another such drama of self-conquest in "Crazy Sunday." In the strangest of all the tales, "A Short Trip Home," Mr. Fitzgerald's obsession drives him to the frankly allegorical: the sinister Joe Varland,

Originally published as "The Perfect Life," *The Nation*, April 17, 1935. Reprinted by permission of *The Nation*, and the Rutgers University Press.

hanger-on of pool-rooms and tracker of women, is the almost abstract embodiment of evil. Indeed, the only exception to the generalization that has been made is the slight and ineffective "Night of Chancellorsville," which would seem to prove that Mr. Fitzgerald is interesting only when he is at grips with the problem of character.

Now the problem of character, which is first and last the moral problem, is not popular with many of the writers and readers of contemporary fiction; it has been relegated to that class of quaint antiquities which includes Malthusianism and the Boston rocker. The reasons for this are obvious enough and need not be rehearsed; but the consequences for fiction have become increasingly more overwhelming during the past two book seasons. For the area of moral conflict, the area which most of the older novelists chose as their terrain, has been substituted the vast, the unchartable, the uncontrollable ocean of the sensibilities. As the tide rises the flood threatens to carry all before it—readers along with writers. The inheritors of the Joycean dispensation, unencumbered by the self-wrought bonds of aesthetic discipline which restrained the master, are intent on submerging the universe. What used to be called character has dissolved in the confused welter of uncoordinated actions, sensations, impressions, and physico-chemical reactions which currently passes for the art of fiction.

Mr. Fitzgerald, in his persistent concentration on "those fine moral decisions that people make in books," is fundamentally, therefore, a rather old-fashioned sort of storyteller. He has more in common, let us say, with George Eliot, Henry James, and Joseph Conrad than with any of the more prominent members of his own generation. One should not be misled by the strong sense of the Zeitgeist reflected in his choice of subjects and characters. Although the experience is as contemporary as that of Faulkner or of Hemingway, the focus on the experience is very different, and the technique that is the result of this focus is different. It is not experience *qua* experience that is important but the ordering of experience, the arrangement of experience according to some scheme of developing moral action. This is the reason why Mr. Fitzgerald in even his worst lapses, such as the story called "Majesty," is always able to sustain a certain interest, to provide the kind of interest that we are accustomed to receive from prose narrative.

The observation that Mr. Fitzgerald is one of the few American writers still occupied with character, and that this is responsible for the distinction of form and technique in his writing, is not equivalent to a definitive evaluation of that writing as a whole. It is of course a temptation to say that stories like "The Last of the Belles" and "Babylon Revisited" are worth a half-dozen novels of more pretentious length and substance published this season. It is the same sort of temptation that has caused certain critics, grateful that anything possessing so many of the features of a great work of fiction could be written in America, to speak of *The Great Gatsby* as if it were *Madame Bovary* or *War and Peace*. But while Mr. Fitzgerald is excellent in tracing the vacillating curve of character in his works, his standard or criterion of character itself is not always easily to be determined. Sometimes it would seem to be the manliness of a Yale football captain, sometimes the innocence of a Middle Western debutante, sometimes no more than the ability to conform to the mores of respectable middle-class society. Especially from "A Short Trip Home" does one derive the impression that evil is always to be found in poverty-stricken back alleys of downtown, and goodness always in the warmly opulent mansions of Summit Avenue. The vision of evil is that of the adolescent suddenly frightened by the glimpse of the great impersonal continent outside the frosted windowpanes of the Twentieth Century Limited. The moral interest in all these stories is acute, but the moral vision is vague and immature. If Mr. Fitzgerald could enlarge his vision to correspond to his interest, he would do much both for his own reputation and for the amelioration of current American fiction writing.

Essays and Editorials

This Side of Paradise

FRANCES NEWMAN

It is not, of course necessary that all American reviewers—critic is a rather lofty word—should have read *Sinister Street* once a month or so during the six years that one has been privileged to do so, and perhaps one official skimming might have been dimmed by the intervention of a fairly prolonged war. But an equally casual skimming of the reviews of *This Side of Paradise* has revealed in only the *New Republic* a glance at Mr. Fitzgerald's "acquisitive eye on 'Sinister Street.'" And as the next line continued "without its obesity," one gathers that this R.V.A.S. has no very tender regard for Michael Fane. But if *Sinister Street* was until very lately the apple of one's eye and if even the discovery of a new apple has not caused one to love it less, the perusal of *This Side of Paradise* becomes nothing less than agony.

Now, naturally, one knows no more of Mr. Fitzgerald's literary affections than he has seen fit to reveal in print, but it rather seems that his memory is much more highly developed than his imagination and that he has no idea how good a memory he really has. As some forgotten writer said when *Queed* was first delighting the world, Mr. Harrison might have imitated Robert Chambers, but he had instead risen to the altitude of imitating the author of *Septimus*, and so one might take it kindly that young Mr. Fitzgerald has hitched his wagon to Mr. Mackenzie rather than to Ralph Barbour, and so, if it were only Mr. Walpole or Mr. Cannan or even Aldous Huxley, one could. But the vulgarizing of one's perfect book is more than can be endured in silence.

Originally published as "Carnegie Library Notes," Atlanta (Ga.) *Constitution*, February 13, 1921. Reprinted by permission of the Atlanta *Constitution*. This text is a slightly shortened version of the original.

Mr. Fitzgerald certainly did not sit down with the desire to write a story of youth and after casting about for a model, say to himself that he would write an American parody of *Sinister Street*. No one in his senses would do that. So it must follow that he has been betrayed by his too retentive memory. The suffering of witnessing the desecration of an idol has made the reading of every one of his words impossible, so it is quite possible that one has missed the most distressing of the affinities between the career of Amory Blaine and Michael Fane—one had not, until the moment of writing them, realized that the names rhyme— and one may also have missed some of Mr. Fitzgerald's felicities, even all of them. This sincere flattery begins at the very beginning, by a caricature of Mrs. Fane, that vague and charming woman, which after being united with some of the less pleasing frailties of Michael's nurse, is called the sophisticated mother of Amory. Mr. Fitzgerald has even provided a dignitary of the Catholic church for Amory to discuss his divergences from other boys with—quite as Michael had his Mr. Viner for the same high use. And just, also, as Michael had his Wilmot to introduce him to Oscar Wilde and Walter Pater and Mademoiselle de Maupin, even to the decadents of another age—Petronius and Apuleius and Suetonius, Amory had his D'Invilliers to discover to him the glories of *Dorian Gray* and Swinburne and Pater, of Gautier, and Huysmans, of "the racier sections of Rabelais, Bocaccio, Petronius and Suetonius." And Michael was called Narcissus by this Wilmot; Mr. Fitzgerald has provided a section entitled "Narcissus on Duty." The first book of *Sinister Street* is called "Dreaming Spires," and most properly since Matthew Armold gave the phrase to Oxford; the entry of Amory into Princeton is heralded by the title "Spires and Gargoyles." Michael was teased by his governess because his sympathies were the sympathies of the late G. A. Henty, even to the point of sympathizing with the American colonists against his own British forbears; Amory had all the "Henty biasses," even to the point of sympathizing with the southern confederacy. Michael was rigid about dividing Oxford into "good eggs and bad men"; Amory's world was divided into "slickers and big-men." And there are endless phrases and incidents that have risen from poor Mr. Fitzgerald's subconscious mind rather than from his observation.

Such a comparison is undoubtedly vain and frivolous, but this young man, in the phrase of his period, has positively "asked for it." To one who cherishes *Sinister Street* and one who cherishes some hope for the American novel, it is impossible to read *This Side of Paradise* without having one's blood-pressure about mount to a dangerous degree and without one's temperature becoming unendurable. And it would not be so very annoying if any number of critics for whom one had high regard had not taken it so very seriously. Such panegyrics as might have greeted the plays of Euripides or the Divine Comedy—but which certainly did not—have flowed from the most respectable sources; the book has had both the success of esteem and the success of popularity.

As for the ways in which *This Side of Paradise* differs from *Sinister Street*, except for a few essentially trivial ones, a comparison would be rather like one between "Irene" and "Tristan and Isolde." There is, however, the fundamental one that Michael Fane, in spite of some eccentricities of ancestry, was a gentleman. And there is also the difference that Mr. Fitzgerald's youths serve Athena and Aphrodite quite interchangeably. . . . But both of these books end with a crisis of youth and a cry in the dark—rather significantly, the darkness of Rome and the darkness of New Jersey.

Of course, Mr. Fitzgerald is young—so young that he thinks eight years passed between the eighteenth amendment and the day when the Fifth Avenue traffic lights were still a subject of conversation—and Dr. Johnson might charitably decide that one should be surprised to find it done at all. But if one must have youth, let us have Daisy Ashford's youth and let us not be confronted with a choice between Mr. Fitzgerald's youthful patchwork and Miss Opal Whiteley's childish labor.

But the crowning glory of *This Side of Paradise* may be regarded as the fact that about his twenty-third year this Amory Blaine "was where Goethe was when he began 'Faust'; he was where Conrad was when he wrote 'Almayer's Folly.' " Now, quite apart from the difficulty of conceiving that Goethe and Conrad were at the same place, one grieves for the loss it is to American letters that this gifted Amory should be only the creation of Mr. Fitzgerald's brain.

F. Scott Fitzgerald

EDMUND WILSON

It has been said by a celebrated person that to meet F. Scott Fitzgerald is to think of a stupid old woman with whom someone has left a diamond; she is extremely proud of the diamond and shows it to everyone who comes by, and everyone is surprised that such an ignorant old woman should possess so valuable a jewel; for in nothing does she appear so inept as in the remarks she makes about the diamond.

The person who invented this simile did not know Fitzgerald very well and can only have seen him, I think, in his more diffident or uninspired moods. The reader must not suppose that there is any literal truth in the image. Scott Fitzgerald is, in fact, no old woman, but a very good-looking young man, nor is he in the least stupid, but, on the contrary, exhilaratingly clever. Yet there *is* a symbolic truth in the description quoted above: it is true that Fitzgerald has been left with a jewel which he doesn't know quite what to do with. For he has been given imagination without intellectual control of it; he has been given the desire for beauty without an aesthetic ideal; and he has been given a gift for expression without very many ideas to express.

Consider, for example, the novel—*This Side of Paradise*—with which he founded his reputation. It has almost every fault and deficiency that a novel can possibly have. It is not only highly imitative but it imitates an inferior model. Fitzgerald, when he wrote the book, was drunk with Compton Mackenzie, and it sounds like an American attempt to rewrite *Sinister Street*. Now, Mackenzie, in spite of his gift for picturesque and comic invention and the capacity for pretty writing that he says he learned from Keats, lacks both the intellectual force and the emotional imagination to give body and outline to the material which he secretes in such enormous abundance. With the seeds he took from Keats's garden, one of the best-arranged gardens in England, he exfloreated so profusely that he blotted out the path of his own. Michael Fane, the hero of *Sinister Street*, was swamped in the forest of description; he

"F. Scott Fitzgerald," *The Shores of Light*. New York: Farrar, Straus and Young, 1952.
Originally published as "F. Scott Fitzgerald," *The Bookman*, March 1922.
Reprinted by permission of the author.

was smothered by creepers and columbine. From the time he went up to Oxford, his personality began to grow dimmer, and, when he last turned up (in Belgrade) he seemed quite to have lost his identity. As a consequence, Amory Blaine, the hero of *This Side of Paradise*, had a very poor chance of coherence: Fitzgerald did endow him, to be sure, with a certain emotional life which the phantom Michael Fane lacks; but he was quite as much a wavering quantity in a phantasmagoria of incident that had no dominating intention to endow it with unity and force. In short, one of the chief weaknesses of *This Side of Paradise* is that it is really not *about* anything: its intellectual and moral content amounts to little more than a gesture—a gesture of indefinite revolt. The story itself, furthermore, is very immaturely imagined: it is always just verging on the ludicrous. And, finally, *This Side of Paradise* is one of the most illiterate books of any merit ever published (a fault which the publisher's proofreader seems to have made no effort to remedy). Not only is it ornamented with bogus ideas and faked literary references, but it is full of literary words tossed about with the most reckless inaccuracy.

I have said that *This Side of Paradise* commits almost every sin that a novel can possibly commit: but it does not commit the unpardonable sin: it does not fail to live. The whole preposterous farrago is animated with life. It is rather a fluttering and mercurial life: its emotions do not move you profoundly; its drama does not make you hold your breath; but its gaiety and color and movement did make it come as something exciting after the realistic heaviness and dinginess of so much serious American fiction. If one recalls the sort of flavorless fodder of which Ernest Poole's *The Harbor* was an example, one can understand the wild enthusiasm with which *This Side of Paradise* was hailed. The novel was also well-written—well-written in spite of its illiteracies. It is true, as I have said above, that Fitzgerald mishandles words; his works are full of malapropisms of the most disconcerting kind. You will find: "Whatever your flare [sic] proves to be—religion, architecture, literature"; "the Juvenalia of my collected editions"; "There were nice things in it [the room] . . . offsprings of a vicarious [vagarious] impatient taste"; "a mind like his, lucrative in intelligence, intuition and lightning decision"; etc., etc. It reminds one rather of:

> Agib, who could readily, at sight,
> Strum a march upon the loud Theodolite.

> He would diligently play
> On the Zoetrope all day,
> And blow the gay Pantechnicon all night.

It is true that Scott Fitzgerald plays the language entirely by ear. But his instrument, for all that, is no mean one. He has an instinct for graceful and vivid prose that some of his more pretentious fellows might envy.

In regard to the man himself, there are perhaps two things worth knowing, for the influence they have had on his work. In the first place, he comes from the Middle West—from St. Paul, Minnesota. Fitzgerald is as much of the Middle West of large cities and country clubs as Sinclair Lewis is of the Middle West of the prairies and little towns. What we find in him is much what we find in the more prosperous strata of these cities: sensitivity and eagerness for life without a sound base of culture and taste; a structure of millionaire residences, brilliant expensive hotels and exhilarating social activities built not on the eighteenth century but simply on the flat Western land. And it seems to me rather a pity that he has not written more of the West: it is perhaps the only milieu that he thoroughly understands. When Fitzgerald approaches the East, he brings to it the standards of the wealthy West— the preoccupation with display, the appetite for visible magnificence and audible jamboree, the vigorous social atmosphere of amiable flappers and youths comparatively untainted as yet by the snobbery of the East. In *The Beautiful and Damned*, for example, we feel that he is moving in a vacuum; the characters have no real connection with the background to which they have been assigned; they are not part of the organism of New York as the characters, in, say, the short story "Bernice Bobs Her Hair" are a part of the organism of St. Paul. Surely F. Scott Fitzgerald should some day do for Summit Avenue what Lewis has done for Main Street.

But you are not to suppose from all this that the author of *This Side of Paradise* is merely a typical well-to-do Middle Westerner, with correct clothes and clear skin, who has been sent to the East for college. The second thing one should know about him is that Fitzgerald is partly Irish and that he brings both to life and to fiction certain qualities that are not Anglo-Saxon. For, like the Irish, Fitzgerald is romantic, but also cynical about romance; he is bitter as well as ecstatic; astringent as well as lyrical. He casts himself in the role of playboy, yet at the playboy he incessantly mocks. He is vain, a little malicious, of quick intelligence and wit, and has an Irish gift for turning language into something iridescent and surprising. He often reminds one, in fact, of the description that a great Irishman, Bernard Shaw, has written of the Irish: "An Irishman's imagination never lets him alone, never convinces him, never satisfies him; but it makes him that he can't face reality nor deal with it nor handle it nor conquer it: he can only sneer at them that do . . . and imagination's such a torture that you can't bear it without whisky. . . . And all the while there goes on a horrible, senseless, mischievous laughter."

For the rest, F. Scott Fitzgerald is a rather childlike fellow, very much wrapped up in his dream of himself and his projection of it on paper. For a person of his mental agility, he is extraordinarily little occupied with the general affairs of the world: like a woman, he is not much given to abstract or impersonal thought. Conversations about politics or general ideas have a way of snapping back to Fitzgerald. But this seldom becomes annoying; he is never pretentious or boring. He is quite devoid of affectation and takes the curse off his relentless egoism by his readiness to laugh at himself and his boyish uncertainty of his talent. And he exhibits, in his personality as well as in his writings, a quality rare today among even the youngest American writers: he is almost the only one among them who is capable of lighthearted high spirits. Where a satirist like Sinclair Lewis would stew "the Problem of Salesmanship" in acrid rancorous fumes, Fitzgerald, in *The Beautiful and Damned*, has made of it hilarious farce. His characters—and he—are actors in an elfin harlequinade; they are as nimble, as gay and as lovely—and as hardhearted—as fairies: Columbine elopes with Harlequin on a rope ladder dropped from the Ritz and both go morris-dancing amuck on a case of bootleg liquor; Pantaloon is pinked with an epigram that withers him up like a leaf; the Policeman is tripped by Harlequin and falls into the Pulitzer Fountain. Just before the curtain falls, Harlequin puts on false whiskers and pretends to be Bernard Shaw; he gives reporters an elaborate interview on politics, religion and history; a hundred thousand readers see it and are more or less impressed; Columbine nearly dies laughing; Harlequin sends out for a case of gin.

Let me quote a characteristic incident in connection with *The Beautiful and Damned*. Since writing *This Side of Paradise*—on the inspiration of Wells and Mackenzie—Fitzgerald has become acquainted with a different school of fiction: the ironical-pessimistic. In college, he had supposed that the thing to do was to write biographical novels with a burst of ideas toward the close; since his advent in the literary world, he has discovered that another genre has recently come into favor: the kind which makes much of the tragedy and what Mencken has called "the meaninglessness of life." Fitzgerald had imagined, hitherto, that the thing to do in a novel was to bring out a meaning in life; but he now set bravely about it to contrive a shattering tragedy that should be, also, a hundred-percent meaningless. As a result of this determination, the first version of *The Beautiful and Damned* culminated in an orgy of horror for which the reader was imperfectly prepared. Fitzgerald destroyed his characters with a succession of catastrophes so arbitrary that, beside them, the perversities of Hardy seemed the working of natural laws. The heroine was to lose her beauty at a prematurely early age, and her character was to go to pieces with it; Richard Carmel, a writer of promise, was to lose his artistic ideals and prostitute himself to the popular taste; and the wealthy Anthony Patch was not only to lose his money but, finding himself unable to make a living, abjectly to succumb to drink and eventually to go insane. But the bitterest moment of the story was to come at the very end, when Anthony was to be wandering the streets of New York in an attempt to borrow some money. After several humiliating failures, he finally approaches an old friend whom he sees with an elegant lady just getting into a cab. This is the brilliant Maury Noble, a cynic, an intellectual and a man of genuine parts. Maury cuts Anthony dead and drives away in the taxi. "But," the author explains, "he really had not seen Anthony. For Maury had indulged his appetite for alcoholic beverage once too often: he was now stone-blind!" But the point of my story is this: though Fitzgerald had been perfectly serious in writing this bathetic passage, he did not hesitate, when he heard people laugh at it, to laugh about it himself, and with as much surprise and delight as if he had just come across it in Max Beerbohm. He at once improvised a burlesque: "It seemed to Anthony that Maury's eyes had a fixed glassy stare; his legs moved stiffly as he walked and when he spoke his voice was lifeless. When Anthony came nearer, he saw that Maury was dead."

To conclude, it would be quite unfair to subject Scott Fitzgerald, who is still in his twenties and has presumably most of his work before him, to a rigorous overhauling. His restless imagination may yet produce something durable. For the present, however, this imagination is certainly not seen to the best advantage: it suffers badly from lack of discipline and poverty of aesthetic ideas. Fitzgerald is a dazzling extemporizer, but his stories have a way of petering out: he seems never to have planned them completely or to have thought out his themes from the beginning. This is true even of some of his most successful fantasies, such as "The Diamond as Big as the Ritz" or his comedy, *The Vegetable*. On the other hand, *The Beautiful and Damned*, imperfect though it is, marks an advance over *This Side of Paradise*: the style is more nearly mature and the subject more solidly unified, and there are scenes that are more convincing than any in his previous fiction.

But, in any case, even the work that Fitzgerald has done up to date has a certain moral importance. In his very expression of the anarchy by which he finds himself bewildered, of his revolt which cannot fix on an object, he is typical of the war generation—the generation so memorably described on the last page of *This Side of Paradise* as "grown up to find all gods dead, all wars fought, all faiths in men shaken." There is a moral in *The Beautiful and Damned* that the author did not perhaps intend to point. The hero and the heroine of this giddy book are creatures without method or purpose: they give themselves up to wild debaucheries and do not, from beginning to end, perform a single serious act; yet somehow you get the impression that, in spite of their fantastic behavior, Anthony and Gloria Patch are the most rational people in the book. Wherever they come in contact with institutions, with the serious life of their time, these are made to appear ridiculous, they are subjects for scorn or mirth. We see the army, finance and business successively and casually exposed as completely without point or dignity. The inference we are led to draw is that, in such a civilization as this, the sanest and most honorable course is to escape from organized society and live for the excitement of the moment. It cannot be merely a special reaction to a personal situation which gives rise to the paradoxes of such a book. It may be that we cannot demand too high a degree of moral balance from young men, however able or brilliant, who write books in the year 1921: we must remember that they have had to grow up in, that they have had to derive their chief stimulus from the wars, the society and the commerce of the Age of Confusion itself.

Two Editorials on Fitzgerald

LOUISVILLE COURIER-JOURNAL

I

The youngness that is F. Scott Fitzgerald permeates the pages of his new book, *The Beautiful and Damned*. It is not a fresh youngness, a distillation of healthy animal spirits. It is post-adolescent, cynical, sour, stale, sophisticated. To discover how savagely old youth can be, cultivate this wise and blasé author. Mr. Fitzgerald has been "about," and his pictures of a decadent and spineless American social set have an air of authority about them.

If there was ever any doubt that Mr. Fitzgerald is superior and supercilious, that he inhales through a sensitive nostril, that he is of the ultra-cognoscenti, that his conception of his own intellect, to use one of his pet words is amazing, that doubt is dispelled by *The Beautiful and Damned*.

For all that, and despite the fact that his hard glitter repels and his snobbery leaves a brown taste, his very arrogance and cocksureness carries you along in a kind of sheer wonder.

It is hardly hazardous to say that *The Beautiful and Damned* is not likely to be more lasting than whisky breaths of its characters. It lacks the simplicity for greatness and it is devoid of a humanity which might have made it endure. Mr. Fitzgerald is a kind of chronicler of a small segment of society, a male gossip, an artistic edition of *Town Topics*.

As fervently as nature abhors a vacuum, so Mr. Fitzgerald abhors the bromide. He struggles to escape its deadening clutch with remarkable success, although the fact that he is struggling is not wholly concealed. Whenever one of the mouthy rubber stamps does escape from his pen, he garbs it in quotation marks—a kind of badge of shame, as though he were disclaiming an unwanted child. Then, too, not contenting himself with polite avoidance of hoary phrases, he wages open war against them and against the sentiments which inspire them.

Originally appeared as "F. Scott Fitzgerald," April 4, 1922, and "Fitzgerald's Future," April 17, 1922. Reprinted by permission of the Louisville *Courier-Journal*.

Thus sourly and with Olympian aloofness, Mr. Fitzgerald sets down his reactions to America's entrance into the war:

> In April war was declared with Germany. Wilson and his cabinet—a cabinet that in its lack of distinction was strangely reminiscent of the twelve apostles—let loose the carefully starved dogs of war, and the press began to whoop hysterically against the sinister morals, sinister philosophy, and sinister music produced by the Teutonic temperament. Those who fancied themselves particularly broadminded made the exquisite distinction that it was only the German Government which aroused them to hysteria; the rest were worked up to a condition of retching indecency.

To make sure that no one will suspect Mr. Fitzgerald of belonging to the common herd, he uses such phrases as "a hysterical area, foul with yellow sobbing and the smells of poor women"; and "from the tenement windows leaned rotund, moon-faced mothers, as constellations of this sordid heaven; women like dark imperfect jewels, women like vegetables, women like great bags of abominable dirty laundry" and "a dozen of these yokels, red-eyed, cheerless as scarecrows."

If this attitude toward his fellow-beings is due less to his youth than to his lack of gentility, his flippant descriptions of death smack on both. This is typical: "his father died with much sweating and grunting and crying aloud for air."

William Shakespeare used to say, "How beauteous mankind is!" Mr. Fitzgerald doesn't like its odors, can't tolerate its contact. He is aloof and untouchable by the common herd. He tries hard not to be a democrat, but he fails utterly to be an aristocrat. He lacks the roast beef of the one, and the gracious mellowness of the other.

What he needs is to pass through the mugginess of his super-sophistication and emerge in that clearer ether which is populated by those who are old enough to understand the wisdom that comes from the mouths of babes.

II

F. Scott Fitzgerald, the *Times'* book reviewer bibulously remarks, is like moonshine, "plenty of kick but mighty hard to swallow." Sympathetically concerned with his future, the recommendation is made that "he should be poured into a large oaken cask, charred on the inside, and left there to age for about ten years. He would then acquire a rich full head, a deep brown color, a delightfully smooth taste and, strange to say, an even more powerful 'kick' than his present brash bitterness can muster."

Some time ago, in these columns, an examination was made of Mr. Fitzgerald, as he appears in his latest work, *The Beautiful and Damned*, and account was taken of his cynical savagery, wholesale disillusion and lack of human sympathy. Whether he shall ever go through that aging and mellowing process must be left to the prophets to decide, but there can be no doubt of the soundness of the *Times'* recommendation.

At any rate, there are reasons to be grateful to Mr. Fitzgerald. He chronicles a segment of society which is unknown to Gopher Prairie and was entirely unsuspected by most of Americans, income-tax and non-income taxpayers alike. What Sinclair Lewis did for Main Street existence, what Edith Wharton did for "high life" in New York, Mr. Fitzgerald has done for parasitic hotel-resident, cafe-frequenter, hard-drinker and do-nothing.

Besides, and this is the cream of a delicious jest, Mr. Fitzgerald, whose abhorrence for bromides is equal to nature's attitude toward a vacuum and who sneers with contempt at honest bourgeois ideals, has become himself the perpetrator of a vast bromide. *The Beautiful and Damned*, for all its fine writing and superciliousness, is built around such hoary and well-worn principles as "The wages of sin is death," "Idleness is the devil's handmaiden," "Extravagance eats the moral fibre," and "The primrose path of dalliance leads but to decay."

Whether or not Mr. Fitzgerald realizes that, instead of bearing the earmarks and intellectual quiver of the cognoscenti, he is in reality purveying the household ideas of civilization under a glittering show of originality, is beside the question. It might irritate him to be accused of dishing up old victuals with nothing but a new and somewhat acrid sauce. But if he were irritated, that would be added proof of his callowness.

That Mr. Fitzgerald, whether unwittingly or not, has espoused the old bromides, which are, let it be said, the truths of life, is something in favor of himself and his literary product. When and if he acquires the rich head the *Times* speaks of, he will be well equipped to take his place among those staid literary gentlemen who throw the weight of their rhetoric to the support of existing institutions, knowing full well and admitting (which Mr. Fitzgerald isn't quite ready to do) that bromides are the salt of the earth.

The Future of Fitzgerald

MINNEAPOLIS JOURNAL

A complimentary headline! For of many writers of Scott Fitzgerald's age it would not be possible to assume that they had a future. The young man is twenty-six; he has published two novels and two volumes of short stories of which the second, *Tales of the Jazz Age,* is only a few weeks old. Moreover, both of the novels have very considerable merit and one, his first, *This Side of Paradise,* is stamped with the unmistakable stamp of a high natural talent. We may safely call it genius, admitting, as we do so, that genius is of many kinds and degrees.

The Beautiful and Damned, Fitzgerald's second novel, had little of the visible inspiration that flashed constantly through *This Side of Paradise,* but as a solid and honest study of decadence it deserves sound praise. The first book of short stories, *Flappers and Philosophers,* is unimportant, but *Tales of the Jazz Age,* in which Fitzgerald says farewell to the flapper, shows very distinctly the author's talent. It also shows terribly what are weaknesses rather than faults. In the field of fantasy he is heir of all that might be expected from an Irish ancestry—"The Diamond as Big as the Ritz" is not perfect, but it is remarkable; "Mr. Icky" shows a talent for straight-out fooling; on the other hand, such a tale as "The Jelly Bean" falls flatter the farther it goes. Fitzgerald may possibly have been misled by the success of earlier work, into believing in his powers as a realist. He has no genuine powers as a realist, and even in *This Side of Paradise* it is not the faithfulness of the Princeton atmosphere that counts, afterward, but the imaginative power, worthy of G. K. Chesterton, which could create the man whose feet were wrong. Similarly, in *The Beautiful and Damned,* the photographic realism does not count for much, unless momentarily, but the imaginative view of Anthony Patch and his Gloria and the splendid irony of the ending count for a good deal.

A story that is told of *The Beautiful and Damned* possibly supports the guess that Fitzgerald has valued too much his realistic skill. It is said, on the best authority, that his first draft of this novel had an ending in

Originally published as "The Future of Fitzgerald," Minneapolis *Journal,* December 31, 1922.

which every conceivable disaster was heaped upon all the characters. So much was this so that the effect was simply laughable, and those who were privileged to read the manuscript had a wild moment wondering if the thing were not a burlesque. When the fault was pointed out to Fitzgerald, he saw it, readily enough, and rewrote the ending.

The little individual prefaces to the stories in *Tales of the Jazz Age* are a happy idea which adds considerably to the book. "May Day" is a tragic story of the bitter sort; "The Lees of Happiness" is another kind of tragedy, the true kind, in which fate stacks the cards and human beings are cheated because they cannot help themselves. There is a take-off on the red-blooded variety of fiction, "Jemina, the Mountain Girl," the spirit of which may be caught from the opening: "It was night in the mountains of Kentucky. Wild hills rose on all sides. Swift mountain streams flowed rapidly up and down the mountains."

Mr. Fitzgerald, with his marked talent, is now apparently destined to choose between two courses, either of which will probably settle his future. He may write the sort of thing he can do better than almost any other American of his generation—imaginative fantasy, imaginative studies of American life with realistic touches—or he may write "smart" stories for American magazines and be as richly rewarded as others who write that kind of article. There was another young man, once on a time, named Robert W. Chambers, who began with much such a gift as Fitzgerald shows. . . . On the other hand, Donn Byrne's last two books show the danger Fitzgerald stands in if his Irish talent for the fantastic runs away with him.

Notes on Personalities: F. Scott Fitzgerald

B . F . WILSON

The strange attraction that a pool of quiet waters has for the boy or man with a stone in his hand is largely a matter of personal curiosity. How far will the ever-widening circles of water spread? What happens when the last wave breaks upon the bank is of no interest to him; his

Originally published as "Notes on Personalities: F. Scott Fitzgerald," *Smart Set*, April 1924.

attention is concentrated upon his own reaction to the disturbance of nature's serenity by his ability to hurl a stone.

This is the story of a boy who, some five years ago, threw a rock into the placid waters of American literature with such force that the splash was heard all over the country, and the waves are still crashing into larger convolutions, bringing in their wake strange matters which continue to absorb the interest of the world at large.

Francis Scott Fitzgerald was the first author to chronicle the younger generation at the moment when youth was becoming supreme and defiant. Pubescence had mushroomed overnight into a powerful factor of every-day existence. A new era was dawning. A new type of girl was being created.

This was the beginning of the Flapper Age, an epoch during which the heroine of *This Side of Paradise* exerted a drastic influence. Her actions, her speech, her manners, her habits and her appearance were under the microscope, and she permeated every phase of life from the school-room to politics.

When it was learned that the author of *This Side of Paradise* was a young man in the first year of voting possibility, the amazement of the reading public turned into something like frenzy. The book became a best-seller in two weeks. Critics raved over the discovery of a new literary personality. Their blurbs on the merits and the depravity of the book were taking up all the space in the daily press. F. Scott Fitzgerald's became a household name; debutantes dreamed on it, hard-boiled critics foamed at the mouth, college youths and faculty members quarreled, mothers sighed, fathers wept, shop-girls envied and country wenches patterned their conduct along the lines exampled by the heroine of the story—in short, something more than a stir was made by the appearance of this incoherent, disconnected, flagellating, first novel which sold into the hundred thousand copies.

Various and contradictory personality paragraphs about the author appeared before the public in every sort of pamphlet. He was an old man; he was a young *roué*, he was a typical Westerner who wore a big sombrero; he was a college youth who wrote only when completely spifflicated on absinthe and gin. He was a bad moral influence for the country. But the wise men of letters sat back and predicted fine things of this infant-in-quills.

Scott Fitzgerald admits them to be right. He is intensely egotistical, but it is the same egotism that a precocious youngster shows to an admiring group of adults. Even as the youngster with smug satisfaction recites his little piece, his tongue in his cheek, so does the blond-haired, blue-eyed historian of the Flapper drive his pen over the blank page. . . .

He has set forth, for instance, in his writing that all the great heroes of the world had blue eyes and yellow hair (as he himself has). It is logical hence to expect the unusual when one meets this good-looking young man. He is vivacious, imaginative, forceful—and slightly unbalanced. The latter is his chief charm. It reveals itself in impulses which would never occur to a more prosaic soul; in his day-dreams; in his worship of the beautiful, and in his creation of characters who linger in one's memory.

He is an actor. The dramatic instinct has been a large part of his character ever since he was a little boy. This trait, intensified by his soaring imagination, is the backbone of his work.

F. Scott Fitzgerald was born in 1896 and was christened for his famous ancestor who wrote our national anthem. His father, a heady young Southerner, followed Greeley's advice and found himself in Minnesota when scarcely more than a boy, penniless but hopeful, and in love with the daughter of a wealthy wholesale grocer. Since this was the age of optimism, the couple married, and for the first twelve years of his life the future novelist lived in St. Paul, as one of the most widely-discussed show pieces of that city. He had to sing and recite to his mother's guests, and in addition it became noised about that he had written a story at seven, and at ten had begun a history of the United States.

His first tragedy occurred when he was six years old, and the episode left a wound which he will never forget. He was giving his first birthday party. The dramatic instinct soared as he saw himself clad in his long-trousered sailor suit assuming the role of host. For weeks he had been revelling in anticipation. It was to mark his formal entrance into society, and he kept meticulous watch over his attire during the hours he had to wait before the party would begin. It started to rain. Nobody came. All the long afternoon he waited silently, and when the rain stopped and the sun came out, he stood on the porch of the house still hoping that the children would arrive. No one came, and finally dusk fell. He went into the house and at the sight of the birthday cake and other refreshments his heart almost broke.

At school he wanted to lead all activities. Unless he was permitted to start the games and was chosen as leader, he was unhappy. This trait is not a very popular one amongst schoolboys unless the desire is reinforced by brute strength, and Scott was a delicate child. Consequently he was unpopular, and on one occasion he was told to "go away," that "he wasn't wanted." The boy's egotistic nature suffered deeply. Furthermore, he had a habit of writing all through class in the back of his geography book, or Latin, or mathematical books. This added to his unpopularity because the boys couldn't understand his absorption. As a result of the eternal scribbling, his studies fell short of parental expectations, and he was sent away to boarding-school.

From his earliest memory Scott Fitzgerald suffered from a pedentia complex. The sight of his own feet filled him with embarrassment and horror. No amount of persuasion could entice him to permit others to see his naked feet, and up until he was twelve this fear caused him a great deal of misery. He refused to learn how to swim. His family accused him of being afraid of the water, but although he endured agony at being called various names which implied lack of courage—he refused to go into the water. He loved the sea, and pleaded that he be allowed to wear his stockings swimming. This complex suddenly disappeared one day without any reason.

When he was eleven he had his first short story published in *Now and Then,* the school organ of the St. Paul Academy. It was called "The Mystery of the Raymond Mortgage." The mortgage in question was mentioned exactly twice in the story: in the title and again in the second paragraph, after which the young author became so engrossed in a lurid murder which one of his characters had committed that the mystery mentioned was never solved.

A year later he wrote "Elavo," a novel in verse, dealing with knights of old, Roman strongholds, drawbridges, et cetera. School requirements at the time included the reading of Walter Scott! It was during this period of his life that he obtained the only historical education he has ever retained. An Aunt Clara, whom he visited during vacations in New Hampshire, was firmly convinced that her nephew was not long for this world, and that the best way he could strengthen his hold on life was to swallow one raw egg every day. To enforce this she bribed him with a twenty-five-cent piece for each egg he could keep down, and when he discovered that with this hard-earned wealth he could purchase a volume of Henty, his distaste for the egg vanished. Each day he would rush down to the local bookshop with his quarter and by night the volume would be finished. . . .

The entire city of St. Paul was thrown into hysterical confusion not long after this by the appearance of a new dramatic genius. A lurid drama, entitled "The Captured Shadow," was presented at a local theatre. The members of the cast were rather young, but so was the author. He was fifteen, and never before had an audience been privileged to witness such a mixture of all the old familiar thrillers. The jokes were pilfered outright from a joke book. The hero, who naturally was played by Scott Fitzgerald, inasmuch as he wrote the drama, drew great applause as he gracefully swooned into the heroine's arms before the final curtain.

But in boarding-school he went off on a new tack. He saw a musical comedy called "The Quaker Girl," and from then on he filled dozens of notebooks with librettos modeled after Gilbert and Sullivan. He discovered that the only collegiate musical comedy flourished at Princeton, and on this information he made his choice of where he was to go to college.

He fell down on his studies during his Freshman year, but he wrote an operetta for the Triangle Club. The play was accepted and produced, and Scott caused great excitement as the most beautiful of the chorus girls.

This aptitude for female impersonation caused a furore at a prom at the University of Minnesota, where one evening appeared an unknown and beautiful young woman. She shocked her dancing partners by guzzling drinks and smoking fiercely, and in addition threw confusion into the host of collegiate youths who had surrounded her in admiration, by playing one of them against the other. After securing written evidence of ardent admiration from some of the most popular boys, she suddenly disappeared, like Cinderella at midnight, and for days the mystery was the choicest bit of discussion in St. Paul.

In the autumn of 1916–17 he embarked for an infantry officers' training camp at Fort Leavenworth—the poetry which he had been furiously writing for some time past in the discard—with a new ambition. This time it was to be the Great American Novel and accordingly every evening, concealing his pad behind his Small Problems for Infantry, he wrote a sort of biographical story of himself and what life meant to him. Despite the fact that this little game was detected and stopped, his burning ambition to finish the novel before he departed for Europe drove him to the Officers' Club, and every Saturday at one o'clock he sat down to his task in a corner of a roomful of smoke, conversation and a thousand-and-one interruptions from facetious fellow-officers. Stimulated by innumerable drinks of Coca-Cola, he wrote one hundred and twenty thousand words during the week-ends of the next three months. The book was aptly enough titled by the author, "The Romantic Egotist," and sent to a publisher's. It was returned with a long letter stating that while the manuscript was the most original received for years, the firm could not publish it. It was too crude and incoherent.

Scott never got overseas. Some six months afterward he came to New York, in the meanwhile having fallen madly in love and become betrothed to Zelda Sayre, a brilliant and beautiful Southern girl whom he met while at camp in Alabama.

He had to make money. But how? He tried to get a job as a newspaper reporter, but no one wanted him. Finally he went to work for Barron Collier, writing advertising copy during the day, and after office hours working on short stories. They were all returned. He made for himself a beautiful frieze which ran around his room out of the one hundred and twenty-two rejection slips which he received from editors. He wrote movies. Song lyrics. Complicated advertising schemes. Poems. Sketches. Jokes. No one bought them. Near the end of June he sold a story for thirty dollars.

The ninety dollars a month which he was earning seemed too silly to waste any more time over, and besides, love was clamoring for recognition. So Scott decided to take a drastic step. He gave up his job, packed his bag and went back to St. Paul. There he announced to a somewhat surprised family that he had come home to write a novel. They took it with as little display of commiseration as possible.

In the next two hot months he sat steadily before his desk, revising, compiling and boiling down "The Romantic Egotist." He changed the title to "This Side of Paradise." It was accepted by special delivery. In the next two months he wrote eight short stories and sold nine. The ninth was accepted by the same magazine that had rejected it four months before. After the appearance of the novel he got married and brought his bride East. . . .

Now they live down at Great Neck, Long Island, where the sovereign of the family is a two-year-old female answering to the name of "Scotty," despite the fact that she had been christened Patricia. Mrs. Fitzgerald writes also. She has a queer, decadent style, luminous in its imagination, and very often Scott incorporates whole chapters of his wife's writing into his own books. He steals all of her ideas for short stories and writes them as his own.

He is at present working on a novel. He wants to write a musical comedy and a play. He utters sentiments like this:

"When I was twenty I wanted to be King of the World, a sort of combined J. P. Morgan, General Ludendorff, Abraham Lincoln and Nietsche, not to omit Shakespeare." There he stops. There is an implication that he has hopes of being all this still.

"I would like to have an awful lot of money with which to buy all the books I want and a Rolls-Royce car."

"I'd like to spend eight months in travel, and have four children. They are cheerful, decorative and amusing to have around the house."

"I'd like to go into politics."

"I am glad I'm a young man in America now."

"I'd like to spend eight months in England during the Regency period. Life was so riotous and colorful and gay then. It was the last of the powder and patch days, and the great spirits like Johnson and Byron were casual figures on the street. Also it was beginning to be possible then for a man to earn his living with his pen."

"And I'd like to have been a young Englishman during the first decade of the present century. The Fabian Society was getting on its feet. Oxford and Cambridge were turning out interesting men, and the inhibitions of the Victorian era were passing away. I would hate to have been a young man between the accession of Victoria and her death."

"I'd like to have been a young Spaniard about 1550 in the glory of the Armada. I would hate to have been a Roman or a Greek of any period. I would like to have been a young Venetian when Venice was the thoroughfare of the civilized world and all the crusaders passed through her gates."

"My heroes? Well, I consider H. L. Mencken and Theodore Dreiser the greatest men living in the country today."

His imagination is the predominant power behind Scott Fitzgerald's pen. He gloats over a good simile as a woman would over a priceless jewel. He loves to roll gorgeous phrases on his tongue. His delight in the beauty of words is sensuous.

He is left-handed, and his chirography is that of a small schoolboy.

He is an earnest worker and when occupied in writing refuses to play. Although he is a boon companion he cannot escape from his thoughts, and in order to avoid hearing the telephone, encountering people, or listening to the every-day noises of his household, he has fitted a room over his garage and daily spends most of the waking hours in hard toil.

The Delegate From Great Neck

EDMUND WILSON

Mr. F. Scott Fitzgerald and Mr. Van Wyck Brooks

Mr. Fitzgerald: How do you do, Mr. Brooks. I'm afraid it's an awful nuisance for you to see me.

Mr. Brooks: Not at all. I'm very glad to. I'm only sorry to have had to put it off. But I've been so frightfully busy with my book that I haven't been able to do anything else.

Mr. Fitzgerald: What's that—the James? I suppose you're hurrying to have it out in time to get the benefit of the publicity of the *Dial* award.

Mr. Brooks: Oh, no: it may take me a long time yet. But it's really rather a complicated job, and I don't like to drop a chapter in the middle or I lose all the threads. I've just come to a breathing-space.

Mr. Fitzgerald: I should think you'd want to rush it right through and get it out now: it might double your sales.

Mr. Brooks: Oh, I couldn't possibly: I still have a good deal of work to do on it.

Mr. Fitzgerald: I suppose you must read hundreds of books, don't you? How many books do you suppose you've read for the James? Two hundred? Five hundred?

Mr. Brooks: Oh, I don't know, I'm sure—everything I could get hold of that threw any light on him.

Mr. Fitzgerald: I suppose you must quote on an average of four or five books on every page of your biographies, don't you?—and you probably refer to four or five others—and you've probably read half a dozen others that you didn't get anything out of. That makes fifteen or sixteen books to a page. Think of it! Reading fifteen or sixteen books just to write a single page! For a book of two hundred and fifty pages that would be—

Mr. Brooks: They're not all different books, you know. One uses the same books again and again.

Mr. Fitzgerald: I know: but even so—it's perfectly amazing! I sup-

"The Delegate From Great Neck," *The Shores of Light*. New York: Farrar, Straus and Young, 1952.
Originally published as "Imaginary Conversations: Mr. Van Wyck Brooks and Mr. Scott Fitzgerald," *New Republic*, April 30, 1924. Reprinted by permission of the author.

pose you must know more about American literature than anybody else in the world, don't you?

Mr. Brooks: Oh, no! Not by any means.

Mr. Fitzgerald: Well, you're the greatest writer on the subject, anyway. That's the reason we've sent you this letter. As I told you, I've been delegated by the Younger Generation of American writers to congratulate you on getting the prize. They chose me as really the original member of the Younger Generation. Of course, there were a lot of people writing before *This Side of Paradise*—but the Younger Generation never really became self-conscious till then nor did the public at large become conscious of it. My slogan is that I am the man who made America Younger-Generation-conscious.

Mr. Brooks: I am certainly very much flattered—

Mr. Fitzgerald: Besides, I'm about the only one who still looks really young. Most of the others are getting old and bald and discouraged. So they picked me out to represent them. They thought they ought to send somebody under thirty.—Well, could you stand to have me read you the letter they've written you or would you rather read it yourself?

Mr. Brooks: No: Certainly—read it. Do!

Mr. Fitzgerald: (*reading*). "Dear Van Wyck Brooks: We, the undersigned American writers, desire to offer you our heartiest congratulations on the occasion of your receiving the *Dial* award. If it is a question of critical service to American letters, we believe that there is no one living to whom it might more fitly be given. We soon found, when we first began writing, that your books were among the few that could help us to orient ourselves."—This first part's pretty heavy—but it gets a little more interesting later on.—I didn't draft the letter myself.

"You yourself had called a caustic roll of the critics whom we found in authority: Professor Irving Babbitt, who, refusing to see in romanticism one of the great creative movements of our time, could do nothing but scold at young writers who derived inspiration from it; Mr. Paul Elmer More, who, for all his sound standards of learning and literary competence—an anti-romantic like Professor Babbitt—had denounced as a form of debauchery what is actually a necessary condition of any artistic activity: the response to irrational impulse, and who thus, if he could have enforced his injunction, would have shut off the arts at their source; and Professor Stuart P. Sherman, who, borrowing the severity of Mr. More's manner without sharing his moral convictions, soon gave out such discordant sounds that he has now been forced to change his tune in the interests of a liberal sweetness. These critics had been preaching restraint to a people bound hand and foot. The country at large may have been suffering, as they thought, from a phase of anarchic expansion; but the failing of our literature was the timidity of the 'genteel tradition.' You were among the first to stand up for the romantic doctrine of 'experience for its own sake' and to insist on the importance of literature as a political and social influence. These ideas are perhaps open to criticism as a definitive aesthetic program; but they have served at least to awaken us to a sense of the drama in which we were playing. Our fathers had been further than our grandfathers from the civilization of Europe, and you goaded us back to our place in the world. You roused us with the cry that the hour had come 'to put away childish things and to walk the stage as poets do.'

"For all this we are forever in your debt, and we have wished to express our gratitude. Do not think us ungracious, we beg, if we accompany it with a plea. You were almost alone, when you first began to write, in taking American literature seriously—in appraising it as rigorously as possible, in comparison with other literatures, and in exhorting us to better our achievements. Yet, in your zeal to confess our deficiencies, you seem sometimes to create the impression that we have so far accomplished nothing. The older generation of critics had fallen down, primarily, as humanists—that is, they had been weak, not in intellect, but in aesthetic sensibility. They had not been able to feel the value of the widely varying forms of beauty which the men of other races and ages had distilled from their varied experience. Can it be that, with more generous intentions than theirs, you, too, with different preconceptions, are tending to fail in appreciation? After all, a good many of the Americans whose inadequacies you have analyzed so damagingly have had each his peculiar sense of life, his particular aspect of America, that he succeeded in getting on paper in some more or less vivid form. Emerson pursuing happy guides through the winey yet fumeless air in his commerce, so blithe and so homely, with the high places of light; Thoreau with his compact prose and his strong and dense colors, like the white of opaque clouds against blue Massachusetts sky, like the clustered green masses of trees around foursquare New England houses —both these men have conveyed to us the beauty of a particular kind of life. We feel in them a freshness and a freedom as of lawns that slope away to fenceless meadows, and we taste a frosty sea-captain sarcasm that seasons ideal and discipline. So Mark Twain has most poignant pages which give us something that we scarcely find in your *Ordeal of Mark Twain*; it is not only the sadness of the Mississippi in the days when life there was poor, but the romance and the humor of the pioneers straying wide across the empty continent; and we recognize in that sadness, that rough romance and that humor, at once genial and cruel, something more than the outlandish product of a particular time and place: we are moved by the troubling compound of life at all times in all places."—

Mr. Brooks: Will you forgive me if I interrupt you a moment? I don't want to find fault so much with your description of the New England writers—though I'm not sure that even there you haven't allowed distance to gild with an imaginary glamor a society that turns out, when we examine it, rather disappointingly barren—but in regard to the West, one is driven, when one comes to look into the subject, to the conclusion that its reputed romance and humor are almost entirely fictitious. The life along the Mississippi that Mark Twain knew in his boyhood was depressing in the extreme—a mere matter of lonely villages scattered along a muddy shore; and such excitement as he afterwards found in Nevada and California was mainly limited to drinking and gambling, with outbursts of violent profanity and occasional outbreaks of murder. The lies and the practical jokes that constituted frontier humor were merely, like those other manifestations, in the nature of hysterical relief from intolerable privations and repressions.

Mr. Fitzgerald: Well, I come from the West—the *Middle* West—myself, and of course it's pretty bad in some ways. But don't you think there must have been still a certain romance about it at the time that Mark Twain went there? Don't you imagine even a pilot on the Mississippi, like Mark Twain was in his youth, must have felt a real thrill at knowing that he was personally playing a part in dominating the American continent? And there must have been a marvellous kind of comradeship in the ranches and the mining-camps—when they called each other Captain and Colonel. I always have a feeling of something heroic in the old songs and stories of the West. Think of the men from New York and New England who first dared to build their settlements in the gigantic ampitheaters of Utah, where the great black rock-ranges wall you round like the ramparts of the world! And the red sandstone hills of Nevada! Can you imagine what it must have been like to try to live the white man's life among those fantastic shapes, in the presence of those faceless prehistoric gods? And the first men who went to California, the prospectors of Mark Twain's sixties—they must have been drunk with the sunshine even more than the San Franciscans today—as well as with liquor, of course. I imagine them shaking off their hardships in a tremendous exhilaration when they first found themselves on that golden coast, where no worry from the old world ever comes, where Time itself seems to have been left behind like some tyrannous medieval institution, where man's life seems restored at least to the primeval leisure of Eden, where it is always summertime and always afternoon! Have you ever seen the mountains turning purple at sunset and the purple-fringed sea? Think of the men from the shacks and the diggings looking out on that new horizon, that new ocean that opened to the Orient, and hearing the drums of the surf that beat out the somnolent rhythms of the reefs and white sands of the South Seas! No older generation and no taboos! Big fortunes easy to make! Don't you think that, if ever Americans have really felt free in America, those early Californians must have?

Mr. Brooks: The condition of survival for the pioneer, even in California, was the suppression of all those instincts which might tend to conflict with his adjustment to his rude environment. You assume that a man of Mark Twain's generation would have been capable of the enjoyment of landscape. But we find no evidence that this was the case. The enjoyment of landscape results in an enrichment of the spiritual soil which bears its fruits in artistic creation, and the generation of Mark Twain—who can doubt it?—throttled its impulse to delight in natural beauty as an interference with its concentration upon its immediate material task. The psychology of the Puritan and the pioneer has always, it seems to me, made Americans rather blind to natural beauty. It may, in fact, be seriously questioned whether America has ever had a writer who can be said to have appreciated it properly. Think of the vital relation to natural objects that one finds in a Ruskin or a Jeffries, and then summon the most distinguished examples that our literature is able to show. How meager, how relatively pale, how lacking in genuine significance, the latter must inevitably appear!

Mr. Fitzgerald: Well, I really oughtn't to try to talk about it because I don't know the subject the way you do.—I dare say that that part of the letter does lay it on pretty thick, but they wanted a purple passage to show you what they meant about enthusiasm.—Shall I go on reading?

Mr. Brooks: Do.

Mr. Fitzgerald: "In the case of Henry James, again, we have been a little disappointed as we have read the published chapters of your forthcoming book about him. What we had hoped for was a definitive study of a novelist of genius who, fortunately for us, happened to be an American; but what we seem to be getting is the tragedy of an American who was rash enough to try to become a novelist. Yet, for all James's partial failures at filling in the outlines of his canvases, he was surely a first-rate artist, one of the few real masters of literature that the United States has produced; and his position as an American expatriate must have given him a peculiar advantage as an international critic of society that made up for whatever he had missed in intimate experience of American life. Must we believe that his social maladjustment as an American of his period had really for his work the disastrous results on which you insist in these chapters? Your first instalment is based on James's own autobiographical volumes; yet what interests us when we read these books is less the record of the provincial background and the writer's relation to it than the wonder and excitement of the artist enchanted by the spectacle of life—life even in the nineteenth century, even in the United States. Do not, we beg you—it is the burden of our plea—lose too much the sense of that wonder!"—

Mr. Brooks: I beg your pardon: but I really do think you overestimate those autobiographical volumes! To me, there has always seemed to be something rather flaccid and empty about them. Think how much more colorful and spirited is Cellini's autobiography! How much more candid Rousseau's! How infinitely much more alive to the intellectual currents of their time the autobiographies of Renan and Mill! How much richer in psychological interest the memoirs of Marie Bashkirtseff! James wrote in his later years, you know, of "the starved romance of my life." And what I feel in his autobiography is the starvation rather than the romance. What American can fail to recognize the inexorable spiritual blight of which James himself spoke so often? Have we not all run up against it—an impotence and a blindness of the soul—like one of those great blank implacable walls that balk the view in American cities?

Mr. Fitzgerald: The Puritan thing, you mean. I suppose you're probably right. I don't know anything about James myself. I've never read a word of him.—Just let me finish this letter; there's not very much more.

"We thus deprecate your gloomy verdicts on the value of the American classics; yet, feeling as we do the force of your criticism of our general culture, we should never have thought of complaining, if we had not lately come to fear that, intent upon the diagnosis of the diseases from which we have suffered, you have ended by becoming inhibited by an a priori theory which prevents you from hoping for improvement. You have discovered so many reasons why artistic achievement should be difficult that you seem to have become convinced that it must always remain impossible. When you write of contemporary literature, it is politely but without conviction: the modern writers who have been most successful in realizing the ideal you proposed have not received your accolade. And the effect, in the long run, has been more than a little discouraging. The other day, one of the youngest of our number, reading your essay *The Literary Life*, broke down into a wild fit of weeping and cursed God for having made him an American."—

Mr. Brooks: Dear me! How distressing! Really—

Mr. Fitzgerald: Oh, that's just a silly joke! It didn't really happen, of course. I made it up myself and had them put it in. It's the only part I wrote.—I'm sorry: I suppose it was bad taste!

Mr. Brooks: No—no: not at all! I see! I beg your pardon. Go ahead.

Mr. Fitzgerald: "It is true that our newer critics tend to err through too easy enthusiasm: it is usually enough for a book to make pretensions to artistic seriousness for them to hail it as a masterpiece. But their indiscriminate excitement hardly compensates us for your indifference. It is certainly a mistake to behave as if all our contemporary writers were equally successful as artists, but we have the uncomfortable feeling that you may think them all equally deplorable—merely the most recent examples of the various depressing ways in which writers fail in America—not the beginnings of a literary renascence but fresh waxworks for a Chamber of Horrors; and we wonder whether your disinclination to write anything about your contemporaries may not be due merely to a delicacy that prevents you from cutting up people before they are quite dead.

"Yet the younger generation of writers have been trying to put your precepts into practice. They have not blenched before the boldness of the European masters, as you accuse their fathers of doing: they have tried to follow great examples. They are interested, as you urged them to be, in the life of their own country; and they have opened their souls to experience. For all their pessimistic pronouncements, they are confident, hopeful and gay. But when they have looked for your snow-white banner flying beside their more motley ones, they have found you still brooding the wrongs of an earlier generation, the defeats of an older army. They find you shivering among the archives, and they shiver at the sight of your chill. Meantime, there is life in America—artistic life even—to warm us all. If we reproach you for failing to enjoy it, we are only giving back to you a gospel we have learned from your own books."

And then the names—I won't read the list—but practically everybody, you see.

Mr. Brooks: It was really awfully kind of you to take the trouble to write me like this. I'm very much interested in what you say.—But I can't reconcile the picture that you draw of yourselves at the end of your letter with the account that you gave me yourself when you were talking about your friends just now. You said, I think, that the younger generation was "getting old and bald and discouraged," and that is not a very cheerful picture. I appreciate your gallant effort to make the best of your situation; but I am afraid that your admirable spirit has already been partly broken by the indifference of a commercial society, that your gestures are lost in the void.

Mr. Fitzgerald: Oh, I was just kidding about that. They're not really old and discouraged. I'm the only one that's discouraged, because I find that I can't live at Great Neck on anything under thirty-six thousand a year, and I have to write a lot of rotten stuff that bores me and makes me depressed.

Mr. Brooks: Couldn't you live more cheaply somewhere else?

Mr. Fitzgerald: Nowhere that's any fun.

Mr. Brooks: I can't help thinking it a pity that a writer as gifted as you should be let in for such heavy expenses. As you say, it lays you open to exploitation by the popular magazines; and, though you charge me with indifference, I can tell you that that is something I regret very much. I should hate to see your whole generation fall a victim to that sort of thing. You are "the man," you told me, you know, at the beginning of our conversation, "who has made America Younger-Generation-conscious." Did you realize, when you used that expression, that you had dropped into the language of advertising? In describing your literary activities, you could not avoid the jargon of business; and it strikes me that the production of books by the younger generation has now become an industry much like another. The first crop of younger writers had scarcely scored their first successes when a new race of editors and publishers met them with open arms, eager to commercialize them—not by turning them into hacks of the old sort who would have had to do work of a kind altogether against their conscience but by stimulating them to write much and often rather than responsibly and well, by putting a premium on their second-best; so that, instead of improving on their first attempts, they have often, it seems to me, sunk below them. A half-educated public has created a demand for half-baked work. And I'm not at all sure that you younger writers are very much better off than your predecessors were: in the eighties and nineties, at least, there was a small cultivated public and not much question of pleasing the rest. I will say of the distinguished writers of the day before yesterday, whom you accuse me of undervaluing, that they usually followed their art with a very high sense of its dignity, so that even their journalism sounds like the work of serious men of letters—and this is true of Stephen Crane as much as of Henry James; whereas, in the case of you younger men, one sometimes cannot help feeling that your most ambitious productions are a species of journalism. Is it possible to resist the conclusion that you are succumbing to our capitalist civilization in a way you could never have foreseen?

Mr. Fitzgerald: I knew that what I said about making America Younger-Generation-conscious sounded like advertising. I was just making fun of the way that the advertising people talk.

Mr. Brooks: Let me remind you that Freud has shown us that the things we say in jest are as significant as the things we say in earnest—they may, in fact, be more significant, because they reveal the thoughts that are really at the back of our minds and that we do not care to avow to the world. I was struck, also, by that other joke, which you contributed to the letter—I mean about the man who cursed God for having made him an American. Who can fail to detect in this desperate image an involuntary tragic cry which contradicts everything else you have been straining so hard to affirm?—Another detail that betrays: I notice that when you mention the signatories, who explicitly include yourself, you always speak of them as "they" instead of "we." In doing so, I can't help feeling, you furnish irresistible evidence that the unity you assume in collaborating is more or less artificial, that you are actually, in spirit and point of view, as isolated from one another as it has always seemed that literary men are bound to be in America. In allowing your art to become a business, you have rendered true unity impossible and have given yourselves up to the competitive anarchy of American commercial enterprise. You can at best, I fear, gain nothing but money and big hollow reputations—each man out for himself—and these things for fifty years in America have brought nothing but disillusion.

Mr. Fitzgerald: Don't you suppose, though, that the American millionaires must have had a certain amount of fun making and spending their money? Can't you imagine a man like Harriman or Hill feeling a certain creative ecstasy as he piled up all that power? Just think of being able to buy absolutely anything you wanted—houses, railroads, enormous industries!—dinners, automobiles, stunning clothes for your wife, clothes like nobody else in the world could wear!—all the finest paintings in Europe, all the books that had ever been written! Think of what it would be like to give parties that went on for days and days, with everything that anybody could want to drink and a medical staff in attendance and the biggest jazz orchestras in the city alternating night and day! I confess that I get a big kick out of all the glittering expensive things. Why, once, when I'd just arrived in New York with a lot of money to spend, after being away in the West, and I came back to the Plaza the first night and looked up and saw that great creamy palace all blazing with green and gold lights, and the taxis and the limousines streaming up and down the Avenue—why, I jumped into the Pulitzer fountain just out of sheer joy! And I wasn't boiled either.

Mr. Brooks: Are you sure you weren't a little hysterical?

Mr. Fitzgerald: No: I've been hysterical, too. This was exhilaration. —Look: I don't suppose you could possibly be persuaded to come down to Great Neck this weekend. We're having a little party ourselves. Maybe it would bore you to death—but we're asking some people down who ought to be pretty amusing. Gloria Swanson's coming. And Dos Passos and Sherwood Anderson. And Marc Connelly and Dorothy Parker. And Rube Goldberg. And Ring Lardner will be there. You probably think some of those people are lowbrow, but Ring Lardner, for instance, is really a very interesting fellow—he's really not just a popular writer: he's pretty morose about things. I'd like to have you meet him. There'll be some dumb-bell friends of mine from the West, but I don't believe you'd mind them. And then there's going to be a man who sings a song called, *Who'll Bite Your Neck When My Teeth Are Gone?* Neither my wife nor I knows his name—but this song is one of the funniest things we've ever heard!

Mr. Brooks: Why, thank you ever so much. I'd like ever so much to go—and I'd like to meet all those people. But I'm really afraid that I can't. I'm not nearly done with the James, and I have to devote all my free time to it. And, since you feel that I'm being unfair to him, I must go over my material again and think about it from that point of view.— You know, I appreciate very much your taking the trouble to write me. I'm sorry you find me discouraging: of course, I don't mean to be. On the contrary, I think that your generation is showing a great deal of promise.

Mr. Fitzgerald: Well, I'm sorry if I've been a nuisance. It was good of you to listen to the letter.

Mr. Brooks: It was very good of you to write it.

Mr. Fitzgerald: Well, I won't bother you any longer.—I'm sorry you can't come down Saturday.

Mr. Brooks: Thank you ever so much. I wish I could!

F. Scott Fitzgerald

PAUL ROSENFELD

The utmost that can be charged against F. Scott Fitzgerald is that too oftentimes his good material eludes him. Of the ultimate values of said material there is no dispute. Certain racehorses run for the pure joy of running, and the author of *The Beautiful and Damned* and *Tales of the Jazz Age* is such an animal. He is a born writer, amusing himself with tales and pictures; and eventually nothing is interesting except the natural bent. Salty and insipid, exaggeratedly poetical and bitterly parodistic, his writing pours exuberantly out of him. Flat paragraphs are redeemed by brilliant metaphors, and conventional descriptions by witty, penetrating turns. Ideas of diamond are somewhat indiscriminately mixed with ideas of rhinestone and ideas of window glass; yet purest rays serene are present in veritable abundance. They must come to this bannerman of the slickers and flappers in a sort of dream, unexpectedly,

Originally published as "F. Scott Fitzgerald," *Men Seen*. New York: Dial Press, 1925.

out of some arcana where they have been concealing themselves, and surprise him by smiling up at him from underneath his pen. For so they startle the reader, unprepared to encounter, in writing as carelessly undertaken, ideas so mature and poignant and worthy of fine settings.

Not a contemporary American senses as thoroughly in every fiber the tempo of privileged post-adolescent America. Of that life, in all its hardness and equally curious softness, its external clatter, movement and boldness, he is a part; and what he writes reflects the environment not so much in its superficial aspects as in its pitch and beat. He knows how talk sounds, how the dances feel, how the crap-games look. Unimportant detail shows how perfect the unconscious attunement: the vignette of a boy drawing gasoline out of an automobile tank during a dance so that a girl can clean her satin shoe; the vignette of a young fellow sitting in his B.V.D.'s after a bath running his hand down his naked skin in indolent satisfaction; the vignette of two bucks from a pump-and-slipper dance throwing hash by the handful around Childs' at six A.M. Not another has gotten flashes from the psyches of the golden young intimate as those which amaze throughout *The Beautiful and Damned*. And not another has fixed as mercilessly the quality of brutishness, of dull indirection and degraded sensibility running through American life of the hour.

Taken as things, nevertheless, both the novels of Fitzgerald, and the majority of his tales as well, lie on a plane inferior to the one upon which his best material extends. He has the stuff for pathos, and this fact he fairly consistently ignores. Certain preoccupations seem to intrude between him and his material, spoiling his power to correctly appreciate it. Hence, instead of the veritable stories he has to tell, there appear smart social romanzas and unhappy happy endings. Of Fitzgerald's preconceptions, the chief sinner appears to be the illusion that the field of his vision is essentially the field of "youth." Now, it would be insanity to deny the author's almost constant preoccupation with exquisite creatures in chiffon and their slender snappy companions, or to deny the jolly subjects of his observations vivacity and frankness of spirit, and perfect elegance of texture. There is a place where an eternal dance proceeds, and this place for the while they occupy, filling it with their proper motions and gestures. And whatever the quality of these, who can for even an instant maintain that it is inferior to that of the dreadful motions and gestures which filled it a generation, or two or three generations ago? What one does affirm, however, and affirm with passion, is that the author of *This Side of Paradise* and of the jazzy stories does not sustainedly perceive his girls and men for what they are, and tends to invest them with precisely the glamour with which they in pathetic assurance rather childishly invest themselves. At the time of the appearance of Fitzgerald's first book, it was evident that to an extent he was indebted to Compton Mackenzie for the feeling with which he regarded the "dreaming spires" of Princeton; and since then it has become apparent that he tends a trifle overmuch to view everything which he sees in the light of Europe's past experiences. His protagonists he observes through the enchanted eyes of a perpetual Maytime, perceiving among the motors and crap-games a wave of cool spring flowers, a flutter of white and yellow ephemeridae. Even when he marks the cruel and shabby side, the decay and ignobility of his objective, he tends to overplay the general attractiveness more than the detail warrants. The couple in *The Beautiful and Damned*, charming and comely enough and yet portrayed at length in the horrible effort to perpetuate a state of narcissistic irresponsibility, we are begged to perceive as iridescently wonderful bodies and souls.

And it is fresh, juicy and spontaneous that the American juveniles of the class described by Fitzgerald exactly are not. Superficially, perhaps. But was not the forest green which Europe called by the name of youth somewhat more a thing of courage? And the number of us willing to face the world without the panoply of elaborate material protections is not overwhelming. It is claimed that in the American South virgins are carefully trained to inquire out the income and prospects of suitors, and nip in the bud any passion which threatens to direct itself upon an unworthy object. But it does not seem probable there is any truth in the report. For such maneuvers can scarcely be necessary. It is undoubtedly physically impossible for any really nice American girl South or North to respond to the desires of a male who does not make the spiritual gesture paralleling the Woolworth Building's. Through either external persuasion or inherent idealism, and which it is we know not, and undoubtedly it is both, the self-respecting damsels early acquire the conviction that splendidly complete orientation onto the business of material increase is the primary characteristic of maleness, and that any offer of love unaccompanied by the tautness for money is the profoundest of insults to the psyche seated in the tender depths of them. And the strapping, college-bred, Brooks-clad youths no less than they share this beautiful innate belief. They too seem unable to face life without having at the back of them the immense upholstery of wealth. Nothing which they might be or do, were they relieved of the necessity of being a worldly success, appears to them capable of making good to the lady the absence of the fur garment and the foreign roadster, and the presence of inevitable suffering. Thus the spirit of the business world is established well before the advent of puberty; and the spirit of business is compromise, which is not exactly it would seem the spirit of youth.

And even the lightest, least satirical of Fitzgerald's pages bear testimonial to the prevalence of the condition. A moralist could gather evidence for a most terrible condemnation of bourgeois America from the books of this protagonist of youth. And yet, *Lieb Vaterland, magst ruhig sein.* It is not a state of immorality in the general sense of the word that might be uncovered. If by morality we mean obedience to the *mores* of the tribe, then Fitzgerald's diverting flappers and slickers are in no sense licentious. By means of necking parties and booze fights of the sort he describes the republic is maintained. Business rests on them. But immorality may be taken to signify a falling away from the ideal spirit of life, and in that sense America is proven the breeding ground of a kind of decay. In all unconsciousness Fitzgerald shows us types of poor golden young too shallow to feel, vainly attitudinizing in the effort to achieve sensation: girls who know they cannot live without riches and men perpetually sucking the bottle for solace. The people aren't young: they are merely narcissistic. Knowledge of life is gotten from books, and the naïveté is not quite lovely. That is all very well; one has no fault to find with it; it is quite sanitary and not at all messy as passion usually is; but why call it spring? And occasionally Fitzgerald drops the light guitar and with cool ferocity speaks the veritable name. "May Day," perhaps the most mature of all his tales, brings the bitter brackish dry taste of decay fully to the mouth. With an air of almost glacial impersonality Fitzgerald gives a curious atmosphere of mixed luxury and rottenness of the heart. Through the entire story there seems to run the brutishness of the two soldiers hiding among pails and mops in the dust closet waiting for some stolen liquor to be handed to them. And in the fantasia "The Diamond as Big as the Ritz," Fitzgerald strikes perhaps quite undeliberately further notes of satire: Mr. Braddock Washington, the richest and most profoundly unsympathetic man in the world, looks dangerously like a jazz-age portrait of the father of the country.

But the world of his subject-matter is still too much within Fitzgerald himself for him to see it sustainedly against the universe. Its values obtain too strongly over him, and for that reason he cannot set them against those of high civilization, and calmly judge them so. Hence, wanting philosophy, and a little overeager like the rest of America to arrive without having really sweated, he falls victim to the favorite delusions of the society of which he is a part, tends to indulge it in its dreams of grandeur, and misses the fine flower of pathos. He seems to set out writing under the compulsion of vague feelings, and when his wonderfully revelatory passages appear, they come rather like volcanic islands thrown to the surface of a sea of fantasy. By every law *The Beautiful and Damned* should have been a tragedy, the victims damned indeed; yet at the conclusion Fitzgerald welched, and permitted his pitiful pair to have the alleviations of some thirty millions of dollars, and his hero tell the readers he had won out. To be sure, a steady growth has been going on within this interesting author. The amusing insolence of his earlier manner of writing has persistently given way before a bolder, sharper stroke less personal in reference. The descriptions in "May Day": the sight of the avenue, the drinking scene in Delmonico's, the adventures of Mr. In and Out, are done with quiet virtuosity. A very genuine gift of fantasy arrives in "Benjamin Button." There are even Lawrence-like strong moments in *The Beautiful and Damned*. And still, in spite of "May Day," Fitzgerald has not yet crossed the line that bounds the field of art. He has seen his material from its own point of view, and he has seen it completely from without. But he has never done what the artist does: seen it simultaneously from within and without; and loved it and judged it, too. For "May Day" lacks a focal point, and merely juxtaposes a number of small pieces. Should Fitzgerald finally break his mold, and free himself of the compulsions of the civilization in which he grew, it might go badly with his popularity. It will be a pathetic story he will have to tell, the legend of a moon which never rose; and that is precisely the story a certain America does not wish to hear. Nevertheless, we would like hugely to hear him tell it. And Fitzgerald might scarcely miss his following.

Prophets of the New Age:
F. Scott Fitzgerald and *The Great Gatsby*

HARVEY EAGLETON

The most outstanding characteristic of the work of F. Scott Fitzgerald is the ability of the older generation to understand what it is all about. When *This Side of Paradise* appeared, it was greeted with enthusiasm by one group, that of Mr. Fitzgerald, and interrogation by another, that of Mr. Fitzgerald's papa and mamma. Said the latter, "It is all very clever and witty and amusing, but, of course not true to life. People aren't like that." Said the former, "Hurrah, here we are in a book. These are the things we think; these are the things we do. We might have written it ourselves if we had only thought about it first."

This Side of Paradise was, of course, not the first college novel, there was *Stover at Yale* years before and *Tom Brown at Oxford*, for that matter, but it was the first college novel to find itself surrounded by a group of imitators, and it is undoubtedly the best college novel. With the exception of the Montross' book, *Town and Gown*, no more realistic picture of undergraduate life and the undergraduate mind has been given us.

One may not approve of the picture, the papas and mammas of Mr. Fitzgerald's flappers and philosophers do not, partly because the picture is a reflection upon themselves and the manner in which they have reared their young, partly because of the ostrich tendency in all of us to hide our heads at what frightens us a little and to try and pretend that the frightening object is not there after all; but to anyone who knows undergraduate life in our great American institutions of higher learning, the picture of that life as drawn in *This Side of Paradise* and *Town and Gown* is only too true. Mr. Fitzgerald jerks his flappers and jellybeans before us and says somewhat cynically, "Here you are. What are you going to do about it?" He offers no solution to the problem, and admittedly it is one, at least to the educator if not to the papas and mammas; he merely presents it.

Originally published as "Prophets of the New Age: F. Scott Fitzgerald," Dallas *Morning News*, May 10, 1925. Reprinted by permission of the Dallas *Morning News*.

But Mr. Fitzgerald, for all his attack on reform and reformers in *The Beautiful and Damned*, is essentially a reformer himself. Most young men with a newly discovered literary talent have also newly discovered the evil of the world, and they use the one to portray the other, loudly calling the attention of the old heads to the strange creatures they have discovered unaided and alone, much to the amusement of the old heads who knew the strange creatures were there all along. It is only a sophomoric stage of development which sometimes lasts over into maturity, witness Byron, Shelley and Jean-Jacques Rousseau. Mr. Fitzgerald is neither a Byron, a Shelley, nor a Jean-Jacques Rousseau, but his agitation and lack of poise show him to belong to the same type, a type representing peculiarly arrested mental development. Mr. Fitzgerald doesn't approve of his flappers and jellybeans. He is secretly very much shocked by them. He assures us he is of them, that his wife, who is incidentally his only heroine, wearing sometimes black hair, sometimes brown, sometimes red, is of them, that his little daughter will be of them, but it is not because he approves of them. It is rather the attitude of the cheap evangelist who tells how hideously he sinned before he got religion in order to impress his hearers with the fact that he knows what he is talking about.

The Beautiful and Damned, Mr. Fitzgerald's second novel, was written purely in the spirit of reform. First he is a reformer of reformers. He has a natural and healthy dislike of gentlemen of Anthony Comstock's ilk, and he attacks them with all the savagery of youth. He doesn't believe in prohibition as a law, but he doesn't believe in drinking either, and he has his hero, a man of promise, completely destroy that promise and almost drink himself to death, giving us to understand that this is what the best of our young men and women are doing, and hinting darkly that it is all due to modern education and the decay of the church in the face of science. Then he is distressed about the ugliness of life, and he shows us picture after picture, scene after scene, of this ugliness, hoping that we shall see it too and do something about it. And there is the weakness of the book, of all Fitzgerald's books, the weakness that prevents them from ever being more than "popular fiction" of the most ephemeral variety. We are to do something about it, but what the something is he knows no more than did Shelley, who was equally seriously concerned about similar matters.

The omission of the constructive in Fitzgerald's work is an indication of his fundamental lack of imagination, for in spite of all his cleverness, and his wit, he has no creative faculty. He has a photographic mind. He can not create beyond himself nor imagine experience very different from his own. He is continuously autobiographic. His heroine, as I have said, is his wife, and his hero is himself. He graduates from college; he writes a novel of college life. He marries; he writes a novel of young married life. He has a little girl, and she appears in *The Great Gatsby*. We know these things because when he can not think of a simple plot on which he can hang his experience, he writes articles about himself and sells them to the *American Magazine*, the *Saturday Evening Post* and the *Woman's Home Companion*.

Having created a type of book however, which has been so widely imitated, Mr. Fitzgerald suddenly finds himself crowded in his own field, a field too small to hold both himself and his followers; and so, in his latest novel, *The Great Gatsby*, he has attempted to get out of his own field and either into a new one or into somebody's else not so crowded as his own. The results have not been happy. He gets into no particular field at all, but hangs up on the fence, leaning, perhaps, in the direction of Mr. Van Vechten's sterile and worthless acres; witness the characteristically unnecessary two-page list of the visitors to the Gatsby Long Island estate and the "literary allusions."

The novel has no plot to mention. Jay Gatz, later changed to Gatsby, from Minnesota, a young man of ability but no opportunity, is filled with the urge to make something of himself. The urge gets him started, but midway in career, when in training in Louisville during the World War, he meets Daisy whom he comes to love passionately. While he is in France winning his way to a captaincy by acts of "high daringdo," Daisy marries another man, and Jay's life is blighted. He comes back to America, makes an enormous fortune by dishonest means, leads a hectic and artificial life, surrounded by noise and vulgarity on his Long Island estate, longing always for Daisy, and finally is shot because he is blamed for Daisy's running over and killing a woman on the road from New York. The book is highly sensational, loud, blatant, ugly, pointless. There seems to be no reason for its existence. Mr. Fitzgerald thinks, quite obviously, that Gatsby is a great and tragic figure, but he merely succeeds in making the reader see him as a rather unbalanced young man who has become a crook. The story is told in first person, Mr. Fitzgerald calling himself Mr. Carraway.

One finishes *The Great Gatsby* with a feeling of regret, not for the fate of the people in the book, but for Mr. Fitzgerald. When *This Side of Paradise* was published, Mr. Fitzgerald was hailed as a young man of promise, which he certainly appeared to be. But the promise, like so many, seems likely to go unfulfilled. The Roman candle which sent out a few gloriously colored balls at the first lighting seems to be ending in a fizzle of smoke and sparks.

The Great Gatsby: It Seems to Me

HEYWOOD BROUN

In the last few months I have not been entirely faithful in reading what the various literary critics had to say, but I hope there has been suitable and proper commotion about *The Great Gatsby* by F. Scott Fitzgerald.

As a matter of fact, I rather fear that there has not been adequate tumult, for nobody yet has stopped me on the street to say "You must" or "Drop everything" or any similar phrase concerning the new book.

To be sure, I am aware of the fact that the cheerleader school of criticism is going out. Blood pressure among reviewers begins to drop. It is the custom now for critics to keep their feet on the ground and their hats on their heads.

Probably this is the better way, but I would like a little of the old extravagance. As it is, I find the newer reticence numbing my arm. A few years ago I would have begun by declaring that *The Great Gatsby* was among the best of all American novels. And it is. But now I have not the recklessness to make any such statement. It is a thoroughly satisfactory book, I say, and let it go at that.

Still, it is not wholly inappropriate that the familiar slogan, "Kindly omit fireworks," should be respected in this instance because there is a

Originally published as "It Seems to Me," New York *World*, August 17, 1925.

new solidity in Scott Fitzgerald. The adjective does not express precisely what I mean. The need is for some word connoting the emergence of Fitzgerald into adult estate. Adultery would do only it means something else.

With the possible exception of John V. A. Weaver, no writer of the day has been so consistently tagged with the qualifying label "young." Before the publication of *The Great Gatsby* each novel and short story was invariably hailed as an addition to the interesting output of "young Mr. Fitzgerald." One was asked to read his books in somewhat the same spirit that you take up the poems of Hilda Conkling. Often the marvel seemed to be no more than that this lad of eight or nine had written a size number twelve novel.

Allowance days are done now. From preciosity Fitzgerald moves to understanding. And, in growing up, gains are marked all along the line. Though he was closer to adolescence when he wrote *This Side of Paradise*, Fitzgerald knew the customs of that country far less completely than he realizes them now in *The Great Gatsby*.

Most startling of all, perhaps, is the improvement in manner. I could see skyrockets in the early books, but I don't care much about skyrockets. The pleasant exhilaration as the sparks fly upward invariably is overcompensated by the dull depression of the far longer period of darkness and the anti-climax of the falling stick. Now Fitzgerald can fling phrases against the sky which catch hold of crevices and hang on and glow against the velvet.

"The lawn started at the beach and ran toward the front door for a quarter of a mile, jumping sundials and brick walls and burning gardens—finally, when it reached the house, drifting up the side in bright vines as though from the momentum of its run."

This is more than a good trick conceit. The picture remains. One sees the rush of green up from the water's edge and forgets to notice the cleverness of Fitzgerald in pointing it out. In the old days one sometimes saw only the shadow of the lecturer across the screen as he moved too frankly between his exhibit and the audience, and in those days he carried a long pointer and pushed a loud buzzer to indicate a transition.

Very few books are more beautifully and smoothly written than *The Great Gatsby*. But it is not likely that many will flock to read a story simply on the recommendation that it is stylistically admirable. I do not feel that they should, and certainly not when this particular opinion is tossed off by one who gives no palpable indications of having any decent conception of the identity of style.

Even that is rather too arrogant. It is much more than possible that I fall below the ability to recognize style when I see it, let alone stumble in attempts to capture it. All I can say is that the sounds of *The Great Gatsby* are not only pleasant but suitable. Never does the language get in the way of the fast and flashing story. Few are the books in which interest is so consistently maintained, and in not many does interest rise in an ascending line so perfectly proportioned.

Fitzgerald has written of a man with "an extraordinary gift for hope, a romantic readiness." Gatsby, his brazen adventurer, is a person of infinite appeal. Roughly, he falls into the class of the "Show-Off," but the novel is developed with a completeness and subtlety impossible in dramatic form.

Most interesting of all is the fine-grained tenderness of Fitzgerald in the treatment of Gatsby. Not once does he fail him in understanding, and upon that solid structure he rears now and again a minaret—of mercy, perhaps—for even understanding cannot reach quite high enough to touch the flesh of any one afflicted.

I suppose Scott Fitzgerald would generally be classed among the group called sophisticated. It is the popular notion that this condition necessarily carries with it a diminution of sympathy. Sophistication is confused with insulation. But, to my mind, it is only the sophisticated who carry in their purse money newer than the thin worn coins of conventional commiseration. After all, sympathy is less than useful if it comes without understanding. There is no point in being sorry about a broken paw if it really is a bloody ear.

And all sorrow is subtle. "I know just how you feel," is an insult and a lie. Mere goodness of heart qualifies no one to make such a mighty boast. But Scott Fitzgerald could say it in all truth to Jay Gatsby.

That Sad Young Man

JOHN CHAPIN MOSHER

All was quiet on the Riviera, and then the Fitzgeralds arrived, Scott and Zelda and Scotty. The summer season opened. There had been talk about their coming. They were coming; they were not. One day they appeared on the beach. They had played tennis the day before, and were badly burned. Everybody was concerned about their burns. They must keep their shoulders covered; they must rub on olive oil. Scott was too burned to go in the water, and much of the time, he sat aside from the rush of things, a reflective, staid paterfamilias.

That the Fitzgeralds are the best-looking couple in modern literary society doesn't do them justice, knowing what we do about beauty and brains. That they might be the handsomest pair at any collegiate house-party, inspiring alumni to warnings about the pitfalls ahead of the young, is more to the point, although Scott really looks more as the undergraduate would like to look, than the way he generally does. It takes some years of training as the best host of the younger set, and as a much photographed and paragraphed author, to be quite so affable and perfectly at ease with all the world.

Scott feels that he is getting on in years, that he is no longer young. It weighs upon him, troubles him. He is almost thirty. Seldom has he allowed a person of such advanced age to enter his books.

"I have written a story. It is not about the younger generation. The hero is twenty-nine."

It must be some comfort to him that he is so superbly preserved, so stocky, muscular, clear-skinned, with wide, fresh, green-blue eyes, hair blond not grey, with no lines of worry or senility, no saggings anywhere. Mrs. Fitzgerald doesn't show her age either; she might be in her teens. Perhaps Scotty does. Yes, there is no denying she looks her four.

There were rumors that Scott had had a sip or two of something up in Paris and had come South to rest. No one could have guessed it, but he is summary with any such doubts:

Originally published as "That Sad Young Man," *New Yorker*, April 17, 1926. Reprinted by permission. Copyright © 1926, 1954 The New Yorker Magazine, Inc.

"Don't you know I am one of the most notorious drinkers of the younger generation?"

There have been whispers certainly. But the young man who drives his publicity manager into a lake, as Scott once did, is bound to get some reputation of that sort. There was no reason on this occasion why he should not have turned the car to the right as most people did, and as the publicity man comfortably expected, but having had perhaps a cocktail or two, it seemed more amusing to turn to the left off the road. The publicity man was not drowned however.

That was after one of those Long Island parties which established his place before the world as a host. If he is worried now about the advancing years he had better buy up two or three Biltmores before he extends that general invitation:

"Grow old along with me!
The best is yet to be—"

This popularity on two continents may explain something of the financial mystery which so appalls him. Ever since *This Side of Paradise*, money has poured in upon this young couple, thousands and thousands a month. And just as fast it has poured out. Where it goes, no one seems to know. Least of all, evidently, the Fitzgeralds. They complain that nothing is left to show for it. Mrs. Fitzgerald hasn't even a pearl necklace.

According to Scott he has known poverty. There was the terrible winter after the war, when he wanted to marry Zelda, and had only a ninety-dollar-a-month advertising job and no prospects. He had gone South to see her, and when they parted at the station he hadn't even enough money for a Pullman. He had to climb into a Pullman, and then sneak through into the day coach.

It was then that he saw that advertising did not pay, and he threw up that job and went home to St. Paul to write a novel. Statistics show that 12,536 young men annually throw up their jobs and go back home to write a novel. This has all come about since Fitzgerald set the example, for the book he wrote that winter was *This Side of Paradise*, and he was launched.

His success as an author was a great surprise to the home circle. He had always lived in St. Paul, but the Fitzgeralds were not what is known as literary people, in spite of their descent from the author of the "Star

Spangled Banner." Scott's father was in business, and Scott was never addicted to prowling about the public library. He was much too attractive a boy to be allowed much seclusion.

However he did enjoy scrawling notebooks full of various suggestions and impressions and witticisms, when the other faithful students of the St. Paul Academy and later those of the Newman School as well were busy adding and subtracting and wondering over what takes the ablative. In the Newman School he decided to run off a musical comedy, and two years later he spent his whole Freshman year at Princeton writing the Triangle Show, which left him no time for algebra, trigonometry, co-ordinate geometry and hygiene. But the Triangle Club accepted the show, and he tutored his way back to college and acted in his own work as a chorus girl.

The war came next, and as Aide-de-Camp to General J. F. Ryan he was able to spend his Saturday afternoons writing a hundred and twenty-thousand word novel, "The Romantic Egotist," which was merely a preparatory exercise apparently. Publishers thought it original and very well written but not quite what they were looking for at the moment. A great many publishers were in that frame of mind about it, but they did not manage to extinguish the writing impetus in him. The winter after the war, before he took up advertising, he collected 122 rejection slips, and by way of encouragement sold one story for $30.

Never has he lived that amorphous affair known as the literary life. He is too active for that, and too gregarious. To the younger set of St. Paul he was known as a dining-out, dancing-out country-club boy, and it was a surprise when it was said about that he wanted to write. But literary people there didn't take his ambitions as a joke. He became a great friend of Charles Flandrau's, who twenty years ago published *Harvard Episodes*, stories of freshmen and sophomores, done somewhat in the Henry James manner. There is no resemblance between the Flandrau book and Fitzgerald's, but with Mr. Flandrau, Scott found a sympathetic and intelligent critic, someone who could understand why he chose rather to write than to sell bonds. He had already begun to work with an energy unflagging in spite of his invitations to dinner. It sustained him even through the arduous business of rewriting *This Side of Paradise*, changing it, at his publisher's advice, from the first to the third person.

Such application, of course, is not associated with the temperament of any merely clever young man. The popular picture of a blond boy scribbling off best sellers in odd moments between parties is nonsense. He's a very grave, hardworking man, and shows it. In fact there is definitely the touch of the melancholy often obvious upon him.

He is wary of the limitations of his experience.

Very deliberately he has taken as the field for his talent the great story of American wealth. His research is in the chronicles of the big business juntos of the last fifty years; and the drama of high finance, with the personalities of the major actors, Harriman, Morgan, Hill, is his serious study. He saw how the money was being spent; he has made it his business to ferret out how it was cornered.

Although Mrs. Fitzgerald once bought a bond, no young people, with such an income, are more far removed from the ordinary affairs of business. A twenty-dollar-a-week clerk must know more of the practical business world than Scott Fitzgerald who cannot live on thirty thousand a year, and yet who earns every cent he has.

His information, to be sure, on the general history of this American phase is remarkable. His most trivial stories have a substantial substratum of information.

It should yield more and more revealing, penetrating pictures of American life as he settles gravely down in the twilight of the thirties.

Handwriting Reveals Character:
F. Scott Fitzgerald

SHIRLEY SPENCER

I once listened to F. Scott Fitzgerald, well-known author, lecture many years ago, and he was so nervous that I still have a vivid picture of him moving from chair to desk, perching nervously on each and making rapid staccato comments. His handwriting looks calm enough at first glance, but a closer examination will reveal a rigid tenseness which is bound to result from nervousness. Each stroke is so blunt and stiff in

Originally published as "Handwriting Reveals Character: F. Scott Fitzgerald," New York *News*, October 16, 1935. Reprinted through the courtesy of the Chicago *Tribune*–New York *News* Syndicate, Inc.

the text of his letter that it looks cold and heavy, but his signature has more flying lines so we know, under the right conditions, he will expand and relax.

His pen pressures is very heavy and muddy indicating the deep sensuousness so often found in the writing of artists. It shows a response to color and all that appeals to the five senses. There is no light skimming of the surface here, but cold, hard facts of reality, earthliness, and unadorned truth. Those who write this type of blunt terminals and inflexible heavy strokes are rarely ever optimists. You will find a note of pessimism in their work, and an undercurrent of tragedy even when they are writing in a lighter vein.

As is so often the case in writing like this the t-bars slant downward. The one in his signature happens not to, but every one in the text of the letter does, another indication that his personality has expanded and that he is more expansive on the surface than he is in reality. These obstinate t-bars have a destructive force behind them. They indicate a critical, analytical mind and temperament.

This is the constructive type of script and resembles the writing of Eugene O'Neill more than any other I have seen. There is creative ability and preoccupation with form. There is nothing soft in this writing. It reflects bluntness, frankness, emphatic expression of opinion, unmitigated by diplomacy. Mr. Fitzgerald believes in saying what he feels and means without embellishments or explanations. There is a tense, tight grip on the pen which shows it is controlled by concentrated energy. There is no natural relaxation. Each down stroke is like a wall —a dam for his emotions.

Parodies

Once More Mother Hubbard—
As Told by F. Scott Fitzgerald

DOROTHY PARKER

Rosalind rested her nineteen-year-old elbows on her nineteen-year-old knees. All that you could see of her, above the polished sides of the nineteen-year-old bathtub, was her bobbed, curly hair and her disturbing gray eyes. A cigarette drooped lazily from the spoiled curves of her nineteen-year-old mouth.

Amory leaned against the door, softly whistling "Coming Back to Nassau Hall" through his teeth. Her young perfection kindled a curious fire in him.

"Tell me about you," he said, carelessly.

He knew about her, of course. She was famous in their generation. Of dances, football games, and house parties, she was the uncrowned queen. It was her good luck that, to date, no one had crowned her.

"There's nothing to tell," she answered wearily, lighting another cigarette. It was a pleasure to watch the movement of her supple young wrist as she tossed the burning match on the floor. "The usual thing—fired from three or four schools—I forget their names. Finished with a year at Bedford. Then a round of dances, clinics, teas, back rooms, motor trips, prize fights—and through them all a clamor of dull, desirous men telling me how beautiful I am. I am a riot, aren't I? In a one-piece bathing suit nobody can tie me. Father gives me ten-thousand a year to dress on, and I manage to break about even on my crap-shoot-

Originally appeared as "Once More Mother Hubbard: As Told by F. Scott Fitzgerald," *Life*, July 7, 1921.

ing. All I care about is knocking the conventions for a goal. I want to live—to live—"

There was a gentle cough, and Mrs. Hubbard appeared apologetically at the door.

"Rosalind, dear," she interrupted, softly, "I think someone ought to feed Prince. He seems to be—"

"Mother, what an old idiot you are," said the girl quietly. She was youth and beauty.

"When I was young," began Mrs. Hubbard, tentatively.

Splash! The washcloth caught her just below the ear. Amory found himself wondering, while he watched Rosalind's young gesture as she threw it, if it were possible for her to make an ungraceful motion.

"I'd better be getting Prince something—"

Mrs. Hubbard's voice trailed vaguely away down the hall.

Rosalind looked languorously down at the cigarette between her nineteen-year-old fingers.

"I was made for love," she murmured.

Amory looked at her through half-closed eyes.

"Could you love me?" he asked idly. It was time to try his line.

There was a soft plashing of water as she shrugged her shoulders.

"How do I know?" she answered. "I haven't even kissed you yet."

Again the gentle cough, preceding Mrs. Hubbard's appearance.

"Isn't that too bad," she said smiling uncertainly. "There isn't a thing in the house—"

"Oh, damn," yawned Rosalind.

The Courtship of Miles Standish—
In the Manner of F. Scott Fitzgerald

DONALD OGDEN STEWART

This story occurs under the blue skies and bluer laws of Puritan New England, in the days when religion was still taken seriously by a great many people, and in the town of Plymouth where the "Mayflower," having ploughed its platitudinous way from Holland, had landed its precious cargo of pious Right Thinkers, moral Gentlemen of God, and —Priscilla.

Priscilla was—well, Priscilla had yellow hair. In a later generation, in a 1921 June, if she had toddled by at a country club dance you would have noticed first of all that glorious mass of bobbed corn-colored locks. You would, then, perhaps, have glanced idly at her face, and suddenly said "Oh my gosh!" The next moment you would have clutched the nearest stag and hissed, "Quick—yellow hair—silver dress—oh Judas!" You would then have been introduced, and after dancing nine feet you would have been cut in on by another panting stag. In those nine delirious feet you would have become completely dazed by one of the smoothest lines since the building of the Southern Pacific. You would then have borrowed somebody's flask, gone into the locker room and gotten an edge—not a bachelor-dinner edge but just enough to give you the proper amount of confidence. You would have returned to the ballroom, cut in on this twentieth century Priscilla, and taken her and your edge out to a convenient limousine, or the first tee.

It was of some such yellow-haired Priscilla that Homer dreamed when he smote his lyre and chanted, "I sing of arms and the man"; it was at the sight of such as she that rare Ben Johnson's Dr. Faustus cried, "Was this the face that launched a thousand ships?" In all ages has such beauty enchanted the minds of men, calling forth in one century the Fiesolian terza rima of "Paradise Lost," in another the passionate arias of a dozen Beethoven symphonies. In 1620 the pagan daughter of Helen of Troy and Cleopatra of the Nile happened, by a characteristic jest of the great Ironist, to embark with her aunt on the "Mayflower."

Like all girls of eighteen Priscilla had learned to kiss and be kissed on every possible occasion; in the exotic and not at all uncommon pleasure of "petting" she had acquired infinite wisdom and complete disillusionment. But in all her "petting parties" on the "Mayflower" and in Plymouth she had found no Puritan who held her interest beyond the first kiss, and she had lately reverted in sheer boredom to her boarding school habit of drinking gin in large quantities—a habit which was not entirely approved of by her old-fashioned aunt although Mrs. Brewster was glad to have her niece stay at home in the evenings "instead," as she told Mrs. Bradford, "of running around with those boys, and really, my dear, Priscilla says some of the *funniest* things when she gets a little —er—'boiled,' as she calls it—you must come over some evening, and bring the governor."

Mrs. Brewster, Priscilla's aunt, is the ancestor of all New England aunts. She may be seen today walking down Tremont Street, Boston, in her Educator shoes on her way to S.S. Pierce's which she pronounces to rhyme with hearse. The twentieth century Mrs. Brewster wears a high-necked black silk waist with a chatelain watch pinned over her left breast and a spot of Gordon's codfish (no bones) over her right. When a little girl she was taken to see Longfellow, Lowell, and Ralph Waldo Emerson; she speaks familiarly of the James boys, but this has no reference to the well-known Missouri outlaws. She was brought up on blueberry cake, Postum, and *The Atlantic Monthly*; she loves the Boston *Transcript*, cod, and her relatives in Newton Centre. Her idea of a daring joke is the remark Susan Hale made to Edward Everett Hale about sending underwear to the heathen. She once asked Donald Ogden Stewart to dinner with her niece; she didn't think his story about the lady mind reader who read the man's mind and then slapped his face, was very funny; she never asked him again.

The Action of this story all takes place in Mrs. Brewster's Plymouth home on two succesive June evenings. As the figurative curtain rises MRS. BREWSTER is sitting at a desk reading the latest instalment of Foxe's *Book of Martyrs*.

The sound of a clanking sword is heard outside. MRS. BREWSTER looks up, smiles to herself, and goes on reading. A knock—a timid knock.

MRS. BREWSTER: Come in.

(Enter CAPTAIN MILES STANDISH, whiskered and forty. In a later generation, with that imposing mustache and his hatred of Indians, Miles would undoubtedly have been a bank president. At present he seems somewhat ill at ease, and obviously relieved to find only PRISCILLA's aunt at home.)

MRS. BREWSTER: Good evening, Captain Standish.

MILES: Good evening, Mrs. Brewster. It's—it's cool for June, isn't it?

MRS. BREWSTER: Yes. I suppose we'll pay for it with a hot July, though.

MILES (nervously): Yes, but it—it is cool for June, isn't it?

MRS. BREWSTER: So you said, Captain.

MILES: Yes. So I said, didn't I?

(Silence.)

MILES: Mistress Priscilla isn't home, then?

MRS. BREWSTER: Why, I don't think so, Captain. But I never can be sure where Priscilla is.

MILES (eagerly): She's a—a fine girl, isn't she? A fine girl.

MRS. BREWSTER: Why, yes. Of course, Priscilla has her faults—but she'd make some man a fine wife—some man who knew how to handle her —an older man, with experience.

MILES: Do you really think so, Mrs. Brewster? (After a minute.) Do you think Priscilla is thinking about marrying anybody in particular?

MRS. BREWSTER: Well, I can't say, Captain. You know—she's a little wild. Her mother was wild, too, you know—that is, before the Lord spoke to her. They say she used to be seen at the Mermaid Tavern in London with all those play-acting people. She always used to say that Priscilla would marry a military man.

MILES: A military man? Well, now tell me Mrs. Brewster, do you think that a sweet delicate creature like Priscilla—

A VOICE (in the next room): Oh, DAMN!

MRS. BREWSTER: That must be Priscilla now.

THE VOICE: Auntie!

MRS. BREWSTER: Yes, Priscilla dear.

THE VOICE: Where in hell did you put the vermouth?

MRS. BREWSTER: In the cupboard, dear. I do hope you aren't going to get—er—"boiled" again tonight, Priscilla.

(Enter PRISCILLA, infinitely radiant, infinitely beautiful, with a bottle of vermouth in one hand and a jug of gin in the other.)

PRISCILLA: Auntie, that was a dirty trick to hide the vermouth. Hello Miles—shoot many Indians today?

MILES: Why—er—er—no, Mistress Priscilla.

PRISCILLA: Wish you'd take me with you next time, Miles. I'd love to shoot an Indian, wouldn't you, auntie?

MRS. BREWSTER: Priscilla! What an idea! And please dear, give Auntie Brewster the gin. I—er—promised to take some to the church social tonight and it's almost all gone now.

MILES: I didn't see you at church last night, Mistress Priscilla.

PRISCILLA: Well I'll tell you, Miles. I started to go to church—really felt awfully religious. But just as I was leaving I thought, "Priscilla, how about a drink—just one little drink?" You know, Miles, church goes better when you're just a little boiled—the lights and everything just kind of—oh, it's glorious. Well last night, after I'd had a little liquor, the funniest thing happened. I felt awfully good, not like church at all—so I just thought I'd take a walk in the woods. And I came to a pool—a wonderful honest-to-God pool—with the moon shining right into the middle of it. So I just undressed and dove in and it was the most marvelous thing in the world. And then I danced on the bank in the grass and the moonlight—oh, Lordy Miles, you ought to have seen me.

MRS. BREWSTER: Priscilla!

PRISCILLA: 'Scuse me, Auntie Brewster. And then I just lay in the grass and sang and laughed.

MRS. BREWSTER: Dear, you'll catch your death of cold one of these nights. I hope you'll excuse me, Captain Standish, it's time I was going to our social. I'll leave Priscilla to entertain you. Now be a good girl, Priscilla, and please dear don't drink straight vermouth—remember what happened last time. Good night, Captain—good night, dear.

(Exit MRS. BREWSTER with gin.)

PRISCILLA: Oh damn! What'll we do, Miles—I'm getting awfully sleepy.

MILES: Why—we might—er—pet a bit.

PRISCILLA (yawning): No. I'm too tired. Besides, I hate whiskers.

MILES: Yes, that's so, I remember.

(Ten minutes' silence, with MILES looking sentimentally into the fireplace, PRISCILLA curled up in a chair on the other side.)

MILES: I was—your aunt and I—we were talking about you before you came in. It was a talk that meant a lot to me.

PRISCILLA: Miles, would you mind closing that window?

(MILES closes the window and returns to his chair by the fireplace.)

MILES: And your aunt told me that your mother said you would some day marry a military man.

PRISCILLA: Miles, would you mind passing me that pillow over there? (MILES gets up, takes the pillow to PRISCILLA and again sits down.)

MILES: And I thought that if you wanted a military man why—well, I've always thought a great deal of you, Mistress Priscilla—and since my Rose died I've been pretty lonely, and while I'm nothing but a rough old soldier yet—well, what I'm driving at is—you see, maybe you and I could sort of—well, I'm not much of a hand at fancy love speeches and all that—but—

(He is interrupted by a snore. He glances up and sees that PRISCILLA has fallen fast asleep. He sits looking hopelessly into the fireplace for a long time, then gets up, puts on his hat and tiptoes out of the door.)

THE NEXT EVENING

PRISCILLA is sitting alone, lost in revery, before the fireplace. It is almost as if she had not moved since the evening before. A knock, and the door opens to admit JOHN ALDEN, nonchalant, disillusioned, and twenty-one.

JOHN: Good evening. Hope I don't bother you.

PRISCILLA: The only people who bother me are women who tell me I'm beautiful and men who don't.

JOHN: Not a very brilliant epigram—but still—yes, you *are* beautiful.

PRISCILLA: Of course, if it's an effort for you to say—

JOHN: Nothing is worthwhile without effort.

PRISCILLA: Sounds like Miles Standish; many things I do without effort are worth-while; I am beautiful without the slightest effort.

JOHN: Yes, you're right. I could kiss you without any effort—and that would be worthwhile—perhaps.

PRISCILLA: Kissing me would prove nothing. I kiss as casually as I breathe.

JOHN: And if you didn't breathe—or kiss—you would die.

PRISCILLA: Any woman would.

JOHN: Then you are like other women. How unfortunate.

PRISCILLA: I am like no woman you ever knew.

JOHN: You arouse my curiosity.

PRISCILLA: Curiosity killed a cat.

JOHN: A cat may look at a—Queen.

PRISCILLA: And a Queen keeps cats for her amusement. They purr so delightfully when she pets them.

JOHN: I never learned to purr; it must be amusing—for the Queen.

PRISCILLA: Let me teach you. I'm starting a new class tonight.

JOHN: I'm afraid I couldn't afford to pay the tuition.

PRISCILLA: For a few exceptionally meritorious pupils, various scholarships and fellowships have been provided.

JOHN: By whom? Old graduates?

PRISCILLA: No—the institution has been endowed by God—

JOHN: With exceptional beauty—I'm afraid I'm going to kiss you. Now.

(They kiss.)

(Ten minutes pass.)

PRISCILLA: Stop smiling in that inane way.

JOHN: I just happened to think of something awfully funny. You know the reason why I came over here tonight?

PRISCILLA: To see me. I wondered why you hadn't come months ago.

JOHN: No. It's really awfully funny—but I came here tonight because Miles Standish made me promise this morning to ask you to marry him. Miles is an awfully good egg, really Priscilla.

PRISCILLA: Speak for yourself, John.

(They kiss.)

(An hour later JOHN leaves. As the door closes behind him PRISCILLA sinks back into her chair before the fireplace; an hour passes, and she does not move; her aunt returns from the Bradfords' and after a few ineffectual attempts at conversation goes to bed alone; the candles gutter, flicker, and die out; the room is filled with moonlight, softly stealing through the silken skein of sacred silence. Once more the clock chimes forth the hour—the hour of fluted peace, of dead desire and epic love. Oh not for aye, Endymion, mayst thou unfold the purple panoply of priceless years. She sleeps—PRISCILLA sleeps—and down the palimpsest of age-old passion the lyres of night breathe forth their poignant praise. She sleeps—eternal Helen—in the moonlight of a thousand years; immortal symbol of immortal aeons, flower of the gods transplanted on a foreign shore, infinitely rare, infinitely erotic.*

* For the further adventures of Priscilla, see F. Scott Fitzgerald's stories in the "Girl With the Yellow Hair" series, notably *This Side of Paradise,* "The Offshore Pirate," "The Ice Palace," "Head and Shoulders," "Bernice Bobs Her Hair," "Benediction" and *The Beautiful and Damned.*

Impious Impressions: F. Scott Fitzgerald

EDWARD ANTHONY

"And now he's going to take a rap
 At Scott Fitzgerald," you say.
A rap? Dear, no! A medium tap,
 And why not, reader, pray?

I might, in starting, say that I
 Know F. S. F. can write.
There isn't a likelier scribbling guy
 (Or I am blind) in sight.

I like the flapperdoodle that
 He serves up steaming hot;
He knows the youthful tabby-cat
 As other scribes do not.

He has a gift of gab for which
 I'd gladly give my shirt.
(I'd offer more if I were rich.)
 But when he starts to squirt

Philosophy, however small
 The dose, I squirm and twist,
And want to holler, "Hire a hall!"
 But simply say, "Desist."

Give me his tales! (They foam and fizz!)
 But though my brain's asleep
At times, I'll do my thinking; his
 Conclusions he can keep.

Originally published as "The Book Factory—Impious Impressions: F. Scott Fitzgerald," New York *Herald*, April 16, 1922.

For when Fitzgerald, all athrob,
A juvenile thought unlocks,
I think he ought to go and bob
His hair and roll his socks.

Paradise Be Damned! by F. Scott Fitzjazzer

CHRISTOPHER WARD

This story was written between 10 P.M. and 3 A.M. of one night while I was playing bridge. *The Swift Set* paid me enough for it to recoup what I lost at bridge and leave me the price of a diamond tiara and two theatre tickets. The movie rights brought me $60,000. It is probably the worst story I every wrote—though, for that distinction, it has many rivals.

GRANDPA AND PAPA

Anthony Blaine's grandfather had all the money in the known world and lived in Tarrytown—a remarkable coincidence. Entirely surrounded by cold cash, he had acquired an austere frigidity of manner and was commonly called "Old Chill Blaine." This relationship made Anthony constantly conscious of social security, since an aristocracy founded sheerly on money postulates wealth in the particular—whatever that means.

His father, an ineffectual aesthete of that prehistoric period known as the Nineties, had died before he was born, apparently thus reversing the customarily usual process of nature—a phenomenon explicable only on the hypothesis that language sometimes obscures the thought it is supposed to elucidate. The fact is that Anthony was a posthumorous child—a kind of practical joke on his surprised mother.

Anthony inherited from his father nothing but his last name, his taper fingers and a million dollars—a miserable heritage.

Originally published as "Paradise Be Damned! by F. Scott Fitzjazzer," *The Triumph of the Nut and Other Parodies*. New York: Henry Holt, 1923. All rights reserved. Reprinted by permission of Holt, Rinehart and Winston, Inc.

MOTHER DEAR

But his mother, Beatrice Blaine! She was a woman!—by curious chance. Born in Boston of the old Puritan family of O'Hara, she was educated in Rome—also in Watertown and Ogdensburg, having been fired from three schools successively. She went abroad and was polished in Poland and finished in Finland.

She learned to smoke Camels in the Desert of Sahara and, at the Hague, to drink the national beverage, double strength. All in all, she absorbed a sort of education and an amount of liquor that it will be impossible ever again to find in this country.

In an absent-minded moment, she married Stephen Blaine, because she was a little bit weary, a little bit sad and more than a little bit pie-eyed. He tried to keep step with her, but in less than a year cheerfully died. So Anthony was born fatherless.

LITTLE CHILD, WHO MADE YOU?

His childhood and youth were spent in the midst of privations—private cars, private yachts and private tutors.

At the age of seven he bit bell-boys, at eight smoked cigarettes, at nine played poker, at ten read Rabelais, at eleven imbibed intoxicants, at twelve kissed chorus-girls, and at thirteen his mother died of delirium tremens. He was sent to school at St. Ritz's.

TOM BROWN AT RUGBY

St. Ritz's isn't Eton but it is pretty strong on drinkin'. Anthony's private stock was recruited from all parts of the world.

"What's 'is pink stuff, Anthony?" asked a fellow dipsomaniac of the fourth form, in the intimacy of intoxication.

"'At's ole genevieve from Geneva. 'At green's grenadine from Granada, an' 'at yellow's yataghan from Yap. Make a fairish cocktail, if you lace it with l'il ole wood-alcohol. Keeps a fella fit, 'is stuff does."

He drank liquors of incomparable strength and iridescent beauty, in whose mysterious depths all the lost lures of Mont Marter and of 42nd and Broadway shivered and shimmied languorously in resplendant redundancy. Also he took a shot of hop now and then.

He read enormously. In his first term he accomplished Rousseau's Confessions, "The Newgate Calendar," Boswell's Life of Johnston, "Frank in the Mountains," Kant's Critique, The Arabian Nights in fourteen volumes, "Ten Nights in a Bar-room," "The Dutch Twins," The Memoirs of Casanova, Petronius, Suetonius, Vitruvius, Vesuvius, Plato, Cato, Keats, Yeats and all the Elsie books.

INCIDENT OF THE IMPUDENT HEADMASTER

Clad in an opalescent dressing-gown, the color of peacock's eyes and emu's fins, Anthony was lying on a luxurious lounge of mauve satin stuffed with eiderdown and aigrettes, reading Ghunga Dhin and drinking Ghordon Ghin. A timid knock on the door preceded the entrance of the headmaster. He stood in the doorway sheepishly, hat in hand, pulling an obsequious forelock.

"Blaine—er—er—Mister Blaine," he said.

"Well, Margotson? What is it?"

"I called—er—to ask you, sir, if—er—er—you wouldn't kindly attend a recitation—er—now and then—er—just as a matter of form, you know?"

"Go to hell!" said Anthony coldly, turning again to his liquor.

"Yes, sir. Very good, sir."

The headmaster faded through the doorway and, doubtless, went as he had been directed.

"Damn his impudence!" muttered Anthony.

INCIDENTAL DIVERSIONS

He was leading man in all school plays, editor of the *St. Ritz Bartenders' Guide*, quarterback on the eleven, first base on the nine, second bass on the glee club, forward on the hockey team and backward in his studies. He carried off first honors in the hundred-yards, the mile, the hurdles, the hammer-throw, the standing long drink, the debating society and the bacchanalian orgies.

Thus Anthony at eighteen, six feet tall and narrow in proportion, green eyes that shone through a tangled mass of tawny eyelashes, scornful of the bourgeoisie and of the proletariat, entered Princeton.

SPIRES AND GURGLES

From the first he loved Princeton, the pleasantest country club in America. He loved the tall, towering tapestries of trees, infinitely transient, transiently infinite, yearning infinitely with infinite melancholy—the dreamy double chocolate jiggers pleasing the palate, drenching the innards with a joy akin to pleasure—the early moon, mistily mysterious, more mysterious than mystery itself—the deep insidious devotion of the dreaming peaks, in their lofty aspiration toward the empyrean—through it all the melancholy voices, singing "Old Nassau," blent in a paean of pain. While over all the two great dreaming towers towered toward the sky, like a gigantic pair of white flannel trousers, reversed.

THE SUB-DEB

The time is in the evening of any day in any month in any year. The place is the front room of an apartment in 52nd Street, New York, the library of a house in 68th Street, the ball-room of the Ritz-Royce, a limousine outside the Country Club in Louisville, the Princeton campus, anywhere else you choose.

Enter Rosalind—kissable mouth, other details unnecessary. Enter to her Anthony Blaine.

HE: Will you kiss me?

SHE: Sure!

(They kiss—definitely and thoroughly—in a most workmanlike manner.)

HE: Did you ever kiss anyone before?

SHE: (Dreamily) Dozens, hundreds, thousands of boys.

HE: Kiss me again.

(They kiss.)

SHE: How old are you?

HE: Nineteen-past.

SHE: I'm sixteen-just.

HE: Kiss me again.

(They kiss.)

SHE: You're some kisser yourself.

HE: Of course—Princeton, you know.

SHE: I knew it. Now, Yale men——

HE: Don't mention the brutes!

SHE: But Harvard men—

HE: Sissies! Kiss me again.

(They kiss.)

SHE: When I was in——

HE: You're so loquacious

(They kiss.)

SHE: By the way, who are you?

HE: Anthony Blaine.

SHE: I've heard—

HE: Don't talk.

(They kiss.)

SHE: I'm—

HE: What difference does it make who you are? Let's get married.

SHE: Can't. I'm engaged.

HE: Whom to?

SHE: What?

HE: To who—who to?

SHE: Oh. Why, to Dawson Ryder and Skeets McCormick and Amory Patch and,—to a boy named Wilson—don't remember his first name and—to a Yale boy I met in the dark and don't know any of his names or what he looks like and to—oh, lots of others.

HE: You love me, don't you?

(They kiss.)

SHE: I love you! I love you! I'm mad about you. I can't do without you.

(They kiss.)

HE: My God! You're spoiling both our lives.

SHE: My God! Am I?

HE: Here! We're losing time.

(They kiss—kiss—kiss.)

SHE: You've broken my heart.

HE: My God!

SHE: My God!

HE: Time's up, I have a date with Cecelia Connage.

SHE: She's my sister. She's not very good at it.

HE: Good-by! You've broken my heart and mussed me all up.

(They kiss. He stumbles toward the exit—a broken man—then—throws back his head with that proud Princeton gesture—and goes out.)

SHE: Oh, God! I want to die!

(She looks about her—misty-eyed—with a deep aching sadness—that will pass—that will pass in time—say, three minutes.—She looks—for her vanity-bag—powders her nose—renews the carmine on those tired lips—)

SHE: Well? Are they going to keep me waiting all night? Next boy, please!

MORE GURGLES

The last light fades and drifts across the land,
The low, long land, the land of towers and spires,
That wanders lonely lest the lurid lyres
Press thy pale petals with a passionate hand—
Enchanted essences and pagan pyres—
Oh, dream that sleeps and sleep that knows no dreaming!
So wert thou wrought in fragrant fadeless fires.
So wert thou wrapt in garments goldly gleaming
And dying knew not what should end this seeming.

The ghosts of evenings haunt these afternoons.
The mid-day twilight shifts with my desire.
Nor yet before my eyes do they conspire
Where to distil the fragrance of the moons
That burn and are consumed with splendid fire,
And hurl them to abide in their abode
Where young Fitjazzer tuned his youthful lyre
And sang to Princeton his melodious ode
Which, what it means, there's no one never knowed.

COLLARS AND TIES

Anthony Blaine paused in the process of adjusting the universe to himself and looked about him—an apartment in a house of murky material, windows that loomed gloomily down upon Fifty-second Street, voluminous chairs, a fireplace of murky black, a flamboyant exotic rug of crimson velvet, an orange-colored lamp—everything suggested the solidarity of wealth, an entré into the best society.

He yawned and sauntered to his bathroom, an enormous room, where he spent most of his time. He usually took five baths a day; on Sundays, seven.

Emerging from his bath, he polished himself with fine sandpaper, finishing with chamois-skin, until his smooth skin shone like satin. From the closets bursting with clothes—underwear for an army, silk shirts for a city, collars and ties for a multitude—he selected his attire.

He taxied to Brook's, to buy him some ties and collars, then to the grill-room of the Jazza.

LIFE IN LARGE CITIES

The grill-room of the Jazza. Anthony seated. Enter Richard Caramel. In person short, in pocket shorter. His figure is round—he is always round where Anthony is buying drinks.

ANTHONY: Hello, Caramel, old sweet!

DICK: Thanks, I will.

ANTHONY: Waiter! Two double Dacharis in tea cups and four more to follow.

DICK: Sounds to me!

ANTHONY: Pour it down, beardless boy! How many can you hold?

DICK: Don't know—never had enough.

ANTHONY: Waiter! two dozen quadruple Dacharis in bath-tubs. Who's the luscious debutante across the room?

DICK: My cousin, Gloria Goodle, the Speed Girl from Kansas City.

ANTHONY: No!

DICK: Yes! These short lines are life-savers, aren't they?

ANTHONY: Indeed. Also this dialogue stuff—so snappy. What were we talking about?

DICK: Gloria Goodle.

ANTHONY: Oh, yes——

DICK: The Speed Girl from Kansas City.

ANTHONY: Aren't we nearly at the bottom of the page?

DICK: Yes, turn over.

ANTHONY: Your cousin?

DICK: Want to meet her?

ANTHONY: Gloria who?

DICK: Goodle.

ANTHONY: Funny name.

DICK: Funny girl.

ANTHONY: What's her line?

DICK: Legs.

ANTHONY: Whose?

DICK: Her own.

ANTHONY: My God! lead me to her!

DICK: Come on.

ANTHONY: Wait a minute. I've got something on my mind.

DICK: Get it off before you meet Gloria.

ANTHONY: Suppose I were an Athenian—too proud to be enigmatic, too supple to eventuate, too incongruous to ratify, too courageous to adorn—

DICK: Cut it! Suppose you were an author too young to be wise, too self-sufficient to learn, too impatient to wait, too successful to stop— that's the kind of bunk you'd write.

GLORIOUS GLORIA

She was dazzling—alright; it was agony to comprehend her beauty in a glance—hair full heavenly glamour—mouth full of gum drops.

"Where are you from?" inquired Anthony.

"K.C., Mo.; Got any gum drops?"

"Gum drops! My God!

The clock on the mantel struck five with a querulous fashionable beauty. Then, as if a brutish sensibility in him was reminded by those thin, tinny beats that the petals were falling from the flowered afternoon, Anthony pulled her to him and held her helpless without breath, with scarcely room to masticate the gum drops, in a kiss like a chloroformed sponge.

The clock struck six.

PASSION VS. GUM DROPS

ANTHONY: Will you marry me, Gloria?

GLORIA: Are you rich?

ANTHONY: Haven't a cent.

GLORIA: Thought you were a millionaire.

ANTHONY: Absolutely stony. Spent it all on neckties and collars.

GLORIA: I must have gum drops.

ANTHONY: Impossible.

GLORIA: My God! How I love you!—but I must have gum drops.

ANTHONY: My God! You've broken my heart!

GLORIA: My God! Have I? Try a gum drop.

ANTHONY: My God! Woman, you're heartless.

GLORIA: I'm Gloria Goodle—the Speed Girl, Coast to Coast Gloria.

ANTHONY: Coast to coast!—ashes to ashes! dust to dust! My love is dead.

(Then a thick impenetrable darkness descended on his mind—though you'd hardly notice the difference.)

THE DAWNING OF A BRIGHTER DAY

At seven-thirty of the same evening, Anthony was sitting on the floor of the front room of his apartment, with three books before him—a child again playing with his stamp-albums—when Gloria and Dick came in.

"Anthony!" she cried, "your grandfather has died and left you a hundred million bucks."

"Go 'way," he answered with petulant gentleness, "I've got a five-pistache stamp of Jugo-Rumania and there isn't any place for it in the damned old book."

"Jugo-Rumania!" gasped Dick. "Ain't that the truth? The poor gink's got 'em. He always was a wet one."

"Never mind," said glorious Gloria gently. "I'll marry him and take him to Arabia where the gum comes from and you can get a decent drink. His trouble ain't so much the humidity as the hooch."

The Rubaiyat of Amory Khayyam
As Translated by F. Scott Fitzgerald

H . W . H .

WAKE! For the bun that scattered into flight
 Dead sober reason all the jazz-long night,
Has gone, and left a hangover to strike
 The aching cortex with a sudden blight.

II

Before the last sub-deb became pie-eyed
Methought a voice within the grill room cried,
 "When all the orangeades are doped with gin,
Why nods the drowsy officer outside?"

This item, transcribed from a clipping in one of Fitzgerald's scrapbooks, has not been located.

XII

A *Vie Parisienne* beneath the bough,
A pocket-flask, some Lucky Strikes—or thou
    Beside me cuddling in the taxi-cab,
Ah, taxi-cab were limousine enow.

XLII

Some for the heavy Wall Street deal, and some
Sigh for the fat inheritance to come.
    Ah, take Dad's Stutz and let the Rolls-Royce Go;
It is the scion's privilege to bum.

Obituary Editorials and Essays

A Last Salute to the Gayest of Sad Young Men

JAMES GRAY

The death of Scott Fitzgerald at 44 is one of those shocking finalities that seems to be especially designed to underscore certain meanings in the quality of our human life. In his neat, epigrammatic style, the late Oscar Firkins once warned a very young student against the inclination "to crowd the beginnings and the middles, lest you leave the ends barren." That advice might have been specifically addressed to Scott Fitzgerald as it was addressed in general to the generation of which he was a brilliant representative.

Scott Fitzgerald did crowd the beginning of his career with success, adulation, excitement. And the middle was crowded, too, though in a different way, with shocks such as few men have to endure, with private griefs of the most poignant and pitiful kind. Throughout all of his later work, beginning with the last novel, *Tender Is the Night*, there runs the appalling theme of youth's bright flame turned suddenly into a sinister, destructive force—the blaze quite out of control. And yet in all of the frank autobiographical writing that he set down during that last phase, he never brought himself to confess quite the most unnerving and demoralizing things that had happened to himself. Painful as that last work was, it must often have seemed to Scott Fitzgerald inadequately candid in its report of the tragedies with which human beings must learn to live. He was letting his public off easily.

Originally published as "A Last Salute to the Gayest of Sad Young Men," St. Paul (Minn.) *Dispatch*, December 24, 1940. This is a shortened version of the original.

There is a kind of rightness to the fact that his death came so early. Having had much of both good and bad, he had surely lived enough. There was brilliance to his success with *This Side of Paradise* when he was a boy just out of college. There was tremendous dramatic impact to the succession of his tragedies during the late thirties and early forties. It would have been unendurable to one of his temperament to have had to face for long the barren end of life in which there was neither pleasurable excitement nor interest of the sort that an intelligent, analytical mind is able to take even in its sufferings. Scott Fitzgerald anticipated all through his life, finding short-cuts through the dull, tortuous paths by which youth is supposed to make its way to success, skipping the monotony of the comfortable middle years, and in the end dying before his time because his whole nature cried out for the reckless expenditure of vitality. He could no more keep from squandering his energies than he could keep from squandering his money.

With Scott Fitzgerald, the twenties were one long, hilarious house-party on Long Island, in Paris, on the Riviera. The thirties were an equally long, uninterrupted clinic over the cost of the previous decade. There was little left for the forties, so he did not bother with them. Perhaps we may comfort ourselves with the thought that, in general, men get the lives that they deserve and the deaths that they want.

Now that he is dead there will be, I suppose, a tendency to dismiss his work merely as a symptom of the nervous irritability of the post-war generation. It will be said that he was a facile entertainer whose gaiety turned sour and left him without an audience.

And that will be cruelly untrue. He wrote one novel, *The Great Gatsby*, which reveals his gift at its most urbane, sensitive and imaginative. It is one of those small masterpieces which inevitably misses tremendous popular success because its implications are more subtle than the casual public cares to disentangle from a melodramatic story. It has missed also the keenest kind of critical appreciation because unfortunately public neglect tends, in our success-loving time, to justify a corresponding neglect on the part of the great arbiters.

There can be no doubt that the Pulitzer Prize has gone to many a novel which is utterly trivial in comparison with *The Great Gatsby*. I even venture the dreadful heresy that the Nobel Prize has gone to writers for a body of work, no one item of which is as beautifully written, as revelatory of significant truths about our American psychology, as creditable in general to the level of our native intelligence and understanding as *The Great Gatsby*.

Perhaps some day it will be rediscovered.

But whether or not justice is ever done his one great literary accomplishment, no one who ever knew him will soon forget the beguiling attraction of his spontaneous generosity.

When Tom Boyd, then of St. Paul, completed the manuscript of *Through the Wheat*, Scott Fitzgerald, wintering here at home, became enthusiastic about it and sent it to his publisher. It was promptly rejected. Scott Fitzgerald immediately got on a train and went to New York. The whole weight of his personal influence with the firm which liked both him and his work was thrown into the struggle to save an unknown writer's work from the discard. *Through the Wheat* was issued by Fitzgerald's publisher and with that debut a useful career began.

So one of the "sad young men" has come to the end of his sorrows.

Not Wholly "Lost"

NEW YORK TIMES

In his later years (they were not very "late" for he was only 44 when he died last Saturday) Scott Fitzgerald compared himself to a "cracked plate," not good enough to be brought out for company but which "would do to hold crackers late at night or go into the ice-box with the left-overs." He bitterly underestimated what he had done and might still have done. He was better than he knew, for in fact and in the literary sense he invented a "generation" and did as much as any writer to form as well as to record its habits.

There were flaws—chasms, indeed—in the theory of the "lost generation." As Fitzgerald described it, it could not include more than a small fraction of American youth, for the simple reason that the life it led was expensive. Moreover, the small fraction never had the unity he ascribed to it, except in a superficial sense. Generations do not come into existence en masse, every ten, twenty or thirty years. They accumulate, day by day.

But he did describe, faithfully, the life and times of a certain section of our society, with the emphasis on youth. He saw clearly what war and other influences had done to such people during the second decade of our century. They thought they had no illusions and surely they had no faith. They were "free" but didn't know what to do with their freedom. They felt cheated, but of what birthright they did not know. They drank and made love, only to find that a combination of these two activities gave no foundation on which to build a career. They grew older and had children of their own and sometimes the children, who took "freedom" for granted as they did their three or four meals a day, laughed at them.

Scott Fitzgerald might have grown up with them. He might have interpreted them, and even guided them, as in their middle years they saw a different and noble freedom threatened with destruction. A *Times* reviewer caught "flashes of wings and sounds of trumpets mingled with the tramp of feet and casual laughter" in his jazz age stories of fifteen years ago. Mystical, glamorous, passionate, shocking—these were some of the adjectives applied to *The Great Gatsby*, published in 1925. It was not a book for the ages, but it caught superbly the spirit of a decade.

But the wings flashed no more, and the trumpets did not blow. For some reason the creative impulse slackened. It might have come back if the still youthful heart had not stopped beating. And it may also be that Scott Fitzgerald, and others of his time, were really "lost"—that they could not adjust themselves, no matter how hard they tried, to the swift and brutal changes of these times. It is a pity, for here was real talent which never fully bloomed.

F. Scott Fitzgerald

BALTIMORE SUN

F. Scott Fitzgerald may have been a writer of "unfulfilled promise," as some of the critics have said. It seems, indeed, that he came more or less to agree with them in the closing unproductive years of his short life. They could not forget the startling brilliance of his first book; he him-

Originally published as "F. Scott Fitzgerald," Baltimore *Sun*, December 24, 1940. Reprinted by permission of the Sunpapers, Baltimore, Md.

self was at last burdened by his early success. Probably he had not the slightest wish to be honored as recorder of the so-called "jazz age," for he had the artist's conscience and the artist's ambition. Having them, he found it hard to see his work perpetually identified with a single period and a transient mood and always judged in light of recollections of his meteoric beginning.

Yet when one looks back at his novels one must question the notion that he never attained the full development of his powers as a writer. For the truth is that his achievement was of a genuinely creative order, and *This Side of Paradise* will, in all likelihood, be enjoyed as a novel when it is forgotten as a "document."

It appeared in 1920. Maybe the "jazz age" had been born then, but certainly it had not reached its brassy majority. Rather the year was one of a renewal of hope, of zest in living, of belief—albeit confused and critical belief—in the future. It was the year of *The Outline of History* and *Economic Consequences of the Peace*, of Aldous Huxley's first published stories and T. S. Eliot's first published essays. It was the year of *Main Street* and *Poor White*, of new novels by Conrad, Edith Wharton and Willa Cather, of new poems by Masters, Sandburg, Lindsay, Robinson and D. H. Lawrence.

But in that crowded year *This Side of Paradise* struck a wholly new note and one that clearly caught not only the echo of the slang and clothes and "subjects" of the day but also the direction of a genuine movement of a young spirit. One can reread it today and find in it far more than a dazzlingly authentic portrait of a vanished day and a forgotten generation. It is a true and a moving story of youth.

Not many first novels possess any such "promise" as this one did. Few represent such "fulfillment." Fitzgerald wrote much that was of lesser consequence—of course, he rode the tide of fortune and fashion. But he also wrote some beautifully turned stories. *The Great Gatsby* was probably his most perfect novel in point of structure and technique. And finally, much later, *Tender Is the Night* embodied a greater and deeper effort than any of his other novels.

These things will last as contributions to American writing. For Fitzgerald had vision and poetry in his work and a feeling for literary and human values that showed in the sensitiveness and often the subtlety of his prose. It may be that, in an age which has again become grim and dark, Fitzgerald's novels seem dated. But that has been the fate of many excellent books as well as merely popular fiction. The difference between the two is that the excellent books outlive the public mood which relegated them to the shelves as well as that which launched them into the best-seller lists. Fitzgerald's books will, we believe, survive.

Fair Enough

WESTBROOK PEGLER

The death of Scott Fitzgerald recalls memories of a queer brand of undisciplined and self-indulgent brats who were determined not to pull their weight in the boat and wanted the world to drop everything and sit down and bawl with them. A kick in the pants and a clout over the scalp were more like their needing, but all of us were more or less goofy then, so they enjoyed a very tolerant public whose sympathy and attempts to understand only encouraged them to eat more live goldfish out of the hotel fountains and whine all the louder. The sensitive young things of whom Fitzgerald wrote and with whom he ran to fires not only because he could exploit them as material for profit in print but because he found them congenial, were fond of a belief that they had been betrayed by some impersonal mass-rouge called their elders who had wantonly and just for the hell of it caused an awful war and the ensuing upsetment and that they, most of all, were the victims of this villainy. Some were veterans of the war, but more were of the group who came of age just after the peace, but we were not taking polls in those days, so we never knew how many they were all told, and may insist, if we like, that the noise they made was far out of proportion to their numbers. After all, there are now living among us millions of men and women in their high 40s and late 30s who were members of that age group and who settled down to work and the responsibilities of life and do not concede that they ever lost their souls.

Of that group or cult of juvenile crying-drunks I have in mind one in particular who obviously seized upon Fitzgerald's writing as an excuse to run his fingers through his pretty, wavy hair and flout every ordinance of morality, responsibility, respectability and manhood. A youth of wealth and high social position, he had joined up for the war in the

Originally published as "Fair Enough," New York *World-Telegram*, December 26, 1940.

spirit of a slummer to drive an officer's car, and afterward wrote to exhaustion of the horror of it all, the disillusionment of his generation, the lack of opportunity for the likes of him in a world disordered by guilty management, collecting, over the course of about 15 years, three wives, a pile of debts the size of a haystack and a cigaret cough which gave him occasion to beat himself delicately on the wishbone and say, "Gas—the war, you know."

Fitzgerald dealt with a group who were not noticeably concerned with noble service but merely petulant, because no one had invented a gin that didn't cause hangover—another grievous failure of the wicked and shiftless elders.

At this distance from Fitzgerald's day there are signs that, just as Saloon Society is exaggerated and overpublicized at present, so then the number, importance and plight of his subjects were vastly magnified. Where are they now, those flappers, male and female, whose problem never was hunger or lack of a job, or rather luxurious comforts, but just a yearning and churning such as every youth is troubled by, but in their great self-pity thought all this was something new? They are not next door, because there were not enough of them to provide neighbors for us all, even discounting the mortality of almost two decades.

Whoever sees one now or knows of one who wouldn't have been a malingering flop and whiner in any generation?

At this point it may be observed that today any legitimate, conscientious effort to regard youth as a section of society and to give special encouragement and aid is certain to be exploited by a relatively small element of youth who will turn pro, so to speak, and either sit down on the curb and quit cold or hop up on a ladder-box and damn the only system under which they are permitted to do so. The majority are minding their business, preserving their self-respect and their individuality as the majority did when Scott Fitzgerald's few were gnawing gin in silver slabs and sniffing about the sham and tinsel of it all.

Talk of the Town: F. Scott Fitzgerald

NEW YORKER

It is our guess that very young men wrote the obituaries for F. Scott Fitzgerald. Not only were they somewhat uninformed (note to the New York *Times: The Beautiful and Damned* is not a book of short stories, and it isn't called *The Beautiful and the Damned,* either) but they were also inclined to be supercilious. He was the prophet of the Jazz Age, they wrote patronizingly, who never quite fulfilled the promise indicated in *This Side of Paradise.* As an approximate contemporary of Mr. Fitzgerald's and, we suppose, a survivor of the Jazz Age ourself, we find this estimate just a little exasperating. He undoubtedly said and did a great many wild and childish things and he turned out one or two rather foolish books; he also wrote, however, one of the most scrupulously observed and beautifully written of American novels. It was called, of course, *The Great Gatsby.* If Jay Gatsby was no more than could be expected of Amory Blaine, Manhattan Island has never quite come up to Peter Stuyvesant's early dreams.

The Great Gatsby was always accepted as his best book, but we have a feeling that Fitzgerald may have preferred *Tender Is the Night,* which he wrote very near the end, perhaps when the end was sometimes too clear to him. It was probably as close to autobiography as his taste and temperament would allow him to come. We read it again the other day when we heard that he was dead, and somehow or other we can't forget the last sentence: "Perhaps, so she liked to think, his career was biding its time, like Grant's in Galena; his latest note was post-marked from Hornell, New York, which is some distance from Geneva and a very small town; in any case he is almost certainly in that section of the country, in one town or another." Scott Fitzgerald knew better than that. The desperate knowledge that it was much too late, that there was nothing to come that would be more than a parody of what had gone before, must have been continually in his mind the last few years he lived. In a way, we are glad he died when he did and that he was spared so many smaller towns, much further from Geneva.

Fitzgerald and the Jazz Age

AMY LOVEMAN

In the death last week of F. Scott Fitzgerald there passed an author whose books, though they are comparatively infrequently read at the moment, had an enormous vogue at the beginning of the twenties and played no little part in the social history of the country. It is hard for the younger generation of today, accustomed to the freedom of social intercourse which is theirs and to the respectful hearing accorded their beliefs and plans, to realize that the freedom and dignity which they have achieved, are in large part the outgrowth of post-war years. Young people in America, from the earliest days of our history, had, to be sure, enjoyed a freedom from social conventions which was at once condemned and envied by the more sophisticated societies of Europe. Except in the cities, that omnipresent figure of European society, the chaperone, was almost unknown, and even on the Atlantic coastboard, where wealth and travel had entrenched European custom, it was only in the larger towns that her rule was observed. The camaraderie of American boys and girls, the good fellowship which marked their school relationships and their fun-making, the informality of their later dancing and courting days were as world famous as the indulgence of American parents to young children and the devotion of American fathers to their daughters. Nevertheless, this was all a freedom within a strictly conventional pattern. So far as taboos on conduct, as differentiated from mere social manners, were concerned, American society accepted Victorian morality wholeheartedly, and expected of its young people conformity to rigid standards of behavior. It was all very well for the young to be unchaperoned, but it was only well because American young men regarded chastity as the priceless jewel of womanhood, and the condemnation of their group as well as the ostracism of society in general was meted out to any wanderer from the paths of virtue.

There had been whispers, of course, before F. Scott Fitzgerald published *This Side of Paradise*, that American youth had entered upon a period of social laxity but it was not until that novel and subsequent tales of flappers, jazz, and gin by Fitzgerald and others made their ap-

Originally published as "Fitzgerald and the Jazz Age," *Saturday Review of Literature*, January 4, 1941. Reprinted by permission of the *Saturday Review*.

pearance that the nation as a whole became aware of the change that was taking place in the code of conduct of the young. Fitzgerald and his fellow authors, since they were novelists writing for dramatic effect and not sociologists investigating national well-being, threw the excesses of the Jazz Age into a prominence which was perhaps as misleading as it was startling; they roused a mortal fear in the parents of the land, and a shocked reaction on the part of the elderly in general. But they did something more constructive than this, for they brought into the open the gathering rebellion of youth against the restrictions of the past, and, by making it apparent and articulate, set it on the way to correction. If now, in the opening lustrum of the forties, our youth is more conservative and far less belligerent than in the first period of the twenties it is because in the decades since the World War it won its freedom from the trammels of the past. Sinclair Lewis and his followers on the one hand, belaboring the restrictions and sterility of small town life, and Scott Fitzgerald and his fellows on the other, showing youth emerging as "beautiful and damned" from the repressions of the Victorian Age, forced a revaluation of social codes upon the country which resulted not only in a salutary broadening of outlook but also in a tolerance of the point of view of the young which deprived them of the necessity of bravado.

Since the twenties youth has gone through the ordeal of the depression, gone through it with shattered hopes and admirable courage, and has emerged from it conscious of itself as a group and united as never before for what it holds good. But it fights now for economic and political ends and no longer for release from outworn social shibboleths. That release it had won for itself by the time the tumult roused by F. Scott Fitzgerald and his fellow writers had somewhat died down. Youth came out of its swaddling clothes with these novelists. They were the publicizers of the new freedom in which the young had come to believe and which they were practicing, and if they showed that new freedom at its worst, they nevertheless helped to initiate the nation into the psychology of youth and thereby to work a transformation in the entire social outlook of the country. The Jazz Age had no more complete expression than in the novels of F. Scott Fitzgerald. That they are already to a great extent unread is perhaps the best testimonial to the fact that the kind of society they portrayed is even now retreating into history.

Salute and Farewell to F. Scott Fitzgerald

ARNOLD GINGRICH

One night in 1934 John Gunther and this editor were discussing American writers. Mr. Gunther, whose name at that time was hardly a household word, was in Chicago on vacation from Vienna, his then post on the foreign staff of the Chicago *Daily News*. On that trip home, his last before becoming famous, he had met the new boss of his newspaper, Frank Knox, and he had arranged a contract with Harpers, to bring out "a book about Europe." The book, of course, was to be *Inside Europe*, that hardy perennial which has been to the best-seller lists what "Tobacco Road" has been to the box-office records.

At that time, before going back to Vienna, there was one American whom John Gunther wanted especially to meet. He was willing to make a side trip to Baltimore, for the purpose, on his way back to New York to sail, and this editor was going to arrange the meeting for him. For the one American John Gunther then wanted most to meet was F. Scott Fitzgerald.

Discussing this, that night, he said, "Hell, I'm just a good newspaperman with a job, or maybe I should say I'm just a newspaperman with a good job, but Scott Fitzgerald's a genius."

It was and is without disrespect to John Gunther that we agreed with that statement then and would again now.

But we couldn't help recalling it with a certain wry bitterness, this Christmastime, when we read the perfunctory obits with which American newspapermen shrugged out the news that Scott Fitzgerald was dead. There may have been some honorable exceptions here and there, but if there were we missed them. All the news stories and editorial comments that we saw ranged from niggardly to nonsensical, as estimates of the stature of Scott Fitzgerald in American letters. From Westbrook Pegler down (or up, depending on which end of the telescope you use in looking at Pegler) everybody seemed bent on remembering him for his worst book, *Flappers and Philosophers*, and forgetting all about the book by which he will be remembered. In most of the newspaper

Originally published as "Editorial: Salute and Farewell to F. Scott Fitzgerald," *Esquire*, March 1941. Reprinted by permission of *Esquire Magazine*. © 1941 (renewed 1969) by Esquire, Inc.

stories *The Great Gatsby* was given mere passing mention, if any at all, while most of the space was devoted to *This Side of Paradise* which compares to *The Great Gatsby* about as George Moore's *Confessions of a Young Man* compares to his *Esther Waters*. And it took the *New Yorker* magazine to tell the great New York *Times* that *The Beautiful and Damned* was *not* "a book of short stories," nor was its name *The Beautiful and THE Damned*.

In general, the American press dismissed the death of the author of *The Great Gatsby* as if he were merely a sort of verbal counterpart of John Held, Jr. Even our own favorite newspaper, the Chicago *Daily News*, could find no more to say of him than this:

"When he died at 44, F. Scott Fitzgerald, hailed in 1922 as the protagonist and exponent of the Flapper Age, was almost as remote from contemporary interest as the authors of the blue-chip stock certificates of 1929. He was still writing good copy, but no one was mistaking a story writer for the Herald of an Era."

Well, the Chicago *Daily News*, which is a highly civilized newspaper, should hardly need reminding that in literature there is no more insecure grip on immortality than that of a Herald of an Era, while a story writer may very well live forever.

It is doubtful that more than one novel and a handful of short stories will endure, out of Scott Fitzgerald's many writings over the past twenty years. Yet nobody, of all the writers of our time, could write as well as he. Almost everybody had as much, or more, to say, but almost nobody could ever say it as well. Scott Fitzgerald drew the finest and purest tone from the English language of any writer since Walter Pater, who also, as fate would have it, never had anything to say half worthy of his incomparable ability to express it.

The great tragedy of Fitzgerald's life was not any one of the several minor tragedies on which, successively, he was wont to blame the wreckage of his life. Other writers have lived lives more sorrow-filled and disappointment-packed than his, with spiritual enrichment to themselves and the world as a result. The Charles Lamb-like career and writings of the late Clarence Day constitute just one of a number of cases in point.

But Scott Fitzgerald's big trouble was that he was a perfectionist in his living as in his writing. He wanted to live his best stories more than he wanted to write them. And in a sense he almost always wrote for his living, at least whenever it came to a choice between that and living for his work.

Then, too, he had a queer Keltic tendency to enjoy ill-luck as some people enjoy ill-health. He liked to dramatize to himself the inevitability of both his latest and his next defeats.

If anything was wrong in his life, and something always seemed to be, even during his Long Island and Riviera days when the world appeared to be his oyster, then everything was all wrong, and he seemed rather to enjoy saying so. He was the same way about a story. In life and letters both he was such a perfectionist that he was always prone to exaggerate minor excellences and minor defects away out of their proportionate importance to the average perception.

Here at *Esquire* he was the seven-year despair of our proofroom. Very seldom did we manage to get to press with any of his writing without receiving from one to four revised versions after the original had been set in type. And every time he wrote a new Pat Hobby story he would want the order of appearance shuffled all over again on all those awaiting publication. More than once we received revised versions of the Hobby stories either on or after the date of their actual appearance on the newsstands. Each time that happened he would act as if his whole career had been torpedoed without warning. Finally we had to send him a sort of ultimatum laying down the deadlines for revision on the various stories in the series. As this is written two of those time-limits have not yet expired. In addition to the two remaining stories that round out the series we have two other Fitzgerald stories, written during the Pat Hobby period but held for later publication to avoid breaking or conflicting with the continuity of the Hobby stories.

So now we have but four more months to devote to keeping his memory green. Two of the stories are up to his best level. Probably neither of the Pat Hobby stories would have pleased him exactly as they stand. Yet, as it happens, they are considerably better than a couple that have appeared in that series to date. For that matter, he didn't like the Pat Hobby story in this issue very well, and twice shoved back its publication date, yet from the time its first version first came in it has been one of our own favorites in the series as a whole. In any case, every word of every one of these last stories has suddenly come to seem precious to us, since his death, and we hope that it will be with some measure of that same feeling that you will read them.

Certainly this sequence of Pat Hobby stories adds up to something considerably short of being a masterpiece. Yet it could hardly be more fitting, as Scott's last word from his last home, for much of what he felt about Hollywood and about himself permeated these stories. Both the first and the last time he left for Hollywood he set out with a sad proud air of resignation, like a young Russian nobleman being banished to Siberia.

Failure always fascinated him. That's why he enjoyed writing about Pat Hobby more than almost any character that came from his pen since that first far away and long ago Amory Blaine. (We are suddenly reminded of a truism with which Scott began one of his early short stories: "Start out with an individual and you find that you have created a type—start out with a type and you find that you have created nothing.") And if your memory goes away back twenty years to *This Side of Paradise* you may be interested to hear that his own favorite scene in that first book of his was the one where the boy holds his classmates breathless while he opens the envelope in which a pink slip will tell him that he stays in Princeton, or a blue slip that he must leave. Waving the failure slip he says "blue as the sky, gentlemen"—a gesture worthy of Cyrano and his plume at heaven's gate.

His last letter to this office, a matter of days before his death, spoke of his new novel, still unfinished in its first draft, as "a book I confidently expect to sell all of a thousand copies." If he had gone on from that one remark for pages more he could not possibly have given better expression to the attitude that was so typical of him, a blend of insouciance and despair.

Remembering how much more he enjoyed living than writing, before the first of those emotional blackouts that used to leave him unfit to enjoy either, and remembering how the bent of his wild and wilful nature always inclined to defeatism, frustration, negation and failure, it is a matter of wonder that he left any perfectly realized work at all, and not that he left so little. The four novels will always be worth reading, but it is doubtful that more than one of them will always be read. *The Great Gatsby* will undoubtedly be read and studied a century hence, when *Gone With the Wind* has long since lived up to its title. Among the four volumes of short stories there are probably not more than a half-dozen tales that will appeal to anthologists of our great-grand-children's day as being (to use Scott's own early phrase) "worth preserving a few years—at least until the ennui of changing fashions suppresses me, my books, and them together."

Oddly enough, or perhaps appropriately enough, his most beautiful book, *Tender Is the Night*, was also his most ugly and was the least perfectly realized piece of work of all four of his novels. It was a magnificent failure in many ways, and it contains passages of haunting loveliness, but it suffered from the very phenomenon with which it was concerned, a split personality. It was really the malformed twin embryo of two books, one of which might have been a masterpiece. That book, which ought to have a prominent place on the shelf of the great unwritten books of lost time, was to have been titled simply *Richard Diver*. It might have been an even better book than *The Great Gatsby* but the story got lost and twisted and came out imperfectly and misshapenly as an unassimilated half of *Tender Is the Night*.

Well, he's gone and we shall miss him. We shall miss both the writer that he was and the one that he might have been. We've no idea what epitaph he might have liked, but we feel that Marlowe's mighty lines were not too good for him, those lines that run: "Cut is the Branch that might have grown full straight, and broken is Apollo's laurel bough."

At any rate we know that he deserved a far better press than he received, although it probably was precisely the kind of press that he himself would have expected. That was the kind of cruel jest that would have given him sardonic satisfaction, in the realization that at least and at last and for once he had not kidded himself.